CW00428279

FROM THE BEAT
TO THE PALACE

175 Years of Gallantry

This book is dedicated to all past and present members of the Metropolitan Police Force. To all those who received the recognition of their bravery by receiving a gallantry award or commendation. To those who never received an award but none the less committed a brave deed. And to those who gave the ultimate, their own lives in the course of their duty.

It is a sad reflection that police officers receive fewer gallantry medals these days, but having said that, most police officers you speak to really love their work, some will even say "it's the fact that you never know what the day will bring, and each day is different".

Even though the police have had their good times and their bad times, this has not stopped the young new generation from going to Hendon and becoming Metropolitan Police Constables. This is a force that is famous around the world. They all feel pride when they finally pass out as a police constable and join their divisions for the first time.

My gratitude to all those mentioned in this book is from the heart.

The Police Helmet badge on the front cover is the copyright of the Metropolitan Police and is reproduced by kind permission of the Commissioner.

FROM THE BEAT TO THE PALACE

175 Years of Gallantry

Jane R. Lawrence

BREWIN BOOKS

First published by
Brewin Books Ltd, 56 Alcester Road,
Studley, Warwickshire B80 7LG in 2005
www.brewinbooks.com

© Jane Lawrence 2005

All rights reserved.

ISBN 1 85858 263 6

The moral right of the author has been asserted.

A Cataloguing in Publication Record
for this title is available from the British Library.

Typeset in Times
Printed in Great Britain by
The Cromwell Press

CONTENTS

ACKNOWLEDGEMENTS

I would like to acknowledge the following for access to, and their permission to use, material from their records.

Metropolitan Police Historical Museum
Public Records Office Kew
Carnegie Hero Fund
Royal Humane Society
London Gazettes
Peel House, Regency Street
Mrs Doris Smith re Pc Francis Stubbs KPM
Wpc Dorothy Bell re Pc William Cole AM
Ps David Pengelly GM
Pc Philip Rainsford QGM
Pc Carl Ritchie
Lorraine Pullen re her father Keith Giles BEM

FOREWORD

This year, the Metropolitan Police celebrates its 175th Anniversary – a remarkable milestone in the long and distinguished history of an extraordinary organisation. In considering that history, it is appropriate that we should remember and honour the officers and members of Met police staff who – throughout those 175 years – have demonstrated courage and a devotion to duty of the very highest order.

The history of this organisation is filled with more stories of gallantry, brilliance and humanity than I could ever tell:

- Stories from two world Wars – including those of 98 Met officers who died during the Blitz;
- Stories of immense courage and sacrifice;
- Stories of ordinary women and men – often doing the most extraordinary things in the most demanding of circumstances.

At a time in the Met's history when so much is being achieved, it is important to recognise that the successes of this organisation have been built on the endeavours of its people: men and women who are amongst everyday heroes and heroines of this city.

Pc Jane Lawrence has invested an enormous amount of her own time and energy in producing this remarkable record of those to whom the people of London owe an enduring debt of gratitude.

It was General Robert E. Lee who said this:

'Duty is the most sublime word in our language. Do your duty in all things. You cannot do more. You should never wish to do less.'

'From the Beat to the Palace' remembers the people who have answered that challenge with immense bravery and a deep sense of commitment to the public we serve. This is their book.

Sir John Stevens
Commissioner
July 2004

PREFACE

Bravery and Gallantry, when ever we see these two words they seem to get our attention. We cannot pass the opportunity by but read on and see what the person did to receive the accolade. Most of the time the person will say 'I was just doing my job', or 'I could not stand by and do nothing' or 'it seemed the right thing to do'. Those who receive the award from HM the Queen say 'I was more nervous receiving the medal than I was when I performed the act of bravery'.

Bravery awards come in many different forms, from a medal or a certificate to a monetary award. But each award is a testimony to the bravery of the individual.

The award for bravery/gallantry is not as we believe a modern concept; the first awards were in fact made during the times of the ancient Greeks; when any gallant act performed by a person was rewarded by a crown and a suit of armour. When a Greek warrior performed an act of gallantry, he was awarded a circular metal badge which he wore on his armour.

The earliest recorded awards in this country were during the Civil War at the Battle of Edgehill on 23rd October 1642. They were awarded to Robert Welch and John Smith who rode to retrieve the Standard of the King's Own Regiment and captured two cannons. Both were knighted on the 'field of battle' and by a warrant dated 1 June 1643, medals in Gold were ordered to be struck as rewards. These men wore their medals on a broad sash of green silk (hence the association of Medal and Ribbon).

This book looks at the awards made to members of the Metropolitan Police Force and deals with the awards of the main medals and the oak leaf cluster of the King's, later the Queen's, commendation for brave conduct (the civilian equivalent of mentioned in despatches).

There are many ways in which police officers received awards for acts of bravery/gallantry. A small selection of the acts concerned are: the arrest of an armed and dangerous criminal, sometimes resulting in the officer being injured; the rescue of occupants of buildings damaged by bombs during both wars; stopping runaway horses and the saving of life from either drowning or from a burning building.

When more than one award is made consisting of different medals, the main medal recipient and citation will be shown and the other recipients cross referred to that entry.

HISTORY OF THE POLICE

Police officers, a name derived from peace officers. This name dates back to the early years of the Saxons. Groups usually of 10 people were called Tythings with a Tything-man as a representative of each group. Larger groups of 10 Tythings then came under a Hundred-man who was then responsible to the Shire-Reeve or Sheriff of the County. Over the passage of time the Tything-man became the Parish constable and the Shire-Reeve the Justice of the Peace to whom all parish constables were responsible.

Back in the 17th and 18th Centuries it was generally adopted that one unarmed able bodied citizen from each parish would be appointed or annually elected to serve for the year as an unpaid parish constable. It was his duty to work with the local Justices in securing the observance of the law and maintaining order.

In 1785 a Bill was put before Parliament, it proposed that all of London's Metropolitan areas including the City of London should be united into a single Police force with its own paid police officers. This Bill was very unpopular and was withdrawn.

To help combat the problems with violence and crime, in 1790 the Bow Street Magistrate Sir Sampson Wright set up foot patrols of 68 men. These were divided into 13 parties of a Captain and either 4 or 5 men. Eight of these squads patrolled the roads leading into London. The remaining five would walk the streets of central London. They did not wear any kind of uniform but were all well armed. The Captain carried a musket and two pistols, the men under his authority wore heavy cutlasses. They all performed their duty at dusk and continued until midnight, or later. Each and every morning the Captains would report the night's events at Bow Street. The patrols were all on standby during the day and were ready to rush to any emergency at the directions of the Magistrate. Before the formation of the Metropolitan Police Force in 1829, the only means of identification of the Bow Street Runners was a tipstaff. The tipstaff was a hollow tube made of wood or metal and would hold a warrant for the arrest of a criminal. After Robert Peel's police force came into being, constables wore a uniform at all times which identified them as police officers. They were given but not required to carry warrant cards. The tipstaff was finally withdrawn in 1880.

In 1792 the Middlesex and Surrey Justices Act created seven new Magistrate offices in London; these would operate in conjunction with Bow Street. Each Magistrate would be paid a yearly salary of £400. Six full time paid constables were appointed to each office, and they were given increased powers of arrest. In those days an idle or disorderly person could be arrested as a vagrant.

In1800 Sir Richard Ford became the Chief Magistrate at Bow Street. On taking up office his first job was to try to tackle the increase of highway robbery on the roads leading into London. He decided to re-create the mounted patrol of 1763. This consisted of 52 armed men who were under the command of two Inspectors. They all carried pistols, a cutlass, truncheon and handcuffs. They wore a uniform consisting of a black leather hat, a scarlet waistcoat, blue trousers and wellington boots. Because of the colour of their uniform they were nicknamed 'the Robin Redbreast'. Their tour of duty was from dawn to dusk, and they could stop any coach with the cry 'Bow Street Patrol'.

London in the early 1800's was a violent and unsafe place in which to live. The districts with the most crime were the City of London, Soho, Covent Garden, and Wapping. In 1822 Robert Peel became the new Home Secretary. On taking up office he said his policy would be to show people that "liberty does not consist in having your house robbed by gangs of thieves". Unfortunately it took him a further seven years to prove this. It was during his time as Chief Secretary for Ireland that he established the successful Irish Constabulary, who were nicknamed 'the Peelers'. He believed that London needed the same system, but the committee set up in 1822 did not agree. Not giving up, he set up within a few months a day patrol at Bow Street of 3 Inspectors and 24 men to work under the Chief Magistrate. They worked until night fall, and became London's first uniformed professional Police.

By 1828 the Home Secretary Robert Peel had 450 policemen under his control. The population of London at the time was 1.5 million so the ratio was one policeman to every 3000 people. There were an additional 4500 watchmen and a small number of private company policemen. Once again Robert Peel set up another committee to enquire into the cause of the increase of commitment in London and Middlesex and into the state of the police of the Metropolis and adjoining districts. This time they found it was absolutely necessary to devise a greater security for both persons and property. Backed by the House of Commons he drafted his Bill for the formation of the Metropolitan Police Force and on 15th April 1829 he introduced his Metropolitan Police Improvement Bill. This time the House of Commons passed the Bill on 25th May 1829. The Act finally received Royal Assent on 19th June 1829 and the Metropolitan Police Force came into being between 5th July and 29th September 1829.

When the Metropolitan Police Force was formed, the first constables paraded for duty at 4 Whitehall Place, better known to us as Scotland Yard. From the onset the force consisted of approximately 1000 men who were responsible for policing 6 divisional areas nearest to Westminster. In 1830 a further 5 divisions were formed and as more men were recruited the number increased to 17 covering the City of Westminster and specified parts of Middlesex, Surrey and Kent, with a total strength of about 3500 men.

By 11 am on the first day 1000 rattles were supplied, these were to remain the only means of rapid personal communication for the man on his beat, the rattle was carried in the coat tail pocket, it was his only means of summoning help or alerting members of the public of any danger, the range of hearing was limited so, on 10th February 1885 each officer was issued with a whistle which replaced the rattle. The whistle gave the constable the added advantage of being heard from a greater distance.

By June 1830 the strength of the force had grown to 17 Superintendents of which 13 were ex warrant officers and 4 civilians from the 'old force'. A Superintendent was paid £200 per annum, an Inspector £100, a Sergeant £58 and a Constable 21 shillings per week. The cost of the Metropolitan Police Force was set at £240,000 per annum. In 1831 two years after the start of Robert Peel's Metropolitan Police Force 378 persons per 100,000 had been taken into custody, sixty years later in the 1890's the rate had dropped to 216 per 100,000. Discipline in the new force was very strict, during the first 9 years nearly 5000 constables had been dismissed for drunkenness and for not matching the required standards.

By the 1880's London was considered the safest Capital City in the World. By the early 1900's the Londoners trust in the familiar Bobby was developing, the policeman on his beat was no longer a member of an alien force. He was a respected community member, a public arbiter and an ally to the weak and the poor.

One of the only means that a constable was able to defend himself was with a truncheon. The original truncheons were made of bamboo or wood and measured 20inches long. They were decorated with the Garter coat of arms and the letters MP in gold on red. In 1846 they were marked with each constable's divisional number. In 1856 the length of the truncheon was reduced to 17inches, most were cut down from the original length thus losing the decoration. Today most police officers carry a friction lock baton, the truncheon being withdrawn in 1996.

THE MEDALS AWARDED

THE ALBERT MEDAL: Instituted on 7th March 1866 for heroic acts performed by mariners and others who endanger their own lives in saving, or endeavouring to save the lives of others from shipwrecks and other perils of the sea. This was extended in 1877 to cover heroic acts performed on land; the medals became known respectively as the Albert Medal of the First Class and the Albert Medal of the Second Class. In August 1917 designations were altered once again, respectively to the Albert Medal in Gold and the Albert Medal. The Albert Medal was replaced by the George Cross in 1971 when recipients of the Albert Medal could exchange their awards. Two awards have been made to Metropolitan Police Officers.

THE GEORGE CROSS: Instituted on 24th September 1940 for heroism for civilians, both men and women; also to members of the Armed Forces, when the instance does not earn or where the situation does not warrant a military award. The George Cross was only to be awarded where the most conspicuous courage was shown and where the recipient himself was in extreme danger. Between the years from its institution until 1947 some 105 George Crosses were awarded with approximately 45 since, the latest award being to the RUC. Five awards have been made to Metropolitan Police Officers.

KING'S POLICE MEDAL: Instituted on 7th July 1909 to reward 'courage and devotion to duty' in the Police and Fire service. The medal was renamed the King's Police and Fire Service medal in 1940. From 1950 the gallantry medals were only awarded posthumously and all medals were discontinued in 1954 when separate awards were established for the two services. 276 awards have been made to Metropolitan Police Officers, of which one bar has been awarded.

QUEEN'S POLICE MEDAL - POSTHUMOUS AWARD: Instituted on 19th May 1954, the Queen's Police Medal for gallantry has been effectively redundant since November 1977 when it was made possible to award the George Medal posthumously. Prior to this the Queen's Police Medal was the posthumous equivalent of the George Medal for Police officers. Five awards have been made to Metropolitan Police Officers.

GEORGE MEDAL: Instituted in September 1940 awarded to both men and women for acts of 'great bravery' intended primarily for civilian personnel, the medal was available to be awarded to military personnel but only when and if the act of gallantry fell outside the scope of any military award. Of approximately 2000 medals awarded 1030 have been awarded to civilians. 138 awards have been made to Metropolitan Police Officers, of which one bar has been awarded.

BRITISH EMPIRE MEDAL FOR GALLANTRY: The British Empire Medal was instituted in December 1922, the gallantry awards were instituted in December 1957. Issued to both men and women, civilian or military. The British Empire Medal was replaced as regards to gallantry by the Queen's Gallantry Medal in 1974. 128 awards have been made to Metropolitan Police Officers, of which one bar has been awarded.

QUEEN'S GALLANTRY MEDAL: Instituted on 20th June 1974 and awarded for exemplary acts of bravery. Although intended primarily for civilians, it is also awarded to members of the armed forces for actions which would not be deemed suitable for a military decoration. With the introduction of the Queen's Gallantry Medal the order of the British Empire came to an end with regards to gallantry. Fewer than 400 have been awarded of which 55 awards have been made to Metropolitan Police Officers, including two bars.

KING'S AND QUEEN'S COMMENDATIONS FOR BRAVE CONDUCT: A description of the various emblems denoting mentioned in despatches and commendations was published as a Supplement to the London Gazette on 27th July 1951. For the King's Commendation after 10th August 1920 a bronze emblem consisting of a single oak leaf. Where no medal has been awarded the emblem was worn on the breast in the position when an appropriate medal ribbon would have been worn. King's or Queen's commendations in respect of bravery granted to civilians for acts during or since the second world war are denoted by a silver emblem in the form of a spray of laurel leaves (this was originally a plastic oval badge). For service during the second world war this emblem was worn on the ribbon of the defence medal. Where no medal was awarded, it was sewn directly onto the coat after any medal ribbons. A total of 71 King's commendations have been made and 271 Queen's commendations.

ROYAL HUMANE SOCIETY: Founded in 1774 for the specific purpose of diffusing knowledge about the techniques of resuscitation and saving life from drowning. From the society's inception large medals were struck in gold or silver, monetary awards, medals, clasps and testimonials were granted to those who saved life, or attempted to save life from drowning, but later the society's remit was broadened to include all cases of exceptional bravery in rescuing or attempting to rescue persons from asphyxia in mines, wells, blasting furnaces or in sewers where foul air may endanger life.

STANHOPE MEDAL (ROYAL HUMANE SOCIETY): In 1873 the Stanhope Gold Medal in memory of Captain C S S Stanhope RN was instituted for award to the person performing the bravest act of life saving during the year.

CARNEGIE HERO FUND MEDAL: Founded in 1908 in Scotland by Andrew Carnegie. The first medallion was awarded posthumously on 26th November 1909. This award does not have a ribbon.

BINNEY MEMORIAL MEDAL: Founded in 1947, instituted in memory of Captain Ralph Douglas Binney who was killed on 8th December 1944 in the City of London while attempting to apprehend two armed robbers single-handedly. It is annually awarded to the British Citizen who displays the greatest courage in support of law and order within the areas under the jurisdiction of the Metropolitan Police and the City of London Police. The medal is not intended to be worn as the medal comes without ribbon.

MEDALS AND AWARDS
FOR SAVING LIFE

The Royal Humane Society Police Medal introduced in 2000 is awarded for an outstanding act of heroism by a police officer. The medal is made of silver gilt and is awarded annually. the first winner was Pc Wayne Martin, of Bedfordshire Police, and in 2001 the medal was awarded to Pc Brown, for successfully rescuing one man from a burning car and trying to save another.

The incident happened on 16 December 2000 at Dagenham in Essex. Pc Brown and a colleague Pc Peter Wilson, were returning to their homes after a fancy-dress Christmas party. The timing was unfortunate – Pc Brown was still dressed as a gangster.

Just off the A13 near Dagenham, the two off duty officers caught sight of a fire. As they got closer they saw an overturned car suspended over railings and it was well alight.

One man had already escaped, but two others were still inside. They were both trapped against the passenger door and one was lying on top of the other. Neither was moving and the fire was spreading rapidly.

Pc Brown tugged frantically at the car door but couldn't open it. So he crawled through the broken windscreen and grabbed one of the men, heavily built and unconscious, by his arm and top of his trousers. he lifted him out and went straight back into the burning car for the second man.

By now the car was engulfed in flames and the heat was intense. Pc Brown pulled the second man out and moved him to safety.

Pc Brown then had the presence of mind to give mouth-to-mouth resuscitation to the first man, whose pulse was very weak. his colleague, Pc Peter Wilson, gave him cardiac massage. In spite of their best efforts, they weren't able to save him, but the other man did survive.

In March 2001 Pc Brown was awarded the Society's Bronze Medal, which he received from the Society's President, HRH Princess Alexandra, at the Annual General Court in May.

Afterwards Pc Brown played down his bravery. "If you know someone's in trouble, you just do it", he said, though he admitted: "I didn't tell my wife what I'd done until the medal ceremony".

TIME LINE FOR THE METROPOLITAN POLICE

1829   Metropolitan Police Force came into being.

1832   Cholera epidemic in London, many police officers died.

1844   CID began when Sir James Graham gave 12 Sergeants the right to work in plain clothes.

1859   Umbrellas were no longer allowed on duty.

1863   The re-formation of the Mounted branch.

1896   A register of all people convicted in the UK held at Scotland Yard.

1898   34 killed during the launch of HMS Albion on the River Thames.

1901   Reliable system devised of classifying fingerprints.

1903   Newgate Prison closed - first prison on this site was opened as early as 1190.

1905   Japanese are teaching the City of London Police Ju-Jitsu.

1906   Several Police stations to be connected to the telephone.

1907   All the Police stations within the Metropolitan Police area installed with telephones.

1910   5 police shot and a Sergeant killed from the City of London Police, at Houndsditch.

1911   Siege of Sidney Street in London's east end after police shot and one killed (see above).

1914   A band of more than 50 Suffragettes stormed Buckingham Palace. Man arrested in the servants' apartments at Buckingham Palace, charged with enclosed premises.

1917   Women's Police service formed.

1918   Metropolitan Police Strike.
Women Police started with 42s a week pay.

1919   15 Police battle against 400 Canadian Soldiers at Epsom Police Station, a Police Sergeant was killed.

1921   Four stripes for a Sergeant were abolished.

1922   Field Marshall Sir Henry Wilson shot dead on the order of the IRA.

1924   As the number of motor vehicles increased it was found essential to institute some means of regulating the flow of traffic. A number of schemes were initiated including one way roads, traffic lights and the introduction of a number of traffic signs.

1926   The General Strike.

1928   The River Thames burst its banks due to heavy rain causing severe floods.

1932   Scuffles broke out between Police and demonstrators in Hyde Park during a rally regarding unemployment. The gathering of 20,000 came as a climax to a hunger march.

1933   Patrol cars were fitted with wireless.

1936	Battle of Cable Street.
1937	Tribute to the new telephone 999 system, suspect arrested within 5 minutes of a phone call.
1940	The Blitz - several George Medals awarded for the rescue of trapped persons.
1946	Police dogs introduced operationally.
1947	Royal wedding of HRH Princess Elizabeth.
	One of the worst winters in living memory from the end of January until the beginning of April Britain in the grip of Arctic weather.
1949	Timothy Evans hanged for the murder of his wife and child (Christie's crime see 1953).
1952	King George VI dies, Queen Elizabeth proclaimed.
1953	Coronation of Queen Elizabeth.
	John Christie arrested for the murders at 10 Rillington Place.
	Derek Bentley hanged for the murder of Pc Sidney Miles.
1955	Riots in Cyprus, UK Police including Metropolitan Police Officers sent out Smog again in London.
	Ruth Ellis arrested for the murder of David Blakely.
	On 13th July Ruth Ellis hanged - last female to be hanged in the UK.
1958	Race riots at Notting Hill.
1961	First arrest and conviction using the new American Identi-kit.
1963	The great train robbery.
1965	State funeral of Sir Winston Churchill.
1966	Timothy Evans granted a free pardon (see 1949).
	Murder of 3 Metropolitan police officers - foxtrot one one.
1968	Ronan Point disaster in east end of London. A gas explosion brought down all the corner flats of a 22 storey tower block.
	Grosvenor Square riots, 246 arrested, 161 casualties of which 117 were police officers.
1969	Capital punishment abolished.
	Kray twins arrested, both sentenced to life imprisonment.
1970	City refuse collectors go on strike.
1972	Britain joined the European Community.
	BEA Trident Papa India crashes at Heathrow Air Port.
1973	London car bombs, Old Bailey and Whitehall (IRA).
1974	Two bombs exploded one at the Houses of Parliament the second at the Tower of London.
1975	Balcombe Street siege (IRA).
1976	Drought, River Thames reached its lowest level in living memory.
1977	Grunwick dispute.
1979	Airey Neave killed by a car bomb while leaving the underground car park at the House of Commons (IRA).
1980	Iranian Embassy siege.
	Fire at Alexandra Palace north London.

1981	Riots in Brixton south London.
1983	Harrods bomb (IRA).
1984	Libyan Embassy siege - Wpc Yvonne Fletcher shot and killed.
1985	Broadwater Farm Riots - Pc Keith Blakelock murdered.
1987	King's Cross underground fire.
	Hurricane hits south of England, London had 94mph winds.
1988	Clapham rail crash.
1997	Death of Diana Princess of Wales and Dodi Fayed.
1999	Paddington rail crash.
2001	Lord Archer jailed for Perjury.
2002	Deaths of HRH Princess Margaret and HM Queen Elizabeth the Queen Mother.
2003	Congestion charge introduced in Central London.
2004	The 175th Anniversary of the Metropolitan Police.

POLICE OFFICER'S PRAYER

Oh Almighty God, whose great power
and eternal wisdom embraces the universe.
Watch over all policemen, women and law enforcement officers.
Father in Heaven please give them the strength,
courage and perseverance to endure
The unjust condemnation, danger,
and physical abuse to which they are at times subjected.
We recommend them to your loving care
because their duty is dangerous.
Dear God, grant these brave men and women your almighty protection,
Unite them safely with their families after duty has ended.

Amen

Chapter One

THE YEARS OF 1820 - 1899

This was the era that saw the end of the famous Bow Street Runners, and the introduction of a new force the Metropolitan Police Force. Its founder being Robert Peel. London established the London Fire Brigade. The penny post was introduced with the first sightings of the famous Penny Black Stamp. The great famine took place in Ireland with their potato crop being blighted.

The country had its fair share of military conflicts, the Crimean War which saw the fatal charge of the Light Brigade, this war saw the introduction of the Victoria Cross for military gallantry. There was also the Zulu wars with the famous battle at Rorkes Drift, and the start of the Boer War. Civil war also broke out in the United States of America and would last 5 years.

The last public executions took place at Newgate Prison, shortly after this, the prison was demolished to make way for the new building, the Central Criminal Court.

London lived under the terror of Jack the Ripper, his reign started in 1888, as we all know he was never caught, and although we all believe we know who he was, this is one of the few mysteries still with us.

The other side of the world witnessed one of the most destructive volcanoes of its time, Krakatoa in Java. It was said that when it erupted it could be heard hundreds of miles away and felt even further.

Police constables were given the authority to have with them handcuffs and rattles when they were on special duty among crowds. This was one of the first entries in Police orders in October 1829. There is also authority given for constables to wear swords when on duty for the protection of St George's burying ground. Obviously a deterrent to anyone who would try to steal newly buried bodies for medical science.

PRE FORMATION OF THE POLICE FORCE

1820 - 1829: ROLL OF HONOUR

MURDER OF A BOW STREET RUNNER

A plot to massacre Government ministers dining at a house was foiled. The Government were aware of the plot as spies had infiltrated the group. When the plotters assembled in a cow shed in Cato Street, Marylebone they were surrounded by armed constables and soldiers.

The lightly armed Bow Street Runners entered the premises unaccompanied. One of the conspirators, the leader Arthur Thistlewood, recognised one of the constables as having arrested him before, and could therefore identify him. He shot the constable and finished him off with a sabre thrust to the stomach. Thistlewood and his gang escaped but were captured the next day.

Six of the leading conspirators were executed at Tyburn.

1829: FIRST RECORDED AWARD FOR GALLANTRY
15 December 1829

The Commissioners have received from a Nobleman £5 to be given to Anthony Wilkinson, Police Constable of St James's Division for having discovered the fire that was likely to take place a few days ago in his Lordship's house and for his assistance on that occasion and the Commissioners give permission for Wilkinson to receive the money.

DISMISSALS
September 1829

Pc William Atkinson, 1 C

Dismissed for being drunk on duty.

11 November 1829

Ps John Candill, 3rd Company

Dismissed from the police force for being asleep in Leicester Square at 3.30am while on duty.

4 December 1829

Pc Cornelius Dickson

Dismissed for asking for broken victuals at Arthur's Club House and talking to a prostitute when on duty.

November 1829

Pc William Robinson, 348 F

For receiving stolen goods.

ROLL OF HONOUR
• Pc Thomas Hart, 3989 T

Drowned in the River Trent.

1830: ROLL OF HONOUR
THE FIRST POLICE CONSTABLE TO BE MURDERED
Pc John Long, G

• The first martyr of Sir Robert Peel's newly formed Metropolitan Police was Pc Long. He was stabbed while following three men who he believed may be committing break-ins in the Grays Inn Road, Theobalds Road area. The man convicted of the murder was John Smith, but known to be burglar William Sapwell.

• Pc Joseph Grantham, D

Kicked in the head while attempting to arrest a drunken man at a disturbance in Somerstown.

1832: ROLL OF HONOUR
• Pc Thomas Hart, 3989 T, aged 42

1833: REWARD GIVEN
16 September 1833
Viscount Melbourne has been pleased to direct the receiver to pay John Brooke and Henry Charles Redwood the sum of Twenty Pounds each as compensation for the severe wounds inflicted upon them while in the execution of their duty in Calthorpe Street on Monday 13 May last.

ROLL OF HONOUR
- Pc Robert Culley, 1044 C

Died of stab wounds at the Coldbath Riots.

1839: ROLL OF HONOUR
- Pc William Aldridge, 13759 R

Died of fractured skull, received when stoned by a mob whilst making an arrest.

1841: ROLL OF HONOUR
- Pc James Carrol, 17546 H

Attacked by a mob and struck with his own truncheon while making an arrest at Shoreditch.

1842: ROLL OF HONOUR
- Pc Timothy Daly, 5277 N

Shot dead while attempting to arrest a man for highway robbery at Highbury.
- Pc James Fulker, 5277 F

Found dead on his beat.
- Pc Charles Reynolds

Drowned in the London docks while on night beat duty.
- Pc Charles Nicholls, 18243 Y

Dropped dead on his beat.

1844: ROLL OF HONOUR
- Pc John Birkmyre, 19748 E
- Pc John Wright, 17357 E

Both were killed at a fire in Guildford Street when the floors of a burning house collapsed on them.

1846: ROLL OF HONOUR
- Pc James Hastie, 21237 R

Died from injuries received after being assaulted by several men in a street disturbance at Deptford.
- Pc George Clark, 22098 K

Brutally beaten and stabbed to death while on night duty at Dagenham.
- Pc George Hall, 21314 K

Injuries received from falling from his horse.

• Pc Charles McCarthy, 10103 K
Knocked down by a horse.

1848: ROLL OF HONOUR
• Pc Daniel Harker Monk, 24816 E
Struck with his own truncheon by a man attempting to free a prisoner at St Giles.
• Pc Henry Morgan, K
Died of injuries received in an affray.

1849: ROLL OF HONOUR
• Pc William Sibley, 13187 S
Collapsed and died from suspected over exertion at a fire.
• Pc John Welch, 26845 B
Suffocated in a sewer while trying to rescue 3 workmen, he died after successfully rescuing 2 of them.

1850: ROLL OF HONOUR
• Pc Alexander Scott, 25983 R
Died during a hospital operation to an injury he had received in an affray at Deptford. He died at Guys Hospital while undergoing an operation where chloroform was administered.

1851: ROLL OF HONOUR
• Pc Henry James Chaplin, 24774 L
Attacked and struck with bricks by a disorderly crowd at Vauxhall Walk.

1852: ROLL OF HONOUR
• Pc Michael Madigan, 24976 V
Found drowned in the River Thames adjoining his beat.

1855: ROLL OF HONOUR
• Pc Francis Stoker, 19183 N
Killed while endeavouring to save the lives of six persons whose house had collapsed.

1856: ROLL OF HONOUR
• Pc Malachi Shannon
Thrown from his horse and died consequently of the injuries he sustained.

1857: REWARD
13/10/1857
Ps 14 Egerton
To be recommended for a reward for the apprehension of a felon.

1858: REWARD
22/2/1858
Pc 28L Worthy
To be recommended for reward for his conduct at a fire at 14 Duke Street.

REWARD
15/9/1858
Pc 212K Donovan
To be recommended for reward for rescuing a child from drowning.

DISMISSAL
Pc 160M Ecclestone
Drinking at the bar of a public house for 1½ hours when off duty, fined 5s, pay to 19th December - 6th report.

1859: REWARD
21/12/1859
Pc George Reeve
The commissioner has much satisfaction in making known to the police force that the sum of £3 has been awarded by the Assistant Judge of the Middlesex Sessions to Police Constable 394S George Reeve, for the courage he displayed in arresting a man for breaking into a dwelling, after a brutal assault had been committed on the constable. This gratuity is in addition to the constables ordinary expenses and 10s is given by the Commissioner.

ROLL OF HONOUR
- Pc William Fuller
Killed while taking a police horse to the station, when it suddenly reared up and fell on him.
- Pc Thomas Randall, 37123 V
Killed in a fight with Pc Wright.

1860: DISMISSAL
Pc 137V Tanner
Complained of for being insolent to a young female when on duty.

ROLL OF HONOUR
- Pc George Brown, 33868 S, aged 25
Killed by falling down an area at Parsonage House, St. Stephen's while in the execution of his duty.

1862: ROLL OF HONOUR
- Inspector William Hard, 16751 T
Died from a fractured skull caused by a fall from his horse.

- Pc Richard Lillicrap, 33960 G

Collapsed from over exertion when in pursuit of a thief in Petticoat Lane.

1863: ROLL OF HONOUR

- Pc William John Davey, T

Shot through the head on his doorstep by a man whom he was investigating for a crime in Acton.
- Pc Frederick William Patrick

Found dead in a barge under Hungerford Bridge having fallen through a hole while on night duty. A note from Police Orders dated 12 December 1863 grants his widow a pension of £15 per annum and a payment of £2/10s to his daughter annually until she reaches the age of 15.

1864: ROLL OF HONOUR

- Pc Charles Pearce

Fell from a police boat and drowned at Devonport Docks.
- Pc Daniel Langford, V

Died from injuries he received when assaulted on duty in 1862.
- Ps George Edward Saunders, 44683 H

Drowned at night in the London Dock while on duty.
- Pc Thomas Jackson, V

Died of injuries received from an assault on duty.

1866: ROLL OF HONOUR

- Pc William Fitzgerald, F

Violently assaulted by a drunken prisoner in Drury Lane.
- Pc Thomas Ley Baker, E

Violently assaulted when apprehending two burglars in 1863.
- Sergeant Henry Collins

Apparently thrown from his horse while on duty in West Drayton.

1867: ROLL OF HONOUR

- Pc Dennis Potter Clarke, M

Assaulted in the execution of his duty in 1864.

1868: ROLL OF HONOUR

- Inspector Daniel Bradstock, 20585 A

Stabbed by an insane prisoner at King Street Police station. Person who stabbed him was called Smith.
- Pc Joseph Eite, V

Died from injuries received by being kicked by a drunken male.

1869: ROLL OF HONOUR

- Pc James Nice, T

Died from kicks received on duty.

1870: ROLL OF HONOUR
- Pc Charles Cox, 43200 T

Accidentally drowned when he fell from the river bank near Kew Bridge while on night duty.
- Ps George Robins, 26863 W

Killed by a kick from his horse while practising mounted drill.
- Pc George Frederick Waring, 51321 G

Died from injuries received when badly kicked by a drunken prisoner in Shoreditch.

1872: ROLL OF HONOUR
- Pc James Bowler

Found drowned on duty in suspicious circumstances in the Limehouse Cut Canal.
- Pc Moses Parrott

Dropped down dead while on duty in Parliament Street from the effects of previous injuries and assaults.

1873: ROLL OF HONOUR
- Pc Alfred Bennett, E

Died following injuries received when assaulted during an arrest.

1875: ADVANCEMENT

Pc Entecott, 53636

Advanced to 1st class, for courageous conduct in rescuing 3 persons from a house on fire.

RESIGNATION COMPULSORY

Pc 208 Meade

Off his beat, and receiving drink from the potman of a public house; telling a deliberate lie, and making a false accusation against his Sergeant; also using threatening language to him when leaving the Superintendent's office, and refusing to return.

ROLL OF HONOUR
- Pc Samuel Bell

Died from injuries received on duty when he was struck on the head by a gate.

1877: ROLL OF HONOUR
- Pc Thomas Groomes

Found drowned on duty.

1878: ROLL OF HONOUR
- Pc Richard Cook, 62602 K

Died of multiple injuries received from his horse falling on him.

1879: ROLL OF HONOUR
- Pc William Stevens Nazer

Drowned while on duty at Chatham dockyard.
- Pc James Collis, 58274 Y

Died from multiple injuries when he was run over by a train while on duty at New Barnet station.
- Pc William Twinn, 62508 E

Died from injuries received when knocked down by a runaway horse.

1881: ROLL OF HONOUR
- Pc Frederick Atkins, 61462 V

Shot three times and fatally wounded when he disturbed an unknown burglar at Kingston Hill.
- Sergeant William Bacon

Accidentally drowned while in the execution of his duty.

1882: STANHOPE MEDAL OF THE ROYAL HUMANE SOCIETY

Jenkins   John   Police Constable   E

Constable Jenkins was on duty on Waterloo Bridge at 2.45 am on 14th July 1882 when he saw a man mount the parapet and throw himself into the river. Without hesitation the constable unfastened his belt and jumped from the bridge after him. Not withstanding a determined resistance on the part of the would be suicide. Constable Jenkins succeeded in seizing the man and supporting him above water until both were picked up some distance down river by a boat which was promptly sent from the Thames Police Station.

The danger incurred in this rescue may be fairly estimated when it appears that the height from which he jumped was 43 feet, the tide was running out under the arches at the rate of 6 mph, and a thick mist covered the river, so much so as to render it impossible to see any object in the centre of the river from either side. The place where the man entered the water was 170 yards from shore.

ROLL OF HONOUR
- Pc William Goddard, 49028 L

Accidentally drowned when he fell into a dock during stormy weather while on duty at Lambeth.
- Pc Henry Fitnum, 14584 R

Drowned while on duty.
- Inspector Joseph Hughes, 46722 T

Thrown from his horse and broke his neck while returning from Sunbury Petty Sessions.
- Pc George Cole, Pc 83N, 65227 N

Shot while trying to arrest a burglar at Dalston.

1883: ROLL OF HONOUR
- Pc William Silvey, 46360 V

Died through falling from a wagon while in the execution of his duty.

1884: ROLL OF HONOUR
• Inspector William Robson, Thames Division, 37083
Accidentally drowned when his police boat was hit by a tug while visiting river patrols near Charlton.

1885: ALBERT MEDAL
From Police Orders Wednesday 28th January 1885
Cole   William   Police Constable
I have today by the personal command of the Queen conveyed to Pc's Cole and Cox Her Majesty's high sense of the courage and devotion which these brave men have shown in the discharge of their duties on the occasion of the recent explosion in Westminster Hall and Her Majesty's hope that they may have a speedy recovery from the serious injuries they have sustained.

"The gallant conduct of Pc Cole who knowing full well the terrible risk he incurred endeavoured at the peril of his life to remove the burning explosive from the building demands a special recognition. That by this daring act of self sacrifice he averted greater disaster cannot be doubted, and I have had the pleasure to inform his that in addition to the professional reward he will receive, it is Her Majesty's intention to confer upon him the distinction of the Albert Medal.

The medal awarded to William Cole is on display at the Palace of Westminster near the riverside canteen.

ROLL OF HONOUR
• Pc Albert Thompson, 59473 B
Run down by a horse and cart he was attempting to stop for traffic offences.

1886: ROLL OF HONOUR
• Pc Harold Richardson, 70324 N
Accidentally drowned on duty when he fell in the canal near Enfield Lock in stormy weather.

1887: ROLL OF HONOUR
• Pc Robert McGaw, 69843 T
Died from a fractured skull after being kicked by his police horse in Fulham Stables.
• Ps David Groombridge, E
Died from injures received when beaten and kicked by two men during an arrest at Kings Cross in 1886.

1888 - 1891: REIGN OF JACK THE RIPPER
The reign of terror began towards the end of the 1880's in London. Some say he started his reign as early as 1887 and others as late as 1891. It remains one of the great mysteries of all time, just who was "Jack the Ripper".

The first recorded victim was found on Friday 31 August 1888 at 3.45am. She was discovered in Bucks Row, Whitechapel. At first the two men thought she was a drunk, so they left her and went to find a policeman. Pc 97J Neil while on his beat came across the body, he used his lamp to signal for help and was joined by Pc 96J Thain. They directed their bulls eye lanterns onto the figure and saw that she was dead. Blood trickled from a deep gash in the throat. The woman was Mary Ann Nichols or "Polly Nichols".

The second victim was discovered on Saturday 8 September 1888 just after 6am in Hanbury Street. She was Annie Chapman also known as "Dark Annie".

On Sunday 30 September 1888 the third victim was found in an unlit courtyard off Berner Street, she was lying on her back, there were deep cuts to her neck, her carotid artery in her neck had been cut. When she was found her body was still warm. She was identified as Elizabeth Stride or "Long Liz", she was a Swedish woman.

At 4.40am the fourth victim was discovered by Pc 881 Watkins. He was patrolling his beat, he walked into Mitre Square and discovered the woman lying in a pool of blood, she like the others was lying on her back her face had been slashed and her abdomen and chest had been ripped open. She was Catherine Eddowes. The sad thing about this victim was that she had only been released from Bishopsgate Police Station at 1am having been arrested for being drunk and incapable earlier the previous evening.

It was November before the Ripper struck again. On a damp and overcast day on Friday 9 November 1888 the owner of Miller Court had become impatient about the non payment of rent at number 13. He sent his young assistant to collect the money. He got no reply at the door so he went to a small broken window, he pulled the curtain to one side, the sight he was to see was most appalling. The Ripper had struck again but this time more brutal than before. The abdominal surface and thighs had been removed, the abdominal cavity emptied, her breasts had been cut off, the arms mutilated the face had been hacked beyond recognition. Her uterus, one breast and kidney were under her head, the other breast was by her right foot, the liver being placed between the feet, the flaps which had been removed from the abdomen were on a table in the room.

These were the five noted victims of the Ripper, but there had been other victims, were they also the work of the infamous "Jack the Ripper"?

- 3 April 1888 Emma Elizabeth Smith was found savagely assaulted in Osborn Street, she died in the London Hospital a little later of peritonitis, before she died she managed to give a description of the gang that had attacked her.
- August 1888 Martha Tabrum was found in George Yard Buildings. She had been stabbed 39 times.
- 17 July 1889 Alice McKenzie also known as "Clay Pipe Alice" was found in Castle Alley, she was still warm when discovered by Pc 272H Andrews.
- 21 November 1888 Annie Farmer claimed she was attacked at 19 George Street, she said she had been attacked by a man who then rushed out of the house.
- 20 December 1889 Rose Mylett's body was found in Clarkes Yard.
- 10 September 1889 an unidentified woman's trunk was found under the railway arches in Pinchin Street.
- 13 February 1891 Frances Coles was found in Swallow Gardens, murdered in the same fashion as the Ripper victims, her throat was cut and her abdomen had been ripped.

Jack the Ripper's reign of terror ended as suddenly as it began. To this day no one knows who he was, we all have our own ideas on the matter, but I am sure this will remain a mystery for ever.

1888: ROLL OF HONOUR
* Pc Michael Lewis, B

Died of a ruptured heart after a violent struggle during arrest of a suspected thief at Chelsea.
* Pc Alfred Ellis, 46391 V

Accidentally drowned on duty when he fell in the river off steps near Barnes Bridge.
* Pc Thomas Dean, 52549 M

Drowned in the Surrey Canal while patrolling his beat on a foggy night.

1890: ROLL OF HONOUR
* Pc William Pasker

Drowned attempting to rescue a man in heavy seas at Margate while off duty.

1891: ROYAL HUMANE SOCIETY BRONZE MEDAL
Elliott   John   Police Constable

At great personal risk, rescued Charles T Pether from drowning in a reservoir at Loughton on the 11th June 1891.

ROLL OF HONOUR
* Pc George Cole

Died when he was run over and fatally injured trying to stop a pair of runaway horses and van on Brixton Hill.

1892: ROYAL HUMANE SOCIETY BRONZE MEDAL
Rowland   Alexander   Police Constable   E

At great personal risk attempted to rescue William F Skinner from drowning in the Thames at Wandsworth on 15th September 1892.

ROLL OF HONOUR
* Pc Arthur May

Died from the effects of injuries received when he fell into a canal while on duty.
* Pc Henry Graham

Died as a result of injuries sustained in an accident while on mounted duty at the Lord Mayor's Show.
* Pc Joseph Daniels

Choked to death when he swallowed his false teeth while assisting in the arrest of a prisoner at Bow Street.
* Ds Joseph Joyce, J

Shot twice and fatally wounded when arresting a burglar at Charing Cross Road.

- Ps David Garner

Collapsed and died from heart disease and other exertion in securing a prisoner.

1893: ROYAL HUMANE SOCIETY BRONZE MEDAL

Berrett   James   Police Constable

At great personal risk rescued John Connelly from drowning in the Regents Canal Dock at Limehouse on 13th May 1893.

ROYAL HUMANE SOCIETY BRONZE MEDAL

Smith   Robert   Police Constable

With Jeremiah Donovan at great personal risk, rescued Daniel Taylor from drowning in the Grand Surrey Canal at Peckham on 9th June 1893.

ROLL OF HONOUR

- Inspector George Dixon

Found drowned on duty in suspicious circumstances at Hampton Court.

- Pc Robert Wright

Killed while searching for persons believed trapped in a burning house in Croydon.

1894: ROYAL HUMANE SOCIETY BRONZE MEDAL

Jones   Edward   Police Constable   E

Saved a woman from drowning in the Channel Sear river (sic) on 6th December 1893.

1895: ROYAL HUMANE SOCIETY BRONZE MEDAL

Rowe   James   Inspector   Y

At great personal risk, rescued George Busby from drowning at Hove on 21st June 1895.

ROYAL HUMANE SOCIETY BRONZE MEDAL

Simmons   Fred   Police Constable

At great personal risk rescued W Mullingier from drowning in the Thames at East Greenwich on 9th February 1895.

ROLL OF HONOUR

- Pc Charles Wright

Crushed while on patrol by the accidental fall of a stack of timber in a wood yard at Dulwich.

1896: ROYAL HUMANE SOCIETY BRONZE MEDAL

Clarke   Albert   Police Constable   457E

Together with Pc George Munro 482E at great personal risk, rescued Mary Williams from drowning in the Thames at Adelphi Stairs on 10th June 1896.

Testimonial on Vellum to Pc Munro.

ROLL OF HONOUR
* Pc Edwin Stone
Collapsed and died from heart disease while assisting in a violent arrest.

1897: ROYAL HUMANE SOCIETY BRONZE MEDAL
Byron   Arthur   Police Constable
At great personal risk rescued Harry Hunt from drowning in the Regents Canal on 19th August 1897.

ROYAL HUMANE SOCIETY BRONZE MEDAL
Crampton   John   Police Constable
At great personal risk rescued Thomas Cole from drowning in the Thames at Wapping on 14th May 1897.

ROYAL HUMANE SOCIETY BRONZE MEDAL
Farrington   W   Police Constable
At great personal risk rescued James Bull, and attempted to rescue Catherine Steward from drowning in the Regents Canal on 13th July 1897.

ROYAL HUMANE SOCIETY BRONZE MEDAL
Green   Henry   Police Constable
At great personal risk rescued Florence Butler from drowning in the Lee at Hackney on 3rd February 1897.

ROLL OF HONOUR
* Dc William James Kemp
Died of internal injuries aggravated through having strained himself while chasing a prisoner.

1898: ROYAL HUMANE SOCIETY BRONZE MEDAL
Cartwright   W   Police Constable
On 16th August 1898 a boy was washed into the river at Hammersmith by the swell of a passing steamer. Cartwright at once dived in, and at great personal risk rescued the lad.

ROYAL HUMANE SOCIETY BRONZE MEDAL
Outram   Herbert   Police Constable
On 27th November 1898 a woman who had wondered from home got into the Thames at the Adelphi Steps, Outram at great personal risk jumped in, the depth being 20 feet and rescued her.

ROYAL HUMANE SOCIETY BRONZE MEDAL
West   Henry J   Police Constable
On 17th September 1898 a boy accidentally fell into Regents Canal, Limehouse. West jumped in fully clothed and rescued him.

ROYAL HUMANE SOCIETY BRONZE MEDAL

Wilson   T   Police Sergeant

On 21st September 1898 Joseph Baker aged 7 was on a floating plank in Williamsons Pond, Tottenham, when he fell in and sank. The pond is very dangerous, with about 8 feet of water and 3 feet of mud. Wilson at great personal risk dived in and recovered the body, but life was extinct.

ROLL OF HONOUR

• Pc James Baldwin, G

Fatally stabbed when attempting to arrest a man for causing a disturbance in the street at Holborn.

1899 ROYAL HUMANE SOCIETY BRONZE MEDAL

Taylor   Ernest   Police Constable

On 7th August 1899 a boy fell into the Thames at Temple Steps, and was being rapidly carried away by the strong tide. Taylor at great personal risk, jumped in fully clothed, and succeeded in rescuing the boy.

Chapter Two

THE YEARS OF 1900 - 1909

The Relief of Mafeking, the end of the Boer War. Queen Victoria dies in 1901, the end of the Victorian era and the beginning of the Edwardian. The first Nobel Prizes are awarded.

The emergence of the Suffragette movement in the United Kingdom, with the leader Emmeline Pankhurst. Disturbances at Parliament and Buckingham Palace.

Man flies for the first time with the invention of the airplane by Orville Wright. An earthquake hits San Francisco, devastating the city.

We see the Tottenham Anarchist Outrage, and the first awards of the new King's Police Medal which was instituted in 1909.

The very first telephone box is introduced into London.

1900

January	The Hippodrome Theatre opens in Charing Cross Road, London.
February	In the UK, Trade Unions create the new Labour Party.
March	Fire destroys part of the roof of Buckingham Palace.
April	In the US the first book of stamps is issued.
May	Rejoicing in UK as the siege of Mafeking is over.
June	In London the central railway 'tuppenny tube' opens from Shepherds Bush in West London to the Bank.
July	In Russia the Tsar abolishes exile to Siberia for punishment for dissent.
August	Britons get their first taste of coca cola, now on sale in the UK 14 years after starting in the US.
September	Bubonic plague is spreading through the City of Glasgow.
October	Soldiers return from the Boer war to a hero's welcome.
November	Front wheel drive mechanism is patented in Germany.
December	Thousands of gallons of beer are being poured down drains after 4 die from poisoning. Glucose supplied to brewers had been contaminated with arsenic.

HITS OF THE YEAR

I'm only a bird in a gilded cage
Goodbye Dolly Gray

ROYAL HUMANE SOCIETY BRONZE MEDAL

Chilcott   Charles   Police Constable

On 17th July 1900 Charles Carter fell into the Regents canal at the Cat and Mutton Bridge. Chilcott jumped in and rescued him in an unconscious state, thereafter applying treatment for his restoration. An award made together with a certificate.

ROYAL HUMANE SOCIETY BRONZE MEDAL

Turner   G T   Police Constable

On 21st August 1900 Constables Meadows Metropolitan Police was in a boat on the Thames at Putney, when some 50 yards from the bank the boat capsized, Turner who was also in a boat, jumped into the river, caught Meadows and swam with him to the bank.

ROLL OF HONOUR

- Pc Ernest Thompson, H

Stabbed in the neck by a man he had moved on after a street disturbance in Whitechapel.

- Pc George Stephen Funnell

Died from injuries received rescuing 3 women from a fire in a public house at Hackney.

- Pc William Goulder

Drowned when he fell in the River Thames at Barnes while on patrol during a foggy night.

- Pc Frederick Kidd

Drowned in Shadwell Dock while on night duty.

1901

January	12 retailers in Manchester were prosecuted for selling beer contaminated with arsenic.
February	Funeral takes place of Queen Victoria.
March	The first diesel motor goes on show in the UK.
April	In the US, actors are arrested at the Academy of Music for wearing costumes on a Sunday.
May	Both Alexandra Park and Alexandra Palace open to the public.
June	Wireless telegraphy is tried at sea for the first time on board the liner 'Lucania' in mid Atlantic.
July	Opening of the first completed section of the London electric tramway from Shepherds Bush to Southall.
August	Important gold strike is made in the Rand, South Africa.
September	Outbreak of smallpox is spreading in London.
October	First submarine is launched by the Royal Navy, the Holland I.
November	The new telephone system for London is completed.
December	Sweden awards the first Nobel prizes.

HITS OF THE YEAR

Just a-wearying for you

Mighty

ROYAL HUMANE SOCIETY BRONZE MEDAL

Cleverley   Harry   Police Constable

On 11th January 1901 Bertha Lawson, who had escaped from a Lunatic Asylum threw herself into the Regents Canal. The night was dark and the depth of water 10 feet. At great risk, Cleverley jumped in and after a hard struggle succeeded in saving her.

ROYAL HUMANE SOCIETY BRONZE MEDAL

Milne   Stewart   Police Constable

On 29th July 1901 a man threw his three children aged 9, 4 and 2 into the Regents Canal at Regents Park the depth being 7 feet and the water very foul. Milne ran 460 yards and plunged in endeavoured to rescue them but failed, as they were dead when brought out by him.

ROYAL HUMANE SOCIETY BRONZE MEDAL

Smith   Albert   Police Constable

On 21 July 1901 Polly Chandler in an attempt at suicide, threw herself into the Thames at London Bridge. At great risk Smith jumped in and after a struggle, succeeded in saving her.

ROLL OF HONOUR

- Pc James Newbold

Drowned when he fell overboard from a patrolling police steam launch.

- Ps Neil MacDougall

Accidentally shot in the neck at the annual police revolver practice in Eltham.

1902

January	In the UK the census shows the population of Greater London at 6,581,372.
February	London Post Office opens its telephone system to subscribers.
March	In London, an Army order gives soldiers the right to wear spectacles on or off duty.
April	Several acres of the Barbican in the City of London destroyed by a massive fire.
May	Thomas Edison the American inventor announces the invention of a new electrical storage battery.
June	A riot nearly breaks out in Watford following the postponement of the Coronation, due to an emergency operation on Edward VII.
July	Lord Kitchener is given a triumphant welcome on his return from South Africa.
August	Coronation of King Edward VII.
September	State of emergency declared in Dublin.
October	It is announced that Windsor Castle will be open to the public when the court is absent.
November	Lord Tennyson is appointed as Governor General of Australia.
December	W W Astor makes a gift of £50,000 to the Great Ormond Street Children's Hospital.

HITS OF THE YEAR
Bill Bailey won't you please come home
In the good old summer time

ROYAL HUMANE SOCIETY BRONZE MEDAL
Hierons   John   Police Constable
On 20th January 1902 Clara Lines accidentally fell from the tow path at Hammersmith, the strong tide running soon carrying her out 50 yards from the bank into deep water. At great risk Hierons swam out and kept her afloat till they were picked up by a boat.

ROYAL HUMANE SOCIETY BRONZE MEDAL
Davies   S   Police Constable
On 27th April 1902, 2 men were in a small boat, which capsized in the Thames opposite the Royal Naval College Greenwich. The accident took place about 30 yards from the bank in 20 feet of water. At great risk, Little swam out and got the man to hold onto the boat but as soon as they became exhausted, Davies swam out and gave assistance till they were picked up by boat.

ROYAL HUMANE SOCIETY BRONZE MEDAL
Ludford   John   Police Constable
On 21 January 1902 a woman named Packham, in an attempt at suicide, threw herself into the Thames in front of the Royal Naval College, Greenwich. It was midnight, and there was 12 feet of water with an ebb tide. At great risk, Ludford who heard the splash plunged in and brought her to safety.

ROYAL HUMANE SOCIETY BRONZE MEDAL
Mills   C   Police Constable
On 28th June 1902 A. Grosvenor a lunatic, in an attempt at suicide, threw himself into the Regents Canal, Shoreditch. There being a depth of 12 feet and the water being very foul. Mills at great risk went in and got him near the side, when police Sergeant Gibson rendered assistance in landing. Testimonial on Vellum awarded to Sergeant Gibson.

ROYAL HUMANE SOCIETY BRONZE MEDAL
Morley   Wm. John   Police Constable
On 28th February 1902 an insane woman in an attempt at suicide threw herself into the Regents Canal at St Marks Bridge. Morley at great risk, jumped in and, after a hard struggle, succeeded in bringing her out.

ROYAL HUMANE SOCIETY BRONZE MEDAL
Plackett   J   Police Constable
On 26th July 1902 Mary A Sagus in an attempt at suicide threw herself into the Regents Canal, Cambridge Heath. The night was dark, the water 9 feet deep and very foul. At great risk Plackett jumped in and succeeded in finding and rescuing her, afterwards restoring her to consciousness.
    An award of a certificate was also made.

ROYAL HUMANE SOCIETY BRONZE MEDAL

Stephens   F   Sergeant CID Scotland Yard

On 27th July 1902 Thomas Palmer in trying to recover a stick fell into the Thames at Vauxhall. There was 12 feet of water with a strong flood tide. At great risk, Stephens jumped from a temporary bridge and rescued the lad.

ROLL OF HONOUR

• Pc Arthur Healey

Fell through a glass roof while checking insecure premises at Kensington.

1903

January	51 die in a fire at a mental hospital at Colney Hatch, North London.
February	Official enquiry launched into traffic congestion in London.
March	Regular news service begins between London and New York using Marconi's new wireless.
April	In Holland, the Government passes a bill punishing the civil service and railway strikers with imprisonment.
May	Kew Bridge over the River Thames opens.
June	16 die in an explosion at Woolwich Arsenal.
July	The Ford motor company in the US sells its first production car, the Model A.
August	Joseph Pulitzer gives $2 million to a Colombia University to start a school of Journalism.
September	Great storms in the SE of England cause deaths and widespread damage.
October	Mrs. Emmeline Pankhurst forms a militant movement to gain votes for women 'The Suffragettes'.
November	US and Panama sign a treaty to build the Panama Canal.
December	Orville Wright flies a heavier than air machine for over 800 feet, the flight lasted almost one minute.

HITS OF THE YEAR

Ida

The Kashmiri song

Sweet Adeline

ROYAL HUMANE SOCIETY BRONZE MEDAL

Barclay   Francis H   Police Constable

On 25th May 1903 Agnes Gibson in at attempt at suicide threw herself into the Surrey Canal at Deptford. At great risk, Barclay jumped in and, after being dragged under water managed to rescue her.

ROYAL HUMANE SOCIETY BRONZE MEDAL
Ennor   W   Police Sergeant Devonport Division
On 23rd September 1903 Charles Drew in trying to pass from one boat to another, fell into
the sea at Torpoint, Cornwall. This took place 70 yards out in 16 feet of water. At great risk
Ennor swam out and supported him till they were picked up.

ROYAL HUMANE SOCIETY BRONZE MEDAL
Russell   G E   Police Constable
On 19th July 1903 a woman threw herself into the Surrey Canal at Peckham. The night being
dark. Russell dived in and rescued her in an unconscious state, and there after succeeded in
restoring her.

ROLL OF HONOUR
- Pc William Campbell
Crushed while on crowd control duties in 1900.

1904

January	In the US Henry Ford sets a new land speed record of 91.37mph.
February	Freak tidal wave swept up the English Channel leaving a trail of devastation in its wake.
March	King Edward VII opens Richmond Park to the public.
April	UK trains run non stop from Plymouth to London in under 4 hours.
May	Mr Rolls and Mr Royce merge to make cars.
June	US President Roosevelt names black Senator Charles Warren Fairbank to second his Presidential nomination.
July	The Royal Horticultural Society opens its new Headquarters in Vincent Square, Westminster.
August	First Atlantic weather forecast is received by wireless telegraph.
September	Detective Inspector Collins of Scotland Yard gives evidence against William Simpson on fingerprints taken at the scene of a crime.
October	Royal Naval ships surround the Russian Baltic Fleet following the Dogger Bank incident.
November	First underwater journey of a submarine across the Solent from Southampton to the Isle of Wight.
December	London's first tube goes electric.

HITS OF THE YEAR
Give my regards to Broadway
Meet me in St Louis, Louis

ROLL OF HONOUR
- Pc Leonard Russell
Collapsed and died while arresting a man for drunkenness at Tottenham.

- Pc James Macey

Collapsed and died following the arrest of a drunken woman at Kennington.

1905

January	It now costs £6 to travel third class by liner to the US.
February	2 Frenchmen land in a balloon at Crystal Palace after crossing the English Channel.
March	Sherlock Holmes is brought back from the dead by public demand.
April	St Petersburg, the Government lifts its censorship of private telegrams.
May	First flight of a motorised aeroplane in Europe takes place in France.
June	Russian Potemkin mutineers kill their officers.
July	Discovery of documents revealing the identity of the original Othello.
August	Severe storms and flooding hit Ireland.
September	The TUC says 1.5 million Britons are in unions and calls for free trade and an 8 hour day.
October	King Edward VII opens the Kingsway and Aldwych, two new roads to ease congestion between Holborn and the Strand.
November	Worlds largest turbine liner, Cunard's 'Carmania' leaves on her maiden voyage.
December	LCC decides to set up the Capital's first motorised ambulance service for traffic victims.

HITS OF THE YEAR

Wait till the sun shines Nellie

ROYAL HUMANE SOCIETY BRONZE MEDAL

Robertson   J   Police Sergeant

On 7 October an unknown man was seen to throw himself into the Thames from Chelsea Embankment. There being at the time a depth of 16 feet, with strong flood tide. At great risk, Robertson plunged in, but was unable to reach him before he sank.

ROLL OF HONOUR

- Pc Thomas William Perry

Collapsed and died at the station after arresting two men for drunkenness at Walworth.

- Pc William Croft

Died in consequence of injuries received when he fell into a pit while chasing burglars at Chiswick.

1906

January	The River Thames catches fire as oil on the surface ignites.
February	HMS Dreadnought is launched, the largest and fastest battleship afloat.
March	London underground opens from Baker Street to Waterloo and is dubbed the 'Bakerloo' line.
April	Earthquake devastates San Francisco, thousands die.
May	Vauxhall Bridge opens in London.
June	Worlds largest and fastest passenger liner 'Lusitania' is launched.

July	A Commons select committee recommends introduction of school meals.
August	Winston Churchill and 100 other eminent people protest at street noise caused by traffic.
September	Thousands help recapture 'Life Guards' mascot bear which escaped in transit to London Zoo.
October	First wireless telegraphy conference agrees to the adoption of SOS as an international distress signal.
November	Noisy London buses are banned from the roads.
December	Suffragettes in Holloway Prison refuse to eat Christmas dinner.

HITS OF THE YEAR
Waiting at the Church

ROYAL HUMANE SOCIETY BRONZE MEDAL
Biggs   Henry   Police Constable
At 2.40am on 3rd September 1906 an old man was seen to throw himself into the Thames at Charing Cross. There being at the time a depth of 30 feet, with an ebb tide and the night dark. At great risk, Henry Biggs, Constable Metropolitan plunged in, and kept him afloat till they were picked up by the police boat, but the man did not recover.

ROYAL HUMANE SOCIETY BRONZE MEDAL
Killick   Harry   Police Constable
On 24 July 1906 a boy named Thomson, while at play fell into the Roding at Ilford, the depth being 10 feet and the water being very foul. Harry Killick police constable Metropolitan ran 60 yards and at great risk plunging in was successful in saving the boy.

ROYAL HUMANE SOCIETY BRONZE MEDAL
Robinson   Geo.   Police Constable
At 11.25pm on 7 July 1906 Louis A Fewings threw himself into the river at the Shadwell entrance to the London Docks, the depth being 23 feet. At great risk Geo. Robinson plunged in, and in spite of his struggles succeeded in saving him.

ROYAL HUMANE SOCIETY BRONZE MEDAL
Cameron   John   Police Constable
On 3rd December 1906 a woman named Andrews threw herself into the Lea at Bow Bridge and sank. The depth being 7 feet and the water very foul. John Cameron police constable Metropolitan dived in, and finding her at the bottom got her out in an unconscious state and then restored her. A certificate was also awarded.

ROLL OF HONOUR

1907
January   Arctic weather hits Europe, in Austria the temperature drops to -30°F.

February	The King and Queen open the new court at the Old Bailey, the Central Criminal Court built of the site of Newgate Prison.
March	72 Suffragettes refuse to pay fines for demonstrating outside Parliament and are sent to prison.
April	Louis Bleriot flies his new mono plane 10 yards.
May	Second reading of a Bill providing an old age pension of 5/- a week to people over 65 years of age.
June	David Lloyd George opens the new Hampstead tube line.
July	Robert Baden-Powell forms the Boy Scouts after the Brownsea Island camp.
August	The uncompleted Singer building is the world's tallest building in New York.
September	UK's first military airship the 'Nulli Secundus' flies at Farnborough.
October	The liner Lusitania breaks all records for crossing the Atlantic in 4 days 19 hours and 52 minutes.
November	Florence Nightingale aged 87 is given the Order of Merit (OM) by King Edward VII.
December	In New York women have to sign affidavits of their age and good character before they marry.

HITS OF THE YEAR
If those lips could only speak

ROYAL HUMANE SOCIETY BRONZE MEDAL
Scott   Conrad   Police Constable
On 26th March 1907 Jennie Hill was thrown into the Surrey Canal at Rotherhithe by her sweetheart. The time being nearly midnight and the water very foul. Conrad Scott police constable went in fully clothed and succeeded in saving her.

ROYAL HUMANE SOCIETY BRONZE MEDAL
Setter   James H   Police Constable
On 27th October 1907 a boy fell from a landing stage into the Thames at Southwark, the depth being 12 feet with a strong tide. James J Setter police constable Metropolitan jumped in and rescued him.

ROLL OF HONOUR

1908
January	In the US the State of Georgia introduces a law prohibiting alcohol.
February	Children's Bill published in London which would penalise anyone allowing children to smoke.
March	Freedom of the City of London conferred on Florence Nightingale.
April	Count Von Zeppelin announces a new airship capable of 47 mph in Berlin.
May	In Washington the Wright brothers patent 'their flying machine'.
June	First visit of an English King to Russia.

July	First criminal appeal against a murder conviction is turned down at the Central Criminal Court.
August	Henry Ford first new Model T is produced in Detroit.
September	The TUC conference in Nottingham says that motor cars should have a fixed maximum speed of 15 mph.
October	New harbour is opened at Dover.
November	International motor exhibition opens in London.
December	Child Emperor Pu Yi accedes to the throne as Hsuan Tung.

HITS OF THE YEAR
Shine on Harvest moon
Oh oh Antonio

ROLL OF HONOUR
•   Pc Joseph Williamson
Died of injuries received when kicked in the head while arresting a violent drunk in 1907.

1909
King Edward VII instituted the King's Police Medal for gallantry

January	3 die and 17 are injured chasing two robbers 5 miles over fields and roads from Tottenham to Chingford - known as the Tottenham Anarchist Outrage - Pc Tyler shot and killed see first entry for 1910.
February	Colour films are screened in public for the first time at Brighton.
March	Selfridge's department store opens in London.
April	Joan of Arc is beatified in Rome.
May	In London the Aeronautical Society presents the Wright brothers with its Gold Medal for achievement.
June	King Edward VII opens the Victoria and Albert Museum in South Kensington.
July	Frenchman Louis Bleriot flies across the English Channel in 43 minutes.
August	In London thousands of slum children leave for a fortnights free holiday in the country organised by charity.
September	First Boy Scout parade takes place at Crystal Palace.
October	Orville Wright flies at a record 1600 feet in Berlin.
November	Naval base planned for Pearl Harbour to defend the US against a Japanese attack.
December	South Pole explorer Ernest Shackleton is Knighted.

HITS OF THE YEAR
Moon struck
I wonder who's kissing her
Has anybody here seen Kelly

TOTTENHAM ANARCHIST OUTRAGE 1909

The murder of a policeman William Tyler, and Ralph Joscelyne a young boy aged 10, and the wounding of a further 21 by 2 anarchist robbers Paul Hefeld and Jacob Lepidus while trying to escape after a wages snatch.

Paul Hefeld and Jacob Lepidus were Latvian immigrants who stole the wages of a rubber factory in Tottenham, North London on 23 January 1909.

There were both armed with pistols and when the vehicle carrying the wages drew up they seized the cash bag. They fired their guns at the driver and a workman who grappled with Lepidus. The shots were heard by Constables Tyler and Newman, who went to the location from the police station. During the long chase the two anarchists fired over 400 rounds at many of their pursuers. A number of officers ran out from the section house to join in the chase, some rode their bicycles.

Pc Newman urged the chauffeur of the wages car to run down the two men but in doing this Newman and the chauffeur were shot and injured, one shot sadly killed little Ralph Joscelyne as he ran for cover.

On hearing that a child had been shot dead and a colleague injured the police smashed open the locked firearms cupboard and took out pistols and joined in the pursuit.

At a railway bridge leading to Tottenham Marshes, Pc Tyler managed to catch up with the two men, Hefeld deliberately took aim and shot him in the face at point blank range, constable Tyler bled to death in a nearby cottage.

The gunmen ran across the marshes and the band of pursuers grew. At one stage the two men commandeered a tram and a milk van. They were eventually trapped behind a high fence, Lepidus managed to scramble over but Hefeld was too exhausted after the long chase and seeing he was about to be arrested put the gun to his head and shot himself, he died 3 weeks later in hospital without speaking to anyone.

Lepidus meanwhile ran into a small development, he pushed the occupants into a lean to scullery, but when the pursuers reached the house he locked himself in a bedroom and used his last bullet to shoot himself. 3 Pc's Eagles, Dixon and Carter broke in and fired shots through the door at him. These officers received the King's Police Medal (see 1910).

A collection of £1,055 was raised for Pc Tyler's widow, and she was granted a pension of £15 a year.

ROYAL HUMANE SOCIETY BRONZE MEDAL

| Deane | James C | |
| Green | A E H | Police Constable |

On 31 May 1909 a man in an attempt at suicide threw himself into the Thames from the Victoria Embankment, the night being dark and the tide running fast. Deane and Green plunged in and between them succeeded in saving him.

ROYAL HUMANE SOCIETY BRONZE MEDAL

| Lambert | W | Police Constable |

On 24th February 1909 a man going on board his ship fell into Debnams dock at Deptford. The depth being 14 feet and the night cold and frosty. Lambert jumped in and succeeded in getting him out.

ROYAL HUMANE SOCIETY BRONZE MEDAL

Saint   Alfred G   Police Constable

On 13th June 1909 George Shepherd fell into the Thames at Long Ditton and sank in 18 feet of water. Saint went in and dived many times but failed to find him.

ROYAL HUMANE SOCIETY BRONZE MEDAL

Taylor   Joseph G   Police Constable

On 4th July 1909 a boy fell into the Thames at Chelsea the depth being 12 feet with strong cross currents running. Taylor plunged in and was able to swim with him to a disused pier, to which he had held till a boat picked them up.

ROLL OF HONOUR

•   Pc William Tyler KPM, N Division

Shot in the head by armed robber Paul Hefeld whom he was chasing in the Tottenham Outrage.

Chapter Three

THE YEARS OF 1910 - 1919

During the early 1910's there were events which involved the Metropolitan Police in their fair share of grief and achievement. The main note was the capture and conviction of an infamous murderer, Dr Hawley Harvey Crippen. This arrest was made possible due to the newly invented radio telegraphy system whereby a ship was able to send a message to London while crossing the Atlantic.

One of the main events which led to better arming and training of the police was the Siege of Sidney Street. Sadly there was loss of life both police and civilian. It was the first time that the Home Secretary was actively involved in police operations and used the military to assist the police in the fire power.

There was a lot of activity by the Suffragette movement 'Votes for Women'. They tried all means to protest including planting bombs, arson, criminal damage and the ultimate protest led to the death of one of their organisation at the Derby. They had even tried to storm Parliament and Buckingham Palace. Several were arrested and some even went on hunger strike.

During the Great War women were allowed to drive buses and taxis. They also did manual labour as the men folk were at the front fighting the war. In 1917 the Women's Police Force was formed, but they were only paid 42s a week.

There was a Police strike in 1918; they were demanding an increase of the war bonus from 12s a week to £1, also an additional bonus of 12%, reinstatement of one of their colleagues who had been dismissed for his militant actions, and finally the recognition of a Union. Due to this strike action the police today are not permitted to strike. So no matter what happens, the police have to work and do their duty as directed by Parliament.

Even though the war ended in 1918, the allied soldiers still remained and one particular incident of note was at Epsom in Surrey. 400 Canadian soldiers stormed the police station to try to release two of the comrades who had been arrested for being drunk and disorderly. Sadly this resulted in the death of a Police Sergeant and several other officers being injured. The Sergeant left a widow and two girls.

This decade also saw a revolution in Russia where the Tsar was deposed, exiled and finally murdered along with his family by the Bolsheviks. We saw the unsinkable liner Titanic sink with the loss of over 1500 passengers and crew.

1910

The first awards of the King's Police Medal were made this year. The first awards for bravery appeared in the London Gazette on 1st January 1910. They were for bravery shown at the 'Tottenham Anarchists Outrage' see page 30 for further information. The names of those awarded the medal can be seen in the next few pages.

January   The wife of Dr Crippen vanishes from their home in Camden Town (see below on the murder by Dr Hawley Harvey Crippen).

February   Hurricane force winds cause several deaths and severe damage through out the UK.

March   Mount Etna erupts causing widespread destruction.

April   Kissing banned on French railways because of the claim it delays trains.

May   A ruling by a Westminster Court states that a cabbie asking for a tip can be prosecuted.

June   Captain Robert F Scott sets sail from London to the South Pole.

July   Police launch a hunt for Dr Crippen after a woman's remains are found in his cellar.

August   Electric street lamps are replaced by 3000 high pressure gas lamps giving more light in the fog.

September   London doctor asserts that if lunacy increases at the present rate, insane will out number sane in 40 years.

October   Launch of the White Star Liner 'Olympic' the biggest vessel afloat.

November   119 Suffragettes are arrested after an attack on the House of Commons.

December   Robbers shoot dead 3 policemen - see 1911 Siege of Sidney Street.

HITS OF THE YEAR
Chinatown, my Chinatown
Ah, sweet mystery of life

DR HAWLEY HARVEY CRIPPEN - 1910
Dr Hawley Harvey Crippen was married to Cora an active socialite of the music hall whose stage name was *'Belle Elmore'*. She would often meet up with her music hall friends for nights out. Theirs was not a happy marriage, she being a brutal domineering wife who often embarrassed him when they went out. They lived at 39 Hilldrop Crescent in North London.

Cora was last seen in January, when suddenly and most uncharacteristically she went to America. She gave no advance warning or prior notice of this to her friends, and she sent no form of communication on her arrival or forwarding address. In February she allegedly informed the 'Music Hall Ladies Guild' of her resignation, as she had to leave for America, she said she was in such haste that she had asked her husband Dr Crippen to write the letter on her behalf.

One month later Dr Crippen announced to all that she was dangerously ill and weak and that her condition was critical, and on 24th March he sent a telegram to one of her closest friends stating that Cora had died, and two days later an obituary notice appeared in 'Eva' the theatrical weekly newspaper.

In the meantime Dr Crippen showed no intention of going to America to deal with the funeral arrangements, but what did seem strange to her friends was that he said that she would be cremated and not buried, they said that this seemed strange as she was a devout

Catholic. On 31st March a friend Mrs Louise Smythson went to Scotland Yard to report her friend's disappearance.

After the visit by Mrs Smythson to Scotland Yard, Chief Inspector Dew was assigned as investigating officer. He went to the address in Hilldrop Crescent. On his arrival he found that Dr Crippen was out at work, but was met by a young woman named Ethel le Neve. He did however notice that she was wearing a distinctive diamond brooch which matched the description of one that had once belonged to Cora. Dr Crippen was later interviewed at his office in New Oxford Street by the Chief Inspector but could only give his statement during his consultations with his patients.

On Monday 11th July the Chief Inspector went to Hilldrop Crescent to clarify a few details with Dr Crippen but was surprised to find the house empty. He then ordered a complete search of the three storey nine room house but nothing of significance was found. Every rose bush in the garden was dug up, every inch of soil was searched. After two full days of searching nothing was found. The only room left was the tiny coal cellar situated at the end of a short gloomy corridor leading from the kitchen.

On removing a few loose bricks and digging about six inches down a nauseating smell filled the cellar forcing Dew and a Sergeant out into the garden. A shallow pit filled with a mass of human flesh had been covered in lime. The cellar grave of Cora revealed that all the bones were removed from the torso and that the head and limbs were missing, they were never found.

Dr Crippen meanwhile had convinced Ethel that they had to leave the house in case the gossip about them started. They also decided before they left that Ethel should disguise herself as a boy so as not to draw too much attention. He crudely cut her long hair short to aid the disguise. They met at Chancery Lane tube and went onto Liverpool Street station where they caught a train to Harwich and then a boat to Holland. They went onto Brussels and to aid in the deception he shaved off his moustache and had Ethel's hair cut properly. After staying in Brussels for ten days he booked two second class berths sailing from Antwerp to Quebec on the 31st July but changed the date to the 20th after reading of the discovery of the body of Cora.

On 20th Dr Crippen and Ethel le Neve boarded the *Montrose* at Antwerp and sailed for Quebec. The second officer being an amateur sleuth noticed the strange couple and having read about the discovery of the body of Cora sent a radio message on the 23rd to the ship's owners who then forwarded the message to Scotland Yard. On 23rd Chief Inspector Dew in disguise left Liverpool on the *Laurentic,* and the chase began. On 25th a radio message was sent to the *Montrose* from London confirming that Scotland Yard had received the radio message regarding the possible sighting of Dr Crippen. On 27th the *Laurentic* overtook the *Montrose* and on the 31st Dr Crippen and Ethel le Neve were arrested at Farther Point in Canadian waters. After due legal process they arrived back in Liverpool under arrest on 28th August.

During the trial it was pointed out that Dr Crippen had made an unusual choice of poison. He used Hyoscine or Hydrobromide of Hyosice; it had never been used before or since. At the time Hyoscine was used as an extremely diluted sedative, and Dr Crippen had bought five grains at a chemist shop and signed for them in the poisons book.

The jury took only 27 minutes to find him guilty of the murder of his wife Cora, and he was sentenced to death by hanging. On 23rd November he was hanged at Pentonville Prison.

KING'S POLICE MEDAL
LG 1/10/10
TOTTENHAM ANARCHISTS OUTRAGE 23/1/1909

Cater	John William	Police Constable 87890	Y
Dixon	Charles	Police Constable	68090 N
Eagles	Charles	Police Constable	90319 V

For conspicuous bravery in connection with the 'Tottenham Anarchists Outrage', on 23rd January 1909.

Two mid-European immigrants, named Jacob Lepidus, and Paul Hefeld, had attempted to rob the wages delivery at a rubber factory in North London. Both men were armed with revolvers and a large quantity of ammunition during which both men fired their revolvers at anyone who stood in their way. The chase lasted for two and a half hours, over six miles, during which a child Ralph Joscelyne aged ten was shot dead. As the men passed in front of Tottenham Police Station, constable TYLER attempted to stop them, but was shot down, and died instantly. In all twenty five persons were injured by the two desperadoes, and over one hundred shots were fired. Towards the end of the chase over open land, Hefeld, exhausted, exhorted his friend onwards, and as the police closed in, put his revolver to his own head. He died in hospital three weeks later. Lepedus went on, and eventually hid in a house. Constables CATER, DIXON and EAGLES, who had been involved in the whole chase, closed in, and as they climbed the stairs, heard a shot from the bedroom. Lepidus had shot himself. All three officers risked their lives in an attempt to arrest this man, knowing that he had already killed two persons, including a police officer. An award to the above was also made from the Bow Street Reward fund.

THE FOLLOWING WERE ALSO AWARDED FROM THE CARNEGIE HERO FUND,

Pc William H Nicod   Pc Charles Eagles
Pc John W Cater   Pc William Dewhurst
Pc Charles Dixon   Pc Charles J Newman
Pc Alexander Ziething

KING'S POLICE MEDAL
LG 1/10/10

Lambert	William	Police Constable 88741 M

At 1am on 24th February 1909, a bitterly cold night, constable Lambert on beat duty in Rotherhithe London, heard shouts coming from the direction of the SS Elaine lying close by in Debnams Dock. He then saw a Swedish seaman Frank Ohlsen, in twelve feet of water in the dock, holding onto the ship's propellor. The constable at once removed his helmet, belt and overcoat, and having unsuccessfully tried to throw a line to Ohlsen plunged into the water and swam to his assistance. In the meantime Ohlsen had managed to reach some nearby barges and was hanging on, unable to climb out. As the constable arrived, another seaman off the Elaine had come ashore, and got down onto the barge, and was holding Ohlsen to prevent him from sinking. The two men then completed the rescue. An award was also made from the Royal Humane Society and a monetary award from the Bow Street fund.

KING'S POLICE MEDAL

LG 1/10/10

Taylor   Joseph George   Police Constable   96320 B

On the afternoon of the 4th July 1909 constable Taylor saw a child in the River Thames. The tide was running strongly, and the constable was not a proficient swimmer. He knew that there was about twelve feet of water, and that the nearest landing point was some two hundred yards away. Without a moment's hesitation, other than to divest himself of his helmet, he plunged into the river, and succeeded in swimming, dragging the boy with him, to the piles of a disused pier, where he was able to cling by his fingertips and hold up the child. When help came after about ten minutes, his fingers were so numb that he was on the point of releasing the child. A monetary award was also made from the Bow Street fund.

KING'S POLICE MEDAL

LG 1/10/10

Young   Alfred   Police Constable   88266 S

On the evening of 15th December 1908 at Swiss Cottage, constable Young observed two men, White and Garcia acting suspiciously. With the help of another constable, Young attempted to arrest them. White immediately pulled out, and attempted to use, a revolver which constable Young tried to wrest from him. White succeeded in pulling the trigger but the weapon misfired and he called on his companion for help. Constable Young however managed to hold onto both prisoners until assisted by the other constable. Both prisoners were found to have black masks in their possession, and Garcia had cartridges, while White had a five chambered revolver, fully loaded. Each was later sentenced to a lengthy term of imprisonment at the Old Bailey. A monetary award was also made from the Bow Street fund.

Constable Young was shot dead in 1915 while attempting to execute an arrest warrant for fraud at Hampstead.

ROLL OF HONOUR

1911

January   Siege of Sidney Street (See over page and appendix 5).
February   First Thames built dreadnought HMS Thunderer launched.
March   France set their time to Greenwich Mean Time.
April   The birch kept as punishment at Eton.
May   The King unveils the Queen Victoria Memorial outside Buckingham Palace.
June   Coronation of King George V and Queen Mary.

July   In the United States 652 deaths in a week during the heat wave.
August   The hottest day in London for 70 years, temperatures reach 97f in the shade.
September   First English Channel swim for 36 years by Thomas Burgess of Rotherham.
October   Winston Churchill named as the new First Sea Lord of the Admiralty.
November   6000 cabbies go on strike in London.
December   Roald Amundsen wins the race to the South Pole beating Capt. Robert Falcoln Scott.

HITS OF THE YEAR
Alexanders ragtime band
I'm 21 today

SIEGE OF SIDNEY STREET

The following gallantry awards were made to the City of London Police Officers in connection with the Siege of Sidney Street the citation below from the London Gazette.

CITY OF LONDON POLICE

Bentley	Robert	Police Sergeant	P
Bryant	William	Police Sergeant	
Choat	Walter Charles	Police Constable	P
Tucker	Charles	Police Sergeant	P
Woodhams	Ernest Charles	Police Constable	

As a result of information received from a member of the public who heard suspicious noises coming from the road of H W Harris the jewellers in Houndsditch, London, late at night on 16th December 1910. Police were called from the nearby station. A number of officers under the charge of Sergeant Bentley went into the Exchange buildings at the rear of Houndsditch. Sergeant Bentley posted the others to keep watch, whilst he went to the door of number 11, Exchange buildings, where a man answered his knock, but did not speak English. The door was closed in the officer's face. Sergeant Bentley opened the door and went inside. Suddenly several shots were heard and Sergeant Bentley fell out of the door mortally wounded. Sergeant Bryant who was standing close behind was also struck in the chest and arm and fell seriously wounded. As the other officers rushed up, an automatic pistol was fired from the doorway, and Sergeant Tucker was hit just above the heart. He died instantly. Constable Woodhams who was on the opposite side of the street was also struck by flying bullets in both legs, his left femur being shattered to such a degree that he was subsequently invalided out of the force. Constable Choat who had been posted to keep watch at the end of the street some thirty yards away ran up on hearing the shooting and grabbed one of the murderers, who was trying to make his escape. This man named Gardstein was the leader of the gang, and one of his compatriots in trying to shoot constable Choat also shot Gardstein in the back. Constable Choat was shot eight times and soon collapsed and died. Gardstein was later found in nearby Grove Street having died from his wounds. The search for the escaped murderers led to the infamous Sidney Street Siege on 3rd January 1911.

The siege of Sidney Street followed the deaths of three City of London Police officers who were shot dead on 16 December 1910. Two other officers were wounded. The officers had attempted to arrest a gang of Latvian burglars who were breaking into a jeweller's shop in Houndsditch, London. The gang escaped into Sidney Street where their leader George Gardstein died of gunshot wounds from one of his own men while evading arrest.

On 2 January police received information that two of the gang were holed up in Mrs Betsey Gershon's flat on the second floor of 100 Sidney Street. In the early house of 3rd January police had cordoned off the area and evacuated several local residents.

Due to the layout of Mrs Betsey Gershon's flat it was not possible to rush it as the gunmen inside could pick off the police as they attempted to enter. Meanwhile armed men had taken Mrs Gershon's skirt and shoes to prevent her from leaving the flat.

At dawn Inspector Wensley of H Division went with a small number of officers to knock on the door, he got no answer so threw some stones at Mrs Gershon's window from which almost immediately came a volley of pistol shots. One of these shots hit Detective Sergeant Leeson. He was carried to a neighbouring house and was immediately removed to hospital.

Such arms that the police had at the time were brought with them, bulldog revolvers, shotguns and rifles fitted with .22 morris tube barrels for use on miniature ranges, these proved completely inadequate for flushing out the gunmen, as they had Mauser pistols capable of rapid fire and deadly fire calibrated to 1000 yards. The Deputy Assistant Commissioner Major Frederick Wodehouse gained the Home Secretary Winston Churchill's permission to send in the Army before going to Sidney Street himself.

500 police were needed to keep back the crowd which had by now gathered. At 10.45am 21 volunteer marksmen of the Scots Guards arrived from their duty at the Tower of London. Three were put on the top floor of a nearby brewery building from where they could fire accurately into the second storey and attic windows from which the gunmen had been shooting. The gunmen were driven down to the lower floors where they came under fire from more guardsmen. In houses across the street the remainder of the guardsmen formed a cordon across Sidney Street firing at the building.

Winston Churchill arrived just before midday to observe the battle, he decided that heavier artillery was needed, but before it could arrive smoke was seen rising from the building. One of the gunmen pushed his head through a window in order to see more clearly, he fell back suddenly, almost certainly shot. The rate of fire from Sidney Street slowed down considerably.

By 1.30pm the building was well alight, the fire brigade arrived but were forbidden by Winston Churchill to extinguish the fire. A maxim gun and another 54 Scots Guards arrived, and a section of Royal Engineers, finally at 2.40pm a troop of the Royal Horse Artillery arrived.

The additional troops were not needed as the last shots from Sidney Street were heard half an hour previously. The fire had gutted the building and its roof had caved in. Two bodies were found inside the building. One of the gunmen had been shot on the first floor while the other had been overcome by smoke on the ground floor.

The failure of the police marksmen and their equipment was duly noted and improved firearms were ordered with better training for officers. This was a very rare case of a Home Secretary taking police operational command decisions.

A letter dated 28 November 1911 from the Metropolitan Receiver authorising payment from police funds of 20 guineas to Dr Nelson Johnstone, £15 to Lewis Levi and £5 to Frank Gascoyne in consideration of the gallantry displayed by them in assisting at the conveyance to hospital of Sgt Leeson who had been wounded in Sidney Street, Stepney.

KING'S POLICE MEDAL
LG 3/1/11

| Cambers | Arthur | Police Constable | 86150 T |

On 26th April 1910, two sewer men, Clark and Ives, entered a manhole with the intention of flushing the sewer in Havelock Road, Southall. A few minutes later Clark was seen lying face down across the flushing tank. Constable Cambers was called to the scene, and assisted Ives down the hold, but after a few feet he was overcome, and had to be hauled out. A second attempt was also unsuccessful. Clark then slipped of the tank, to the bottom of the sewer into water about fourteen feet down. The constable tied a handkerchief across his mouth, and with a rope around his body was lowered to Clark. He was unable to tie a rope round Clark, before he too was over come by fumes. He was hauled out unconscious. A smoke helmet had meanwhile been brought, and constable Cambers was dissuaded from going down again, due to his exhausted condition. Clark was eventually brought to the surface but he was dead. An award was also given from the Royal Humane Society of a bronze medal and a monetary award from the Bow Street fund.

KING'S POLICE MEDAL
LG 3/1/11

| Deniham | William | Police Constable | 93406 V |

Shortly after midnight on the 1st March 1910 constable Deniham heard shouts coming from the direction of the river at Queens Promenade, Kingston, and on his arrival found that a man had jumped into the river. The constable threw off his helmet and greatcoat, jumped into the river, which at this spot was about eleven feet deep, and swam about ten yards from the bank to the man whom he seized, but was compelled almost immediately to release him owing to his struggles. He again seized the man, and managed to swim with him to the bank, where with the assistance of spectators, got him onto the bank. The rescued man, being unconscious, was restored by artificial respiration applied by the constable. An award was also given from the Royal Humane Society of a bronze medal and a monetary award from the Bow Street fund.

KING'S POLICE MEDAL
LG 3/1/11

| Gatland | George | Police Constable | 97045 L |

On the 18th December 1909 a horse drawn greengrocers van was standing outside premises in Brixton Hill, South London, when the animal took fright and bolted. In trying to stop it, the driver pulled the bit from the horses mouth, leaving the bridle hanging around its neck. Constable Gatland, who was some distance down the hill jumped into the rear of the van as it passed him, and climbed onto the back of the galloping horse, finding the bridle useless, the constable pulled on the animals neck and succeeded in guiding it sufficiently to avoid a collision with numerous vehicles on the road. After proceeding in this manner for about 150 yards the constable was compelled to pull into the near side to avoid an approaching tramcar, and in doing so the van collided with a street lamp, and overturned. The constable was thrown onto the foot way, but regained his feet, and seized the horse by the nostrils, and held it until the bridle was replaced, and the horse brought under control. A monetary award was also made from the Bow Street fund.

KING'S POLICE MEDAL
LG 3/1/11

| Haytread | George | Police Constable | 95320 M |

On 26th December 1910, at about 1am, constable Haytread was patrolling his beat when he heard a police whistle, and he saw a man walking quickly away. Upon following him, the man began to run, and on realising that he was being pursued by the constable, stopped, turned and fired three revolver shots at his pursuer. Undeterred the constable caught up to the man who fired a further shot, and whilst struggling, succeeded in placing the revolver against constable Haytread's head and pulling the trigger but providentially the weapon failed to fire. Constable Haytread's pursuit and arrest under such desperate conditions displayed remarkable tenacity and courage. He was valiantly assisted by Mrs. Frances Wright, who without hesitation, and well aware of the risk, came up and struck the man in the face with her fist, and then took the constable's whistle and blew it. During the fierce struggle Mrs. Wright again hit the man, cutting her hand on his teeth. Her screams no doubt, responsible for bringing more assistance. An award was also made from the Carnegie Hero fund and a monetary award from the Bow Street fund.

A member of the Public Mrs. Frances Maude Wright who went to the assistance of the constable was awarded the Albert Medal 2nd Class.

KING'S POLICE MEDAL
LG 3/1/11

| Jessiman | William | Police Constable | 91872 J |

A horse pulling a light spring cart driven by a Miss Quick, took fright and bolted along Holloway Road, London on 30th June 1910. The lady tried to alight, but unfortunately caught her skirt in the step, and was dragged along in close proximity of the horses' hooves. Constable Jessiman reacted to the situation by seizing the near side rein, which was trailing, but was knocked down by the galloping horse. Even so he retained a hold of the rein, and after being dragged along the ground for some 20-30 yards, succeeded in bringing the animal to a halt. Both the lady and the constable were beneath the cart and seriously injured. A most serious accident had narrowly been averted, for near the spot where the horse had been stopped were a number of school children. A monetary award was also made from the Bow Street fund.

KING'S POLICE MEDAL
LG 3/1/11

Joslin	Joseph	Police Constable	80329 V

Sergeant Joslin went to the assistance of a 15 stone woman who had fallen from a burning fire escape at a store in Clapham, London on 20th December 1909. At first he had to retreat owing to the intense heat, but putting a coat over his head, he returned to the woman, who was badly injured, the skin of her arms peeling off with her clothing. He dragged her away from the fire escape, which by this time was collapsing around her. A fireman who came to their assistance was also beaten back by the heat. The Sergeant then got the woman to the opposite side of the road, and eventually, with the help of the fireman took her into a shop. Whilst awaiting the arrival of the ambulance, the Sergeant put olive oil on the woman's severely burnt arms and face. She was also suffering from a fractured left leg, and cuts to her face. She was subsequently taken to Bolingbroke Hospital where she died on 22nd December. An award was also made from the Society for the Protection from Fire and a monetary award from the Bow Street fund.

KING'S POLICE MEDAL
LG 3/1/11

Purfett	Alfred	Police Constable	93809 V

On the 9th July 1910 constables Purfett and Gordon were patrolling the bank on the River Thames when they heard an alarm raised that a child was in the water. They ran the 50 yards to the scene, and saw the child go down for the third time, and remain underwater. Constable Purfett jumped into the water, which was about nine feet deep, and was successful in bringing the girl to the surface, but owing to the strong outgoing tide, he was unable to reach the bank with her. Constable Gordon then jumped in and together the two constables succeeded in bringing the child ashore. They gave her artificial respiration, with the result that the child recovered. An award was also made from the Royal Humane Society and a monetary award from the Bow Street fund.

ROYAL HUMANE SOCIETY BRONZE MEDAL

Root	Joseph	Police Constable

At 1.35am on 5th September 1911 a woman either fell or threw herself into the Thames at the Victoria Embankment. Joseph Root police constable jumped in and caught her, and they were picked up by a boat.

CARNEGIE HERO FUND
7/12/11

Smith	Clive	Police Constable

At serious risk to himself stopped a pair of runaway horses near Blackfriars Bridge.

ROLL OF HONOUR
• Pc Frederick William Free
Drowned while operating a security boom at the Royal Gunpowder factory, Waltham Abbey.

1912

January	National Telephone Company is taken over by the Post Office.
February	The big freeze, temperatures drop as low as -35f.
March	King George V lays the foundation stone for County Hall.
April	RMS Titanic sinks after hitting an iceberg on her maiden voyage, over 1500 die.
May	40,000 jammed into Trafalgar Square to hear union officials regarding the Dock Strike.
June	Suffragettes start window smashing campaign at Post Offices and Labour Exchanges.
July	Board of Trade inquiry into the Titanic disaster finds Captain Smith who went down with the ship guilty of negligence.
August	Air mail service opens between London and Paris.
September	22 injured in a tube collision on the Piccadilly line, this is the first ever accident on the underground.
October	Opening of the new tunnel linking Woolwich and North Woolwich under the River Thames.
November	Vickers Machine gun introduced to the British Army.
December	Discovery in Sussex near Lewes of apparent human ancestor nicknamed 'Piltdown Man'.

HITS OF THE YEAR

Waiting for the Robert E Lee
It's a long way to Tipperary

KING'S POLICE MEDAL GEORGE V ISSUE

KING'S POLICE MEDAL

LG 2/1/12

Baldwin	Walter	Police Constable	98393 L

At about 11pm on 13th October 1910, whilst constable Baldwin was on duty on the tow path of the Grand Surrey Canal, Camberwell Basin, he saw a man jump into the water with the apparent intention of committing suicide. The constable, who is a fairly good swimmer at once took off his belt, and tunic, and dived in after him. On reaching the would be suicide, the constable seized him, but he struggled so violently that it was several minutes before he was brought to the bank, and landed on the tow path. The rescued man was taken charge of by onlookers, and having become calm, was allowed to stand. He at once knocked one man over, and jumped back into the water. Constable Baldwin shouted to the others to get assistance, and again jumped in to the rescue, a second struggle, similar to the first, taking place. The man was however brought to the side again by the constable and helped out. Witnesses said that the constable was apparently exhausted when he helped out the first time, and they were surprised to see him jump in again before he had time to recover. When he was helped out the second time, he was completely exhausted, and scarcely able to breathe. The basin is wide and deep at the spot where the rescue took place, and is stagnant and filthy. An award was also given from the Royal Humane Society of a bronze medal and a monetary award from the Bow Street fund.

KING'S POLICE MEDAL
LG 2/1/12

Barry	Michael	Police Constable	88195 L
Springett	George	Police Constable	74190 L

A fire occurred at 1 am on 4th March 1911 at 5 Angel Street, Walworth, London, a four roomed house occupied by a labourer, Arthur Julian, his wife and children, Phyllis aged 9 and Arthur Ernest aged 5. The fire was first noticed by constable Springett who blew his whistle, and with the aid of constable Barry, who soon arrived, began to arouse the occupants. The constables forced the street door, but were beaten back by the flames which engulfed the passage and stairs. Arthur Julian (senior) appeared at the first floor window and handed down his daughter to constable Springett, who was standing on the window sill of the ground floor room. The man was then overcome by smoke, and fell out of the window to the street below. Julian then told the constables that his wife and boy were still in the house, so constable Springett with the help of his colleague, climbed to the first floor window, and entered the smoke filled room. He found Mrs Julian unconscious on the floor, carried her to the window, and handed her to constable Barry and safety. However he was overcome by smoke, and forced to leave the room. The boy was seen at the window, trying to climb out, but he fell back into the room, which was now alight. Constable Barry standing on Springett's shoulders pulled himself into the room, and found the boy, and got him out. Tragically the boy was so severely burnt that he died shortly afterwards. The Fire Brigade had, in the meantime arrived and extinguished the blaze, but not before the house was totally destroyed. An award was also given from the Royal Humane Society and a monetary award from the Bow Street fund.

KING'S POLICE MEDAL
LG 2/1/12

Clapp	William	Police Sergeant	78139 J

A pair of horses, left unattended in Victoria Park Road, Hackney, took fright and bolted towards Mare Street. A serious accident seemed inevitable, but Sergeant Clapp, on duty nearby, seized the reins of the near side horse, and pulled hard, moving them clear of an electric tramcar, but in so doing was crushed between the cart the horses were pulling and a lamp standard, sustaining serious injuries to his arm, back and abdomen. He was placed sick for some time afterwards. He averted a collision, and after being dragged for some distance eventually succeeded in bringing the horses to a stop. A monetary award was also made from the Bow Street fund.

KING'S POLICE MEDAL
LG 2/1/12

Ryall	Sidney	Police Constable	95238 W

Constable Ryall saw a man named French, acting suspiciously in Normanton Road, Croydon at 12.30am on 8th October 1911, and arrested him in the front garden of a house.

The prisoner struggled violently, and succeeded in escaping, but the constable chased and caught him in a neighbouring field. French then struck the officer a violent blow to the side of his head with a heavy iron case opener about 15 inches long, knocking him down and partially stunning him. In spite of the fact that blood was streaming down his face, constable Ryall again chased the prisoner, and catching him a second time, took the weapon from him and overpowered him. Then with the aid of other constables who had arrived on the scene, French was taken to the police station. A monetary award was also made from the Bow Street fund.

CARNEGIE HERO FUND
20/7/12

Taylor   Joseph   Police Constable

Endeavoured to rescue a boy from drowning in the River Thames near Albert Bridge, Chelsea.

ROLL OF HONOUR
•   Inspector Alfred Deeks

Collapsed and died after dispersing youths causing a nuisance outside a church while off duty in West Ealing.

•   Ps Walter James Heath

Died after being accidentally shot while unloading a revolver used on night duty at Greenwich.

1913
This appears to be the year that the Suffragette movement was most active, with several members being imprisoned and one even dying from injuries received when she jumped in front of the King's horse at the Derby.

January	2 die as black fog descends on London.
February	The bodies of Captain Robert Falcon Scott and two of his party were discovered in their snow covered tent.
March	Mobs attack suffragettes in Hyde Park and at Wimbledon.
April	Peking opens the first China Parliament.
May	10 mph speed limit imposed at Hyde Park, the world's busiest road junction.
June	Emily Dawson is appointed as the country's first woman Magistrate.
July	A woman wearing a split skirt is seized in Richmond, London.
August	Police stop a football match in Kasimov, Russia saying it is an illegal assembly.
September	In Paris the aviator Bleriot performs the first loop the loop.
October	Aero bus aeroplane sets new record by carrying ten people including the pilot at Hendon.
November	Charles S Chaplin makes his film debut in Mack Stennets 'Making a living'.
December	A couple are arrested in New York for kissing in the street on Christmas Day, they were fined $15.

HITS OF THE YEAR
You made me love you
Hello, Hello who's your lady friend

KING'S POLICE MEDAL
LG 1/1/13

Ravening   Thomas   Police Constable   97277 G

On 11th October 1911, a horse attached to a railway van suddenly took fright and bolted along City Road, London at a very fast pace. After colliding with, and damaging a tramcar, and a van, the runaway continued unchecked until it reached Castle Street, where constable Ravening was standing. He at once jumped at the horse's head and seized the reins, but was knocked down, and kicked in the chest. He managed to keep hold of the reins, and after being dragged along the road for a considerable distance eventually brought the horse to a standstill. A monetary award was also made from the Bow Street fund.

KING'S POLICE MEDAL
LG 1/1/13

Root   Joseph   Police Constable   88965 E

At 1.35am on 5th September 1911 constable Root was on duty on the Victoria Embankment, London when he heard shouts for help coming from the river. He saw a woman struggling in the water, threw off his helmet and tunic, and plunged in to her rescue. There was a strong ebb tide running, but the constable was a strong swimmer, and on reaching the woman, both were carried downstream between a pier and the steam tug Hampton moored alongside. A boat was manned and both the woman who had been continually struggling and the constable were hauled in. There was a great danger of them being carried under the steamers moored at Waterloo. It transpired that the woman had accidentally fallen into the river. An award was also given from the Royal Humane Society and a monetary award from the Bow Street fund.

KING'S POLICE MEDAL
LG 1/1/13

Silver   William   Police Constable   76758 W

At about 1.50pm on 25th May 1912 a man named Mark Despard called at the offices of a moneylender in Brixton, London and was interview by the manager, from whom he requested a loan. During the interview he produced a large revolver, and levelled it at the manager's head. The manager was able to escape, and ran into the street, and secured the assistance of Constable Silver. Despard, meanwhile, escaped from the house, and was pursued by the constable and several other persons, who eventually caught up with him, whereupon he again pointed the revolver this time at his pursuers. Constable Silver advanced straight towards him, and when he was about ten paces from the man, he levelled the weapon straight at the constable, who dashed straight at him, and tackled him. Witnesses and even the prisoner, expressed surprise at the officer's courage. Had the weapon been discharged the constable would surely have been mortally wounded. A monetary award was also made from the Bow Street fund.

KING'S POLICE MEDAL
LG 1/1/13

| Spencer | Bertie | Police Constable | 99361 J |

At about 7 pm on 18th July 1912, a horse attached to a brewer's van, left standing outside the George IV public House, in Holmes Road, North London, took fright, and bolted towards Kentish Town Road. The van boy managed to hold it for a short distance, but he was thrown off the van, and rendered unconscious. Two private persons tried to stop the runaway, but one was killed in the attempt, and the other injured. The horse, a heavy and powerful animal, passed the police station where constable Spencer was on duty, and he managed to seize the reins, and shaft. His efforts to stop the horse were hampered by the fact the bit was outside the animal's mouth. The constable ran with it for some time, then stumbled and fell. He got up, chased the horse again, seized it by the nostrils, and nose band, and after a great effort succeeded in bringing it to a stop in Islip Street. A monetary award was also made from the Bow Street fund.

KING'S POLICE MEDAL
LG 1/1/13

Waters	Edmund	Police Sergeant	90870 H	
Little	Thomas	Police Constable	98274 H	
Winton	Albert	Police Constable	99222 J	DCM

At 12.20 am on 29th January 1912 a fire broke out at 196 Mile End Road, London. Constable Little kicked open the door of the house, and with Sergeant Waters entered a smoke filled passage. Flames were bursting through a door to the shop, where the fire had started. The officers saw a Mr. Bluefarb, the occupier with his wife and friend, who had been in a back room, and while constable Little went upstairs with Mr. Bluefarb to get the children, Sergeant Waters took Mrs. Bluefarb, by this time hysterical, and her friend, into the street. The Sergeant then went and searched the second floor, which appeared unoccupied, and then on the first floor heard a child's voice cry out. In the back room, he found Esther aged 5. He picked her up, but owing to the smoke and darkness, lost his way in the room. After groping about in the darkness, during which time the child became unconscious he felt himself falling, but managed to blow his whistle before collapsing. A fireman managed to gain entry to the room, and passed the child out, and the with difficulty, rescued the unconscious Sergeant. Meanwhile constable Little had brought out Dora aged 9 and Phillip aged 7. He then attempted to return, but was overcome by smoke and heat, collapsed on the foot way. Constable Winton having arrived later went into the house and brought out Yetta aged 10 together with the children from the first floor. This constable again entered the house, but on reaching the top of the stairs, his lantern went out and he slipped and fell down the stairs in the darkness, just managing to crawl out to the street before collapsing. An award was also made from the Society for the Protection of Life from Fire and a monetary award from the Bow Street fund.

Constable Winton had been awarded the DCM and was mentioned in Despatches (MID) during the War in South Africa 1899 - 1902.

CARNEGIE HERO FUND
10/12/13
Roberts   George   Police Constable
Injured while attempting to stop a pair of runaway horses in Norwood Road, West Norwood.

CARNEGIE HERO FUND
8/9/13
Watt   Joseph   Police Constable
In consequence of injuries received in endeavouring to stop a runaway horse in High Street, Romford. A grant was also made by the *Ancient Order of Foresters*.

ROLL OF HONOUR
•   Ps George Ernest Spooner
Drowned when his police motor patrol boat was hit by a barge at Southwark Bridge.

1914
This is one of the most infamous years of our history, it is the year of the Great War, the war to end all wars. It was believed that the war which began in August would be over by Christmas.

January   Queen Victoria Memorial in front of Buckingham Palace finally completed.
February   Marconi announces that he can light a lamp six miles away by wireless.
March   Sylvia Pankhurst is arrested on her way to a demonstration in Trafalgar Square.
April   Electricians strike in London for shorter hours.
May   57 protesters arrested as they attempt to reach Buckingham Palace to present a petition of 'Votes for Women' to the King.
June   Worst thunderstorm in memory causes several deaths as four inches of rain fall in three hours in London.
July   Several European countries mobilize their armies.
August   Britain's declaration of war on Germany.
September   500,000 more men were required to sign up for war.
October   First bomb dropped on London.
November   700 die when HMS Bulwark blows up in the harbour at Sheerness, Kent.
December   Truce in the trenches - see below.

HITS OF THE YEAR
Keep the home fires burning
St Louis Blues

CHRISTMAS TRUCE IN THE TRENCHES
They called it a war to end all wars.
   The war had begun in August 1914 and the whole nation believed it would all be over by Christmas. On Christmas Eve the Western Front began to freeze with temperatures dropping well below zero, and in some places snow was beginning to fall.

Although no official order was given, each side decided to hold a truce, a truce for the duration of Christmas. It was obvious that all the soldiers only had thoughts for their families over this time, families so far away. Along some areas of the trenches strange lights appeared. Behind the German lines small Christmas trees were being put up. Singing was heard; some of the voices sounding like angels.

In place of gunfire shouts were heard between enemy lines of 'Happy Christmas' and carols were being sung the sounds drifting over no mans land. At one particular point a German soldier was heard playing carols on his violin. Both the German and British anthems were played to the delight and applause of the men.

Eventually soldiers from both lines climbed from their trenches and faced each other in no mans land. They walked towards each other, they shook hands and exchanged gifts. Beer was exchanged for bully beef, laughter was heard and singing of popular carols in both languages. Not a single shot was fired this day in honour of this special holy day.

The truce was probably observed by at least two thirds of the British and German lines, it was also a chance for both sides to collect and bury their dead.

Commanding Officers on hearing of this fraternisation ordered an immediate end to it. The soldiers simply said their goodbyes and returned to their own lines and within a couple of days the war resumed, heavy gun fire and bombing. Three more years would pass before the war would end, no more Christmas truces would take place by order of the British Generals who threatened serious punishment.

KING'S POLICE MEDAL
Assassination attempt on Metropolitan Police Commissioner
LG. 1/1/14

English   Albert   Police Constable   84676

On 27th November 1912, Sir Edward Henry, the Commissioner for the Metropolitan Police, was entering his private residence, when a man, armed with a fully loaded revolver, ran up, and fired three shots in rapid succession at him. Constable English who was acting as the Commissioner's chauffeur, immediately ran up the steps of the house, and after a struggle succeeded in wrenching the weapon from the man, and holding him, until further assistance arrived. The Commissioner was uninjured, although shocked. A monetary award was also made from the Bow Street fund.

KING'S POLICE MEDAL
LG. 1/1/14

Jameson   George   Police Constable   72985 J

Constable Jameson was on duty at Cambridge Road, Hackney on the 9th November 1912 when at about 11.30pm he had occasion to disperse a disorderly crowd, and whilst he was so engaged, a man produced a revolver and fired two shots into the air. The constable arrested him, and the man then fired another shot directly at the constable's head. The force of the shot knocked his helmet off. A struggle ensued between the two, during which the constable forced the arm with the revolver downwards, but the man fired two more shots, one of which struck the constable on the inner side of his left thigh just below the groin. The bullet caused little injury however, the force of it having been spent passing through the constable's greatcoat and other uniform clothing. A monetary award was also made from the Bow Street fund.

KING'S POLICE MEDAL
LG. 1/1/14

| Jones | Noah | Police Constable | 98383 H |
| Goodwin | Cornelius | Police Constable | 91698 H |

In the early morning of 24th January 1913 a fire broke out at a shop in Commercial Road, East London. Constable Jones arrived to find the premises well alight and full of smoke. He went in and climbed the stairs through dense smoke to the bedroom on the first floor. There he found a woman with a babe-in-arms, and two other children. He carried the children down the narrow stairs, and handed them to constable Goodwin who had now arrived on the scene. Constable Jones returned to help the one with a small child. He took the child out and returned with constable Goodwin to help the two women from the now fiercely burning house. One woman was unconscious, and the stairs were ready to collapse in the flames. After reaching the street with the women, the two officers were too overcome with heat and smoke. The four other lodgers in the house were rescued by the fire brigade, although two of them subsequently died. An award was also made from the Society for the Protection of Life from Fire and a monetary award from the Bow Street fund.

KING'S POLICE MEDAL
LG. 1/1/14

| Lockwood | William | Police Constable | 101135 N |

At 5.50pm on the 13th June whilst on duty at West Green Road, Tottenham, constable Lockwood saw a runaway horse attached to a van, galloping towards him, the reins dragging on the ground. He grabbed the reins as the horse passed, and tried to stop the animal, but after a few yards, he fell and the near side rear wheel of the van went over his leg. The constable, despite the injury, kept hold of the reins, and was dragged a further 20 yards before the horse fell, with the result that the van wheels went over the constable's back. The constable was on the sick list for some considerable time. This incident took place near to two schools, and there were many children in the vicinity at the time. A monetary award was also made from the Bow Street fund.

KING'S POLICE MEDAL
LG. 1/1/14

| Porter | George | Police Constable | 91690 T |

At 4pm on 19th August 1913 constable Porter was patrolling along Lower Mall, Hammersmith when he was informed that a six year old boy had fallen into the River Thames. Although he had only recently learned to swim, constable Porter jumped into the water from a wall, where the water was some 10 feet deep, with a swiftly running tide, and dangerous currents around some moored barges. The constable could not dive, but groped around below the surface, grasping the boy's ankle, and pulling him above the water. He was unable to land due to the height of the wall, but kept the boy's head up, until he was being drawn down by the strong currents. A spectator took off his belt, and the constable held onto it until help arrived, and both he and the boy were saved.

KING'S POLICE MEDAL
LG. 1/1/14

| Stiff | Arthur | Acting Sergeant | 77290 J |

At about 11.20am on the 10th September 1912 a bay mare, attached to a cart was being driven down a hill near the Chingford Hotel, Chingford, Essex, when the animal suddenly bolted towards Epping New Road, the occupants of the cart being thrown out. The animal had covered a considerable distance when acting Sergeant Stiff saw it, and seized the reins, as the cart ran over his leg. The horse was pulled up, and restrained, before the Sergeant was taken to hospital where he was treated for his injuries. A monetary award was also made from the Bow Street fund.

CARNEGIE HERO FUND
8/6/14

| Burfield | Sidney | Police Sergeant |

Rescued a lunatic from drowning in the River Roding at Ilford.

CARNEGIE HERO FUND
28/12/14

| Dew | John | Police Constable |

Received injuries while stopping a runaway horse.

CARNEGIE HERO FUND
28/8/14

| Drabble | Fred | Police Constable |

Sustained injuries while stopping a pair of runaway horses.

ROLL OF HONOUR
• Spc James John Christopher Popps

Collapsed and died after assisting officers in the arrest of a violent prisoner while off duty.

• Spc John Quinnell

Drowned when on duty at Winchmore Hill pumping station.

• Pc George Johnson

Died from the effects of injuries received in the execution of his duty on Clapham Division.

• Chief Inspector Francis Harry Rolfe

Died from blood poisoning following an elbow injury sustained by a fall while in the execution of his duty at Shrewbury.

• Pc Alfred Smith

Died as a result of injuries received in the execution of his duty on Kensington Division.

1915

January	The Military Cross (MC) introduced as a decoration for Gallantry in the armed forces, the first awards made this year.
February	London announces 104,000 UK casualties to date in the war.
March	Government creates a Woman's Army Battalion in the UK.
April	Over 33,000 women sign up for war service.
May	Liner Lusitania sunk off the Irish coast, over 1400 die.
June	VC for Flt Sub Lt Reginald Warneford who brought down a Zeppelin with bombs.
July	German submarine sinks 4 British steamships off Cornwall and Ireland.
August	Total UK casualties to date 381,983.
September	600 Austrians and Germans interned at Alexandra Palace, London.
October	Women can apply for licences to be bus and tram conductors.
November	Women first employed on permanent staff at Scotland Yard.
December	Hugo Junkers builds the first all metal aeroplane in Germany.

HITS OF THIS YEAR
Pack up your troubles in your old kit bag

KING'S POLICE MEDAL
LG. 1/1/15

Brown	Frederick	Police Constable	89201 X

On the morning of 10th December 1913 constable Brown was informed of a fire at 27 Bute Street, South West London. On his arrival at the house, he learned that there was a woman in the front bedroom on the second floor. He ran up the stairs to the room, but owing to the density of the smoke, was compelled to leave. He then placed a wet cloth over his mouth, again entered the room, and by crawling on his hands and knees, he managed to reach the bed, on which he found a woman aged 83, whose clothing had been burned on her. The constable eventually got the woman out of the house, and she was conveyed to hospital, where she unfortunately died later that day. An award was also made from the Society for the Protection of Life from Fire and a monetary award from the Bow Street fund.

KING'S POLICE MEDAL
LG. 1/1/15

Brown	Henry	Police Constable	102935 B

At 12.15am on the 21st March 1914 constable Brown was on duty at Ladbroke Grove, West London, when he heard screams coming from the Grand Union Canal. He looked over the bridge, and saw a woman struggling in the centre of the canal. The constable wearing full winter clothing, jumped from the parapet into the water, some 18 feet below. With difficulty he succeeded in reaching the woman and brought her to the bank, where she was assisted from the water, but the constable had to wait a while, due to the weight of his wet clothing. The woman was semi conscious, and the constable, after he was pulled out of the water exhausted, applied artificial respiration until she had sufficiently recovered to be removed to hospital. The water at this spot is about 15 feet deep in the centre and 6 feet at the banks. The water was at freezing point.

KING'S POLICE MEDAL

LG. 1/1/15

Burfield   Sidney   Police Sergeant   85479 T

At 11.30 pm on 8th June 1913 a fire was discovered at 6 Queens Terrace, Isleworth in a four roomed cottage. When Sergeant Burfield arrived at the premises, they were well alight, with dense smoke issuing from windows and doors. On learning that a child was in the house, he went in and upstairs to the bedroom, but returned quickly as the staircase was about to collapse. He went in again with a wet apron over his face, and crawling on the floor reached the back room, where, after difficulty he found the child and brought it into the street. The child died the following evening. Sergeant Burfield was burned, and suffered from smoke inhalation. An award was also made from the Society for the Protection of Life from Fire, the Carnegie Hero fund, and a monetary award from the Bow Street fund.

KING'S POLICE MEDAL

LG. 1/1/15

Roberts   George   Police Constable   96056 W

A pair of horses attached to a milk van, took fright and bolted along Norwood Road, South London on 10th December 1913. Constable Roberts on seeing this, grabbed the reins on the near side of the horses, and ran alongside for some distance trying to bring the animals to a halt, eventually he was dragged off his feet. He held onto the reins for a further 20 yards and then was compelled to release his grip, falling to the ground, and the near side wheels of the van ran over him. However his efforts had checked the horses sufficiently for them to be turned into a cul-de-sac, where they came to a stop, and were secured. The constable was so seriously injured that he was obliged to retire from the force. A monetary award was also made from the Bow Street fund.

KING'S POLICE MEDAL

LG. 1/1/15

Walker   John   Police Constable   103024 L

At about 2.55am on the 23rd March 1914 constable Walker saw two men acting in a suspicious manner. He questioned one of them, who produced a lead mallet with which he aimed a blow at the constable's head. Constable Walker drew his truncheon and while parrying blows with his assailant, the second man came up and tried to get behind the constable, but being unsuccessful ran away. The first man then also ran away, and the constable gave chase, and after another constable arrived and tried to arrest the man, he was felled by a blow from the mallet. Constable Walker then closed with the man, but was also felled with the mallet. Eventually, with other assistance, the man was arrested. Both constables were on the sick list for several weeks.

KING'S POLICE MEDAL

LG. 1/1/15

West   Frederick   Police Constable   96344 B

On the evening of 29th April 1914 a boy aged 5 was playing on the steps of Battersea Bridge, when he fell into the River Thames. Constable West was called to the scene, and found the boy being carried away on the tide, which was running strongly. He thereupon plunged fully clothed into the water from the parapet of the bridge, and swam out to the boy, who was by this time some 20 feet from the bank. The water was about 10 feet deep and running strongly. After reaching the child, the constable could not swim back to the bank, so he swam with the tide, until he reached the wall some distance downstream, where he clung, until rescued by boat. A monetary award was also made from the Bow Street fund.

KING'S POLICE MEDAL
LG. 1/1/15

Wright	Thomas	Police Constable	102591 N

On the early morning of 15th December 1913 constable Wright saw a man attempting to force the catch on the window of a house in Springfield Road, Stoke Newington, London. He seized the man as he was in the act of climbing a fence, and pulled him back to the ground. The man then kicked the constable in the face and threatened to murder him, and then struck him with a shoemaker's knife. The constable was cut on the face and thumb during the struggle as the man attempted to stab him. The struggle lasted for some 15 minutes until other officers arrived and the man was arrested. Constable Wright was off duty on the sick list for two weeks. A monetary award was also made from the Bow Street fund.

CARNEGIE HERO FUND

Carpenter	Walter	Police Constable

Sustained injury while attempting to stop a pair of runaway horses.

CARNEGIE HERO FUND

Smithers	Cecil	Police Sergeant

Assisted by another man, succeeded in rescuing a soldier from drowning in the Thames at the Albert Embankment.

CARNEGIE HERO FUND

Goodman	William A	Special Police Constable	006506

Rescued a child aged 2 from the ruins of a house which was demolished during a hostile air raid.

CARNEGIE HERO FUND

Hughes	Albert	Police Constable

Sustained injury while stopping a pair of runaway horses.

CARNEGIE HERO FUND

Kemp	Charles	Police Constable

Rescued a boy from drowning in the Thames at Union Wharf, East Greenwich.

ROLL OF HONOUR

- Pc William Williamson

Knocked down by a motor bus while on duty observing search lights.

- Dc Alfred Young KPM

Shot dead when attempting to execute an arrest warrant for fraud at Hampstead.

- Spc Alexander Addison Marnie

Slipped between a wharf and a vessel fracturing his skull at Southwark.

- Spc J A Wiley

Collapsed and died while going to the assistance of an Army bi-plane which had made a forced landing at Thames Ditton.

1916

January	House of Commons voted overwhelmingly for Military conscription.
February	Major German assault of Verdun in France.
March	Zeppelin raids on eight counties in England 12 killed.
April	Military Medal (MM) introduced for gallantry in the armed forces.
May	Commons give backing to daylight saving plan by putting the clocks forward one house in summer - the start of what is now known as British Summer Time (BST).
June	King George V states the Military Medal can be awarded to women.
July	Battle of the Somme - starts on 1st July.
August	American chewing gum goes on sale in France.
September	Zeppelin raid on UK causes 2 deaths and 13 injuries, one ship being shot down near to London.
October	Captain T E Lawrence (Lawrence of Arabia) backs the Arab revolt.
November	Government announces appointment of food controller to regulate food consumption.
December	Lloyd George becomes the new Prime Minister.

HITS OF THE YEAR

If you were the only girl in the world

Take me back to dear old blighty

KING'S POLICE MEDAL

LG. 1/1/16

Carpenter   Walter   Police Constable   84470 G

On 20th July 1915 constable Carpenter was escorting the Chairman of the County of London Sessions to the Sessions House in Southwark when a pair of cob horses, attached to a van standing by the roadside, bolted and ran away. Constable Carpenter immediately attempted to stop the horses, but was knocked down, and the near side wheels of the van passed over his body, seriously injuring him. An award of a Medal from the Royal Society for Prevention of Cruelty to Animals, and a monetary award from the Bow Street fund.

KING'S POLICE MEDAL

LG. 1/1/16

Dew   John   Police Constable   89274 F

On 28th December 1914 a horse attached to a light covered van in Longridge Road, Kensington, London suddenly took fright while the driver was absent, and bolted along several streets. Having collided with several other vehicles, the horse was seen by constable Dew, who was on point duty, and he tried to stop it, but was knocked over. He quickly recovered, and jumping onto a passing cab, gave chase, overtook the cart, and again tried to grab the horse, but slipped and fell. The constable again mounted the cab, and on his third attempt, seized the horse's reins, fell under the animals legs, but managed to hang on, and pull the horse and van to a stop. A monetary award was also made from the Bow Street fund.

KING'S POLICE MEDAL

LG. 1/1/16

Drabble   Fred   Police Constable   97982 F

On 28th September 1914 a pair of horses attached to a covered van took fright, and bolted. Constable Drabble who was on traffic point duty grabbed the reins of the offside horse, ran with them a few yards, and then fell. He succeeded in regaining his feet, and continued to attempt to being the horses to a standstill, but was knocked down, and went under the wheels. He had succeeded in slowing the horses sufficiently for them to be brought under control. Constable Drabble sustained a broken leg, and two small fractures in his right foot. A monetary award was also made from the Bow Street fund.

KING'S POLICE MEDAL

LG. 1/1/16

Hughes   Albert   Police Constable   99509 W

On 8th July 1915 a pair of horses with a van which had been left in the charge of a van boy took fright and bolted. Constable Hughes on nearby traffic point duty grabbed the reins as it passed, and tried to turn the horses into a side road. He failed to turn them, but hung onto the head of the near side horse, and pulled it to the ground, causing the other horse to pull up. Constable Hughes unfortunately was run over by the van, the wheels passing over his legs and back. A monetary award was also made from the Bow Street fund.

KING'S POLICE MEDAL

LG. 1/1/16

Kemp   Charles   Police Constable   052978R

On 1st July 1915 a boy aged 5 years who was playing on the steps leading down to the River Thames at Greenwich, fell into the water, and was being carried away on the tide, when the alarm was raised. Constable Kemp heard the alarm, and ran down the steps, and into the water fully clothed. He swam out about 12 yards and reached the boy, bringing him to the shore, from where he was taken to the Police station, a distance of about a quarter of a mile. There he was given first aid and recovered quickly. This was a particularly dangerous spot, as the tide turns very quickly, and there are dangerous eddies caused by the piles in the river.

The constable was a police pensioner who had been recalled for duty during the Great War. An award was also made from the Royal Humane Society, the Carnegie Hero fund and a monetary award from the Bow Street fund.

Charles Kemp was a first generation police constable, the only police pensioner recalled to the police for war duty to receive a gallantry award. Both his son and grandson were to become serving Metropolitan police constables.

KING'S POLICE MEDAL
LG. 1/1/16

Smithers	Cecil	Police Sergeant	93752 A

On 25th January 1915 Sergeant Smithers was off duty, but in uniform, travelling home on the top of a tramcar over Westminster Bridge, when he heard a police whistle being blown. He immediately got off, and went to the bank of the river, where he saw two men in the centre of the river calling for help. He took a life belt from outside the County Hall, and went down the steps into the water, and swam against the tide to the men, who were in an exhausted condition. The three of them were carried downstream to some barges, where they hung on, until rescued by a police launch sent from Westminster Pier. After one was lifted into the boat, the Sergeant tried to swim back with the other man, but was too exhausted and they were both brought in by boat. An award was also made from the Royal Humane Society, the Carnegie Hero fund and a monetary award from the Bow Street fund.

ROYAL HUMANE SOCIETY BRONZE MEDAL
Cook	Charles	Police Constable

On 2nd April 1916 a man and a woman were in a boat which was capsized on the Lea at Clapton. The depth being 15 feet. Cook swam out and kept both afloat until a boat reached them.

ROYAL HUMANE SOCIETY BRONZE MEDAL
Hancock	Frederick	Police Constable

On 21st October 1916 a man in the intense darkness fell into the canal at Enfield Lock, the depth being 30 feet. Hancock jumped in and caught him, but when he got out he did not recover.

ROYAL HUMANE SOCIETY BRONZE MEDAL
Siddall	Harold	Police Constable

On 18th January 1916 a man in an attempt at suicide threw himself into the Thames at Chelsea, the depth being 6 feet and the night dark. Siddall went in, and with the help of a buoy succeeded in saving him.

CARNEGIE HERO FUND
22/3/16

Archer	Herbert	Police Constable

Rescued a boy from drowning at Rosyth, Dunfermline.

ROLL OF HONOUR
* Pc Frank Ricketts

Drowned when going to the assistance of a drowning boy at Teignmouth while off duty.
* Spc William Alfred Ellis

Drowned when he fell from a footbridge into the Regents Canal Lock while on patrol on a stormy night.
* Insp Daniel Hubbard

Killed in a road accident when he was run over by an omnibus at Putney.

1917

January	350 dies when HMS Laurentic is sunk by a mine in the Atlantic.
February	Government allows women to become taxi drivers.
March	Tsar abdicates, the revolution grows in Russia.
April	91 German ships are seized in New York harbour.
May	German aeroplanes kill 76 in bombing raids along the South East coast of England.
June	King George V orders members of the Royal Family to drop German titles. Saxe-Coburg-Gotha becomes Windsor and Battenberg becomes Mountbatten.
July	London 37 die in German air raids.
August	Ex Tsar and his family removed from Petrograd to Siberia.
September	108 die in German air raids on the Isles of Sheppy and Thanet.
October	Chequers mansion and estate become the official residence of the Prime Minister.
November	War office agrees to supply British troops in France with Christmas puddings.
December	new Bolshevik Government begins peace negotiations.

HITS OF THE YEAR
For me and my gal

Goodbye-ee

KING'S POLICE MEDAL
LG. 1/1/17

Archer   Herbert   Police Constable   100876

At 5.20am, on 22nd March 1916 a boy aged 14 years residing in Rosyth, Scotland, was crossing the emergency entrance caisson on the docks, when he slipped and fell into the water inside the caisson chamber. A companion shouted for help, and constable Archer, a London constable seconded to the Royal Dockyards, who was on duty nearby, ran to the spot, but was unable to see the boy, as the water was some 10 feet below ground level, and it was dark at the time. The constable threw off his greatcoat and helmet and lowered himself by the framework, into the water, which was about 40 feet deep and very cold. Having located the boy by the noise of splashing, he caught hold of him and shouted for a rope to be lowered. However the person holding the rope found the weight of the constable and the boy too great, and dropped the rope. The constable then swam to the end of the caisson and held onto the stonework until assisted out of the water by some workmen. The boy could not swim, and the rescue was effected in darkness on a wintery morning after the constable had been on duty for over seven hours. There was considerable danger to the constable from the framework of the caisson. An award was also made from the Royal Humane Society and the Carnegie Hero fund.

KING'S POLICE MEDAL
LG. 1/1/17

| Askew | Arthur | Detective Sergeant | 93408 S |

On 14th July 1915 Detective Sergeant Askew accompanied by a constable went to a private house to arrest a man called Gorges, both officers being aware that the man might be armed, and that he had already threatened to kill police, Gorges was seen inside the house, and both officers entered, and went along a dark passage down a badly lit staircase to the basement. Halfway down, Gorges stood with his hands behind him, close to the wall. The Sergeant noticed he was fumbling with something, and fearing danger, threw himself at Gorges, endeavouring to clasp him round the arms and body. He failed to secure the man's right arm, and the man fired a revolver which killed the constable instantaneously. The Sergeant struggled with Gorges and forced him down onto the stairs, eventually getting a grip on the revolver. Other people in the house then assisted the Sergeant and the man was overpowered, and disarmed. A monetary award was also made from the Bow Street fund.

KING'S POLICE MEDAL
LG. 1/1/17

| Bowles | George | Police Constable | 104037 D |

At 12.58am on 19th May 1916 constable Bowles observed flames coming from the first floor bedroom window of 127 Cleveland Street, Marylebone, London which was occupied by two Rumanians. Having directed another constable to call the fire brigade, he was unsuccessful in an attempt to arouse the inmates. He then climbed onto the railings, and standing on an iron support bar, climbed onto the window sill some 14 feet above the ground. He opened the window, entered the room and closed the window to prevent a draught. He pulled down the burning curtains, and extinguished them. After closing the window in the next room as well, he found a semi conscious woman, whom he wrapped in a cloak, and carried out onto the landing. He then obtained some water, and put out the fire, which was taking a hold of the bedding. The constable then returned to the woman, who had sustained slight burns on her arm, and burns to her head, and tended her until the regained consciousness. She was eventually rescued, and taken to hospital. An award was also made from the Society for protection of life from fire, and a monetary award from the Bow Street fund.

KING'S POLICE MEDAL
LG. 1/1/17

| Burton | George | Police Constable |

A Naval Stoker of a torpedo boat, which was lying in the tidal basin alongside the North Wall Jetty in Portsmouth Dockyard, was crossing the brow, going aboard his vessel at

6.55pm on 5th November 1915, when he suddenly became dizzy and fell overboard into 30 feet of water. Constable Burton a London Officer seconded to the Royal Dockyards witnessed the incident and immediately ran to the scene, shouting 'man overboard'. He took off his greatcoat and helmet, dived into the water, and held the stoker, who was unconscious, above water, until a rope was thrown from the boat. The constable then fastened the rope round the man's shoulders, and both the victim and the constable were hauled aboard. The man recovered, after some attention. An award was also given from the Royal Humane Society and a monetary award from the Bow Street fund.

KING'S POLICE MEDAL
LG. 1/1/17

| Longhurst | William | Police Constable | 97308 |

On 25th August 1916 at 9.15am, a miner of the building works department of the Royal Arsenal descended a manhole of the main sewer to clear away an obstruction, when he collapsed from the effects of sewer gas. Another miner went down to his assistance, and he was also overcome by the gas, but was able to shout for help. With the assistance of a labourer, a rope was lowered and secured round the first man, who was hauled up. The labourer got out, but the second miner became unconscious, and was left behind. Constable Longhurst arrived at this juncture, and although warned of the danger and advised not to descend, at once went down the hole, and attached a rope to the unconscious miner who was then drawn to the surface. The constable himself almost overcome by the gas, but succeeded in getting out himself. Both the miners recovered after being given first aid and being removed to hospital. Constable Longhurst also received an award from the Carnegie Hero Fund trust and a monetary award from the Bow Street fund.

KING'S POLICE MEDAL
LG. 1/1/17

| Slipper | Thomas | Police Constable | 89865 W |

Whilst on beat duty in the Wandsworth road, London at 4.45pm on 29th March 1916, constable Slipper saw a pair of horses, attached to a covered van, galloping towards him. There was no driver on the van, and in attempting to stop the runaways, he seized the offside reins, but was knocked over and dragged 150 yards down the road, before the horses came to a stop. The constable was seriously injured in this action. A monetary award was also made from the Bow Street Fund.

KING'S POLICE MEDAL
Posthumous
LG. 22/6/17

| Greenoff | Edward George Brown | Police Constable | 96389 K |

On Friday 19th January 1917, a fire broke out at the Silvertown Chemical Works which were being used for the purification of TNT, and it was almost certainly known to Constable Greenoff that there was a large quantity of high explosives in the buildings, which, in case of fire, would explode and lead to a much more serious disaster. Constable Greenoff was on beat duty outside the works when the fire first broke out. He could easily have escaped, as many who were nearer to the explosion when it came, did, but he remained where he was in order to warn others to keep their distance. As a result of the subsequent explosion, he was fatally injured, and died in hospital.

CARNEGIE HERO FUND
Greenoff   Edward G B   Police Constable
Sustained fatal injuries while urging people to flee from the scene of an explosion at a munitions factory.

This was an immediate award at the suggestion of H.M. King George V.

CARNEGIE HERO FUND
9/10/17
Davies   David   Police Constable
Rescued a man who had been overcome by gas in a manhole at Mitcham.

CARNEGIE HERO FUND
25/1/17
Landy   Matthew   Police Constable
Rescued a Doctor on the occasion of a fire which occurred at 211 Francis Road, Leyton.

CARNEGIE HERO FUND
12/3/17
Ralph   Augustus   Police Sergeant
Rescued an old woman on the occasion of a fire which occurred at the Christian Union Alms House.

CARNEGIE HERO FUND
Posthumous
13/6/17
Smith   Alfred   Police Constable
Lost his life while urging employees of a factory to take cover during a hostile air raid.

ROLL OF HONOUR
• Pc Edward George Brown Greenoff KPM - see above entry
• Ps Lawrence Quibell
Killed during fire engine practice at Rosyth Dockyard.
• Pc Michael Donovan
Drowned while on patrol during a stormy night at Chatham dockyard.
• Stn Ps William James Wheeler
Died from the effects of injuries received in the execution of his duty on Greenwich Division.

1918

January	Government orders restaurants and eating houses not to serve meat on two days each week.
February	In London meat, butter and margarine are rationed.
March	British MP's voted to raise the school leaving age to 14 for all children.
April	The budget puts up taxes and abolishes the Penny Post.
May	Government takes control of London central markets.
June	London reports that the British have shot down 4102 German aeroplanes in the past year against 1213 British losses.
July	Frenchman Captain Sarret makes the first ever parachute drop from an aeroplane falling 800 feet.
August	London police go on strike, over 2000 policemen marched from Scotland Yard to Tower Hill.
September	Spanish flu takes its toll in Britain.
October	T E Lawrence leads Arabs into Damascus.
November	Germany signs the armistice - the Great War is finally over.
December	Women vote for the first time in UK election.

HITS OF THE YEAR

Till we meet again

If you could care for me

ALBERT MEDAL

Wright   Frederick   Sub Divisional Inspector

On the occasion of an enemy air raid which took place on the 19th October 1917 a bomb fell on two adjoining houses, killing 10 persons and imprisoning 18 others under the wreckage. When helpers arrived it was found that some of the persons who were imprisoned in the basement of one of the houses were alive, but the work of rescue was exceedingly dangerous, for escaping gas in the basement became ignited and set fire to the debris above. Inspector Wright with an axe made a small opening in the floor over the basement which was in a slanting and tottering condition. The joists which supported it were broken, and through this opening though with much difficulty 13 persons were rescued. It was then ascertained that two children were left in the basement, Inspector Wright with Police Constables Robert Melton and Jesse Christmas dropped into the basement through the opening and searched for the children under very dangerous conditions. In addition to the fumes of the escaping gas which was suffocating and the fire raging above there was a possibility of further movement of wreckage which might have proved fatal to all below. The space was so confined that they were barely able to reach the back of the premises. The children were found to be dead.

Inspector Wright on reaching the open air collapsed overcome by the fumes and by his exertions, but after medical care he recovered sufficiently to be sent home. He returned to the scene of the disaster shortly after and continued his work of rescue throughout the night.

Police constables Melton and Christmas both received the KPM.

KING'S POLICE MEDAL
LG. 10/5/18

Brocklehurst	Fred	Police Constable
Hodgson	William Bramwell	Police Constable
Moffat	D'Arcy Benson	Police Constable
Newsham	Richard	Police Constable
Oakes	George Albert	Police Constable
Sloan	Daniel Devine	Police Constable
Wearing	William Andrew	Police Constable

"On account of their gallant conduct on the occasion of fire which occurred at a munitions factory on 1st October 1917."

KING'S POLICE MEDAL
LG. 1/1/18

Bence	Alfred	Police Constable	96827 B

Whilst on duty on Oakley Street, Chelsea on 11th October 1916, constable Bence was informed that there was a body floating in the River Thames. On reaching the embankment he saw an object floating, but because it was dark, he could not see clearly. He ran along the bank and down some steps onto the foreshore where he saw some ripples on the surface of the water. Without removing any of his uniform, he entered the water and swam some 20 yards out, and drifted to where he had seen the ripples. He then put his hand under the water and came into contact with a woman's clothing. He grasped the body, and swam to the beach, and pulled her ashore. Although exhausted, he applied artificial respiration until a doctor arrived, and pronounced life extinct. The constable had only recently learned to swim, and it was dark, with a strong tide running. Constable Bence was also awarded with a medal and certificate from the Royal Humane Society and a monetary award from the Bow Street Fund.

KING'S POLICE MEDAL
LG. 1/1/18

Dednum	Charles	Police Constable	102815 C

At 3.30pm on 8th October 1916 a fire occurred at 58 Frith Street, Soho, the ground floor used for storage of films, and the upper storeys for dwellings. On hearing police whistles being blown, constable Dednum went to the house, and found dense smoke coming from the windows and door. On being informed that some residents were still inside, he placed a handkerchief over his mouth, entered the house, and crept on hands and knees along the passage to the stairs. Hearing voices, he went up to the fourth floor, where he found a man trying to get through the skylight. By this time the smoke was really dense, and poisonous fumes were coming from the burning film. Constable Dednum lifted the man through the skylight, and with difficulty followed him onto the roof. The constable revived in the fresh air, but the man was overcome, and the constable partially revived him, and then helped him onto the roof of the next house, down through the skylight, and out to the street. Unfortunately the man died later in hospital, and constable Dednum was affected for several

days by the fumes. He was also awarded a silver medal from The Society For Protection of Life from Fire and a monetary reward from the Bow Street fund.

KING'S POLICE MEDAL
LG. 1/1/18

Hardy   James   Police Constable   78653 F

On 30th November 1916 at 12.15am constable Hardy was called by a gamekeeper, who had heard several shots fired in Ruffetts Wood, West Wickham. After a short time, the constable, and the gamekeeper saw two men approaching. The gamekeeper flashed a torch in the face of one of the men who immediately raised the gun he was carrying by the barrel, and knocked the constable's helmet off. The man then felled the constable with a violent blow to the head, which broke the gun in two. The other man escaped, and in the darkness the gamekeeper mistook the constable for one of the poachers, and a struggle ensued during which the constable's assailant also escaped. By this time, the gamekeeper had realised his mistake, and sent his dog after the poacher. The dog found the man hiding, whereupon the constable, although severely wounded, and bleeding profusely, closed with the man, and with the assistance of the gamekeeper arrested him. A monetary award was also made from the Bow Street fund.

Constable Hardy was killed in a road accident on the eve of the Royal Investiture for the King's Police Medal.'

KING'S POLICE MEDAL
LG. 1/1/18

Landy   Matthew   Detective Constable   99801 J

On 25th January 1917 at about 9.20 pm police were informed that a doctor's house in Francis Road, Leyton was on fire, and on arrival found the premises full of smoke. The front door was forced and groans and heavy breathing could be heard from upstairs. But although several attempts were made by the officers to mount the stairs, the volume of smoke pouring down made it impossible. Constable Landy dipped a cloth in water, put it over his mouth and nostrils and rushed upstairs to the first floor landing, where he found the doctor on the floor. The constable succeeded in dragging the unconscious doctor to the stairs and carried him down, but at the foot of the stairs, the constable collapsed, and fell into the arms of other officers. Both the doctor and the constable received medical attention and recovered. An award was also made from the Society for Protection of Life from Fire, a Medal from the Order of St John of Jerusalem and a monetary award from the Bow Street fund.

KING'S POLICE MEDAL
LG. 1/1/18

Penn   Charles   Police Constable   91252 G

During an enemy air raid on the morning of 13th June 1917 several bombs were dropped in Shoreditch, killing and injuring many people, also causing damage and several fires. There was total confusion with people running in every direction and several horses frightened by the blast also took fright and bolted. Constable Penn was on point duty in Tabernacle Square, when a pair of horses attached to a railway cart raced towards him. He caught hold of the reins and after running 70 yards with them he managed to bring them to a halt. After securing the horses, he returned and began to attend an injured woman, when he saw another horse and heavily laden van, bolting down the road. He dashed forwards and succeeded in pulling that to a stop as well. Although bombs were still dropping around him, the constable paid no heed to his own safety, and shouted to people to take shelter. He stopped two more runaway horses before assisting in removing more injured people to hospital.

An award was also made from the Royal Society for Protection of Animals from Cruelty and a monetary award from the Bow Street fund.

KING'S POLICE MEDAL
LG. 1/1/18

| Ralph | Augustus | Police Constable | 98153 D |

On the night of 12th March 1917 a fire occurred in one of the rooms of the Christian Union Almshouse, Crawford Place, London. Constable Ralph, who was off duty, saw the flames through the window of an upper room, and after raising the alarm, entered the house and went upstairs to the room which was on fire. He was told the occupier was out, but being doubtful of this, he twice tried to enter the room, but was driven back by heat and smoke. He then tied a wet handkerchief round his mouth and nostrils, and threw water on the flames. He entered the room, and found an old woman lying on the floor, unconscious, and her clothes alight. She was a heavy woman, but he dragged her to the door, and with assistance put out the burning clothing. Unfortunately the woman died three days later in hospital. An award was also made from the Society for Protection of Life from Fire and a monetary award from the Bow Street fund.

KING'S POLICE MEDAL
LG. 1/1/18

| Wilson | Robert George | Police Constable | 87252 G |

At 10.40am on 7th July 1917 during an attack by hostile aircraft, a horse attached to a covered van bolted along Finsbury Pavement, the driver having taken shelter. Constable Wilson who was on traffic duty, seized the reins, and eventually succeeded in stopping the horse. A few minutes later, the constable saw another horse and van galloping down Chiswell Street, and also stopped that, just as a bomb fell, killing the horse and rendering the constable unconscious. A monetary award was also made from the Bow Street fund.

KING'S POLICE MEDAL - ZEPPELIN RAID OVER LONDON

| Melton | Robert Melton | Police Constable | 94328 L |
| Christmas | Jesse | Police Constable | 95206 L |

On the occasion of an enemy air raid which took place on the 19th October 1917 a bomb fell on two adjoining houses, killing 10 persons and imprisoning 18 others under the wreckage. When helpers arrived it was found that some of the persons who were imprisoned in the basement of one of the houses were alive, but the work of rescue was exceedingly dangerous, for escaping gas in the basement became ignited and set fire to the debris above. Inspector Wright with an axe made a small opening in the floor over the basement which was in a slanting and tottering condition. The joists which supported it were broken, and through this opening though with much difficulty 13 persons were rescued. It was then ascertained that two children were left in the basement, Inspector Wright with Police Constables Robert Melton and Jesse Christmas dropped into the basement through the opening and searched for the children under very dangerous conditions. In addition to the fumes of the escaping gas which were suffocating and the fire raging above, there was a possibility of further movement of wreckage which might have proved fatal to all below. The space was so confined that they were barely able to reach the back of the premises. The children were found to be dead.

This was one of the many Zeppelin raids that took place over London.

Sub Divisional Inspector Frederick Wright received the AM.

CARNEGIE HERO FUND
11/8/18
Bellamy   Arthur Richard   Police Constable
Attempted rescue of a woman from drowning in the River Lee between Cheshunt and Waltham Abbey.

CARNEGIE HERO FUND
18/5/18
Bryant   Frank   Police Constable
Rescued a lunatic from drowning in the River Roding at Ilford.

CARNEGIE HERO FUND
13/8/18
Kidd   Charles   Police Constable
Rescued a boy from drowning in the River Thames.

ROLL OF HONOUR
• Pc George Henry Richard Judge
Fatally injured while on night duty at Cricklewood by a motor car which failed to stop.
• Pc James Hardy KPM
Killed in a cycling accident on the eve of investiture for his KPM.
• Pc Herbert Berry
Died from injuries sustained while making an arrest in the Euston Road.
• Pc Henry William Sawyer
Died from the effects of injuries received in the execution of his duty on Peckham Division.
• Pc Edward William Swan
Died from the effects of injuries received in the execution of his duty on Greenwich Division.

1919
January   The Atom was split.
February   Passengers flew between London and Paris for the first time.
March   Invention of a wireless telephone enabling air pilots to talk in flight.
April   Petrol now costs around 3/6d a gallon.

May   Government launches enquiry into London traffic problems.

June   200 feared dead after a tornado strikes Fergus Falls in Minnesota USA.

July   Sir Edwin Lutyens new war memorial the 'Cenotaph' is unveiled in Whitehall.

August   Beginning of daily flights to Paris, the world's first international schedule daily air service.

September   Lord Leconfield gives Scafell Pike to the nation in memory of the Great War dead.

October   6 Sinn Fein prisoners escape from Strageways Prison.

November   Nancy Astor is elected as the first woman MP.

December   RAF Commander Sir Hugh Trenchard presents proposals for making the force permanent.

HITS OF THE YEAR

Don't dilly-dally on the way

I'm forever blowing bubbles

EPSOM POLICE STATION SIEGE - 1919

A police Sergeant Thomas Green was killed during a riot at Epsom Police Station in June 1919. Seven other officers were injured.

It all began when a large group of Canadian soldiers from the Woodcote Convalescent Camp made an attack in force on 18th June 1919 at Epsom police station in an attempt to rescue 2 of their comrades who had been arrested for being drunk and disorderly. 15 police defended the police station against a large mob of between 400 and 500 soldiers. Station Sergeant Green rallied his men after the rioters had battered down the iron gates of the station, he led them in a charge against the crowd but was struck on the head by an iron bar and sadly died later in hospital.

The angry mob some armed with large blocks of wood which they used as battering rams, others collected stones and started bombarding the station. All the lights both inside and outside were smashed and the battle continued throughout in darkness. The angry mob managed to free one of their colleagues, the police then released the other in the hope that the situation would quieten down before any further injuries or loss of live occurred.

At the camp head quarters, a military court of enquiry was held and certain men under suspicion were confined to camp but not arrested.

Sergeant Green left behind a widow who was an invalid in the National Hospital for Paralysed in Bloomsbury and 2 daughters aged 16 and 18. He had served 7 years in the Royal Horse Artillery and had 24 years in the police and was due to retire on pension in March 1920.

Officers who were at the station for the siege were presented with inscribed watches and medallions.

KING'S POLICE MEDAL

LG. 1/1/19

Bellamy   Arthur Richard   Police Constable   86920 N

On 11th August 1918, constable Bellamy, whilst off duty was walking along the bank of the River Lea between Cheshunt and Waltham Abbey when he noticed a woman walking about

300 yards ahead of him suddenly disappear. He hurried to the spot an old bathing hole which had been unused for some time due to its dangerous nature, and seeing bubbles rising in the water, threw off his hat and coat, and plunged in. Owing to the rank growth of weeds, he couldn't find the body, so he returned to the bank, and threw off the remainder of his clothes and made two further attempts without success. A drag was brought up and constable Bellamy was then able to recover the body.

KING'S POLICE MEDAL
LG. 1/1/19

Bryant	Frank	Police Constable	84871 K

At 4.10 am on 18th May 1918 a woman brought word to Ilford Police station that her husband who was deranged had escaped from his home and had run off towards the River Roding. Constable Bryant saw him soon afterwards, and went towards him, whereupon the man ran along the river bank flourishing an open razor, and then suddenly jumped in the water. Constable Bryant followed him into the water fully clothed, and seized the man, who drew the razor across his own throat, causing severe injury and then attacked the constable. After a struggle, the razor was knocked out of the man's hand, but the constable was pushed under the water. Fortunately with some assistance the constable dragged the man to the bank, and he was taken to hospital. The constable was in a state of collapse, as he was not a strong swimmer.

Constable Bryant died of the injuries he received in this rescue attempt.

KING'S POLICE MEDAL
LG. 1/1/19

Davies	David	Police Constable	91506 W

At 3.40 pm on 9th October 1917 two workmen were engaged in cleaning a sewer at Tamworth Villas, Mitcham. One of them, Simmons, descending a manhole some 12 feet deep, was partially overcome by sewer gas, and obliged to return. When near to the top, another man Lemon caught his hand but was unable to retain hold and Simmons fell back into the sewer. Lemon at once went down but was also overcome. The alarm was raised, and a soldier who was standing nearby, attempted to rescue the two men, but he was also overcome. Lemon then grasped a rope which was lowered, and was rescued. Simmons was lying in 4 inches of water. Constable Davies who was off duty, arrived on the scene, and although warned against it by a doctor, descended into the sewer with a rope. He came up for fresh air on one occasion, then went down again, and succeeded in placing the rope round Simmons, and both were brought to the surface, unconscious, but they eventually recovered.

KING'S POLICE MEDAL
LG. 1/1/19

Kidd	Charles	Police Constable	83745 E

At 7.40 pm on 13th August 1918 constable Kidd was on duty at the Victoria Embankment when he heard shouts from the direction of Cleopatra's Needle, and he found a boy aged 8 years in difficulties, and struggling in the water, about 10 yards from the stops. Constable Kidd removed his uniform and jumped in, swan to the boy, and catching him by the

shoulders succeeded in bringing him to the steps. The water at this spot was about 20 feet deep, and constable Kidd was 47 years old, and a poor swimmer, with no experience in methods of saving persons from drowning.

KING'S POLICE MEDAL
LG. 1/1/19

Stubbs	Francis	Police Constable	97726 R

At 1 am on 12th May 1918 constable Stubbs arrested a man whom he recognised as being an army absentee, but the prisoner broke away, hit the officer a heavy blow in the mouth and decamped. The constable overtook him, and then was kicked in the testicles, before the man ran away again. Constable Stubbs although in severe pain, again attempted to arrest the man, who then flourished a pocket knife and warned the officer to take care. Constable Stubbs closed with the man, who stabbed the officer in the thigh, but in spite of the wound, and the pain he was suffering, constable Stubbs forced the man to the ground, blew his whistle, and held him until assistance arrived.

CARNEGIE HERO FUND
7/4/19

Lambert	Frederick	Police Constable	**Posthumous**

Sustained fatal injuries while attempting to stop a runaway horse in Stanford Hill.

CARNEGIE HERO FUND
6/2/19

Staines	Police Constable
Hill	Police Constable
Avery	Inspector
Harper	Police Sergeant

Rescued 2 young ladies on the occasion of an explosion at Battersea.

ROLL OF HONOUR
- Pc Frederick William Lambert

Killed when he was run over attempting to stop a runaway horse and cart in Stamford Hill.
- Station Ps Thomas Green

Struck on the head and killed by a mob during the Epsom Police Station Siege.
- Pc Frank Bryant KPM

See above entry
- Pc Thomas Eldred Briggs Rowland

Died from a fractured skull after being assaulted while attempting an arrest at Walworth, South London.
- Chief Inspector Frederick James Rivett

Killed when he fell from his horse and fractured his skull whilst on duty at Westminster.

Chapter Four

THE YEARS OF 1920 - 1929

During this decade again many achievements were made, speed records were set and broken both mechanical and physical. Inventions came along and the weather decided to prove a point or two. We saw a new dance craze come from America 'the Charleston', new fashions came along 'the Oxford bag trousers', and the hem lines of ladies' skirts finally rose.

Not long after the men returned from the Great War unemployment hit new records. The soldiers having been discharged from the military made up at least one third of million or so unemployed.

Trouble was brewing in Europe, the rise of Mussolini's Fascist party, and of Hitler's Nazis. The USSR saw the rise of Joseph Stalin.

The trouble in Ireland was in the news most months during the decade. Riots in Belfast, the assassination of Field Marshall Sir Henry Wilson by the IRA in London, Civil war in Ireland and, during the years, over 600 died in the troubles.

Prohibition started in the United States of America, Mary Pickford married Douglas Fairbanks, Roscoe 'Fatty' Arbuckle, a successful film comedian, was charged with rape and murder. He was found not guilty of the charge but it was enough to finish his career. Charlie Chaplin was still the most popular silent screen film star. Towards the end of this decade the 'talkie' came in with Al Jolson painting his face black and appearing in The Jazz Singer, a highly acclaimed film with sound.

There was one infamous murder and trial, the murder of a police constable in Essex, the two offenders being convicted on the evidence of a ballistic expert.

The number of motor vehicles had increased so much that traffic controlling systems started to be introduced, lines in the middle of the road, traffic lights, speed restrictions and finally making the driving test compulsory. One of the busiest road junctions in the world at the time was Hyde Park Corner, which is still very busy to this day.

There was a general strike which brought the country almost to its knees, again nothing has changed. We had severe flooding and freezing Arctic weather making white Christmases quite normal.

All in all, this is an interesting decade of change.

1920

January   The manufacture and sale of alcohol is banned in the United States of America, prohibition had begun.

February   In London the police are told that they will get cars instead of horses.

March   Queen Alexandra unveils a monument to Nurse Edith Cavell next to the National Gallery in London. Nurse Cavell was shot as a spy during the Great War.

April	140 killed when a tornado sweeps across the Southern United States of America.
May	Government proposes a car tax of £1 per horsepower.
June	King George V opens the Imperial War Museum housed at Crystal Palace.
July	New air mail service starts to Amsterdam costing 3d per ounce of mail.
August	First two night bus services introduced in London.
September	Roscoe 'Fatty' Arbuckle charged with rape and murder.
October	King George V approves the burial of the Unknown Soldier in Westminster Abbey on Armistice Day.
November	Unknown French soldier is buried under the Arc de Triomphe, Paris.
December	Martial law declared in large areas of Ireland.

HITS OF THE YEAR
Wyoming lullaby
Avalon
Margie

KING'S POLICE MEDAL
LG. 1/1/20

Bird	Royal	Police Sergeant	93337 A
Richardson	George	Police Constable	98951 L
Riches	Frederick	Police Constable	101415 L
Williams	William	Police Constable	102953 B

Constables Richardson and Williams were sent to Waterloo Railway Station on 20th September 1918 to meet a train and arrest a man whom the Surrey Police wanted for housebreaking. When confronted the man resisted violently, and produced an automatic pistol. He shot and disabled constable Richardson. Constable Williams then closed with him and endeavoured to get the pistol, but the man shot him in the thigh. Constable Williams closed with him again, but was thrown down, and could not rise, the prisoner ran away. Sergeant Bird and constable Riches had by this time arrived, and chased the man through several streets, finally coming upon him in a wash-house, where they arrested him. The pistol was found in the wash house still containing five live cartridges.

KING'S POLICE MEDAL
LG. 1/1/20

Carr	Percy	Police Constable	92939
Mewton	William	Police Constable	93291
Monnery	William	Police Constable	78027

On 10th June 1919 a train of 26 trucks all loaded with explosives was standing beside a magazine at Woolwich Arsenal, when a truck full of small arms ammunition caught fire. Constable Carr who was patrolling nearby at once ran to the nearest fire hydrant, and connected the hose. Constables Mewton and Monnery came up and Monnery took the hose, and went up to the burning truck. Bullets and cartridge cases were exploding, and flying in all directions, and the tarpaulin covering the next truck, loaded with boxes of fuses had by this time caught light. As soon as the water had been turned on, constables Carr and Mewton helped constable Monnery to play the water onto the fire. They first put out the tarpaulin, and then the small arms ammunition, unfastening the side of the truck in order to reach the inner contents.

KING'S POLICE MEDAL
LG 1/1/20

Darke	Gilbert	Police Constable	84510 R
Moore	Francis	Police Constable	100734 R

On the 13th June 1919 the manager of a bank had been threatened with a revolver by a man who had then decamped. Constable Darke was sent to pursue the man and he caught up with him on the edge of a wood, but the criminal got behind a tree, and fired at the constable, the bullet going through his helmet. The man escaped into the wood. Constable Moore then joined constable Darke, and the two officers searched until the man was found hiding in some shrubs. He aimed the revolver at constable Moore who threw his helmet in the criminal's face before he could pull the trigger, and then struck him with his truncheon. Constable Moore then closed with the man and struggled with him for possession of the revolver, the man succeeding in firing it, but shot and wounded himself by mistake. He was then overpowered and arrested.

KING'S POLICE MEDAL
LG. 1/1/20

Hearn	Walter	Police Constable	96204 P

Whilst constable Hearn was on duty in Catford, on the 25th June 1919 a pair of horses with a carrier's van bolted. The horses galloped at full speed along the street, and as they approached the point where the constable was standing he attempted to seize the reins, but the horses swerved. He did manage however to grab the tailgate of the van, and hang on, and then climbed into the van, over the goods, and got to the driver's seat, where he took the reins and pulled the horses to a standstill.

KING'S POLICE MEDAL
LG. 1/1/20

Ost	Frederick	Police Constable	102444 S
Wright	Frederick	Police Constable	98430 S

On 29th June 1919 constables Ost and Right were on duty in plain clothes and keeping observation on two suspected burglars. Constable Ost went to arrest one of the burglars when he suddenly pulled out a revolver, and fired three shots at the constable from a distance of 5 or 6 yards. Constable Right immediately went to his colleague's assistance, leaving the other burglar, the man then fired four more shots at close range, and then ran away. After a chase, the two constables caught up with the man, and arrested him and took away the revolver. It was found later that both officers had been hit by the shots, but the force of the bullets had been spent passing through their clothes, and as a result they were not seriously injured.

KING'S POLICE MEDAL
LG. 1/1/20

Sullivan   Maurice   Police Constable   98083 W

On 13th June 1919 constable Sullivan chased two burglars into the gateway of a house, when one of them turned and fired three shots at him. He took cover for a moment and then crept along to the gateway, where two more shots were fired at him. The burglars escaped. However, constable Sullivan together with another constable who had come to his assistance, found one of them in a nearby garden. The man struck at constable Sullivan with a jemmy, but the constable dodged to one side, and it missed. The man was immediately arrested.

KING'S POLICE MEDAL
LG. 1/1/20

Webber   Albert   Police Constable   97964

A gas explosion took place in the lower compartments of the German battleship 'Baden' which was in dock at Invergordon, Scotland on 5th August 1919. Constable Webber a London constable seconded to the Royal Dockyards was on duty on the ship and hearing that two or three workmen were still in the shaft alley, he offered to rescue them. He and two workmen with lines round them went down to a compartment near the shaft alley, where one workman was lying unconscious. It was a dark area, and full of poisonous fumes, but after torches had been lowered to them, they got the man out. All the rescuers also came out safely. No other workman was found below.

KING'S POLICE MEDAL
LG. 1/1/20

Williams   Harry   Police Constable   92336

On 2nd July 1919 constable Williams was on duty in Grosvenor Square, when he heard shots being fired in nearby Grosvenor Gardens Mews. When he arrived there he found a United States Marine, very drunk, armed with an automatic pistol. The Marine had fired five shots when the constable approached him, and then fired at the constable's feet, before running off around the corner. Constable Williams took cover and hid until the Marine returned, and then he sprang on the Marine, threw him to the ground, and disarmed him. The constable overpowered the Marine after a fierce struggle.

CARNEGIE HERO FUND
4/6/20

Hayes   Harry   Police Constable

Rescued a girl from drowning in the River Lee.

ROLL OF HONOUR
• Pc Alfred James Tyler

Knocked down by a motor van while on patrol in Hampstead.

- Pc James Kelly

Shot 3 times and killed while pursuing a burglar he had disturbed in Acton.

- Pc Page M Janeway

Injured at the Epsom Police Station Siege in June 1919 and subsequently died from cancer in the shoulder believed aggravated by the blow.

1921

January	Six policemen are killed in Ireland by the IRA.
February	Aviator Etienne Oehmichen makes the first ever flight in a helicopter.
March	State of emergency declared in the UK after a coal strike is called.
April	In London the police patrol on motorcycles.
May	Concerns as skirts rise and morals decline, no more long skirts for women.
June	Rainfall ends the 100 day drought in the UK.
July	1,363,121 people in the UK are on poor relief, the highest number ever recorded.
August	27 Britons and 16 Americans die when the airship ZR11 explodes during a trial flight at Hull.
September	Charlie S Chaplin returns home to London.
October	First German war criminal Karl Heynen sentenced to 9 months in jail for cruelty to Prisoners of War.
November	Unknown soldier arrives in the US from France for reburial at Arlington National Cemetery.
December	Discovery of insulin gives hope to diabetics.

HITS OF THE YEAR

The fishermen of England

Three o'clock in the morning

KING'S POLICE MEDAL

LG. 1/1/21

Abbott	John	Police Sergeant	90645
Churchyard	Wallace	Police Constable	102391 W

On 28th January 1920 Sergeant Abbott and constable Churchyard were on duty in South Croydon when they were informed that there was an armed lunatic at No 10 Moreton road, Croydon. As they approached the house, they saw the man pointing a rifle at them in a threatening manner, and muttering something inaudible. The officers rushed him throwing the barrel of the rifle upwards, and after a brief struggle, overpowered him, and disarmed him. When the rifle was examined, it was found to be loaded and the man had several cartridges in his pocket.

KING'S POLICE MEDAL

LG. 1/1/21

Allison	Bertram	Police Constable	105771 P

On 19th September 1919 constable Allison saw a youth removing dentist's equipment from the front of a house in Camberwell road, South London. The youth ran away along several streets pursued by the constable, during which he drew a revolver from his pocket and threatened to shoot constable Allison. Despite the threats he continued to follow until the youth stopped, turned round and fired a shot at the constable, which fortunately missed. The youth was finally run to ground in an outhouse and arrested.

KING'S POLICE MEDAL
LG. 1/1/21

Day	George	Police Constable	94624

On 25th July 1920 constable Day a London officer seconded to the Royal Dockyards, saw a man in the water in Portsmouth Harbour throw up his hands and sink. The constable dived in and swam 70 yards to where he had seen the man disappear, and groping round under the water found him. The man was still alive, and struggled violently, and constable Day had to use force to quieten him. It was dark at the time, but constable Day swam back to the steps with him, and got him ashore.

KING'S POLICE MEDAL
LG. 1/1/21

Hayes	Harry	Police Constable	106505 N

On 4th June 1920 at 11pm constable Hayes was informed that a little girl had fallen into the River Lea at Tottenham, North London, and was shouting for help. Arriving at the spot, he plunged into the water in full uniform, and found the girl in mid stream, and brought her back safely to the bank. The river is over 60 feet wide in the area.

KING'S POLICE MEDAL
LG. 1/1/21

Jaffray	Alexander	Police Constable	98927 E
Sweet	Percy	Police Constable	107769 E

On 20th March 1920 constable Sweet was called to a house in Endell Street, London where he found a man holding a woman by the throat. He struggled with the man, who tried to hit the constable with a poker, tongs and a chair. Eventually he was quietened, and agreed to go to the police station. As he got to the door of the house, the man pushed the constable into the street and closed the door. Constable Jaffray had arrived when suddenly the door was opened by the owner, and the man was seen on the stairs holding a poker. Both officers rushed in chasing the man into a kitchen, where he had grabbed the woman again, and was twisting her arm. He threw the woman down, and after a short but fierce battle, he was knocked down with a truncheon. The man was taken to the police station, biting and kicking the officers all the way.

KING'S POLICE MEDAL
LG. 30/12/21

Buchanan	Thomas	Inspector	83289 M

At 10.15pm on 29th December 1919 the manager and the lady cashier of the Electric Palace Theatre, Deptford were depositing the takings in the safe, when John Pratt and another man

entered the office, pointed an automatic pistol at them and demanded the money. The lady cashier ran out of the office and called for help. The second robber decamped. The manager then knocked Pratt over, and ran out of the officer slamming the door, and, holding it tight, kept the man prisoner. Station Sergeant (Now Inspector) Buchanan on hearing screams ran to the scene where he saw the manager who explained the situation. The officer opened the door, and rushed din, pinning the man against the wall, and awaited the arrival of assistance. When the office was later searched, the automatic pistol was found hidden.

KING'S POLICE MEDAL
LG. 30/12/21

| Burton | William | Police Constable | 111046 E |

At 9.35 pm on 12th November 1920 a bitterly cold and very foggy night, constable Burton was on duty at Victoria Embankment, when he heard cries near to the Adelphi Steps, Westminster, that someone was in the river. He immediately blew his whistle, and ran to the steps, where he saw a woman in the water, being carried by the flood tide towards Charing Cross Bridge. The constable took off his greatcoat, tunic and helmet, and swam out tot he woman. Lifebuoys had been thrown into the water and not being a good swimmer, the constable put one round the woman, and used the other himself. He supported the woman, whilst clinging to a boat moored about 20 feet away from the bank, until both were taken on board a police launch. Despite artificial respiration the woman died.

KING'S POLICE MEDAL
LG. 30/12/21

| Green | Percy | Police Constable | 110124 M |

At 5 pm on 27th April 1921 one of the wheels came off a single horse phaeton, which was being driven along London Road, Southwark. The animal took fright and bolted, colliding with a stationary motor car, and then becoming detached from the cart. It galloped along the foot way knocking down and injuring 12 people. Constable Green attempted to stop the horse by grabbing the reins but was knocked down. Although dazed he commandeered a passing motor car, and jumped on the running board. After a chase of about a quarter of a mile, he came alongside the animal and managed to grab the reins and although dragged for about 30 yards he brought the horse to a standstill.

KING'S POLICE MEDAL
LG. 30/12/21

| Hall | Charles | Police Constable | 104283 |
| Lewis | Jack | Police Constable | 109192 |

At 12.15 pm on 16th June 1921 constables Hall and Lewis received information about four fugitives, and after arming themselves with revolvers went to Burnt Ash Lane, Bromley where they observed a taxicab coming towards them. Constable Hall stepped out into the road and signalled the driver to stop. In the cab were four or five men who on being interrogated failed to give satisfactory replies. The constable then ordered the driver to get out and covering the others with their revolvers ordered them out of the cab

one by one. The first man had alighted and a second was about to do so, when constable Lewis called 'search him'. Constable Hall apparently misunderstood, and turned from the first man to the second. In the confusion, the first man produced a revolver, and fired two shots at constable Hall. The constables returned the fire, and during this exchange of fire, the other occupants of the vehicle escaped. All four men were arrested. This incident involved **Sinn Fein.**

KING'S POLICE MEDAL
LG. 30/12/21

Powell	Harry	Police Constable	99354 N
Taylor	Samuel	Police Constable	80128 N

At about 12.10 am on 27th November 1920 constable Powell saw smoke coming from the doorway of No 1 Fore Street, Edmonton, a furniture shop, with living accommodation above. The constable immediately gave the alarm, and constable Taylor and another officer arrived. An onlooker said that there was a woman and children sleeping in the house. The constables immediately forced the door and searched the house. As the Fire Brigade arrived constable Powell was at the second floor window preparing to jump, but he was rescued by the Fire Brigade. As the flames were brought under control, a ladder was put up to the first floor, and a fireman found constable Taylor crouched, unconscious in a corner. With assistance he was also brought out safely. A subsequent search of the premises proved that the alarm that persons were trapped was false. Both constables received severe burns to their hands and faces.

KING'S POLICE MEDAL
LG. 30/12/21

Smith	George	Police Constable	108011 L

At 1.15 am on Wednesday 17th August 1921 constable Smith was on duty in Bollingbroke Grove, Battersea, when he heard loud screams, and saw a servant girl standing on the roof of a house calling 'Help. Police, Burglars'. The constable blew his whistle and after other officers arrived the building was surrounded. Constable Smith climbed a high wall, and then by a difficult and dangerous route, reached the roof, where he found the girl in a hysterical condition. As he approached, she tried to descend the other side of the roof, which was 30 to 40 feet above the ground. The constable managed to grasp her wrist, and was able to pacify her. The constable then carefully helped her down from the high roof, onto a lower one, but although she was still very emotional he managed to bring her safely to the ground.

KING'S POLICE MEDAL
LG. 30/12/21

Thomas	John	Police Sergeant	95461 D

At 11.45 am on 10th January 1921 Sergeant Thomas was called to 22 High Street, Marylebone, where he was told by the landlady that a tenant, Miss Ida Todd, was acting strangely. The Sergeant found she had locked herself in her room, and was threatening to throw herself from the window. She refused to open the door. Sergeant Thomas went into

another room, and got out onto a 10 inch wide ledge, 40 feet above the ground, and then positioned himself outside the woman's window. As the door was forced open by other constables Miss Todd went to the window, but was prevented from jumping by Sergeant Thomas, standing precariously on the ledge outside. She then attacked Sergeant Thomas with an iron curtain rod, but he was able to defend himself with his truncheon. She was overpowered and taken into custody.

CARNEGIE HERO FUND
12/12/21
Mace   Benjamin   Police Constable
Stopped a pair of runaway horses in Waterloo Road.

CARNEGIE HERO FUND
17/8/21
Smith   George   Police Constable
Rescued a girl from a perilous position on a roof about 40 feet from the ground.

ROLL OF HONOUR
•   Pc William George Hallett
Killed on patrol in Drury Lane by a car driven by a drunken driver.
•   Pc David Wroth
Died from the effects of an accidental injury received in the execution of his duty on Croydon Division.
•   Pc Baseby 101053 T
Fatally injured while on duty through the skidding of his bicycle causing him to fall in front of a steam wagon.
•   Pc Pike 87352 Y
Received injuries as a result of a blow from a violent prisoner.

1922
January	804 deaths reported in the UK from influenza.
February	8,500 cattle, 1,000 sheep and 2,500 pigs slaughtered as 477 foot and mouth outbreaks are reported.
March	Annie Oakley shoots a record 98 out of 100 clay targets from 16 yards in the US.
April	6 die when two aircraft of the London to Paris air service collide over Poix on the Somme, France.
May	Highest May temperatures for 50 years 88°F in the shade in London.
June	Police arrest 20 men in connection with the murder of Field Marshall Sir Henry Wilson in London - shot by the IRA - KPM awarded see entry 1923 gallantry awards.
July	Johnny Weissmuller became the first man to swim 100 metres in less than a minute.
August	Government decides to provide 500 aeroplanes for home defence.
September	Telephone toll exchange system is inaugurated in London.

October   BBC formed.
November   Sir William Horwood, Metropolitan Police Commissioner poisoned by arsenic filled chocolates.
December   In the United States 57 reported lynchings this year 18 in Texas alone.

HITS OF THE YEAR
Limehouse blues
Chicago

CARNEGIE HERO FUND
24/4/22
Hutchings   Harry   Police Constable
Stopped a runaway horse in Blackfriars Road.

CARNEGIE HERO FUND
8/6/22
Tribe   William   Police Constable
Attempted to stop a runaway horse and thereby sustained injury.

ROLL OF HONOUR
• Pc Albert E Cordwell
Pensioned as a result of a non-accidental injury received in the execution of his duty on Holborn Division from which he subsequently died.

1923
January   Engagement announced of Prince Albert Duke of York to Lady Elizabeth Bowes-Lyon.
February   Cox's bank merges with Lloyds bank.
March   Telegraphic links established between the UK and Afghanistan.
April   Duke of York and Lady Elizabeth Bowes-Lyon marry.
May   BBC opens their new wireless studio at Savoy Hill, London.
June   £1 now worth 600,000 German marks.
July   MP Lady Astor's liquor bill passed - banning sale of alcohol to people under 18yrs.
August   £1 now worth 15,000,000 German marks.
September Huge earthquake devastates Tokyo 300,000 die.
October   BBC recommends 7/6d wireless licence.
November   First transatlantic wireless broadcast to the US.
December   Agreement reached on formation of Imperial Air Transport Company.

HITS OF THE YEAR
Who's sorry now

KING'S POLICE MEDAL
LG. 1/1/23

Bush	Walter	Police Constable	106323 B
Duff	James	Police Constable	112231 B
March	Walter	Police Constable	106179 B
Sayer	Cecil	Detective Constable	103316 B

On 22nd June 1922 Field Marshall Sir Henry Wilson was assassinated in the street by two men. There was an immediate hue and cry, and a large crowd followed the men as they ran away. Constable March who was at the corner of Eaton Terrace, Chelsea heard the commotion, and as he ran into Eaton Place West he confronted the two armed men. The constable rushed at the taller one and grappled with him, but the other man fired a shot which hit constable March in the stomach. He collapsed but was able to give a good description to other officers. Constable Sayer was in Elizabeth Street when he heard the shots and found constable March. He took up the chase, and was fired at several times. He kept in close contact with the men, and threw his truncheon which hit one of the men on the head. At this point one of the men turned, aimed and fired a shot which hit constable Sayer in the leg, and disabled him. Constable Duff who was off duty, and Bush were at Gerald Road Police Station when the alarm was raised. They ran out and found the fugitives in Ebury Street, where they were fired on by the men. Constable Duff threw his truncheon which hit one of the men, and followed up and tackled him, and arrested him. Constable Bush at the same time rushed straight at the other man, and felled him with a punch to the jaw, and overpowered him. Both men had fired numerous shots at police and onlookers, wounding several people before they were arrested.

Field Marshall Sir Henry Wilson was shot dead on his door step on the orders of the IRA. The two suspects Reginald Dunne and Joseph O'Sullivan were both ex soldiers, both were hanged.

KING'S POLICE MEDAL
LG. 1/1/23

Carter	Frederick	Police Constable	109044 Z
Hayes	John	Police Constable	110539 Z

On 23rd March 1922 a barmaid at the Green Dragon Public House, High Street, Croydon was bolting the front door to the public bar, when a man called John Wallace forced his way inside, and drew a pistol. The alarm was raised, and the man ran away. Constable Hayes pursued the man, who after 30 or 40 yards, turned and aimed a shot at the constable which missed. The chase was then joined by constable Carter and the man fired at them twice from close range, failing to hit either of them. Eventually he turned into a cul de sac, and went into a house. Constable Carter rushed in, and tackled the man as he drew the pistol and pushed it into constable Carter's stomach. A struggle ensued, but both constables overpowered him.

KING'S POLICE MEDAL
LG. 1/1/23

Geer	Edward	Police Constable	111636 B

On 24th September 1921 a van was being driven down a gradient in Grosvenor Road, when the horse's bridle came off, and the horse bolted. Constable Geer commandeered a motorcycle combination driven by a civilian and gave chase. One overtaking the runaway, the constable stood up in the sidecar, and seizing the nostrils of the horse in one hand and the shaft with the other, jumped out of the sidecar, and after several yards dragged the horse to a standstill.

KING'S POLICE MEDAL
LG. 1/1/23

Hutchings	Harry	Police Constable	110125 M

On the evening of the 24th April 1922 constable Hutchings was on duty in Blackfriars Road, when he saw a runaway horse without a bridle, pulling a van, galloping towards him. He ran into the roadway, seized the shafts of the van and with one hand, and the horses nostrils with the other but the horse seemed to gather speed. Constable Hutchings then tried to swing his leg over the horse's back, and mount it, but his foot caught in the harness, and he fell underneath the horse, catching the horse's foreleg, causing the horse to stumble to its knees. As it struggled to get up, it kicked the constable in the head, which rendered him unconscious.

KING'S POLICE MEDAL
LG. 1/1/23

Martin	Charles	Detective Constable	96366 A
McDoull	Percy	Detective Constable	108433 A

On the evening of 15th November 1921 constables Martin and McDoull were concealed on the premises in the Brownie Restaurant in Victoria Street to await the arrival of a man called Percy Lane. On the previous evening this man had aroused the suspicion of the lady cashier by stating that he was a police officer, and that he wished to examine the treasury notes in her possession. He was asked to call again the following day. Eventually Lane arrived and whilst examining the bank notes, was challenged by constable Martin as to his identity. He failed to satisfy the officer, who then informed him he would be arrested. Lane then made a swift movement towards his trouser pocket. The constable seized his hand, and a large calibre Webley revolver was found. A fierce struggle took place which constable McDoull joined in, and the constable had his head pushed through a glass window.

CARNEGIE HERO FUND
3/4/23

Mountney	Harry J	Police Constable

Stopped a runaway horse in Roadway North, Royal Albert Dock.

ROLL OF HONOUR

1924
January	UK Submarine L-34 sinks off Weymouth, 43 die.
February	Miss Helena Normanton is first woman barrister to practise at the Old Bailey.
March	Public vehicles are allowed in Hyde Park for the first time since 1636.
April	BBC begins broadcasting to schools.

May	Sir Edward Elgar is appointed as Master of the King's Musick.
June	Hugo Junkers and Henry Ford meet to discuss the building of an all metal aeroplane.
July	Police warn cyclists to avoid roads heavily used by cars following a steep rise in fatal accidents.
August	Agreement reached to allow 3,000 UK families to emigrate to Canada.
September	Moscow reports that a bomb has been found in Lenin's tomb.
October	Ministry of Health bans preservatives in cream, butter, margarine and other food stuffs.
November	US Texan elects its first woman State Governor Miriam Ferguson.
December	Imperial Airways aircraft plummeted to the ground seconds after take off from Croydon aerodrome, 8 are killed.

HITS OF THE YEAR

Fascinating Rhythm

It had to be you

KING'S POLICE MEDAL

LG. 1/1/24

| Allen | Joseph | Police Constable | 99067 J |

At about 5 pm on 16th October 1922 a black mare attached to an uncovered trolley, was being driven along Epping New Road, Loughton, when the bit slipped from its mouth, causing the animal to bolt. The mare galloped along the road for about two and a half miles before constable Allen made an attempt to stop it, but as he did no he was knocked down as the near side shaft of the trolley struck his chest. He got up, winded and took up the chase, firstly on motorcycle, and then a motor car, being given lifts in each case by the drivers. He eventually caught the animal and brought it to a stop.

KING'S POLICE MEDAL

LG. 1/1/24

| Beesley | Alfred | Detective Sergeant | 96655 CO C1 |
| Hobbs | Walter | Detective Sergeant | 90661 CO C1 |

At about 10.30 am on 5th July 1922 Detective Sergeants Beesley and Hobbs were in the vicinity of Denmark Terrace, Horsney road, keeping observation on two men suspected of stealing and receiving stolen bicycles, when one of the suspects mounted a bicycle and rode away. The second man was stopped and questioned by the officers, and being unable to satisfy them, he was arrested by Sergeant Beesley. On the way to the police station, the prisoner attempted to put the Sergeant off his guard, and then wrenched himself free. As Sergeant Beesley went to seize him, the prisoner produced a pistol and fired two shots, wounding Sergeant Beesley in the leg. Sergeant Hobbs was following behind, rushed forwards and assisted his wounded colleague to overpower the prisoner. During the struggle four or more shots were fired, which fortunately were ineffective, due mainly to Sergeant Hobbs holding the prisoner's pistol against the pavement.

KING'S POLICE MEDAL

LG. 1/1/24

Cooper   John   Police Constable   109452 Y

At about 12.50 pm on 20th August 1923 a pair of horses attached to a van was left temporarily unattended at the junction of Coleridge Road and Broadway, Hornsey, when the offside horse began to plunge and kick, frightening its companion, with the result that both horses bolted. Constable Cooper saw this happening and rushed forwards to grab the bridle of the offside horse, and after being dragged for 30 yards, he was able to turn the horses into the near side of the roadway. One of the animals fell, throwing the constable to the ground, and then it kicked him on the knee. Both horses started to plunge again, and mounted the foot way, pinning the constable to a wall, injuring his left side and shoulder.

KING'S POLICE MEDAL

LG. 1/1/24

Cozens   John   Police Constable   107938 L

At 5.35 am on 20th March 1923 a fire occurred at 6 Frere Street, Battersea. Constable Cozens who was off duty, and who resides in the same street, was awakened by cries of 'fire'. Partially dressing, and without putting his boots on, he rushed to the scene. He saw a woman holding a child out of a second floor window. He burst open the front door, scrambled through the smoke and darkness up the stairs to the second floor, and took control of the child from the woman. Having injured his foot on the way up, and in severe pain, he descended the stairs, which collapsed whilst he was on them causing him further injury. However he continued, with the child in his arms, to make his way carefully to the street and safety, where he handed the child to a bystander. Then in a dazed state and with seriously burned feet, he went home.

KING'S POLICE MEDAL

LG. 1/1/24

Dubber   John   Police Constable   83792 P

At 4.20 am on 3rd August 1922 constable Dubber's attention was drawn to an unusual light shining in a jeweller's shop in Sydenham Road, Croydon. Going to the rear of the premises, he saw two men on a low roof, who on seeing the constable, jumped to the ground and began to make off. Constable Dubber approached one of the men, who pointed a loaded revolver at him, and pulled the trigger, but it misfired. The constable leaped at the man, who fired again, but the weapon misfired a second time. Constable Dubber struck the man with his truncheon, and shouted for assistance. Another constable arrived, and together they disarmed the man, and took him to the police station.

KING'S POLICE MEDAL

LG. 1/1/24

Flint   Albert   Police Constable   105469 A

At about 5 pm on the 18th September 1922, constable Flint was on duty near Victoria Gate, Hyde Park, when he saw a woman lying on the grass, with a man standing over her. As he approached the man ran away. Constable Flint chased the man and after some distance the man turned and attacked the constable with a knife. In the ensuing struggle constable Fling was stabbed several times, and although severely injured hung onto the prisoner until help arrived. The man was subsequently charged with robbery and attempted murder. The constable received wounds to the throat, neck, chest and legs.

KING'S POLICE MEDAL
LG. 1/1/24

Lovegrove	Henry	Police Constable	103653 J

At 7.10 am on 14th June 1922 a horse drawing an uncovered van being driven along Stoke Newington road, took fright and bolted, throwing the driver from the seat. Constable Lovegrove was on duty further down the street, and attempted to stop the animal, but it collided with a light standard, and caused him to release his hold. The horse then broke away from the van, and continued its flight. Constable Lovegrove was given a lift on a passing lorry, and as he drew alongside, he jumped from the running board, grabbed the reins, and after being dragged for about 40 yards, pulled the animal to a stop.

KING'S POLICE MEDAL
LG. 1/1/24

Rutherford	John	Detective Constable	103146 G

At about 10.30 pm on 28th July 1922 constable Rutherford while off duty, was in the saloon bar of the 'Red Bull' public house, Grays Inn Road, when six men entered, three of whom he knew belonging to a local gang known as the 'Camden town Gang'. As the men entered, members of a rival gang, already inside the pub, moved towards them and forced them into the street. The constable followed, and saw one man fire a revolver. Most of the men were carrying firearms, and as the two gangs went down Portpool Lane followed by the constable, several shots were fired in his direction. One of the leaders shouted 'go back Rutherford' and fired a shot at him. Constable Rutherford caught the man who said 'go away or I'll do it again'. Rutherford then knocked the man down, took his revolver away, and arrested him.

KING'S POLICE MEDAL
LG. 1/1/24

Sadgrove	Charles	Police Constable	89105 P

At 11 pm on 5th May 1922 constable Sadgrove was informed that there were horses in a burning stable in Endwell Road, Brockley, South London. The stable was well alight, and although the Fire Brigade had not arrived, and no water was available, the constable pulled open the stable door, and plunged through the flames to the animals. The first horse was turned out into the yard, but the second was lying amongst burning straw. The constable desperately tried to get the horse to its feet, and eventually succeeded, but not before he was severely burned on his hands and almost overcome from the smoke. Both horses were later destroyed due to their injuries.

ROYAL HUMANE SOCIETY BRONZE MEDAL

Hickman   Police Constable   H

Has been awarded a Bronze medal and certificate by the Royal Humane Society for assisting to rescue a girl from drowning.

CARNEGIE HERO FUND

28/5/24

Harris   Arthur W   Police Constable

Rescued a man from drowning at St Katherine's Docks, London

ROLL OF HONOUR

*   Pc Edward Lock

Knocked down by a motor car after stopping a cyclist at Kingston Hill.

*   Pc Arthur Holdaway

Knocked down by a tram while on traffic duty at Camberwell, and died after retiring from the service because of his injuries.

1925

January	Capital of Norway, Christiana, is renamed Oslo.
February	London Zoo to install lights to cheer the animals during the London fogs.
March	Fire destroys 2 floors of Madame Tussauds waxworks museum.
April	Orville Wright gives his first aeroplane to the Science Museum in London.
May	King George V opens the rebuilt Great West Road from Chiswick to East Bedfont.
June	First aerial murder takes place, when a London gem dealer is thrown out of an aeroplane.
July	Reported that 10 million people listen to the BBC.
August	Charlie Chaplin's film 'The Gold Rush' opens in London.
September	Traffic lights introduced at Piccadilly London.
October	Police raid the Head Quarters of the British Communist Party, 6 arrested and documents seized.
November	Sub M-1 lost in the English Channel all 68 on board perish.
December	First Motel opens in California, USA.

HITS OF THE YEAR

Show me the way to go home

Always

Manhattan

KING'S POLICE MEDAL

LG. 1/1/25

Fisher   George   Police Constable   105825 J

At 1.45 pm on 27th January 1924 a horse attached to a van laden with eggs, was left unattended outside a shop in Askew Road, Shepherds Bush, when it slipped its bridle and bolted. Constable Fisher on seeing the runaway approach him, ran into the roadway, and by grasping the shaft of the van, was dragged along for about 25 yards, and he then put his fingers in the horse's nostrils, and brought it to a standstill. The horse again bolted, with constable Fisher hanging on, and this time he guided it into a side street, before assistance arrived.

KING'S POLICE MEDAL
LG. 1/1/25

Harding	Robert	Police Constable	107307 C

At 10.30 am on 25th July 1924 an unattended horse attached to a heavy van loaded with ice, took fright in Oxford Street, and bolted. Constable Harding who was on traffic duty at Oxford Circus tried to stop the animal, but could not do so. However, he managed to get onto the horse's back, and tried to stop it by holding onto its head. The animal was in collision with three other vehicles, before the constable was able to stop it in this very busy thoroughfare.

KING'S POLICE MEDAL
LG. 1/1/25

Norman	Percival	Police Constable	112531 B

At 7.20 pm on 23rd July 1924 a horse attached to an empty coal cart, was left unattended in Eaton Terrace, when it took fright, and bolted towards Sloane square. Constable Norman saw the horse, with its bridle trailing on the ground, and ran in the same direction as it for a short distance before grabbing the shaft of the cart with one hand, and the nostrils of the horse with the other. He continued to run like this for about 50 yards, before the animal ran into a lamp standard, causing the constable to lose his grip. He continued the chase, and brought the horse to a stop after another collision.

KING'S POLICE MEDAL
LG. 1/1/25

Peckover	Harold	Police Constable	112235 B

On the morning of 24th June 1924 a pair of horses drawing an army van was being driven out of Chelsea Barracks when it was involved in a collision, and the horses bolted. Constable Peckover, was in Sloane Square when he saw the runaway horses, and after snatching three children to safety, ran after the horses, and grabbing the reins, pulled the horses to a standstill.

KING'S POLICE MEDAL
LG. 1/1/25

Vincent	Harold	Police Constable	104678 G

At 11.10 pm on the 6th December 1923 constable Vincent found that the padlock had been forced from the door of a lock up shop at 137 Lever Street, East London. He went into the premises, and saw a man called Bert Smith, who on seeing the police officer, pointed a revolver at him and said 'hands up'. The constable ignored the threats and moved towards the man, and talked him into putting the weapon down. As soon as the man had done so,

the constable took possession of it, and arrested the man. When it was later examined the weapon was found to be fully loaded, and Smith had a further 10 rounds of ammunition in his pocket.

ROLL OF HONOUR
• Pc John Lloyd
Pensioned in 1921 and subsequently died from the effects of a non accidental injury received in the execution of his duty on Southwark Division.

1926
January	John Logie Baird demonstrates moving pictures transmitted by wireless.
February	Flooding in suburbs of London after 18 days of continuous rain.
March	One way traffic system comes into operation at Hyde Park Corner.
April	One way traffic system introduced at Trafalgar Square.
May	UK General strike begins.
June	100,000 women go on a march for peace.
July	Lightning strikes a US Navy munitions dump causing an explosion visible for 30 miles.
August	First traffic lights in London come into operation at Piccadilly Circus.
September	Northern line extension from Clapham Common to Morden opens.
October	The Motor show opens at Olympia.
November	Bookies strike at Windsor in protest of the new betting tax.
December	Novelist Agatha Christie disappears from her Surrey home.

HITS OF THE YEAR
Black bottom
Bye bye blackbird

KING'S POLICE MEDAL
LG. 1/1/1926

Bonner	Richard	Police Constable	111300 K
Gravett	Albert	Police Constable	100385 K

At 12.15 am on 12th September 1925 constables Bonner and Gravett were informed that a serious disturbance had broken out amongst the inmates of the Asiatic Seaman's Home, West India Dock road, Limehouse, London. On their arrival, they found the occupants of the house rushing about, and shouting. The main staircase was in semi-darkness darkness. Many of the men were half naked, and some were stained with blood. All were panicked and excited, as they were being chased by a man called Ali Jan, who was mad with drink, stripped to the waist, and armed with a knife. He had blood pouring from a wound on his arm. The two constables without hesitation, approached the man, wrenched the knife away, and overpowered him. A furious fight ensued, but the officers escaped serious injury before they finally arrested the man.

KING'S POLICE MEDAL

LG. 1/1/1926

| Hedges | James | Police Sergeant | 101340 H |

At 10.15 pm on the 6th January 1925 a dark and foggy night, thieves broke into the warehouse at 59 Hassard Street, Bethnal Green, London. Police were called, and Sergeant Hedges saw, and gave chase to a man called Alfred Coggins, who endeavoured to evade capture by running along the top of a wall at the rear of the houses in Hassard Street, and then climbing onto a roof. The Sergeant took off his greatcoat, climbed onto a flimsy pigeon loft, and walked along a narrow plank 20 feet from the ground, and onto the roof from where Coggins was throwing roof tiles. The chase then continued over several roofs until Coggins was arrested. At the moment of arrest the roof collapsed, and Sergeant Hedges and the prisoner fell through onto the rafters. During a further struggle, the ceiling collapsed and they both fell into a bedroom, where the prisoner was overpowered.

KING'S POLICE MEDAL

LG. 1/1/1926

| Hopkins | William | Police Constable | 112325 J |

At 12 noon on 7th July 1925 a greengrocer's van was left unattended outside the Swan Hotel in Bayswater Road, when the mare took fright and bolted towards Marble Arch. Constable Hopkins was on duty at Victoria Gate and as the horse approached he sprang forwards and grabbed at the bridle, but missed. He then caught the back of the van, and got in, clambering along over the produce, and along the shaft to secure the reins, which were dragging along the ground. After some 200 yards in this precarious position the constable brought the animal to a standstill.

KING'S POLICE MEDAL

LG. 1/1/1926

| Mead | Thomas | Police Constable | 112869 K |

At 1.25 am on 2nd March 1925 a heavy milk van was being loaded in the Eastern Counties Dairy Co. yard in Stratford, East London when the horses took fright and galloped out of the yard, colliding with and damaging three vehicles and a lamp standard. Constable Mead saw the runaways, and dashed towards them, and without hesitation, grabbed the bridle of the near side horse, causing it to slacken speed. The horse then fell, dragging the constable underneath it for several yards, resulting in serious injuries, from which he eventually recovered.

KING'S POLICE MEDAL

LG. 1/1/1926

Ward	Albert	Divisional Detective Insp.	85473 L
Bellinger	James	Detective Inspector	92322 L
Ellis	Robert	Detective Sergeant	98377 L

At 11.15 pm on 28th March 1925 Inspectors Ward and Bellinger with Sergeant Ellis went to 76 Waterloo Road, where they believed a James Walsh was located. He was a dangerous criminal wanted in connection with numerous crimes all over the country, including stealing firearms, robbery and escaping from Cork Gaol in December 1923. They found Walsh in a

back room and Inspector Ward was about to challenge him as to his identity, when Walsh produced a revolver, and shouted 'stand back'. Regardless of their personal safety the three officers rushed at the criminal, who pulled the trigger of the weapon, which fortunately misfired. Before he could make a second attempt he was overpowered and arrested.

CARNEGIE HERO FUND
12/11/26

Marshall	William	Police Constable
Dunn	Duncan	Police Constable

Rescued a woman after an outbreak of fire in Newman Street.

ROLL OF HONOUR
• Ps Tom L Whitney

Died from the effects of a non accidental injury received in the execution of his duty on Paddington Division.

• Pc Victor J Wilson

Pensioned in 1924 from the effects of non accidental injury received in the execution of his duty on Lambeth Division and subsequently died.

1927

January	Number of telephones in use is now estimated to be 500,000.
February	Morris motors buy Wolseley motors for £730,000.
March	Petrol prices drop to 1s 4d per gallon.
April	Teachers call for the school leaving age to be raised from 14 years to 16 years.
May	Lindbergh is the first to fly the Atlantic solo in his aircraft 'the Spirit of St Louis'.
June	First time for 200 years a total eclipse of the sun can be seen in the UK.
July	20 Players Navy Cut cigarettes now cost 11d.
August	Covered top buses are allowed to run past Buckingham Palace for the first time.
September	UK summer is the worst since 1879 as up to 80% more rain fell than normal.
October	Black faced Al Jolson stars in the first talkie 'The Jazz Singer'.
November	First automatic telephone exchange installed at Holborn, London.
December	A white Christmas as Britain is swept by freezing blizzards.

HITS OF THE YEAR
Among my souvenirs
Ain't she sweet
Wings

MURDER OF POLICE CONSTABLE GEORGE GUTTERIDGE 1927
FREDERICK GUY BROWNE AND WILLIAM HENRY KENNEDY
Robert Churchill an expert in ballistics won the major achievement of his career in the case of Browne and Kennedy after the shooting of Police Constable George Gutteridge. It was the first time that such evidence was given in an English Court of Law.

The body of constable Gutteridge was discovered in a quiet country land between Romford and Ongar in Essex. He had been shot four times, twice through the left side of his face and once through each eye. He was still clutching his pencil and his report book was at his side, this gave the impression he was making enquiries with a person or possibly a motorist when he was shot and that he died between 4 and 5 am.

It was discovered that a car had been stolen at about 2.30am from the garage of a Dr Edward Lovell of Billericay 10 miles from the spot where the constable was killed. The car was later found abandoned in Foxley Road, Brixton. Forensic examination revealed bloodstains on the cars running board and a spent cartridge case was found under one of the seats.

There were no further developments for a few months then an incident occurred in Sheffield when another car was stolen and driven in such an erratic manner that it forced another motorist off the road damaging the vehicle. The driver had made a note of the car's number and reported the incident to police. Unfortunately the number plate proved to be false, but it did provide the police with the first of a series of clues which led police to the Globe garage, a business at Clapham Junction run by Frederick Guy Browne. Browne was known as a small time crook whose speciality was car theft, he also had a violent temper and an unreasoning dislike of the police.

It was on one of Browne's regular periods of imprisonment at Dartmoor that he met and teamed up with Scottish born William Henry Kennedy. On Kennedy's release from prison he made his way to London and joined Browne at the Globe garage. Three months later when stopped driving a recently stolen car they shot dead constable Gutteridge, at the time of the murder Browne was 47yrs old and Kennedy 36.

Early in 1928 Browne arrived back at the garage in a recently stolen car, he was arrested and charged with car theft. Once in custody Detective Inspector Barker ordered a thorough search of the garage and of Frederick Browne's home in Lavender Hill and as a result a veritable arsenal of hand guns and ammunition was found. All in all the police found four weapons including a Webley revolver loaded with bullets of the same type as those which had murdered constable Gutteridge. The armoury was subsequently handed over to Robert Churchill, a forensic gun expert.

In the meantime Kennedy had been arrested in Liverpool where he had fled with his wife. While in custody he made a confession placing the whole blame on Browne. He said that they had stolen the vehicle and were driving it to London via the quiet back lanes, they saw a policeman who signalled with his lantern for them to stop. Browne who was driving ignored his signal and the constable took out and blew his whistle. They stopped the car and the constable approached taking out his note book and pencil, when he drew level with the car Browne raised the revolver and shot the officer twice in the head. He then got out of the car walked over to him and shot at close range through each of the eyes (*it was an old superstition that the last image a dying person saw was photographed onto their eyes*).

The trial opened at the Old Bailey on 23rd April 1928, the balance of evidence tipped in favour of the prosecution especially by the expert testimony of Robert Churchill. Mr Churchill had carried out test firings with the gun and ammunition suspected of being used in the killing, and a close examination with a comparison microscope of the slugs taken from the body and those fired in the tests showed the same identical rifling marks. The powder discoloration on the victim's skin around the entry wounds matched the black powder used in the cartridges in Browne's possession.

Both Browne and Kennedy were convicted of the murder of Police Constable George Gutteridge and executed on 31st May 1928, Frederick Browne at Pentonville Prison and William Kennedy at Wandsworth Prison.

KING'S POLICE MEDAL
LG. 1/1/27

Cunningham   Alexander   Police Constable   112728 H

At 1 am on 27th September 1925 constable Cunningham heard screams for help coming from Old Gravel lane, Wapping. He ran to the swing bridge over the entrance to Wapping Basin and saw a man struggling in the water. The constable took off his tunic and helmet, and dived 15 feet from the swing bridge into the water and grabbed the drowning man who struggled violently. The other constables arrived but were unable to render immediate assistance, however they shone their lanterns, and guided constable Cunningham 70 yards to a small iron ladder at the end of the wall. A line was lowered and the man was tied to it, and then hauled up the side of the dock to safety, where artificial respiration was successfully applied. The water in the basin was over 20 feet deep, and the surface littered with driftwood.

KING'S POLICE MEDAL
LG. 1/1/27

Green   Alfred   Police Constable   90992 Y

At 11.50 am on 7th September 1926 constable Green was off duty in plain clothes when he heard a cry for help from a shaft 22 feet deep, which had been sunk in connection with sewer working at Potters Bar. When he looked down the shaft, he saw the body of a young workman lying at the bottom, and a strong smell of coal gas. Despite the obvious danger, he descended the shaft, and when he got to the bottom, he put his cap in his mouth to avoid being overcome by the gas. The young workman was unconscious, but with the aid of a rope lowered to him, constable Green tied it round the youth, and then he was pulled up to safety by others at the top. A second man then crawled out of a tunnel, and collapsed, and the constable rescued him also, before coming to the surface and rendering artificial respiration to the youth, whilst instructing others to give similar treatment to the second man.

KING'S POLICE MEDAL
LG. 1/1/27

Jones   Christopher   Police Constable   110632 D

At 7.50 pm on 26th January 1926 a horse attached to an empty van being driven along Oxford Street, took fright and bolted. Constable Jones was on traffic duty, and signalled all traffic to stop before he made an unsuccessful attempt to stop the animal. He then mounted the footboard of a motor car, and directed the driver to chase the horse. He made two further attempts to stop the animal before bringing it to a standstill, and avoiding a serious accident in a busy street.

KING'S POLICE MEDAL
LG. 1/1/27
Lyddon   Leslie   Police Constable   114736 E
At 11.20 am on 3rd August 1926 constable Lyddon was on the Thames Embankment when he saw a boy struggling in the water near Cleopatra's Needle. He immediately took off his jacket and helmet, jumped into the water, and swam to the boy. He was taken a long way downstream by the strong current, but kept the boy afloat until both were rescued by the River Police Launch.

KING'S POLICE MEDAL
LG. 1/1/27
Wood   Wallace   Police Constable   111138 J
At 7.30 pm on 26th October 1926 constable Wood received information that two men had been overcome by bitulac gas whilst working in a water main at Feltham. The constable and two other men descended a ventilation shaft 20 feet deep leading to the main. Accompanied by one of the men, constable Wood crawled along the main for about 100 yards when he found one of the workmen in a helpless condition. They dragged him to the foot of the ladder, and with help, got him to the surface, where he recovered. Having obtained gas masks from the nearby army depot, constable Wood returned to the scene, and with the help of three soldiers rescued the second workman, who was found a further 250 yards along the water main. The main at this point is only 52 inches wide.

CARNEGIE HERO FUND
7/10/27
Cook   Edwin P   Police Constable   **Posthumous**
Along with David R Williams, lost their lives while attempting to rescue a man who had been overcome by gas at the bottom of a shaft.

CARNEGIE HERO FUND
10/1/27
Lyddon   Leslie G   Police Constable
Recovered a man from the River Thames.

CARNEGIE HERO FUND
27/6/27
Stone   Frederick M   Police Constable
Rescued a man from drowning in the River Thames.

CARNEGIE HERO FUND
30/4/27
Turpin   Albert   Police Constable
Rescued a servant after an outbreak of fire in a house at Blackheath.

ROLL OF HONOUR

- Ps Leonard Carter

Fell into an uncovered pit when searching a basement near Pall Mall.

- Pc Percy Edwin Cook

Overcome by fumes while attempting to rescue workmen from a long disused inspecting chamber in Notting Hill.

- Pc Thomas E Moulton

Died from an injury on duty on Whitechapel Division.

- Stn Ps Anthony Sullivan

Died from an accidental injury on duty on Brixton Division.

1928

January	466,000 over 65's receive the first UK state pension of 10s a week.
February	11 killed as gales sweep across Britain.
March	Blizzards sweep Britain up to -9F in London.
April	London Zoo acquires a 100 year old Chilean tortoise.
May	Piccadilly Circus tube station is to get 11 escalators, the largest number at any station in the world.
June	Amelia Earhart becomes the first woman to fly across the Atlantic.
July	Captain de Haviland sets a world record by flying his plane Gypsy Moth at 21,500 feet.
August	Morris Motors launch their latest model the Morris Minor.
September	Penicillin is discovered by Professor Alexander Fleming.
October	Worlds largest airship Graf Zeppelin lands in New Jersey after an 111 hour flight from Germany.
November	First Pound and Ten shilling notes come into circulation.
December	House of Lords approve a bill making driving tests compulsory.

HITS OF THE YEAR

A room with a view

I can't give you anything but love, baby

Ol man river

KING'S POLICE MEDAL

LG. 1/1/28

Clayden	Alfred	Police Sergeant	92301 D
Pegler	Henry	Police Sergeant	103564 D

In January 1927 a Bench Warrant was issued for the arrest of a man called Harridan, who had failed to surrender to court for trial, on a charge of receiving stolen property. Harridan was known to be a dangerous criminal, and information was received that he was in possession of a loaded firearm. On 18th January 1927 Sergeant Clayden and Pegler were off duty in plain clothes, in the saloon bar of a public house, when Harridan walked in, but on seeing the officers, he ran off. The two Sergeants having recognised him followed and on being stopped, Harridan drew a revolver and threatened the two officers. He pointed the gun at Sergeant Pegler and pulled the trigger, but the weapon misfired, and at the same time both the officers jumped on Harridan and arrested him.

KING'S POLICE MEDAL
LG. 1/1/28

Dunn	Duncan	Police Constable	115196 D
Marshall	William	Police Constable	111453 D

Early on the morning of 12th November 1926 a fire occurred at a flat in Newman Street, London, in which four persons were sleeping. Three of the occupants escaped through a window onto the roof, but the fourth, a woman became hysterical as she clung to the window sill, with her feet resting on the guttering, some 70 feet above the street. Constables Dunn and Marshall who were off duty and in plain clothes rushed up to the top of the building, but were unable to get into the flat owing to the flames. However they opened a window off the staircase, and constable Marshall got out and stood on the guttering, and whilst constable Dunn held him, he edged his way along to the woman. As he caught her, she fainted, and constable Marshall took her full weight as he was pulled slowly and carefully back by constable Dunn. Eventually, the two constables were able to get the woman to safety. During the whole of the rescue, both constables were in imminent danger of falling to their deaths.

KING'S POLICE MEDAL
LG. 1/1/28

Hainsby	George	Police Constable	108758 B

Late at night on 11th July 1927 constable Hainsby was told that a woman was floating in the river opposite the Royal Hospital Grounds, Chelsea. He took off his helmet and tunic, and dived into the water, and after swimming about 30 yards out, succeeded in grasping the woman. He then tried to return to some steps, but the strong tide prevented him, however two life buoys were thrown in, and constable Hainsby put one round the woman, and the other on himself, and they were then pulled into the embankment wall.

KING'S POLICE MEDAL
LG. 1/1/28

Roberts	Percival	Police Constable	106118 C

On 13th April 1927 a man named Roscher entered a public house in Glasshouse Street, London and produced a pistol, and placed it on the counter. He was ordered to leave the premises, but he refused, and police were called. Roscher pointed the pistol indiscriminately at the customers, and ordered them to leave. As constable Roberts arrived, the customers were streaming down the stairs in panic. As the constable entered the bar Roscher pointed the weapon at him, and pulled the trigger. The weapon misfired, and as he was about to try again, constable Roberts jumped at him, and in the violent struggle, Roscher was disarmed and arrested. A monetary award was also made from the Bow Street fund.

KING'S POLICE MEDAL

LG. 1/1/28

Stone   Frederick Mark   Police Constable   111658 A

Shortly after midnight on 28th June 1927 constable Stone was informed that a man had jumped into the river from Westminster Bridge. On reaching the bridge, he saw the man floating in the water, and immediately took off his boots, helmet and tunic, and climbed onto the parapet, and jumped into the river. He succeeded in reaching the man, and swimming across the tide, made for the steps of the London County hall, a distance of 100 yards. The man began to struggle, and constable Stone disabled him, by hitting him with his fist. Owing to the tide, constable Stone was swept past the steps, but grabbed a chain hanging from the wall, and held on until rescue by the River Police Launch. An award was also made from the Royal Humane Society.

Constable Stone was later awarded the George Medal via LG. 12.2.52, and he subsequently received the BEM for meritorious service.

KING'S POLICE MEDAL

LG. 1/1/28

Turpin   Albert   Police Constable   105955 R

On 30th April 1927 a serious fire occurred at Shooters Hill road, Blackheath. A servant girl who was sleeping in a second floor bedroom immediately above the fire, escaped onto a veranda roof. Constable Turpin who had been called to the fire, arrived just as she was about to jump some 35 feet to the ground. He told her to stay where she was, and then rushed into the house, up the stairs and guided by her cries, found her in a state of collapse. The constable put her over his shoulder, and descended the stairs through the dense smoke, feeling his way down the burning banisters, until nearly at the bottom, when the stairs collapsed. Both of them fell to the bottom of the stairs, but were removed by the Fire Brigade. The constable also received awards from the Carnegie Hero Trust and the Society for the Protection of Life from Fire.

ROLL OF HONOUR

• Pc Raymond Mitchell

Struck by a motorcycle combination when on traffic duty at Wallington.

1929

January	1.6 million telephones in Britain - 3.6 for every 100 people.
February	Charles Lindberg and his fiancee escape almost unhurt when their plane overturns on landing in the United States.
March	5000 mile airmail service opens serving India, Egypt, Palestine and Iraq.
April	Sir James Barrie donates 'copyright fee' of his novel Peter Pan to Great Ormond Street Hospital for Sick Children.
May	Experiment in Oxford Street, London using traffic lights finally approved.
June	Actor Douglas Fairbanks Jnr marries actress Joan Crawford.
July	Pope Pius XI became the first Pope to leave the Vatican since 1870. He blessed the crowd from an altar on the Basilica steps.

August   London policemen to get radios in their cars.

September   Traffic signals in 21 British provincial towns to be standardised, green will mean go, red stop and amber will warn of a coming change.

October   Wall Street crashes in New York.

November   London Government warns it will ban any new coaches capable of achieving 60 mph.

December   First public telephones come into service in London.

HITS OF THE YEAR
Tip toe through the tulips

KING'S POLICE MEDAL
LG. 1/3/29

Farrance   Thomas   Police Constable   111144 S

On 10th November 1927 a pair of horses attached to a heavy uncovered van were being driven along Alanby Street, London, when they took fright at a sheet of newspaper blowing along the street, the driver lost control, and the horses shied and bolted. Constable Farrance seeing that the driver was helpless, ran into the road as the animals approached, and seized the bridle of the near side horse with his right hand, forcing his left hand into the horse's mouth and grabbing its tongue. After some 75 yards the horses came to a standstill.

KING'S POLICE MEDAL
LG. 1/3/29

Newing   Cecil   Police Constable   114173 J

At 2.15 am on 10th October 1928 a serious fire occurred at South Woodford, originating in an Oil and Colour warehouse, above which were two flats. A passing motor cyclist notified the police station, and constable Newing went to the premises, which were by this time blazing furiously. On being told that a woman and child were in one of the flats, the constable went into the building and up the smoke filled stairs. Following the sounds of the screams, he found the woman and her child in the kitchen, and carrying the child in his arms, and with the woman holding onto his shoulders, he guided them down to the street. Immediately afterwards the whole of the shop front collapsed.

KING'S POLICE MEDAL
LG. 1/3/29

Sparkes   Henry George   Police Constable   111604 M

On 19th March 1928 a horse attached to a heavy van loaded with straw, took fright and bolted along Rotherhithe New Road, throwing the driver from the van. Constable Sparkes on seeing the animal approach, ran into the roadway, and endeavoured to seize the reins. He was unable to get hold of them, and in his attempt he fell and the van wheels ran over him. The horse continued running on for another 150 yards before stopping of its own accord outside the owners stables. The constable was taken to hospital with severe injuries, and was off duty for 133 days.

ROLL OF HONOUR

- Inspector Arthur Vistor Tullett

Killed when a motorcycle driven by a colleague collided with a lorry.

- Pc David Ford

Fell through a glass roof while pursing a suspect in Westminster Bridge Road.

- Pc John Arthur Self

Violently struck to the ground by a man he was questioning in Golders Green.

- Pc William G Benton

Knocked down by a motor car in September 1927 while engaged on traffic duty at Chiswick and subsequently died from his injuries.

Chapter Five

THE YEARS OF 1930 - 1939

Just like the years 1910 - 1919 this decade also brought the world into conflict, the second world war would begin. Like before, it would last for over four years, bringing misery, hope and human valour to its peak, and would prove how inhumane one man could be towards another.

Depression and unemployment were witnessed throughout the western world. The crash of Wall Street was still evident. Hunger strikes were made and battles fought in Hyde Park with gatherings of over 200,000.

The rise of the Nazi party under the lead of Adolf Hitler was gathering support from both the unemployed as well as big businesses. By the beginning of 1933 Hitler became Chancellor of the German Reich, this was the beginning of the end for peace in Europe.

The main event in our own history was the death of King George V. His successor was King Edward VIII, but he was never crowned as monarch, due to his love for a divorced American, Wallis Simpson. He could not marry her and make her Queen so he abdicated. The speech was given in December 1936 so this made our new King, King George VI. On becoming King, King George VI made Edward the Duke of Windsor. During his life the Duke of Windsor made a controversial visit to Germany in October 1937 and was entertained by Adolf Hitler and other Nazi leaders.

Prime Minister Chamberlain returned from Germany waving in the air the famous piece of paper which he said would guarantee 'peace in our time'. He was driven to Buckingham Palace to appear with the Royal Family on the balcony. A few days later Germany invaded Poland and the War began.

One major break through with regards to crime and a tribute to the new 999 telephone system was the arrest of a suspect just five minutes after a phone call being made.

1930

January   Women civil servants vote in favour of compulsory retirement of women on marriage.
February New planet discovered - named Pluto.
March   The Channel Tunnel committee approves the building of a tunnel from England to France.
April   Amy Johnson aged 27 is the first woman to fly solo from Britain to Australia.
May   BBC forms its own permanent symphony orchestra.
June   Trade unionists protest at the 'invasion' of industry by women.
July   Airship R100 begins its maiden flight across the Atlantic.
August   24 die in the heat wave, temperatures in London soar to 94F (34c).

September   Hitler denounces the peace treaties saying he wants to build a huge conscript German Army.

October   R101 the world's largest airship explodes in a fireball in France - over 44 killed.

November   Over 30 injured when four elephants stampede during the Lord Mayor's Show in London.

December   A draft highway code is issued.

HITS OF THE YEAR
The king's horses
On the sunny side of the street

KING'S POLICE MEDAL
LG. 1/1/30

Bacon   Charles   Police Sergeant   104017 M

At 9.15 am on 10th August 1929 Sergeant Bacon was on holiday at Yarmouth, when he heard a shout and saw a boy in the sea being quickly carried away by the tide. He immediately took off his jacket, dived in and swam to where he had seen the boy, but he had disappeared. The Sergeant dived three times, and eventually brought the boy to the surface, and swam to the quay. A jacket was lowered, and the boy grabbed the sleeve, and was being pulled out of the water, when the sleeve ripped, and he fell back into the sea. Sergeant Bacon had been carried away by the tide, but swam back, and after diving again found the boy, and swam further down to the quay, where the boy was hauled out by a rope. The Sergeant swam a further 20 yards to some steps, and landed safely.

KING'S POLICE MEDAL
LG. 1/1/30

Beacham   Henry   Police Constable   108149 M

At 3.30 am on 13th January 1929 constable Beacham saw a motor car containing five men turn into a side street off the Old Kent Road, where it stopped, and the men got out. He hid in a dark doorway, and saw four of the men go to a shop, whilst the other kept watch. One of the men forced the door with a large jemmy, and then constable Beacham ran across the road, with the intention of arresting all of them, but all the men jumped back into the car and made off. The constable drew his truncheon and jumped on the running board, and hit the driver, which caused him to stall the engine. The five men got out and attacked the constable. Fortunately he avoided a blow aimed at his head, and when a taxi driver went to his assistance, he too was attacked. The men then ran off pursued by constable Beacham, who caught one of them after some 500 yards.

KING'S POLICE MEDAL
LG. 1/1/30

Cole   James   Police Constable   116839 D

At 1 am on 26th May 1929 a fire occurred at a tenement house at 50 Molyneux Street, Marylebone. When constable Cole arrived, smoke was pouring out of the windows and there were people shouting for help. He at once entered the building, and went to the top floor from where he had heard the screams. Owing to the smoke, he could not see, but groping about, he found a man, two women, and a child. Taking the child in his arms, he directed the others to hold onto his belt, and then guided them all down the staircase into the street. He handed them all into the care of bystanders, and then re-entered the building with another constable, and when they got to the top floor again, constable Cole who was by this time exhausted, collapsed. He was assisted out by his colleague.

KING'S POLICE MEDAL
LG. 1/1/30

Hall   Harry   Police Constable   104237 Y

At about 10 am on 5th October 1928 the constable was informed by two County Court Officers that they intended to execute a distress warrant on the goods of a Mr Rawlins, of Lowman Road, Holloway, and requested that the constable remain in the vicinity to prevent any trouble. Mrs Rawlins saw the bailiffs arriving, and tried to stop them entering the house, but they forced their way into the passage. After a few moments, Rawlins appeared at the top of the stairs with a revolver, threatening to shoot, unless they left the house. He then fired into the ceiling to emphasise his intent. Constable Hall on hearing the shot, entered, and saw Rawlins leaning over the banisters waving the revolver about. He rushed upstairs, drawing his truncheon, with which he aimed a blow at Rawlins, but missed. Rawlins, not wanting any trouble with police, surrendered the weapon to his wife, and was taken into custody. He was later found to be of unsound mind.

KING'S POLICE MEDAL
LG. 1/1/30

Highgate   Albert   Police Constable   91109

At 2.15 pm on 14th July 1929 constable Highgate a London constable attached to the Royal Dockyards was off duty, but in uniform on a ferry between Portsmouth and Gosport. As the boat was about to dock an 11 year old boy fell into the water, between the ferry and the dock. Constable Highgate immediately jumped into the water, and saw the boy trapped under the tanks, supporting the landing stage. He swam underwater caught hold of the boy, and pulled him out into open water, from where he was helped out. After artificial respiration was applied to the boy, he recovered. It was particularly dangerous as the landing stage rises and falls with the swell of the water.

KING'S POLICE MEDAL
LG. 1/1/30

Jones   Reginald Granville   Detective Constable   106274 L MM

At about 12.15 am on 15th August 1929 constable Jones and another detective constable saw five men acting suspiciously in Doon Street, Southward. As the detectives approached them, one of the suspects named O'Brien pointed a revolver at constable Jones and threatened to shoot. The other detective stepped behind the corner of a building as O'Brien rushed forwards, and then as he was close, detective constable Jones pounced on him and caught his wrist, just as O'Brien pulled the trigger and fired. The bullet went into the air, and constable Jones threw the man to the ground, and after a brief struggle overpowered him. Constable Jones had won the MM during the first world war.

KING'S POLICE MEDAL
LG. 1/1/30

| Lovejoy | Ronald King | Police Constable | 112639 A |

At 7.30 pm on 19th April 1929 a man called Mahoney was seen floating in the River Thames, having apparently jumped from the Embankment Wall. Constable Lovejoy having been told of the incident, ran across Westminster Bridge, to the steps, at St Thomas's Hospital, where he took off his helmet, tunic and boots, and after diving in, swam to the would-be suicide. It was dusk, a strong tide was running, and it was windy, causing the water to be very choppy. Constable Lovejoy lost sight of the man, and after swimming around for some time, climbed into a dinghy moored off the embankment. Meanwhile, Mahoney had been pulled out of the water by the Deputy Pier Master at Westminster Pier. Constable Lovejoy was taken to hospital before being allowed home.

KING'S POLICE MEDAL
LG. 1/1/30

| Ockey | Edward Michael | Detective Inspector | 96446 |

At 1 am on 24th July 1929 Inspector Ockey with other officers in an unmarked police car, followed three men acting suspiciously, in a Vauxhall motor car, through several streets, until the men stopped and went up to a shop. As the officers drove up, the men jumped back into their car and drove off at high speed. At one stage the police car drew alongside, and Inspector Ockey jumped from the police car, onto the running board of the other calling on them to stop. They increased speed, and as Inspector Ockey hung on with both hands, one of the men hit him on the hands and head with a jemmy, forcing him to release his grip, and fall into the roadway. The police car just avoided running over him as he lay unconscious. Eventually the Vauxhall skidded and crashed, and the occupants were arrested. Inspector Ockey eventually recovered.

ROYAL HUMANE SOCIETY BRONZE MEDAL
CARNEGIE HERO FUND
12/4/30

| Jacobi | Ernest | Police Constable | L |

Along with another man sustained serious injury while endeavouring to rescue a woman from drowning in the River Thames.

ROYAL HUMANE SOCIETY BRONZE MEDAL

| Adamson | | Police Constable | A |

For courage and tenacity of purpose in attempting to rescue a woman from drowning in the River Thames.

ROYAL HUMANE SOCIETY BRONZE MEDAL
Couthart   Police Constable B
For courage and promptitude in saving a man from drowning in the River Thames.

CARNEGIE HERO FUND
16/7/30
Barnett   Harold   Police Constable
Sustained injury while attempting to stop a runaway horse at Kilburn.

CARNEGIE HERO FUND
29/4/30
Denton   Albert W   Police Constable
Sustained injury while preventing 2 boys from being run over by a motor car.

CARNEGIE HERO FUND
19/5/30
Minnis   Robert H   Police Constable
Sustained injury while preventing a child from being knocked down by a motor car.

CARNEGIE HERO FUND
18/3/30
Murphy   Dennis   Police Constable
Sustained injury while preventing a boy from being knocked down by a motor car.

CARNEGIE HERO FUND
17/3/30
Sweet   Ernest A   Police Constable
Sustained injury while stopping a runaway horse attached to a van.

CARNEGIE HERO FUND
22/9/30
Tyson   Albert W   Police Constable
Sustained injury while stopping a pair of runaway horses attached to a van.

ROLL OF HONOUR
• Pc Arthur Lawes
Deliberately struck by a hit and run driver in an unlit stolen car at Tooting.

1931
January   Road Traffic Act comes into force in the UK.
February   In Japan the first television broadcast is made of a baseball match.
March   Court of enquiry claims that a gas leak caused the R101 disaster.
April   Publication of a bill that legalises Sunday openings of Cinemas.

May	28,000 people visit Whipsnade Zoo which opened on the 23rd causing chaos.
June	Britain's most violent earthquake on record is felt from the English Channel to the Scottish Highlands.
July	First trolley buses to run in London, 20 years after making their debut in Yorkshire.
August	14 die as gales and floods hit Britain.
September	First night of trial floodlighting of important buildings in London causes traffic chaos.
October	Oxford Streets new traffic lights are reported to speed up the evening's rush hour by up to 90%.
November	Rolls Royce buys Bentley Cars.
December	Following London's experiments, traffic lights to be used all over Britain.

HITS OF THE YEAR
Goodbye
The peanut vendor
Just one more dance

KING'S POLICE MEDAL
LG. 1/1/31

Adamson	James Dunsmore	Police Constable	118247 A

At 4 pm on 2nd August 1930 constable Adamson was informed that a woman had jumped into the River Thames. He ran to Vauxhall Bridge and saw the woman struggling in midstream. The incoming tide was running swiftly, and had carried her about 150 yards towards Chelsea. Handing his helmet and truncheon to a bystander, the constable mounted the parapet, and jumped 50 feet into the water, narrowly missing a stone buttress of one of the arches. Hampered by his clothes, and boots, he almost reached the woman when she threw up her arms, and disappeared. He made two unsuccessful attempts to locate her by diving, but was forced to abandon the efforts due to exhaustion. During his swim back to shore, he was twice carried under by the tide, and found difficulty in getting a foothold on the muddy bank, before coming ashore.

KING'S POLICE MEDAL
LG. 1/1/31

Baker	Robert Henry	Police Constable	109347 K
Irvine	Alexander McLeod	Police Constable	115905 K

At about 3 am on 27th March 1930 constable Irvine heard the sound of wood splintering, and with constable Baker he climbed a five feet high fence and gained access to the rear of a shop, where they discovered four men, two of whom were armed, in the act of removing a panel from the back door. Two of the men immediately pointed revolvers at the constables, and threatened to shoot them if they advanced. Without hesitation, both officers leapt at the man, and after a very fierce struggle overpowered three (the fourth running away) and detained them. At this point another officer arrived, and located the fourth man hiding nearby in a lavatory.

KING'S POLICE MEDAL
LG. 1/1/31

Colvin   George Charles   Police Sergeant   108729 J

On 17th January 1930 Sergeant Colvin and Sergeant Clarke were called to an address where a man was believed to be mentally deranged. They went into the house and saw the man standing on the stairs apparently quite rational, and then without warning he kicked Sergeant Clarke in the head, and rushed out into the street. Sergeant Clarke remained on the premises, whilst Sergeant Colvin took up a position outside the front door. Shortly afterwards the man appeared at the front of the house, and seeing Sergeant Colvin he drew a revolver, and fired at him twice. The Sergeant immediately closed with the man, who then hit him on the head with the gun. A fierce struggle ensued in which several people joined, and eventually the man was overpowered and detained.

KING'S POLICE MEDAL
LG. 1/1/31

Jacobi   Ernest   Police Constable   106752 L

On 12th April 1930 constable Jacobi was told that a woman had fallen into the River Thames. He ran to the spot, took off his greatcoat, jacket and helmet, and dived into the water, which was about 18 feet deep, and reached the woman who was by then unconscious. He got a life belt around her, and swam to a boat moored off the Embankment. On reaching it however he could not lift the woman in, or climb up himself, without releasing her, so he clung on to the boat with one hand, supporting woman with the other until rescued by a police boat.

    Ernest Jacobi also received a Carnegie Silver Medal on 31 July 1930 and a Royal Humane Society Medal on 19 August 1930. He died in 1972 aged 81.

KING'S POLICE MEDAL
LG. 1/1/31

James   Alfred Charles   Police Constable   115271 J

Early on the morning of 11th July 1930 constable James saw a stationary motor car, which he recognised as one reported stolen earlier, and a man standing beside it holding the spare wheel. The constable questioned the man as to his ownership of the vehicle, but being dissatisfied with his explanation, the constable told the man he would be arrested, and suddenly the man produced a pistol, thrust it close to the constable's body, and threatened to shoot. Constable Jones immediately struggled with the man, and with the assistance of two civilians, overpowered the man, and took him to the police station.

KING'S POLICE MEDAL
LG. 1/1/31

Kenwood   Thomas Jack   Police Constable   113673 E

On the night of 7th April 1930 constable Kenwood was told that the body of a woman was floating in the River Thames near Cleopatra's Needle. He went to the spot and with the aid of a police lamp, saw the woman being carried downstream, on the ebb tide. He took off his greatcoat and helmet, and dived into the water, and reached the unconscious woman. Although hampered by his wet clothing, he swam with the woman to the steps and with assistance got her out. Artificial respiration was given by another officer, and a member of the St Johns Ambulance Association, and the woman later recovered.

KING'S POLICE MEDAL
LG. 1/1/31

Minnis	Robert Henry	Police Constable	155455 T

On the afternoon of 19th May 1930 the officer was on traffic duty, and he was escorting four school girls across the road. They stopped on the centre refuge, but then one of them a four year old suddenly dashed out into the road in front of a car, which was only 20 yards away. Realising that an accident was inevitable, constable Minnis dashed out, and pushed the girl away from the front of the car, but he was caught by the wing of the car and seriously injured. The girl escaped injury. The whole incident was witnessed by His Royal Highness the Duke of York who arranged for his detective to call an ambulance.

KING'S POLICE MEDAL
LG. 1/1/31

Muggeridge	Frederick George	Police Sergeant	95588 R
Bertram	John Laidlaw	Police Constable	115379 R

At 3.30 am on 4th October 1930 a lady saw a man attempt to enter her bedroom window. She called the police, and these two officers attended the address by police car. As they approached the house, they saw a man on the pavement near the house, and went to question him. The man ran away, followed by Sergeant Muggeridge, but he turned and pointed a revolver at the officer, threatening to shoot. The Sergeant refused to be intimidated, and continued towards the man, who then fired a shot, and ran off. He fired three more shots on the run, all missing their target. Constable Bertram saw the man behind a tree, and ran towards him, as the man levelled the weapon, and pulled the trigger but it misfired. The two officers then struggled with the man, who produced a second weapon but was unable to use it. He was arrested and subsequently sentenced to 10 years imprisonment.

KING'S POLICE MEDAL
LG. 1/1/31

Murphy	Dennis Henry	Police Constable	111170 S

At about 7.20 pm on the 18th March 1930 the officer was directing some traffic round some roadworks, when three boys attempted to cross the road. The constable shouted a warning to them, and two stopped, but the third, a boy aged 11 years ran across the road, into the path of a motor car. Seeing the imminent danger, constable Murphy rushed out into the road, and pushed the boy clear, but at the same time the car swerved, and knocked the constable down. He was conveyed to hospital with extensive injuries from which he did not fully recover.

KING'S POLICE MEDAL

LG. 1/1/31

| Raymond | Walter Ernest | Police Constable | 399 L 101443 |

On 21st May 1930 constable Raymond was informed that a woman was standing on the parapet of a house, apparently intending to jump and commit suicide. The constable entered the house, took off his tunic and helmet, and placed a white towel over his shoulders, and put on white traffic sleeves. He got through an open window which led to the roof, and beckoned to the woman, pretending to be a doctor. Whilst her attention was distracted he caught hold of her, and a struggle took place between them, on the narrow ledge only 18 inches wide, but 40 feet above the ground. Constable Raymond restrained her, and then carried her in his arms for some 20 feet along the narrow gutter between a sloping roof, and a ledge, back to the open window, from where she was taken to hospital.

Walter Raymond joined the Metropolitan Police 6 April 1908 and retired in 1933, he died on 10 July 1960.

ROYAL HUMANE SOCIETY BRONZE MEDAL
CARNEGIE HERO FUND
JERSEY HUMANE SOCIETY SILVER MEDAL

| Juniper | Police Constable | H |

An inscribed silver watch by the Carnegie Hero Fund Trust, a bronze medal and certificate by the Royal Humane Society, and a silver medal by the Jersey Humane Society, for exceptional courage and resourcefulness in rescuing a man from drowning on 29th July 1930 while on annual leave at Greve-de-Lecq, Jersey, Channel Islands, whereby he sustained personal injury.

ROLL OF HONOUR

- Pc William George Ware

Drowned when a tug struck a police motor boat at Chiswick.

- Pc Harry Cautherlay
- Pc George William Allen

Killed in an accident in Beckenham while pursuing a car on a motorcycle combination.

1932

January	US Hoover electric cleaner Co. decides to build a factory at Perivale, Middlesex.
February	Bill introduced to improve youth courts, raise the age of juveniles and ban whipping of under 14's.
March	Charles Lindberg's baby kidnapped from his home, the baby's body discovered in May.
April	London Peers approve Motor Traffic Bill making drivers who kill guilty of manslaughter.
May	BBC's new HQ opens in Portland Place.
June	World's fastest train 'Cheltenham Flier' reaches record average speed of 81.6 mph over 77 miles.

July   King George V opens Lambeth Bridge.

August   Three letter number plates appear, the first in London is AMY1.

September   Mersey tunnel opened from Liverpool to Birkenhead costing £77 million.

October   London - Police pay to be cut by another 5% making 10% in all.

November   UK the actors union 'Equity' votes to operate a closed shop from 1933.

December   King George V makes first Christmas day broadcast to the Empire.

HITS OF THE YEAR

Love is the sweetest thing

Forty second street

The sun has got its hat on

KING'S POLICE MEDAL

LG. 1/1/32

Barwick   Harry Claude Vivian   Police Constable   111611 T

At 12.15 pm on 11th August 1931 whilst on the sick list through a foot injury, constable Barwick saw a boy aged 10 years in the River Thames about 80 yards from Teddington Weir, and about 12 feet out from the bank. Taking off his jacket, the constable dived into the water and managed to clutch the boy as he was sinking. He then swam with the boy to the bank, but the boy grabbed him round the neck, and both went under the surface. Fortunately the constable was able to grasp a pile in the river, and dragged both of them to the surface, after which they were assisted out of the water exhausted. The constable further injured his foot during the rescue.

ROYAL HUMANE SOCIETY BRONZE MEDAL

Prout   Police Constable   V

Has been awarded a bronze medal and certificate by the Royal Humane society, for courage and devotion to duty, while off duty in plain clothes, in assisting to rescue a woman from drowning in the River Thames, whereby he was subsequently placed on the sick list suffering from the effects of the immersion.

CARNEGIE HERO FUND

24/8/32

Haynes   Thomas J   Police Constable

Sustained severe injuries while stopping a runaway horse.

CARNEGIE HERO FUND

11/2/32

Smith   Harry   Police Constable

Sustained injury while attempting to render assistance to the occupants of a house after an outbreak of fire.

ROLL OF HONOUR

1933

January	In London a report says betting on greyhounds should be banned.
February	Gunman shoots at US President Franklin D Roosevelt, but he escapes assassination.
March	Hitler orders a boycott of Jews and Jewish shops.
April	Four Britons make the first flight over Mount Everest.
May	Traffic lights being installed in the Capital at the rate of one set a day.
June	Hitler bans all opposition parties.
July	London opening of Richmond, Chiswick and Hampton Court Bridges.
August	UK drought threatens as temperatures touch 90°F.
September	Forest fires rage through Dorset and Hampshire.
October	US the research ship Atlantis returns to port with evidence of life in the deepest parts of the ocean.
November	Examination of the skeletons of the alleged 'Princes in the Tower' indicates they died in the reign of Richard III.
December	Prohibition ends in the USA.

HITS OF THE YEAR

Smoke gets in your eyes
Stormy weather
Who's afraid of the big bad wolf

KING'S POLICE MEDAL

LG. 2/1/33

Cain   William   Detective Inspector   98297

At 11.15 am on 15th March 1932 the Inspector together with three other police officers, were keeping observation in a police 'Flying Squad' car, on three men in another motor car. The men were seen to draw up near an unattended motor car containing leather goods, and then one of the men got into the vehicle, and drove quickly away. The police gave chase, and eventually the police car was pulled across the road forcing the other cars to stop. Inspector Cain jumped on the running board, but was knocked to the ground. As the car accelerated away, he again jumped on the car, and after a fierce struggle forced the driver to stop, and all three suspects were arrested.

KING'S POLICE MEDAL

LG. 2/1/33

Cockburn   Herbert   Police Constable   119089 D

At 11.40 am on 29th December 1931 a horse attached to a light van bolted in Edgware Road. Constable Cockburn made a determined effort to stop the vehicle but was knocked down. Jumping into a passing taxi he gave chase, and when he was alongside, he jumped and caught hold of the horse's bridle, but as he did so the van collided with a bus, and the impact threw the constable to the ground. Although badly shaken he resumed the chase, and eventually brought the horse to a stop.

KING'S POLICE MEDAL

LG. 2/1/33

Pattenden   Sidney   Police Constable   111614 V

At 2.30 am on 25th September 1931 constable Pattenden was in plain clothes keeping observation, with another officer on a tennis pavilion at Thames Ditton, when two men approached and tried to force the door. The two officers at once tackled the men, and a violent struggle took place during which constable Pattenden was shot three times through the arm, neck and body, the latter shot passing close to his heart. Hearing the shots, the other constable stopped chasing his suspect and returned to find the man standing over constable Pattenden, and threatening to shoot, before he made good his escape. As a result of his injuries constable Pattenden was pensioned as unfit for duty about 5 months later.

KING'S POLICE MEDAL

LG. 2/1/33

Scheide   Alfred   Police Constable   103656 T

At 1.15 pm on 1st November 1931 constable Scheide was directing traffic at the Great West Road and Boston Road, Brentford when he saw a 10 year old girl begin to cross the road in front of a car. He ran forward with the intention of pushing her to safety, but the car killed the girl and seriously injured the constable.

KING'S POLICE MEDAL

LG. 2/1/33

Swan   Robert   Police Constable   115132 L

At 3 am on 17th May 1932 at Rodney Road, Walworth, South London constable Swan's suspicions were aroused by the actions of a man outside a grocery store. Looking through a side window, the constable saw two other men inside the store, tampering with the safe. There was an explosion, and the two men rushed out of the store, brandishing jemmies. Constable Swan caught hold of both men, but was hit with a jemmy on the head and hands and knocked to the ground. Although severely injured the constable gave chase, and caught up with one of the criminals and arrested him after a struggle.

KING'S POLICE MEDAL

LG. 2/1/33

Wallen   Robert   Police Sergeant   94365 E

At about 8.40 am on 17th March 1932 Sergeant Wallen was escorting children across Clerkenwell Road, at the junction with Great Saffron Hill, when he saw a young girl crossing the road on her own, and in front of a fast approaching car. It seemed she would certainly be knocked down. The Sergeant ran into the road, and succeeded in pushing the child to safety from in front of the car, but he was knocked down and seriously injured. As a result of his action, Sergeant Wallen was pensioned as unfit for further service on 6th October 1932.

ROYAL HUMANE SOCIETY BRONZE MEDAL

Morgan   Police Constable   98931

A bronze medal and certificate by the Royal Humane Society for exceptional courage and devotion to duty in assisting to rescue a man from drowning and immediately afterwards rescuing another man from drowning while on annual leave at Broadstairs on 12th August 1933. Also commended by the Coroner at an inquest and also commended by the Commissioner

ROLL OF HONOUR

•   Pc Frederick Percy

Crushed by a van during a collision when he was on traffic duty in Chelsea.

•   Pc Albert E Pecker

Pensioned in 1932 in consequences of a non accidental injury received in the execution of his duty on Greenwich Division from which he died.

1934

January	Road signs to be standardised, including a sign for 'Main Road Ahead' but no 'Stop Sign'.
February	23 reported dead after tornadoes sweep through the Southern United States.
March	Road Traffic Bill, tests will have to be taken for all new drivers, and for the first time pedestrians may be penalised for walking dangerously.
April	126 have died in road accidents since 7th April but some traffic lights have cut the number of accidents in London.
May	British author H G Wells stands by his prediction of another major war by 1940.
June	Dismantling of the old Waterloo Bridge begins, it will be offered for sale.
July	The King opens the Mersey Tunnel, the longest underwater tunnel in Liverpool.
August	UK 1,246,000 people have been rehoused and 2,328,000 houses built since 1918.
September	Evangeline Booth becomes the Salvation Army's first woman General.
October	18 month baby is kept alive in a hospital 'oxygen bed'.
November	The Flying Scotsman reaches a record speed of 97.5 mph between London and Leeds.
December	US Olympic swimmer Johnny Weissmuller to star for first time at 'Tarzan of the Apes'.

HITS OF THE YEAR

Isle of Capri

I only have eyes for you

You're the top

KING'S POLICE MEDAL GEORGE V AND VI ISSUE

KING'S POLICE MEDAL

LG. 1/1/34

| Blundell | Frederick Gilbert | Police Constable | 115820 L |

At about 1 pm on 27th November 1932 a fire broke out in a room on the second floor of a house in Lambeth Palace Road, opposite St Thomas's Hospital. Constable Blundell, who was on sick leave, saw the fire as he was leaving hospital after undergoing a minor nasal operation. He hurried to the house, ran up the stairs to the fiercely burning room. The mother of the family living there had already rescued one of her children, and constable Blundell met her on the point of collapse, with another child in her arms. The constable took her downstairs, and hurried with the child to hospital. On his return he tried to crawl into the burning room to attempt to rescue the remaining child, but after being choked and scorched by smoke and flames, he withdrew. The child was later found dead. Constable Blundell had to return to hospital for treatment, he was off sick for 6 weeks.

KING'S POLICE MEDAL

LG. 1/1/34

| Bunce | William | Police Constable | 116430 B |
| Hawkes | Frederick Ernest | Police Constable | 117005 B |

At about 6.15 pm on 20th June 1933 a jeweller's shop in Sloane Street was raided by two men named Colbard and Johnson, who after injuring one of the employees, decamped with jewellery to the value of £280. Constables Bunce and Hawkes saw the thieves running away, and with the assistance of a passing motorist caught them as they got into a taxi in Lowndes Street. Colbard broke a window and threatened to shoot constable Hawkes with a double-barrelled 'sawn off' shotgun. The constable tackled him with his truncheon, meanwhile Johnson struck at both constables with a knife, and in the struggle constable Hawkes was cut on the hand and jaw. Both suspects then ran away, but Colbard was soon arrested. Johnson was overtaken by constable Johnson and he was disarmed and arrested. Both constables received a monetary award from the Bow Street Fund.

KING'S POLICE MEDAL

LG. 1/1/34

| Haynes | Thomas John | Police Constable | 100193 M |

At about 4.45 pm on 24th August 1932 two heavy draught horses attached to a van bolted along Paradise Street, Rotherhithe, a narrow crowded thoroughfare. Constable Haynes was in the police station when he heard shouting and ran out into the street just in time to push a woman to safety from under the horses' hooves. He the seized the reins on the offside horse and ran alongside for some 40 yards but was unable to stop the horses, due to a loose trace which eventually tripped him causing him to fall, pulling the offside horse down on top of him. He was dragged along the ground some distance, and the wheels of the van passed over him, severely injuring him. The constable received a monetary award from the Bow Street Fund. He was off sick for 4 months.

KING'S POLICE MEDAL

LG. 1/1/34

King   William Frederick   Police Constable   102477 K

At about 1.30 pm on 14th February 1933 a fire broke out in an upstairs room of a house in Chadwell Heath, where an old lady was bedridden. The housekeeper had tried to drag the old lady out, but had been unsuccessful, and then constable King crawled into the room through thick smoke and flames. He found the woman lying on the floor partly covered by smouldering bedclothes and a burning night-dress. Constable King rolled her along the ground to put out the flames, and then with great difficulty, owing to her weight, dragged her from the room onto the landing. He was then overcome by smoke, and had to go out for some air. Others then brought the woman downstairs, and she was taken to hospital where she later died. An award was also made from the Society for the Protection of Life from Fire and a monetary award from the Bow Street Fund.

KING'S POLICE MEDAL

LG. 1/1/34

Lemmon   James   Police Constable   99346 W

At about 3.45 pm on 21st April 1933 a heavy horse attached to a four wheeled coal lorry bolted from St Johns Hill, Battersea, after an accident with a motor lorry. Constable Lemmon was in Northcote Road when he saw the horse approaching, and although the animal was at full gallop, ran alongside it for some distance hanging onto the mane. He realised that he could not stop it this way, so he released his grip on the mane, and gripped the animal's nostrils with his left hand, and at the same time pulled with all this weight on the horse's head. Eventually the horse came to a standstill after some 300 yards.

KING'S POLICE MEDAL

LG. 1/1/34

McLaren   Laurie Andrew   Police Constable   117840 E

At about 12.30 am on 18th January 1933 constable McLaren was on the Victoria Embankment when he heard shouting, and looking over into the river, saw some clothing floating on the water. He ran down the slipway onto a pier, and taking off his greatcoat, jumped into the water but as it was low tide he had great difficulty in moving through the water and thick mud to the spot where he had seen the clothing. He saw a foot sticking out of the muddy water, but was unable to pull the body out. He persevered for some time, in the extreme cold, and darkness, with the waters rising, and eventually totally exhausted, was assisted from the water by onlookers, who had pushed a ladder out to him. Had it not been for their assistance he may have got stuck himself and drowned.

KING'S POLICE MEDAL

LG. 1/1/34

Robins   William Albert   Police Constable   120786

Shortly after midnight on 27th February 1933 constable Robins was on plain clothes duty in Clapton, East London, when he chased a suspect he had disturbed breaking into a garage with another man. After running for over a mile, the man finally jumped into the River Lea in an attempt to escape. The river was in flood, and the man soon got into difficulties. He called for help, and the constable dived fully clothes into the river, and brought the man to the bank. As he was pulled out of the river, the man struggled violently and constable Robins in effecting the arrest hurt his knee.

KING'S POLICE MEDAL
LG. 1/1/34

| Todd | Walter Henry | Police Constable | 110231 J |

In the early hours of 25th February 1933 constable Todd saw two men enter a garage and on his approach they ran away. The constable chased them, and whilst he was talking to them, one a known criminal named Smith, pulled out a revolver and fired at the constable from close range. Both men ran away in different directions, and constable Todd followed the other man called Stansell, who it was later discovered was also armed, and after a chase during which the man tried to jump onto a passing lorry, he was arrested, Smith was arrested later. A monetary award was also made from the Bow Street Fund.

CARNEGIE HERO FUND
2/7/34

| Glasby | Harold | Police Constable | **Posthumous** |

Lost his life while endeavouring to rescue his wife and 2 children from drowning in the lake at Danson park, Bexley Heath. He was also awarded the ***Royal Humane Society 'In Memoriam' Bronze Medal.***

CARNEGIE HERO FUND
17/12/34

| Morris | Edward | Police Constable |

Along with four other men assisted in the stopping of a pair of runaway horses.

ROLL OF HONOUR
• Ps Harold Glasby

Drowned while saving the lives of his wife and sons after their boat capsized.

• Pc James Robert Carter

Knocked down by a car when on traffic duty in Hampstead.

1935

January	Mary Pickford divorces Douglas Fairbanks Snr.
February	The BBC says it will start the world's first public television service.
March	30 mph speed limit in built up areas introduced in the UK and police cars will have gongs in order to halt offenders.
April	Glass reflectors or 'cats eyes' invented by Percy Shaw are first used on British roads.
May	Leicester Square underground opens with the world's longest escalator.

June	Stanley Baldwin becomes Prime Minister.
July	Ministry of Transport says dipped headlights will be compulsory.
August	On Hitler's orders the Nazi swastika becomes the German National Flag.
September	200 die when a hurricane hits Florida.
October	Rolls Royce announce their new 50 hp 12 cylinder Phantom III at a cost of £1,850.
November	Prototype of the Hawker Hurricane fighter makes its maiden flight.
December	Charles Lindberg to start a new life in England with his wife and 2 yr. son.

HITS OF THE YEAR
Blue moon
Red sails in the sunset
Cheek to cheek

KING'S POLICE MEDAL
LG. 1/1/35

Morris	Walter	Police Constable	100484 R

At about 6.45 pm on 30th June 1934 constable Morris hearing cries for help, hurried to the gardens alongside Greenwich Tunnel, where he saw a child struggling in the River Thames about 20 feet from the bank. The constable climbed the railings, and jumped fully clothed into the water and swam to the child, holding her above the water. He was unable to swim back to the shore, but caught a rope thrown to him from a ship nearby, and hung on until they were both rescued by some men in a rowing boat. A monetary award was also made from the Bow Street Fund.

KING'S POLICE MEDAL
LG. 1/1/35

Ruddock	Bertram Wellesley	Police Constable	119015 L

At about 4.45 pm on 30th June 1934 a horse attached to a four wheeled van bolted whilst the driver was adjusting the bridle. The man jumped on the van and tried unsuccessfully to stop the horse. Constable Ruddock was in New Church Road, Peckham and saw the runaway approaching at the gallop, with the civilian standing on the van shouting, and waving his arms. Constable Ruddock grabbed the horse around the neck, and after some 75 yards brought it to a standstill. A monetary award was also made from the Bow Street Fund.

KING'S POLICE MEDAL
LG. 1/1/35

Russell	Arthur George	Police Constable	97828 M
Timmins	Harry	Police Constable	118990 M

At 4 am on 17th October 1933 constables Russell and Timmins were searching the vicinity of Fountain Stairs, Bermondsey for a woman reported missing, who was feared might commit suicide, when they saw her jump into the river. Both constables immediately took off their greatcoats, and dived in. The water was about 8 feet deep, and there is an obstruction at this point, which made the water race. The woman had been carried out about

18 feet by the ebb tide, but with considerable difficulty the constables brought her to shore, and commenced artificial respiration until she recovered. Constable Russell aged 50 years was pensioned from the police on 31st July 1934 as unfit suffering from phlebitis and thrombosis as a result of his actions. Each received an award from the Royal Humane Society and a monetary award from the Bow Street Fund.

KING'S POLICE MEDAL
LG. 1/1/35

Shelah   Edward Er Onan   Police Sergeant   108115 L

At about 5 pm on 22nd July 1934 a horse attached to a van, bolted and galloped along Brixton Road, South London. Sergeant Shelah was off duty in plain clothes, and standing at a bus stop. He tried to stop the horse by grabbing its head, but he was knocked down. He tried a second time to grab the horse and succeeded in holding on to the horse's head as it galloped up the pavement and towards a bank. In danger of being crushed against the bank wall by the shafts of the van, the Sergeant managed to force the horse away, and eventually after being carried some considerable distance along the busy road, brought it to a stop. A monetary award was also made from the Bow Street Fund.

KING'S POLICE MEDAL
LG. 1/1/35

Smith   Claude Douglas   Inspector   107080 J

At about 9 pm on 9th February 1934 Inspector Smith with two other officers entered some office premises in Poplar, London, where a suspect named Hester had been seen to enter. Hester was seen descending some stairs holding a revolver. Inspector Smith challenged him, and in an ensuing struggle, one of the constables fell to the ground. Hester immediately fired two shots at the fallen constable, but fortunately missed. Hester broke free and ran into the street, followed by the Inspector, and the other constable. During the chase, Hester turned and fired the revolver three more times at his pursuers, before Inspector Smith got close enough to challenge him again. Hester then aimed and fired at the Inspector, but although there was a click, it did not fire, and Hester was overpowered. A monetary award was also made from the Bow Street Fund.

CARNEGIE HERO FUND
24/9/35

Green   Gordon J   Police Constable

Along with another assisted in rescuing a woman and her three children from a burning house.

ROLL OF HONOUR
- Pc James Warrender Thompson KPM
- Pc Henry Arthur Groves

Thrown by his horse as he was forcing it to avoid bolting into Trafalgar Square.
- Pc Joseph Diboll

Collapsed and died after attending to an injured woman in the street on Brixton Division and going with her to hospital.

1936

January	King Edward VIII becomes Monarch.
February	London figures show 2,581,027 registered cars on the road.
March	New Spitfire fighter aircraft makes its maiden flight.
April	Lindberg's baby killer executed.
May	Fashion craze for pierced ears sweeps London.
June	Gatwick Airport opened.
July	Assassination attempt on King Edward VIII, special constable Anthony Dick grabs the man and wrestles the revolver away from him.
August	BBC makes the first television broadcast from Alexandra Palace.
September	Big new film studios opens at Pinewood.
October	Jarrow jobless march starts to London.
November	Fire destroys Crystal Palace.
December	King Edward VIII abdicates for the love of Mrs Wallace Simpson.

HITS OF THE YEAR

The way you look tonight

When I'm cleaning windows

BATTLE OF CABLE STREET

Britain had its own 'Black shirt' movement demonstrating against the Jewish population. The British Fascist Party was led by Sir Oswald Mosley and used to parade through the East End of London chanting anti-Jewish slogans. For their own protection the marchers were surrounded by large groups of Police.

On Sunday 4th October 1936 Mosley announced a major East London rally, inviting black shirts from all over England to the East End of London. He was to inspect the troops and march along Commercial Road through the heart of the East End.

All police leave was cancelled and mounted police sent to the area. Approximately 300,000 people had gathered waiting for the fascists. There was a massive police presence, and drawing their truncheons managed to make some headway through the masses so that the fascists could march.

At Gardeners Court there was a solid human mass jamming the route. Trams and road blocks were set up. Another route was available via Cable Street. A barricade was erected using the contents of a builder's yard. Marbles were thrown under the horses' hooves, paving stones and bricks were thrown at the police. The windows and roofs of buildings were crowded with women who hurled bottles at anyone in uniform.

The police were captured and temporarily imprisoned in shops. Barricades were broken down only to see new ones erected. The police finally admitted defeat and the march through the East End had to be abandoned.

The following weekend the fascists returned, they smashed the windows of all Jewish shops in the Mile End Road. The abandonment of the march saw the start of the decline of the Black Shirts, they never again marched in uniform in such force. During the skirmishes 70 people were injured many being police officers, and a total of 88 arrests were made.

KING'S POLICE MEDAL
LG. 1/1/36

Airton	James	Police Constable	122833 A
Waldren	Percy	Fireman - London Fire Brigade	

On 11th July 1935 a fire broke out at Ashley Place, Westminster. When constable Airton arrived he found dense smoke and flames coming from an underground cable box. With some assistance he extinguished the flames by throwing several barrel loads of sand into the hold. He then learned that a man who had been working down the hold was still there. Despite the dense smoke and impossible visibility, and the danger from the high voltage cables, constable Airton went down into the hold and found the man at the end of a tunnel, after searching in the darkness He was overcome by smoke and had to come out for air. As he did so, the Fire Brigade arrived, and fireman Waldren went down into the hold and with difficulty brought the man to the surface. The man was badly burned and subsequently died. A monetary award was also made from the Bow Street Fund.

KING'S POLICE MEDAL
LG. 1/1/36

Densham	Alan	Police Constable	104529 V

At about 1.30 pm on 20th August 1934 at the junction of Malden Road and Dukes Avenue, New Malden the constable saw a runaway horse attached to a milk float galloping towards him. The horse had bolted from a road about half a mile away. As it came alongside him, constable Densham seized the reins and ran with the horse, but he was soon pulled off his feet. Despite being dragged for several yards, he hung on, and eventually the horse came to a stop. A monetary award was also made from the Bow Street Fund.

KING'S POLICE MEDAL
LG. 1/1/36

Fox	Charles Edmond	Police Constable	117505 B

On 24th March 1935 constable Fox who was off duty, was walking along Millbank, Westminster when he noticed a seven year old boy had fallen in the river. He immediately took off his overcoat and dived in. He reached the boy, who was about 12 feet out, and then was carried towards Lambeth Bridge on the strong tide, but swam on his back to reach the shore. The boy was taken to hospital. An award was also made from the Royal Humane Society and a monetary award from the Bow Street Fund.

KING'S POLICE MEDAL
LG. 1/1/36

Green	Gordon Jack	Police Constable	122456 C

At about 9 pm on 24th September 1935 a fire occurred at 18 Charlotte Street, Soho. The fire began in the basement but spread rapidly all through the house. Constable Green who was off duty, hurried with other officers to the scene. A woman and three children on the third floor were completely cut off by the flames. Unable to get through a padlocked door, constable Green climbed out of a window in an adjoining house, and onto the roof. Sliding down the other side he was able to reach a small ledge from which with assistance, he was able to reach out and take the children from the mother, and hand them to safety, then with difficulty due to her weight, he helped the woman to safety over the roof. A monetary award was also made from the Bow Street Fund.

KING'S POLICE MEDAL
LG. 1/1/36

| Morris | Edward | Police Constable | 105282 G |

At about 6.20 pm on 17th December 1934 constable Morris saw a pair of draught horses in Cropley Street, Shoreditch, harnessed to a heavy four wheeled wagon, take fright and bolt towards him. He ran into the road, and shouted to some children to get out of the way, and then he waved his arms to try and stop the horses. However the horses galloped towards him, and as he grabbed the nearest horse and hung on, he was dragged for some distance along the road. He was able to grab the nose harness of the horse,, and after several efforts to pull the horse to a stop, he was able to steer them into a side street, where they were brought to a halt. A monetary award was also made from the Bow Street Fund.

KING'S POLICE MEDAL
LG. 1/1/36

| Robinson | Charles Frederick | Police Constable | 110037 M |

At about 4 pm on 10th April 1935 constable Robinson heard a loud explosion come from a shop some 30 to 40 yards away from him in London Road, Southwark. He saw a wall facing the road bulge outwards, and bricks began to fall to the pavement. The constable immediately ran to the spot, where a man who had been passing below the wall was struck down by falling masonry and rendered unconscious. In spite of the falling bricks and masonry, constable Robinson continued to remove debris from off the man, and, when he felt the man's pulse, he was dead. It was later discovered that 22 tons of debris has fallen during the time the constable was attempting to rescue the man. A monetary award was also made from the Bow Street Fund.

KING'S POLICE MEDAL
LG. 1/1/36

| Steele | Kenneth Walter Lawrence | Police Constable | 123382 E |

At about 12.55 am on 13th March 1935 constable Steele and another constable were told of a fire, and that a woman was trapped on the second floor. Both constables ran to the house and found the door of the room locked. They broke it down, and were met by a wall of flames and smoke. The woman could be seen some 10 feet into the room. Whilst the other constable went to call the Fire Brigade, constable Steele put a wet handkerchief over his nose and mouth, and entered the room, locating the woman in a collapsed state. After several attempts, he managed to drag her to the door, but she became jammed against a chest of drawers. The constable was then overcome with the smoke and had to leave. The Fire Brigade arrived and took the woman out, but she was dead. Constable Steele sustained severe burns to his face and hands. He also received an award from the Society for the Protection of Life from Fire.

KING'S POLICE MEDAL
Posthumous
LG. 1/1/36

Thompson   James Warrender   Police Constable   112399 S

'At about 11.35pm on 7th September 1935 Constable Thompson was at the Great North Road, Barnet Hill, at the junction of Mays Lane, where he was regulating traffic at the end of the Barnet Fair, being held nearby. There was a large crowd of people crossing the road to the tram stop, and although the tram was full, there were many people in the roadway. A heavy lorry loaded with 6 tons of cement suddenly appeared out of control on the hill, heading straight for the crowd. Constable Thompson saw this, and began to push pedestrians clear of the road, shouting at them to jump clear. The lorry ploughed into the crowd, killing Constable Thompson and three others, and injuring many more. By his action he saved the lives of many people.

CARNEGIE HERO FUND
27/2/36

Hood   Joseph   Police Constable

Sustained serious injury while stopping a runaway motor car.

CARNEGIE HERO FUND
12/8/36

Mounce   Reginald   Police Constable

Suffered physically as a result of attempting to rescue a young boy from drowning in the Grand Surrey Canal.

CARNEGIE HERO FUND
2/4/36

Perigo   Lawrence   Police Constable

Sustained serious injury while stopping a runaway horse.

CARNEGIE HERO FUND

Green   Police Constable   122456 C

For exceptional courage, promptitude and resourcefulness displayed while off duty in assisting to rescue four persons from a burning house. Also received an inscribed gold wrist watch.

ROLL OF HONOUR
• Pc Joseph Alfred Allaway

Knocked down and killed by a car while on duty at Harlington.

1937

January Horse drawn traffic is banned from a wide area of the West End of London.
February Artificial fibre 'Nylon' is patented in the US.
March   New 12 sided three penny piece introduced.

April	King George VI opens the National Maritime Museum at Greenwich.
May	Coronation of King George VI and Queen Elizabeth.
June	Duke of Windsor marries Mrs Wallis Simpson.
July	Ex rector of Stiffley dies after being mauled by a lion at Skegness amusement ground.
August	GEC announce a new television for under £50.
September	In Palestine 100 Arabs arrested for the murder of two British Officials.
October	First London motor show opens at Earls Court.
November	Typhoid breaks out in the suburbs of London.
December	General Viscount Gort is made Chief of the Imperial General Staff.

HITS OF THE YEAR
A nice cup of tea
September in the rain
The folks who live on the hill

KING'S POLICE MEDAL
LG. 1/2/37

Hood   Joseph Henry   Police Constable   109183 Z

A police car, which had been left temporarily unattended facing down hill, outside Gypsy Hill Police Station on 8th October 1936, started to move off downhill. Constable Hood who was on duty in plain clothes ran to the car, leaped onto the running board and grabbed the steering wheel. Although the constable could not drive a car, he remained on the running board. The car swerved about on the road, and hit a bicycle and then overturned a milk barrow, and mounted the pavement. The car struck several other vehicles as well as a wall and a hoarding on its way down the long steep hill, before constable Hood was able to steer it towards a field. With a pedestrian in the way, the constable had to swing away from the field, and in so doing hit two motor lorries and overturned. As a result of the injuries he received in the action constable Hood was pensioned as unfit for further police service.

KING'S POLICE MEDAL
ROYAL HUMANE SOCIETY BRONZE MEDAL
CARNEGIE HERO FUND
LG. 1/2/37

Mounce   Reginald Ernest Ralph   Police Constable   118026 L

At about 4.40 pm on 12th August 1936 some children were playing on three barges moored side by side in the Grand Surrey Canal, Peckham, when one of the boys aged 7 fell into the water. A labourer from a wharf side yard dived in, but could not find the boy. In the meantime police had been called, and constable Mounce took off his outer clothes and dived in. On diving for the third time found the boy under the middle barge, and brought him to the side, where he was helped by other officers. Artificial respiration was applied and was successful for a time, but the boy died later in hospital. The canal is particularly polluted and the bottom overgrown with weeds, and with a great deal of debris.

KING'S POLICE MEDAL
LG. 1/2/37

Perigo   Lawrence Austin   Police Constable   1222264 H

Constable Perigo saw a heavy draught horse attached to a four wheeled covered van galloping driverless towards Durwand Street, Whitechapel. As the horse drew abreast of him, he ran into the road, and caught hold of the reins and the offside shaft, and ran alongside pulling the reins. He was dragged for some distance, still holding on until the shaft broke, striking him in the back and knocking him to the ground. The constable got up and although in great pain, pursued the runaway, catching it again, and eventually stopping it. It was later discovered that constable Perigo had sustained a cracked base of the spine in the incident, and he was off sick for over three months.

CARNEGIE HERO FUND
17/11/37

McKitterick   Arthur J   Police Constable

Along with another man suffered physically as a result of extricating 3 people from a house after a serious explosion.

ROLL OF HONOUR
• Pc Bernard Tutt

Crushed as he attempted to push children clear of the path of a motor vehicle which had been involved in a collision in Marylebone.

• Spc Frederick Parncutt
• Pc Albert Taylor

Drowned on duty near West India Docks when a tug was in collision with a police patrol boat.

1938

January	Walt Disney's Snow White shown for the first time, the first feature length cartoon film.
February	John Baird demonstrates a large screen prototype colour television.
March	Flogging should be abolished a London committee recommend.
April	UK police recommend that all bicycles should be fitted with rear lights.
May	Scotland Yard says it is to start using police dogs.
June	US a new comic strip has appeared this month, it is called Superman.
July	The Government orders 1000 Spitfire fighters.
August	A gearless, clutchless car is tested.
September	There is a rush among Londoners for new gas masks as international tension escalates.
October	Germans march into Czechoslovakia.
November	Jews are given 48 hours to quit Munich or face concentration camps.
December	Government plans to spend £200,000 on air raid shelters.

HITS OF THE YEAR
You can't take it with you

KING'S POLICE MEDAL
LG. 1/1/38

Cavalier	Cecil Frank	Police Constable	109064 Y MM
Swayne	Ernest Walter	Police Constable	106257 Y

On the morning of 19th May 1937 the verger of a church entered the adjoining parish hall, and was walking towards the stage when shots were fired at him. He ran out as more shots were fired at him. The vicar soon arrived, and looking into the hall was shot in the face. He died four days later. The police were called, and two unarmed officers, constables Cavalier and Swayne, arrived on the scene. They had every reason to believe that a dangerous criminal was hiding in the hall, but nevertheless they immediately entered and whilst one searched the left side of the hall the other searched the right side. Constable Swayne climbed a ladder leading to a platform above the stage, which was in complete darkness, and saw a man who appeared to be crouching down. Thinking he was about to attack, the constable jumped on him, but realised he was dead. The man had shot himself, the gun lying nearby. Constable Cavalier had won the Military Medal in World War I.

KING'S POLICE MEDAL
LG. 1/1/38

Chesterman	John William	Police Constable	104988 E

At about 12.10 am on 27th February 1936 constable Chesterman who was off duty and in plain clothes, noticed a motor car containing five men driving slowly down New Compton Street, Soho and he recognised one of them as being a convicted thief. The car stopped in Denman Street, and two of the men got out, and whilst one kept watch, the other stole a suitcase from the rear seat of an unattended motor car, then both hurried back to their car and drove off. Constable Chesterman who had concealed himself in a doorway to watch, immediately jumped out, and onto the running board of the car, shouting that he was a police officer and telling them to stop. The driver accelerated, and as a result constable Chesterman slipped from the running board, however he regained his balance and held on, despite the drastic efforts by the driver to dislodge him. Eventually he was thrown off into the road, but he immediately got up, and ran to a telephone and called Scotland Yard with the information. As a result, the car was soon stopped and the men arrested.

KING'S POLICE MEDAL
LG. 1/1/38

Freeland	Edward Ernest	Police Constable	122696 E
Perry	Howard James	Police Constable	124816 E

On 23rd August 1937 an old dwelling house at 9 Cumberland Terrace, WC1 was fumigated by hydrogen cyanide gas. At about 9.30 pm a Miss Smith who resided in a flat backing onto the address, went to her neighbour's flat, and found her lying unconscious on the floor.

Constable Freeland arrived, and saw the woman Mrs Jenkinson, lying on the floor in the basement. He called for assistance, and then kicked in a shutter and dragged the woman out into the basement area. However he was overcome by the gas, and collapsed, along with the man who was helping him. Constable Perry arrived from the police station, and found all three unconscious. He climbed over the railings into the basement area, and lifted all three over the railings to safety, before he then made a search of the basement flat for any other persons. As he came out of the flat, he too was overcome by fumes and collapsed. The ambulance soon arrived, and took everyone to hospital, where all but Mrs Jenkinson recovered.

KING'S POLICE MEDAL
LG. 1/1/38

Hearn   John   Police Constable   107107 J MM

In the afternoon of 17th October 1936 a man attempting to evade arrest, jumped about 15 feet into the West India Dock. Constable Hearn sprang, fully dressed, into the water, which was dirty and slimy, and swam over to the man, turning him on his back. The constable then caught a life buoy which had been thrown to him, and he was pulled to the edge, where he had great difficulty in keeping the man who was now unconscious above water. Both were hauled out and taken to hospital. He was off sick for 5 days. Constable Hearn won the Military Medal during the First world war.

KING'S POLICE MEDAL
LG. 1/1/38

Starkey   Robert Macintyre   Police Constable   123165 E

At 4.10 am on 1st May 1937 constable Starkey and another constable were on duty in plain clothes when they noticed flames coming from the basement room of a house in Frederick Street, WC2. Whilst the other constable went to call the Fire Brigade constable Starkey kicked the door open and went in to arouse the occupants. He saw two men in the basement flat, and he made his way down into the basement where there was thick smoke. He made two attempts to enter the room, and finally was able to get in, and search the room, only to find that the two men had escaped by another route. The constable then went upstairs, where he was able to rescue a young girl before he collapsed from the smoke, and was taken to hospital suffering from burns and injuries to his eyes. He was off sick for 10 days.

KING'S POLICE MEDAL
LG. 1/1/38

Turnell   Harry Joseph   Police Constable   119672 R

On 9th November 1936 a civilian found an empty pram on the bridge over the main railway lines between Lewisham and Blackheath railway stations. When he looked over the parapet, he saw what appeared to be a bundle trapped between the live rail, and the running rail, which was sparking. Suspecting something unusual, he reported it to police. Constable Turnell arrived at the bridge, and then climbed over the parapet, and down an almost perpendicular embankment to the tracks. Trains were still passing by making this manoeuvre more dangerous. On reaching the child, the constable found that its head was under the live rail, and sparks were flashing between the rail and the child's body, burning the flesh. Trying to pull the child free, the constable received a violent shock, which threw him backwards, but although badly shaken he tried again to free the child, and on the second attempt was successful. He then ran with the child in his arms along the track to Blackheath station, a distance of about 400 yards, from where the child was taken to hospital and later recovered. The child's father was later convicted of attempted murder.

ROLL OF HONOUR

• Pc George Shepherd

Thrown from the running board of a car whose driver he was seeking to stop when the suspect collided with a bus in Hampstead.

1939

January	London, the committee on Nursing Services reports that nurses are overworked and under paid.
February	Hunt for IRA terrorists following bomb blasts at Tottenham Court Road and Leicester Square tube stations.
March	Prime Minister Neville Chamberlain denounces Hitler and recalls the British Ambassador from Berlin.
April	Britain's largest aircraft carrier HMS Illustrious is launched at Barrow.
May	The Military Training (conscription) Bill introduced.
June	First military conscripts enrolled.
July	A five year boy reported to have been chosen as the new Dalai Lama.
August	All movable treasures are taken to safety from the major museums, galleries and Westminster Abbey.
September	War is declared on Germany.
October	HMS Royal Oak is sunk by a German U-boat at Scapa Flow, 800 die.
November	Imperial Airways and British Airways merge to form British Overseas Airways Corporation (BOAC).
December	German Battleship Graf Spee is scuttled by her crew when trapped in the River Plate.

HITS OF THE YEAR

Washing on the Siegfried line
Over the rainbow
Gone with the wind

KING'S POLICE MEDAL

LG. 2/1/39

Bailey	Ronald Tom	Police Sergeant	112832 G

On 5th November 1937 Sergeant Bailey was with another officer in plain clothes were in Golden Lane, Finsbury when they noticed two men loitering, one of whom was wearing a chauffeur's cap. The Sergeant and his colleague kept the men under observation and after a few minutes a young woman carrying a music case and a handbag was seen being followed by a third man. Suddenly two of the men snatched the handbag and music case from the woman and made off in a car driven by the man in the chauffeur's cap. Sergeant Bailey and the other officer chased after the fugitives by commandeering two private cars. Sergeant Bailey then jumped from the private car onto the running board of the fugitive's car whilst in motion, and forced them to stop. Two of the men ran away, but the third was arrested, and the music case and handbag containing £139 was recovered.

KING'S POLICE MEDAL
LG. 2/1/39

Bursnall	Matthew	Police Constable	114370 D

Constable Bursnall was standing at Lancaster Gate Underground Station, Bayswater when he was informed that a taxi driver needed assistance to deal with some men who were fighting in his cab. The constable saw a man who was involved in the fight cross the road and climb over some iron railings. The constable followed this man, and realising that he was drunk, decided to arrest him. As he was about to do so, there was a sudden loud report and he felt a stab of pain and realised he had been shot. The man broke away from the constable, but despite his wound, the constable drew his truncheon, ran after the man, and hit him on the head. The man fell to the ground, and the constable fell on top of him until he got some assistance. The constable was immediately taken to hospital, where he was found to be severely wounded, but after a delicate operation to remove the bullet, the constable recovered.

KING'S POLICE MEDAL
LG. 2/1/39

Charmichael	Alexander	Police Constable	119057 X

Early in the morning of 28th November 1937 constable Carmichael and another officer heard unusual sounds coming from a kiosk on the platform of Dollis Hill Railway Station, which was closed at that hour. As they approached they saw two men run away. One man jumped onto the railway tracks, and disappeared into a ditch. Constable Carmichael running in pursuit, saw the man lying face down in the ditch, partly concealed, with a revolver in his hand. Although threatened by the revolver, the constable jumped at the man and as he did so, he was shot in the left leg. Despite the wound, the constable struggled with the man. The man threatened to shoot both constables but he was overpowered and arrested. The suspect was sentenced to 7 years imprisonment.

KING'S POLICE MEDAL
LG. 2/1/39

Champs	Frederick Henry	Police Constable	110541 X

At about 10.55 pm on 25th September 1937 constable Champs and an Inspector were told that a man had jumped from a railway bridge onto the lines at Sunbury. The Inspector drove to Sudbury Town railway station, in order to have trains stopped, whilst constable Champs scrambled down the embankment, during which he fell and lost his torch. He saw the man lying on the tracks some 20 feet away. Owing to the darkness, and the loss of his torch, the constable was very cautions in avoiding the live rails. As he was nearing the man, someone shouted that a train was coming, and on seeing the train lights very close by, he grabbed the man, and pulled him away from the track as the train passed. The man later died in hospital.

KING'S POLICE MEDAL

LG. 2/1/39

Cosham	Albert Edward	Police Constable	119693 S

On 1st July 1938 constable Cosham discovered that some men had broken into a post office, and had made off in a dark saloon car. With another constable, he went in pursuit in a police car, and for over 40 miles and at very fast speeds he chased the vehicle. The driver of the fugitive car drove recklessly, totally ignoring traffic signs, and attempting on several occasions to wreck the police car. Eventually the car was stopped, and two of the four men inside were arrested.

KING'S POLICE MEDAL

LG. 2/1/39

Hemley	George Edward	Police Sergeant	117424 K
Rackham	Cecil	Police Sergeant	114609 K
Ground	Frederick William	Police Constable	121225 K
Pillar	Elliott	Police Constable	122883 K

On the evening of 28th February 1938 two troopers deserted from the 12th Royal Lancers stationed at Tidworth, Hampshire taking with them two revolvers and ammunition. They held up two local police officers and stole their car. Later they forced a Royal Air Force officer to drive them to London.

On 1st March constable Pillar was off duty standing by his private car at Woolwich Ferry, when the two deserters climbed into his car, and pushed a revolver into his side, and told him to drive. The constable drove as directed, but as he passed Barking Police station, he jammed on the brakes and crashed the car into a lamp post. A fight followed between the constable and the men, all three falling onto the pavement. One of the men fired his revolver twice at the constable but missed. The two Sergeants and constable Ground appeared from the police station and chased the men, who fired their revolvers repeatedly at the officers. Eventually both men were overpowered and arrested, but not before Sergeant Hemley had been shot in the arm.

KING'S POLICE MEDAL

LG. 2/1/39

McKitterick	Arthur James	Police Constable	105606 B

In the early hours of 17th November 1937 an explosion occurred in a house at Fulham. Constable McKitterick, who lives in the same street was off duty in bed when he heard the explosion. He immediately put on some clothes and ran to the scene, where he found the front of the house collapsed, and the occupants crying for help. He climbed into the debris, and made two separate rescues. There was a strong smell of gas, but hearing groans, the constable re-entered the house and found an old man buried beneath the debris. A fire broke out as he was pulling the man out, and with gas still escaping, the constable then ran to the nearest telephone box, called the Fire Brigade and then returned to complete the rescue of the old man, who unfortunately died later in hospital.

KING'S POLICE MEDAL
LG. 2/1/39

Paxton   William Dale   Police Constable   126224 M

At about 10 am on 25th January 1938 constable Paxton was patrolling the Albert Embankment, alongside the River Thames, when he heard a splash and saw a man in the river. He blew his whistle, and then without waiting for assistance took off his greatcoat, belt and helmet and dived 10 feet into the water. He swam out to the unconscious man, and brought him into the side, but was unable to reach a ring on the wall. With no assistance arriving, the constable had no means of getting out of the water and after some five minutes the constable became totally exhausted and released the man. After several more minutes his shouts for help were answered and he was picked up by a passing tug. The man's body was later recovered.

CARNEGIE HERO FUND
29/5/39

Evans   Charles   Police Constable

Along with another man rescued 3 schoolboys from drowning in a disused ballast pit.

ROLL OF HONOUR
• Pc George Rodney Southworth
Fell attempting to put out a light in the blackout in Harley Street.
• Wrpc Jack Morgan (also known as Israel Abrahams)
Knocked down crossing tramlines to deal with an accident on Victoria Embankment.

Chapter Six

THE YEARS OF 1940 - 1949

The world was in the grip of yet another world conflict. There were gallant efforts by small ships in going across to Dunkirk in France to bring back our beleaguered troops who were forced almost into the sea by the advancing German army.

London suffered during the Blitz and many gallantry awards of the George Medal were awarded to Metropolitan Police officers for their aid in digging out persons trapped in bombed out buildings. Even Buckingham Palace did not escape the bombing, and one police officer was killed during one of the raids on the Palace.

The war raged not only in the UK but in Italy and the western deserts. The USA suffering at the hands of the Japanese in the bombing of their base at Pearl Harbour.

One of the most noted dates in this decade was 6th June 1944 better known as D-day. This was the day when the allied invasion took place where troops landed in vast numbers on the beaches of Normandy.

The final part of this dreadful conflict was the liberation of the concentration camps and the sight of the suffering of the inmates, some too weak to stand or even move. Not only did the liberating army see the walking skeletons but the piles of as yet unburied corpses, the piles of clothing, shoes, false teeth, spectacles even a vast pile of gold rings.

The first atomic bombs were dropped, one on Nagasaki and the other on Hiroshima, this finally ended the Japanese involvement, and brought about their surrender.

Even though the war ended in 1945 rationing still took place in the UK.

Conflict started in the Middle East with the formation of Israel, the Arab nations became hostile towards the Israelis and the British, this resulted in many British soldiers being killed by the Palestinians.

1940

In September of this year King George VI instituted both the George Cross and the George Medal for valour and outstanding gallantry. The George Cross was awarded to the Island of Malta .....'To Honour her brave people I award the George Cross to the Island Fortress of Malta to bear witness to a heroism and devotion that will long be famous in history'..... Also starting this decade we see the King's Commendation for Brave Conduct.

January	The River Thames freezes for the first time since 1888 as a cold wave strikes the country.
February	Birmingham, 2 IRA men are hanged.
March	Two seater fighter bomber the Mosquito makes its maiden flight.
April	Adolf Hitler invades Denmark and Norway.

May   First evacuated troops arrive from Dunkirk.
June   The Government bans all strikes.
July   German bombers carry out their first daylight raid.
August   First German plane brought down over London.
September 400 deaths reported in renewed Luftwaffe bombing but the BBC says that 185 German aeroplanes have been shot down over the City in a single day.
October   Winston Churchill elected leader of the Tory Party upon the resignation of Chamberlain, on grounds of ill health.
November   Historic cave paintings discovered at Lascaux in the Dordogne.
December   10,000 fire bombs dropped on the City of London on a single night.

HITS OF THE YEAR
Nightingale sang in Berkeley Square
Whispering Grass

KING'S POLICE MEDAL
LG. 1/1/40

| Tarry | William | Police Constable | 120694 P |
| Wright | Maurice Henry | Police Constable | 122246 P |

At about 4.30 am on 27th September 1938 constables Tarry and Wright heard noises coming from the interior of a house at Cheslehurst, and decided to deep observation. After some time a man came out carrying a bundle in one hand and a rifle in the other. The two officers ran towards the man who dropped the bundle and threatened the constables with the rifle. As the constables rushed the man, he pointed the weapon at constable Wright and pulled the trigger, but there was no report. The man then used the rifle as a club, swinging it around, and hitting both constables on the head. After a short struggle the man was overpowered, and the rifle was found to be unloaded although the officers did not know this before.

KING'S POLICE MEDAL
LG. 1/1/40

| Walton | Frederick Charles | Police Constable | 108015 W |

Constable Walton was in the High Street, Colliers Wood when he saw a driverless horse and van galloping towards him. The horse had thrown its bridle, so the constable jumped on the back of the van, and clambered forwards until he was astride the horses back, standing on the shafts, from where he could grab the reins. He pulled the horse off the side of the road, and eventually a lorry driver, seeing the position, drove alongside, and forced the horse and van to mount the kerb, where the van collided with a power pole and came to a stop.

KING'S POLICE MEDAL
LG. 1/1/40

| Fabian | Robert Henry | Detective Inspector | 111858 C |

At about 10 pm on 24th June 1939 Detective Inspector Fabian was in his office in Vine Street Police Station, when he heard a loud explosion. He went to nearby Piccadilly Circus and found that a bomb had exploded there, but then he found a second bomb in the debris. Ordering people to stand back, he slowly dismantled the bomb, removing the detonator, and putting it in his pocket. He then took the gelignite, and other remains of the bomb back to the police station and immersed them in water. The device contained 40 oz of explosives.

KING'S POLICE MEDAL
LG. 1/1/40

| Hayward | Ernest Victor | Police Constable | 107767 C |

During the early hours of 4th May 1939 constable Hayward was in Tottenham Court Road when he discovered a brown paper parcel in the window of a shop. He removed the parcel to the edge of the pavement, unwrapped it, and saw a blue rubber balloon containing liquid. Beside the balloon was a round paper package with a fuse protruding from one end. He immediately separated the balloon from the package, and keeping them apart, put them in a bucket of water, he then carried the bucket with its contents to the police station. On examination it was found that the parcel contained a stick of gelignite with a time fuse and detonator attached to a double rubber balloon containing acid.

KING'S POLICE MEDAL
LG. 1/1/40

| Morrison | Gordon Donald | Police Constable | 126075 R |

In the early morning of 24th February 1939 a cyclist riding in an erratic manner was stopped and questioned as to the ownership of the bicycle. He was unable to give a satisfactory account of his possession of some property, and he was taken to Woolwich Police Station, from where he escaped. Constable Morrison who was off duty, and other officers chased him, but the man pulled an automatic pistol from his pocket. Constable Morrison threw himself at the man, and knocked the pistol from his grasp. The man was taken back to the police station, where it was found that the pistol was loaded.

KING'S POLICE MEDAL
LG. 1/1/40

| Shepherd | Thomas Charles | Police Constable | 120915 Z |

During the early hours of 5th August 1938 constable Shepherd with other officers on patrol in a police car saw a large car stop outside several shops in Croydon and anticipating a shop breaking, they kept observation on the men, on foot. The suspect car stopped outside a jeweller's shop, and whilst one remained in the driver's seat, the other two got out, and threw bricks through the shop window. As the officers approached, the offenders ran off, one was caught immediately, the other got into the car, which drove off. Constable Shepherd jumped onto the car, and reached in and got hold of the driver round the neck, jerking him back, causing the car to crash. All three men were arrested.

BRITISH EMPIRE MEDAL FOR GALLANTRY

LG. 15/11/40

Gahan   Edward Raymond Riordan Station Inspector   X

Since the commencement of the heavy nightly aerial bombardment, station Inspector Gahan has visited and dealt with no less than 22 incidents of varying magnitude, being a real leader and stimulus to all with whom he has come in contact. On one occasion, two heavy bombs demolished three houses and damaged a very large number of others. Several persons were killed and a large number sustained injury. The station Inspector, efficiently organising soldiers and civilians into a 'chain gang' soon had three persons rescued after wholesale removal of debris. On another occasion incendiary bombs were dropped causing several fires. One of these fires at a factory proved to be serious and fire services were in attendance. An H E bomb then fell on the premises causing the fire to spread to an adjoining factory and other premises. Small fires also began to break out in many places and the water supply was affected by explosions. The station Inspector obtained four stirrup pumps and organised local teams of residents to obtain buckets of water from neighbouring houses. In this manner he succeeded in stopping several fires from spreading, being assisted in these efforts by women as well as men. He had also organised a number of evacuations, following unexploded bombs and land mines. In one particular instance a very large excavation was necessary which was carried out efficiently and methodically.

BRITISH EMPIRE MEDAL FOR GALLANTRY

LG. 15/11/40

Iusignea   Herbert Charles   Inspector   V

Night after night the Inspector has taken charge of all incidents in his station, and exhibited an inspiring leadership to all ranks serving under him. When he dealt with two unexploded bombs of a new type, the first in the division, he realised their potential danger, closely examining them at great personal risk and organising evacuation of local residents on a large scale, involving two to three thousand people. This operation was carried out without a hitch.

GEORGE MEDAL

LG. 15/11/40

Hack   William George   Police Constable   J

During an air raid a crude oil bomb was dropped on a factory, a huge fire resulted and dwelling houses became enveloped. 6 persons were trapped in a shelter by debris. Despite the heat he managed to move the debris and release those trapped. Continuing along the road he found a man trapped by debris, and after a short time he too was released.

GEORGE MEDAL

LG. 15/11/40

Kerrison   Edward Phillip   Police Constable   L DCM

Rescue of terrified occupants of a public house that had been hit by a high explosive bomb and completely demolished. One woman lying across a bath that was protruding over a deep crater caused by the bomb.

GEORGE MEDAL
LG. 15/11/40

Lees	Bernard	Police Constable	G
Gunn	Richard	Police Constable	G
Nicholson	Charles	Police Constable	G

A large number of buildings were demolished during an air raid. They entered one building where people were trapped. Crawling through the debris, managed to clear the wreckage and rescue the occupants.

GEORGE MEDAL
LG. 15/11/40

Rose	Sexton	Police Constable	D

During an air raid a house had been hit by a high explosive bomb. He managed to dig out the family trapped. The constable was working in hazardous conditions, a burst water pipe pouring over him, a concrete slab wedged against a glass door was the sole support of the whole of the upper floors.

GEORGE MEDAL
LG. 15/11/40

Jackson	Edward William Thomas	Police Constable	L
Parsons	Albert George	WR Police Constable	L

A high explosive bomb burst in South East London, Jackson and Parsons rescued several people from debris. They were told of a man trapped on the top floor, they found him pinioned by fallen debris and next to a leaking gas pipe. Jackson plugged the pipe, and using their shoulders to support the fallen roof they rescued the man.

GEORGE MEDAL
LG. 15/11/40

Young	Harold Isaac William	Station Sergeant	L

After an air raid a large number of houses had been demolished. Gas main was fractured near to electric cables. The Sergeant regardless of personal safety entered the area to rescue people trapped. They could not use lights as enemy aircraft were circling overhead. On another occasion 2 parachutists were seen falling in the same neighbourhood, when he was a short distance away there was a loud explosion. This was caused by land mines the parachutists were carrying. Young was blown off his feet.

KING'S COMMENDATION FOR BRAVE CONDUCT
LG. 15/11/40

Atkins	Richard Harry MacDonald	Police Constable	V
Carpenter	Harry Gordon Peppiatt	Police Constable	X
Comley	Sidney John	Police Constable	J
Franklin	Charles Frederick	Police Constable	X
George	Ernest Walter	Inspector	X

Hammerton	Richard David	WR Police Constable	L
Hogarth	Thomas	Police Sergeant	G
Kelly	Brian Corkery	Police Constable	N
Lewin	Robert Frederick William	Police Constable	X
Lowery	Bernard	Police Constable	X
Lowes	Alfred Thomas	Police Sergeant	S
McKechnie	Albert	Stn Police Sergeant	M
Mawer	Stuart	Police Constable	X
Mulliken	Robert Edward	Police Constable	V
Murphy	Joseph Alston	Police Sergeant	F
Osborne	Alexander David	Police Sergeant	J
Shipton	Alfred Leonard	Inspector	X
Smith	Stephen	Police Constable	G
Stevens	Maurice Arthur	Police Constable	D
Thompson	James Easton	Police Constable	J
Trim	Harry Richard William	Police Constable	G

For Civil Defence

ROLL OF HONOUR

* Wrpc Ernest Taylor

Fell from a wall while extinguishing a light during the blackout in Chelsea.

* Pc Alexander McKinnon,

113807, Y, aged 37

* Pc Alexander Bruce
* WRPC, 08567, X, aged 40
* Pc Thomas O B Cockbury
* WRPC, 08573, X, aged 44
* Pc Henry Thomas Brooks

Accidentally shot with a police revolver at Chelsea Police Station.

* Wrpc Jack William Avery

Stabbed by a man sketching gun emplacements in Hyde Park.

* Spc Herbert George Ross-Myring

Killed on duty in a cycling accident on Croydon Division.

1941

January	German actress Marlene Dietrich becomes a US citizen.
February	War is now costing Britain £11 million a day.
March	London and the South East becomes the main target for the Luftwaffe's spring night raids.
April	The war budget raises income tax to around 50%.
May	German Battleship Bismark is sunk.
June	The RAF reveals that 'radio location' has been Britain's key weapon against German bombing.

July   London has 15 hrs and 48 mins of sunshine making this the capital's sunniest day of the century.

August   Soviet air force carries out its first raid on the German capital Berlin.

September   Jews are ordered to wear a yellow Star of David when out in public in Germany.

October   Hitler nears the gates of Moscow.

November   HMS Ark Royal is torpedoed by an Italian Submarine, finally sank while under tow.

December   The Japanese attack Pearl Harbour.

HITS OF THE YEAR
Boogie-woogie bugle boy
White cliffs of Dover
How green was my valley

KING'S POLICE & FIRE SERVICE MEDAL GEORGE VI ISSUE

KING'S POLICE MEDAL
LG. 1/1/41

Bridge   William Alfred   Police Constable   110180 B

At about 1.30 pm on 30th August 1939 at Wyfold Road, Fulham, constable Bridge and another officer were keeping observation on a Jaguar motor car, which they had been informed was being used by two well known criminals. A short time later, a Humber motor car drew up, and one man got out of it, and got into the Jaguar. Constable Bridge ran up, and seized the man, but after a violent struggle, the man broke away and got back into the Humber. The constables jumped on the running board, and tried to get the man out. However the car accelerated away, with constable Bridge hanging on, as the driver swerved from side the side, trying to throw him off. Eventually the car was stopped and two of the occupants arrested. When the two cars were searched, it was found that both contained a large quantity of stolen jewellery. A monetary award was also made from the Bow Street Fund.

KING'S POLICE MEDAL
LG. 1/1/41

Myers   George Thomas   Special Constable   007906 H

At about 5.20 pm on 22nd January 1940 a pair of horses attached to a van, bolted along Vallance Road, Stepney towards Bethnal Green Road. Special constable Myers was some distance away, when he saw the horses approaching at a fast speed. As they entered Squirries Street he ran into the roadway, and threw himself across the neck of the offside horse and grabbed the reins. He was dragged along for about 250 yards, before bringing the horses to a standstill. It was a dark evening, and there were many pedestrians about. A monetary award was also made from the Bow Street Fund.

KING'S POLICE MEDAL
LG. 1/1/41

Pateman	Alfred John	Police Constable	122542 G

At about 1.10 am on the 24th December 1939 constable Pateman was in Bethnal Green Road when he saw that a gate at the entrance to a shop had been broken open. He was just pulling aside a curtain hanging over the shop doorway, when he was hit in the face, and two men came out of the doorway. The constable seized one of them, the other running away. After a short struggle, the man was arrested, and as constable Pateman was taking the prisoner to the police station, three other men attacked him, and he received several severe blows to the face, breaking a tooth, and his nose. The constable dragged the prisoners into a doorway, and felt for his whistle, but found that it had been wrenched from his coat. For several minutes the men set about the constable who refused to let his prisoner go. Eventually a passer-by telephoned for assistance, and when a police car arrived the most violent attacker was chased and caught. A monetary award was also made from the Bow Street Fund.

KING'S POLICE MEDAL
LG. 1/1/41

Barton	James Thomas	Police Constable	113708 V
Pritlove	Thomas Joseph	Police Constable	119079 V

On 22nd December 1940 at about 5 pm two armed men entered the post office at Petersham Road, Ham, Surrey and robbed the postmistress of cash and a purse. Constables Barton and Pritlove were patrolling in a police car nearby, when they saw two men running from the post office in a suspicious manner. Being unaware of the robbery at the time, they decided to stop and question the men. Constable Barton got out of the police car and called on them to stop, but as they did, one of the men pointed a sawn off shotgun at the constable and the other growled 'give it to him in the guts'. Constable Pritlove drove the police car at the men, and as they were distracted, constable Barton grabbed the gun from the criminal. As constable Barton called to his colleague to get the rifles from the police car, the men surrendered without further resistance. Both officers received a monetary award from the Bow Street Fund.

GEORGE MEDAL
LG. 9/5/41

Coker	Frederick George	Inspector	S
Hite	Vernon Thomas	Special Police Constable	S

BRITISH EMPIRE MEDAL FOR GALLANTRY

Lee	Charles Henry	Special Constable	S
Orr	Charles Robert	Sub Inspector	S
Payne	Gerald Frederick	Sub Div Inspector	S

When severe damage was caused by enemy action Inspector Coker went to the scene with other officers and took charge of police arrangements. He assembled his men and began a systematic search of bombed houses, rescuing people, extinguishing fires and arranging for evacuation where necessary. Despite the fact that they had no equipment of any kind, many splendid and heroic rescues were achieved by these officers, who continually risked their lives in appalling conditions.

BRITISH EMPIRE MEDAL FOR GALLANTRY
LG. 9/5/41

| Brown | James Wilson | Police Constable | L |

Bombs demolished dwelling houses and a water main was fractured. The street and gardens flooded to a depth of nearly two feet and bomb craters rapidly filled with water. Pc Brown and Warden Bird waded to the wrecked premises and found people marooned on the tops of Anderson Shelters. The depth of water was increasing and some elderly people were still inside the shelters in water up to their waists. The two men assisted them on to the tops of sheds and carried the women and children through the partly demolished houses to higher ground. Eventually forty five people were brought to safety.

BRITISH EMPIRE MEDAL FOR GALLANTRY
LG. 20/6/41

| Jackson | Alfred William | Inspector | N |

Inspector Jackson has displayed outstanding initiative and leadership throughout the whole period of intense enemy air activity. By his coolness and courage he has set a splendid example to the men under him.

BRITISH EMPIRE MEDAL FOR GALLANTRY
LG. 15/8/41

| Grey | Herbert Frederick | Police Sergeant | H |

Several houses were completely demolished and a number of others severely damaged during an enemy attack. Police Sergeant Grey accompanied by other officers, immediately went to the scene and organised his party in the rescue of trapped persons. There was every likelihood of a further collapse of debris and there was also a strong leakage of gas but the Sergeant led his men with great confidence and skill and their combined efforts were successful in releasing many trapped persons. Many of the rescued owe their lives to the splendid efforts of Sergeant Grey who has shown courage and outstanding qualities of leadership throughout the period of enemy air activity.

BRITISH EMPIRE MEDAL FOR GALLANTRY
LG. 26/9/41

| Bartlett | Gilbert James A | Sub Div Inspector | L |

Bombs demolished several houses under which people were sheltering. Inspector Bartlett made a tunnel ten feet long into the mass of unstable debris and found two injured women. He rendered first aid and then pulled them slowly out. Renewing his search he discovered more casualties whose injuries were such that under the direction of a doctor he administered morphia. He was joined by Leaders, Searle and Smith. Owing to the confined space it was necessary for the three men to work lying down and while so doing debris and masonry was continually falling on them. After four hours strenuous effort six persons were released.

BRITISH EMPIRE MEDAL FOR GALLANTRY

LG. 26/9/41

Cockburn	Herbert	Police Sergeant	B

A bomb demolished dwelling houses and a woman was trapped in the debris. Sergeant Cockburn took charge of the rescue operations and, lying full length, started tunnelling. After working for an hour sufficient debris was removed to enable him to reach the victim but she was pinned in a chair by surrounding timber which was supporting the mass of rubble overhead. Sergeant Cockburn, at great risk to himself, cut through the wood and arm of the chair and the woman was finally released.

BRITISH EMPIRE MEDAL FOR GALLANTRY

LG. 26/9/41

Sloan	William	Inspector	G
Bond	Henry Lauriston	Police Constable	G

A bomb hit a block of flats and people were buried. Inspector Sloan and constable Bond released ten people from beneath the debris and then organised a search for a man known to be buried in a ground floor flat. After digging for half an hour the victim was located. A wall and concrete floor above them were swaying dangerously but the rescuers shored up the mass of concrete and brick with roof joists. A hole was made between two of the blocks but the man could not be reached. A small hole was made through a fourteen inch wall of the adjoining ground-floor flat and, although gas was escaping, Inspector Sloan and constable Bond crawled in and with great difficulty managed to free the victim. As he was removed a mass of debris came down on to the place where he had been lying.

BRITISH EMPIRE MEDAL FOR GALLANTRY

LG. 3/10/41

Honour	William Albert	Superintendent	B
Nightingale	John Cyprian	Station Inspector	B
Watkins	Wyndham Vavasor	Police Constable	B
Falk	Alan David	Warden Civil Defence	

A bomb caused damage to property and fires started. A man was trapped under debris on the second floor of a building, the roof and top floor of which had fallen in. The outer wall had been blown out and the remaining wall was likely to collapse. In addition a fire was raging in the adjoining house and another at premises opposite. Superintendent Honour, with Nightingale, Watkins and Falk, reached the second floor and found the victim lying on a bed covered with plaster and other debris from the floors above. The heat from the fires increased but the four men began to remove the debris with their hands. Great care was necessary to ensure that no undue vibration was caused. After a time the man was partially uncovered but he was still pinned down by a broken joist which had fallen across the upper part of his body. The removal of this joist was attended by considerable danger as any movement was likely to cause a further collapse of the wall. Great gallantry was shown by the rescuers and after they had worked for an hour the trapped man was released without having suffered any serious injury.

GEORGE MEDAL

LG. 31/1/41

Bass   Harry   Police Sergeant

Two heavy bombs partially demolished a large 4 storey building. He immediately crawled into the basement and rescued an injured woman. On another occasion he led a party to rescue a man buried 12 ft below a pile of debris and also assisted a party to rescue a small boy also buried.

GEORGE MEDAL

LG. 31/1/41

Crump   John Henry   Police Constable

A bomb demolished a house causing a fire and trapping a number of people. He was off duty at the time, eventually rescued a 70 yr. woman. On another occasion at a block of flats hit by a high explosive bomb he managed to free a woman buried in the debris.

GEORGE MEDAL

LG. 31/1/41

Davison   Jackson Sweeting   Police Sergeant

Three houses demolished by enemy bombing. The rescue of the trapped occupants, he rescued a small girl from the second floor, but she died later.

GEORGE MEDAL

LG. 31/1/41

Bates   Harry Jesse   Inspector

Rescue of 3 young children and a woman from a house that suffered a direct hit. He had to tunnel under the debris to reach the trapped. All four were eventually rescued alive.

GEORGE MEDAL

LG. 14/2/41

Douglas   William Edward   Station Sergeant

While off duty he assisted in the rescue of a man and 2 girls trapped beneath the debris of a house. Douglas found a small gap beneath the ceiling and started to worm his was towards the trapped people. He found the 2 girls pinned beneath brickwork, he was able to free one girl, eventually the second girl was freed, unfortunately the man was dead.

GEORGE MEDAL

LG. 14/2/41

Burgess   Frederick Maurice   Police Sergeant   J

Rescue of 8 persons trapped in wreckage in the basement area of a dwelling. They were unharmed but a water pipe had burst and was gushing in. He managed to enter via a hole and helped the 8 onto a ledge from which they were pulled to safety.

GEORGE MEDAL
LG. 14/2/41

Burgoyne	Henry	Police Constable	D
James	John Phillip	Police Constable	D

A block of flats was demolished and a large gas leak was evident. James had commenced searching for victims but was overcome by the gas and had to seek treatment. After Burgoyne arrived a cry was heard. Constable Burgoyne began to clear away debris from the roof and went to the area where the cry came from. James now recovered and went to assist Burgoyne. The roof was shored up, they eventually extricated a woman but she died on the way to hospital. After great difficulty another female who was unconscious was freed, she recovered.

GEORGE MEDAL
LG. 14/2/41

Allen	William Henry	Police Constable	G

A high explosive bomb exploded resulting in the demolition of property. So extensive was the devastation that the rescue squad were of the opinion that any person trapped must be dead. After hearing faint cries Allen crawled into a hole and found 2 elderly men and 2 young girls pinioned beneath debris. The 2 girls and one man were rescued uninjured. The other had serious injuries. After first aid was administered the second man was rescued. When he was sure that no more were trapped inside Allen crawled to safety.

GEORGE MEDAL
LG. 17/2/41

Almond	Charles Frederick	Special Police Constable

He tunnelled below a mass of overhanging debris and managed to uncover a man buried sufficiently for a hypodermic injection to be given. The man was later rescued and fully recovered.

GEORGE MEDAL
LG. 14/3/41

Grigg	David Lionel	Police Sergeant	P

German aircraft crashed into 2 dwelling houses burying the residents. Four persons were rescued slightly injured. Several bombs still attached to the aircraft were amongst the debris, 2 more occupants buried underneath. The bombs had to be removed before they could be rescued. Grigg volunteered to carry the bombs from the wreckage. He then crawled beneath the debris and located a trapped victim who was eventually rescued.

GEORGE MEDAL
LG. 21/3/41

Dean	George Herbert	Police Constable	
Mead	John William Turner	Police Constable	
Slowley	Roy Victor	Police Constable	127948
Tricker	Ernest John	Police Constable	

A factory premises received a direct hit by high explosive bombs, the whole building quickly caught fire. Mead Tricker and Slowley arrived and were joined by Cain a boy aged 15 yrs., he knew several people were trapped in the private basement shelter directly underneath the fire. Eventually they found their way in, passing burning wreckage, paint, water and live electric wires dropping around them. They speedily freed 6 men from the wreckage and carried them on doors and planks to safety. A few minutes after the 6th was removed the whole interior of the building collapsed.

Constable Slowley joined the RAF as a Flight Sergeant and was killed in 1944 on active service.

GEORGE MEDAL
LG. 28/3/41

| Griffiths | Willis | Police Constable | Y |

Bombs practically demolished a house and fractured a gas and water main. A woman was trapped inside. Slowly crawling through, Griffiths removed debris enough for a doctor to reach the woman. The woman was trapped by a spring mattress. Pliers were given to Griffiths who managed to release the woman and take her to safety.

GEORGE MEDAL
LG. 7/4/41

| Deacon | Graham | Special Police Constable |

A man of 60 yrs. was trapped in a ground floor room of a ruined house. The only access was a small hole. Being a small man Deacon volunteered to enter, he reached the man and stayed with him for 2 hours and helped the doctor in giving first aid. Both were finally rescued.

GEORGE MEDAL
LG. 25/4/41

| Gilbert | Ernest Frederick | WR Police Constable |
| Whitmore | George | Police Constable |

A man and his wife were trapped in the basement of a 3 storey house which had collapsed. The man was quickly freed. In order to reach the woman they burrowed with their bare hands. With much difficulty she was taken out by the tunnel they had dug.

GEORGE MEDAL
LG. 9/5/41

| Finbow | Leslie Ernest | Police Constable | E |

Rescue of 3 women from a demolished building, they took a further 4 hours rescuing a man, fires were breaking out, heavy debris had to be moved also gas was escaping from a fractured pipe.

GEORGE MEDAL
LG. 13/6/41

| Flett | James Frederick John S | Police Constable | K |
| Stone | Leon | Police Constable | K |

A high explosive bomb exploded trapping a little girl. Stone made a hole in the debris and Flett was lowered down. He first extinguished a fire burning in the fire place. Stone then entered and a search was started for the child. She was found pinned beneath a slab of brickwork. With a crowbar they levered up the brickwork and extricated the child who was taken to hospital.

GEORGE MEDAL
LG. 18/7/41

Bridle	William Henry	Police Constable	M

A high explosive bomb demolished a building, Bridle without hesitation reached the wreckage and found a man almost buried in the rubble. He cleared the rubble from his face so that morphine could be administered. He then made a hole 6 feet deep and a small tunnel, he then reached the man. After a long struggle the man was released. Bridle had to cut through a steel bed which was pinning down the casualty.

GEORGE MEDAL
LG. 27/7/41

Coomber	Sidney Cyril	Detective Constable	D
Grose	Reginald George	Police Constable	D
Pope	Edwin John	Police Constable	D

Buildings were damaged, Coomber and Grose entered one house and found several men lying severely injured and one man trapped. They removed all of them to safety. On the second floor, on removing debris one man was released and lowered to the ground. A third man was found and eventually rescued. Pope who was on duty nearby was thrown to the ground by the force of the explosion, he attended to two severely injured, and helped seven to safety. The officers were rescuing while an air raid was in progress.

GEORGE MEDAL
LG. 8/8/41

Foster	George Edmund	Police Sergeant	M

A building was completely demolished by a high explosive bomb and people were trapped inside. Gas and water was escaping from fractured mains, the water rising rapidly. Foster at once took charge aided by 2 others who were off duty at the time. Gradually tunnelling towards the cellar 3 women were rescued. The officers unable to find the 2 men trapped left just as a wall collapsed.

GEORGE MEDAL
LG. 22/8/41

Block	Ralph Cyril	Police Constable	B

Several houses were demolished by bombs and several people were trapped. A faint cry for help was heard. Block along with an ARP warden tunnelled towards the sound. They eventually reached a woman who was pinned down by rafters. The men cut through the rafters with a saw. Gas and water was escaping along with ammonia fumes from a damaged fridge, but after 2 hours she was extricated and carried to safety.

GEORGE MEDAL

LG. 29/8/41

Gordon	Albert Victor	WR Police Constable	W
Young	William Henry	WR Police Constable	W

A high explosive bomb partially demolished a house and a woman was trapped. Despite the danger, Young burrowed a hole large enough to work in and after 2 hours they cleared sufficient rubble to extricate the woman. In the meantime Gordon entered the wreckage from another direction, he remained in a cramped space and comforted the woman until she was rescued. An air raid was in progress at the time.

GEORGE MEDAL

LG. 5/9/41

Cox	William George	Police Sergeant	E
Rosie	George Murdoch	Police Sergeant	E

A high explosive bomb damaged a house, the upper two floors collapsed and a fire broke out. The two Sergeants climbed through a ground floor window and found a man pinned under a large boulder and considerable debris. They began to remove the rubble with their bare hands and after half an hour liberated the man. The whole structure collapsed shortly afterwards.

GEORGE MEDAL

LG. 12/9/41

Burrows	Charles Henry	Police Constable	E

A block of flats was partly demolished by bombs. He went to the rear of the flats where persons were injured and trapped. He directed several civilians who had accompanied him to remain outside while he went in to look for casualties. He found men, women and children, some severely injured and pinned under piles of debris. He rendered first aid to the more seriously injured and carried them to the outside of the building.

GEORGE MEDAL

LG. 19/9/41

Brandon	Henry James Burke	Police Constable	N

Bombs demolished several houses and fractured gas and water mains. He climbed up the remains of a staircase and was able to release 4 people who were trapped. In another house he made a small hole to where a woman was trapped, a strong escape of gas from a broken main was evident, he crawled through but was overcome by the gas and had to withdraw. When he had recovered he re entered and managed to free the woman. While dragging the woman out some debris was dislodged and fell on his head stunning him.

GEORGE MEDAL

LG. 21/11/41

Blake	Frederick John	Station Sergeant	H
Edwards	Walter Rees	Police Constable	H
Hall	Leonard Dennis	Police Constable	H

A bomb fell on a warehouse and the whole structure collapsed onto a large public shelter, the roof blown and all the entrances blocked. Hall and Edwards who were off duty volunteered to attend under the leadership of Sergeant Blake. Many tons of debris was piled around the shelter and there was a constant danger of collapse. The three men tunnelled their was through the debris and found 4 trapped and injured people, these were freed and carried out. On continuing their search they found and rescued several more people.

GEORGE MEDAL
LG. 13/6/41

Hales   Charles Arthur   Police Sergeant   K

A cinema was set on fire during an air raid. Hales with other officers and a fireman entered the building. Bombs were dropped and all the men were thrown to the ground. Hales the first to recover picked up one policeman and carried him down the stairs to the street. He then returned and brought out a war reserve police officer in the same manner. The building now well alight he again entered and found the fireman unconscious, Hales was too exhausted to carry him so he dragged him to safety.

GEORGE MEDAL
LG. 31/1/41

Hughes   Leslie Francis   Police Constable

A large building was hit by a high explosive bomb, he entered the rubble and rescued 2 women who were trapped. He also managed to extricate an imprisoned first aid worker who was taken to hospital in an unconscious condition.

GEORGE MEDAL
LG. 28/3/41

James   Evan John   Police Sergeant   M
Riddle   Matthew   Police Constable   M

Bombs were dropped on a garage near where people were sheltering. Fires were started and oil containers exploded. James and Riddle forced their was through the flames which were several feet high and searched the whole premises. When they were sure no one was inside they turned their activities to preventing the fire reaching the petrol tank. With the help of a working party they also managed to move nearly 100 vehicles which would have been destroyed.

GEORGE MEDAL
LG. 7/2/41

Johnson   Stanley William   Police Constable

Several houses were destroyed by high explosive bombs. Two people were trapped, one so deep it was necessary to tunnel under the debris. Johnson volunteered for the work and eventually managed to rescue the man. He then burrowed still further and reached a woman, she too was eventually rescued.

GEORGE MEDAL

LG. 31/1/41

Keery   William James   Police Constable

After a heavy bomb demolished a large part of a block of dwellings he entered and managed to rescue 7 occupants by clearing debris and dropping down into a hole.

GEORGE MEDAL

LG. 27/7/41

Leslie   James William Crichton   Police Constable   L

A high explosive bomb partially demolished a house and a little girl was trapped. He tunnelled beneath the debris towards the girl but was unable to reach her. Finally by removing debris piece by piece he reached the girl. Her arm was trapped; it took one and a half hours to eventually rescue her.

GEORGE MEDAL

LG. 25/4/41

Mahir   Thomas Edward   Station Inspector   H

Goff   John Aidan Hastings   Junior Station Inspector   H

BRITISH EMPIRE MEDAL FOR GALLANTRY

Sneddon   Alexander   Police Sergeant   117762 H

When a bomb demolished two houses, the roof and chimney stack of one house fell across the ruins of the other and the whole formed a heap of wreckage about fifteen feet high. Station Inspector Mahir and Junior station Inspector Gott tore away debris and found a hole down which Mahir crawled. A man, buried up to the chin was pinned down by a rafter, in a cavity about seven feet deep and two feet wide. Goff had the mouth of the hold widened and then crawled down to join Mahir. They reached the man who informed them that a friend was below him and Mahir crawled out to investigate while Goff took on his shoulders the weight of the debris above the mans head. At this point Sergeant Sneddon arrived from another incident and Mahir showed him where the other man was thought to be whilst he himself returned to relieve Goff. Sneddon sent his men to collect buckets from nearby houses to carry away the rubble and organised their work so well that the man was soon released.

There was a lot of rubble and the strain on the two Inspectors was greatly increased. The whole of the pile was nearly brought down on to the three men when outside tried to dig through to them. Mahir and Goff used the broken rafter to shore up the cavity and sawed through a bedstead and a sofa, eventually releasing the victim who was only slightly injured.

Mahir, Goff and Sneddon were throughout subjected to being crushed by shifting rubble and from leaking gas. At one time water from the burst main in the crater outside threatened to overflow into the hole in which the two inspectors were working.

The inspectors showed resourcefulness, courage and determination and were ably supported by Sergeant Sneddon.

GEORGE MEDAL

LG. 25/4/41

Mann   Charles George Toni   Police Constable   L

A man was trapped 30 feet from the ground on first floor of a house which had been partially demolished by a bomb. The ladder only reached 18 feet. Constable Mann mounted the ladder and managed to reach the man by stretching and placing his foot on the damaged frame work of the window. The man was encouraged to climb out backwards and lower himself. The constable took most of the man's weight on his right hand and lowered him onto his shoulders. He then climbed down the ladder.

GEORGE MEDAL

LG. 31/1/41

Martin   Albert Victor   Police Sergeant

He crawled through debris to rescue a woman trapped beneath the wreckage. While inside the wall of an adjoining property collapsed on them. The female became hysterical, but eventually both were rescued.

GEORGE MEDAL

LG. 5/9/41

Martin   Jasper   Police Sergeant   V

A high explosive bomb caused extensive damage to a house. A man and his mother were trapped underneath a partially demolished stair case. Sergeant Martin crawled into the wreckage and succeeded in rescuing the injured man. He then re entered in an attempt to rescue the woman, she was pinned down by masonry and after ascertaining she was dead he crawled out of the debris, reaching safety just before the wall collapsed onto the staircase.

GEORGE MEDAL

LG. 12/9/41

McFarlane   Neil Robertson   Police Sergeant   G
Sherlaw   James Alexander   Police Sergeant   G

A bomb was dropped outside a building the basement of which was used as a public air raid shelter. Water from a burst main flooded into the basement. McFarlane, on removing some debris, he saw a warden trapped in the cellar below who was in danger of drowning. He managed to get a rope round the victim and eventually succeeded in dragging him to safety. In the meantime Sherlaw working up to the waist in water, cleared some debris and extricated several women who were moved to safety. They again entered and saved two more men. Shortly after leaving the premises the roof collapsed.

GEORGE MEDAL

LG. 5/9/41

McKenning   John Ernest   Police Constable   B
Oakes   Reginald Ivor   Police Constable   B

High explosive bombs fell on a building leaving a chasm 12 ft across and 40 ft deep. Cries for help were coming from a room on the opposite side. They obtained a plank of wood 9 inches wide and passed it over the gap, they crossed to the other side. They reached a room where 4 people were trapped. They helped them out of the room across the plank and to safety.

GEORGE MEDAL
LG. 31/1/41

Morrison   Thomas Arthur   WR Police Constable

A block of flats demolished by high explosive, after some hours police attended, after they had left a delayed action bomb exploded killing a number of members of the rescue and demolition party. Police entered the premises and found a man trapped. Morrison supported him while others removed the debris, he was eventually rescued. Approximately one hour later the remainder of the building collapsed.

GEORGE MEDAL
LG. 5/9/41

Noble   Ronald   Junior Station Inspector   X

A high explosive bomb caused extensive damage to property and people were trapped in the wreckage. Noble who was off duty was blown over by the blast but quickly went to the scene. On the first floor of a block of flats he found a woman in a hysterical condition. Hooking his legs round a beam hanging upside down he managed to lower her to the ground. He then heard shouts from another home, he cleared the rubble and found an unconscious woman whom he pulled to safety.

GEORGE MEDAL
LG. 25/4/41

Pedrick   Brinley Thomas   WR Police Constable   L

BRITISH EMPIRE MEDAL FOR GALLANTRY
Bignal   WR Police Constable   14560 L

A family were trapped in the rubble of a demolished house, gas and water services had been disrupted, and there was a danger of flooding and asphyxiation. Tunnelling into the premises using only a pocket knife the man was released. Pedrick continued and found the woman unconscious, she was dragged to safety.

BRITISH EMPIRE MEDAL FOR GALLANTRY
Tarbit   Osmond Edward Albert   Inspector   113004 S

Inspector Tarbit has displayed excellent leadership and efficient control on all occasions during air raids. He has dealt with unexploded time bombs in a fearless and capable manner. His disregard of personal danger his cool demeanour were praiseworthy and set his men a magnificent example.

BRITISH EMPIRE MEDAL FOR GALLANTRY

Hill   Basil Edward   Police Constable   127375 E

A block of flats was severely damaged by a bomb. Police constable Hill heard cries of help coming from beneath the wreckage, on top of which was lying a huge slab of masonry. Wardens and police succeeded in lifting the end of the slab and a man's hand was then exposed It was only possible for one person to work under the slab and constable Hill immediately started removing debris and passing it backwards in this way he gradually reached the victim who was in a cavity but unable to move. While he was working several bombs fell and there was a considerable danger that the wreckage would slip and crush the constable.

GEORGE MEDAL

LG. 6/6/41

Porter   Lambert Ernest   WR Police Constable   X

High explosive partially demolished a number of houses. Porter heard a small child crying under the debris. The child was buried under a sloping portion of a wall which was liable to collapse at any moment. He commenced to remove the debris and refused to cease work until the child was released. The child was only 12 months old.

GEORGE MEDAL

LG. 28/3/41

Pulham   John Charles   Inspector

Rescue of an elderly woman trapped in a bedroom by climbing a partially destroyed staircase. He carried her to safety. On another occasion he went to the rescue of a man trapped in a demolished building, he managed to wriggle under the wreckage and lifted it in such a way as to take the weight off the casualty.

GEORGE MEDAL

LG. 7/3/41

Schurmuly   William Joseph Conrad   Police Constable
Tanner   Thomas   WR Police Constable

Some houses were demolished by bombing, both were off duty, Tanner being in bed on the sick list. They went to the scene on hearing the explosion. Three women were extricated and carried to safety. They entered a second building where 5 women were rescued. While carrying out one of the casualties from the third floor the staircase collapsed, throwing them a distance of about 25 feet. The woman was fortunately thrown clear without injury but the two officers were injured.

GEORGE MEDAL

LG. 9/5/41

Taylor   Walter George   Police Constable

Several people were trapped in a demolished house. Taylor who was off duty assisted 2 women to safety, searched for a man trapped under the debris. Taylor at one stage had to support a large piece of masonry on his back while wreckage was pulled clear. As this was being done the ceiling fell on them partially burying them. Taylor was knocked insensible but quickly recovered. On re-entering the premises to continue his rescue work he collapsed and had to be taken to hospital.

GEORGE MEDAL

LG. 25/4/41

Thorne   Leonard Wilfred   Police Constable   C

A heavy bomb wrecked buildings, set them on fire and burst a water main. Thorne was standing in a shop doorway at the time of the explosion and was thrown into the road. Although badly shaken he reported the incident then began to search for casualties. On hearing cries for help from a public house, he released 3 men with the help of an ARP warden. They found a man beneath the debris and rescued him and continued to search for more casualties.

GEORGE MEDAL

LG. 14/2/41

Voizey   George Alfred John   WR Police Constable   F

Being the smallest member of 3 officers at the scene of bomb wreckage he volunteered to enter a small opening to try to reach trapped persons. A gas main had been fractured. He reached the victims, administered first aid, he tried to clear away the debris. He was gradually falling under the effects of the coal gas. One of the two women was eventually brought out alive.

KING'S COMMENDATION FOR BRAVE CONDUCT

LG. 21/3/41

Shillingford   Stanley James   Special Constable   V

For Civil Defence

KING'S COMMENDATION FOR BRAVE CONDUCT

LG. 9/5/41

Cummin	Arthur Stephen	Police Constable	E
Freston	Stanley George	WR Police Constable	K
May	Percival Thomas Frederick	Police Constable	E
Parker	William John	Police Constable	K
Telfer	Robert	Police Constable	S

For Civil Defence

KING'S COMMENDATION FOR BRAVE CONDUCT

LG. 13/6/41

Bedwell	Edward Miles	WR Police Constable	K
Gibson	Arthur	Inspector	X
Mulvaney	Thomas Frederick	Police Constable	K
Murray (Deceased)	Charles Edward	Police Sergeant	K

For Civil Defence

KING'S COMMENDATION FOR BRAVE CONDUCT
LG. 5/9/41

Candlish	William Basil	WR Police Constable	B
Hibbitt	Charles Edward	WR Police Constable	D
Lee	Charles George	Police Sergeant	B

For Civil Defence

KING'S COMMENDATION FOR BRAVE CONDUCT
LG. 12/9/41

Hardy	Alfred	WR Police Constable	G
Levy	Isaac	WR Police Constable	G
Phillips	John Alfred	WR Police Constable	G

For Civil Defence

KING'S COMMENDATION FOR BRAVE CONDUCT
LG. 19/9/41

Bennett (Deceased)	Frederick Ernest	Sub Division Inspector	K
Dalby	Charles Henry Alfred	Police Constable	Y
Davison	John	Police Sergeant	Y

For Civil Defence

KING'S COMMENDATION FOR BRAVE CONDUCT
LG. 26/9/41

Murphy	Donal John Francis	WR Police Constable	W
Quincey	John Josiah	Sub Division Inspector	G
Robinson	James	Police Sergeant	B
Sample	George Rennell	Police Constable	G
Smith	Malcolm McLennan	WR Police Constable	B

For Civil Defence

CARNEGIE HERO FUND
19/11/41

Hamovitch	Joseph	WR Police Constable

Suffered physically as a result of rescuing an elderly woman from drowning in the Grand Surrey Canal.

ROLL OF HONOUR
• Spc Arthur Cecil Guest
Killed accidentally by an instructor during a firearms training class.
• Spc William Sutch
Killed on duty in a cycling accident on Hammersmith Division.

1942

January	Japan laid siege to Singapore.
February	Sir Arthur Harris takes over as head of the RAF bomber command.
March	BBC broadcasts its first daily Morse code news bulletins to the French resistance.
April	Government in London bans embroidery on women's underwear and night wear.
May	US Navy signs up its first ever Black recruit.
June	Eisenhower to lead US forces in Europe.
July	UK sweet rationing begins and driving vehicles for pleasure is banned.
August	New Waterloo Bridge built through the blitz is opened.
September	The German SS slaughter the Jews in the Warsaw ghetto.
October	General Montgomery triumphs at El Alamein.
November	In the US coffee rationing begins.
December	Board of Education states it plans to make school meals permanent.

HITS OF THE YEAR
This is the army Mr Jones
White Christmas
We'll meet again

KING'S POLICE MEDAL
LG. 1/1/42

Kane	John	Station Sergeant	116727 CO

At about 11.20 pm on 15th March 1941 a man wearing soldier's uniform, who had been drinking and was suspected of being a deserter, was being taken to Streatham Police Station when he suddenly drew a revolver from under his coat, and pointing it at one of the officers threatened to fire. Station Sergeant Kane came out of the police station, and pursued the man down the street. Entering s shop doorway the man pointed the revolver at the Sergeant and threatened to shoot, but without hesitation the Sergeant closed with the man, and grabbed the revolver. On arrival of other officers, the man was overpowered and taken into custody. The weapon was found to be fully loaded and the man had 35 rounds of ammunition in his pocket. A monetary award was also made from the Bow Street Fund.

KING'S POLICE MEDAL
LG. 1/1/42

Collyer	Sidney	Police Constable	106158 Z
Lee	Frederick Walter	Police Constable	111639 Z

On the afternoon of 7th March 1941, constables Collyer and Lee who were in plain clothes were hiding in the front garden of a house in Carshalton keeping watch on a suspect. After he was seen knocking on the door, the man picked up a stone and broke a window. The two officers left their hiding place and went to arrest him, as he was putting his arm through the window. As he turned, the constables seized him, and held his arms, and arrested him. As he struggled he got one arm free, and immediately pulled out a revolver from his coat pocket, and put it into constable Lee's stomach threatening to kill him. Constable Collyer pushed the weapon down as the man pulled the trigger and the shot went into Lee's thigh. The man immediately turned and fired at Collyer, hitting him in the stomach. He then fired a second shot into constable Lee's leg and ran off. Both officers, although wounded, chased him, and caught the man and held him down after a violent struggle until other officers arrived and overpowered him, and took him to the police station. Both officers were detained in hospital with bullet wounds.

KING'S POLICE MEDAL
LG. 1/1/42

Barnes   Douglas Martin   Police Constable   127419 C

At about 11 pm on 2nd April 1941 constable Barnes was with another officer, and they had been given the description of two soldiers who had committed a robbery at a shop in Piccadilly that day. They saw a group of soldiers leaving a public house in Dean Street and followed them into Wardour Street, where in view of their rowdy behaviour, constable Barnes advised them to go away. The party dispersed except for two soldiers, and suspecting one of them might be a deserter, constable Barnes went to question him, but he made off. After following the men for some time, constable Barnes stopped one of the men, who pulled out a gun and fired twice at him, and then ran off. The man fired again on the run, and eventually was tackled by a civilian whom he had shot in the leg to get away again. After a further chase, during which the man continued to fire on the constable until the weapon was empty, whereupon he threw it at the constable. The man was caught, and overpowered, and subsequently identified as one of the robbers.

KING'S POLICE MEDAL
LG. 11/6/42

Bannister   John   Police Sergeant   122507 N

At about 3.40 am on 15th October 1941 Sergeant Bannister was told that fire had broken out at a house in Farleigh Road, Stoke Newington, and some people were believed to be trapped. He immediately gave the alarm at the fire post, then ran to the scene. The house was burning fiercely, and he was told of three people trapped on the upper floor. He dashed through the front door, climbed the burning staircase, and entered the bedroom where he saw a woman and child lying on the bed, with another woman on the floor nearby. He grabbed the child aged 7 and carried her out to safety, returned to the bedroom and picked up one of the women and carried her out, before he was overcome and collapsed. Help came too late for the other woman, and she was dead when found. An award was also made from the Society for Protection of Life from Fire and a monetary award from the Bow Street Fund.

KING'S POLICE MEDAL
LG. 11/6/42

McVernon   John   Detective Constable   123992 B

On 11th September 1941 detective constable McVernon went to a house in Bessborough Street, Pimlico to question a man and a woman about a larceny case. After denying any knowledge of the offence, the man suddenly produced a revolver. The constable went towards the man and told him to put the gun down, to which the man threatened to shoot if he did not sit down. The constable sat on the arm of a chair and the man then backed away, out of the door and ran downstairs. Detective constable McVernon followed, and the man fired a shot at him, which missed. There then followed a long chase through several streets, until the man stole a pedal cycle and rode away. The officer jumped on a passing motor car and directed the driver to follow and eventually the driver knocked the fugitive off the cycle with the front of the car. The man then ran into some flats, whereupon the detective constable obtained assistance and when the flat was entered it was found the man had shot himself in the leg. A monetary award was also made from the Bow Street Fund.

KING'S POLICE MEDAL
LG. 11/6/42

| Monteith | William | Detective Constable | 121500 Z |

On 5th November 1941 detective constable Monteith suspecting that a youth, who had previously escaped from custody, was in a house in Wallington, decided to search the premises. He went into an upstairs bedroom, where he found the youth hiding in a wardrobe. As the officer approached, the youth stood up and pointed a revolver at him, saying that he was going to shoot. The officer told him not to be foolish, but he again threatened to fire. As the officer moved forwards, the youth pushed the weapon against his body, and a short struggle took place, as a result of which the officer got possession of the weapon and the youth was arrested. A monetary award was also made from the Bow Street Fund.

KING'S POLICE MEDAL
LG. 11/6/42

| Oliver | William | Police Sergeant | 118153 Z |

Sergeant Oliver, in company with a constable stopped two men in South End, Croydon at 12.15 am on 4th February 1942 and asked them for their identity cards. The men were questioned about a box of stockings they were carrying, but could not give a satisfactory account, so they were taken to a police box so that transport could be summoned. As the Sergeant finished the call to the station, one of the men drew a revolver pointed it at the Sergeant and said 'stick them up you bastard, I've got one in the spout and I'm going to put daylight through you'. The Sergeant shouted a warning to the constable and jumped on the gunman forcing him to the ground. During the struggle the man again stuck the gun in the Sergeant's ribs, but with the help of the constable, the gun was wrestled away, and both men were arrested.

KING'S POLICE MEDAL
LG. 11/6/42

| Potter | William | Police Sergeant | 115615 |

At about 1.20 pm on 27th February 1942 Sergeant Potter who was in plain clothes along with two constables, was in South Mimms when he was approached by a man who asked the way to Hatfield. Sergeant Potter noted that the man's description was similar to that of a Canadian soldier wanted for the murder of a police Sergeant in Bognor Regis. He also noted the man had a Canadian accent. The Sergeant asked him to produce his identity card, and the man produced one in the name of Kathleen Meathrel, with an address in Bognor Regis. Sergeant Potter concluded that his was the wanted man, but as he did so, the man pulled a revolver, pressed it into Sergeant Potters side and said 'I've just shot two, I'll shoot you as well'. The man then took the Sergeant hostage, and began to walk him along the road. The constables ran to call assistance, which arrived quickly and one constable arrived with a pistol. After a few minutes when threats were exchanged, the man's attention was momentarily distracted. Sergeant Potter quickly grabbed the weapon and disarmed the man and he was arrested. A monetary award was also made from the Bow Street Fund.

CARNEGIE HERO FUND

Lewis   WR Police Constable   14723 L

For courageous conduct in rescuing a woman from drowning in the Grand Surrey Canal, Camberwell, also a monetary award of £10.

CARNEGIE HERO FUND

Bannister   Police Sergeant   122507 N

For outstanding bravery in rescuing two persons from a burning dwelling house, also received £15 reward.

ROLL OF HONOUR

- Ps Edwin Towers

Died after being concerned in an accident while travelling on a prison van.

- Spc William Grout

Killed on duty in a cycle accident on Wood Green Division.

1943

January	In the UK only standard grey or blue school uniforms will be allowed to save on dye.
February	US Actor Errol Flynn cleared of 3 rape charges.
March	178 crushed to death at air raid shelter at Bethnal Green tube station.
April	Government to introduce a unified National Health Service.
May	617 Squadron RAF bomb the dams on the Ruhr, led by Wing Commander Guy Penrose Gibson.
June	King George VI goes to Algiers to meet the allied troops.
July	Government introduces PAYE tax.
August	Uprising in the Jewish ghetto of Bialystock.
September	Poland reports that concentration camp inmates are being used for medical experiments.
October	Court of appeal in the UK rules that savings from the house keeping money belong to the husband.

November   RAF Wellington bombers using new techniques to allow night time precision bombing.

December   German battleship Scharnhorst sunk by the Royal Navy.

HITS OF THE YEAR
You'll never know
My heart and I
Casablanca

KING'S POLICE MEDAL
LG. 1/1/43

Beavis	Frank George	Inspector	108037 A
Drew	Ernest	Police Constable	122255 G

At about 10 pm on 2nd May 1942 a police officer in Diss Street, Shoreditch heard rifle shots being fired in a nearby street. As a result of initial enquiries, he called for assistance. Inspector Beavis together with constable Drew went to the scene, and as they approached two further shots were heard. The Inspector knocked on the front door and called for the man to open the door, stating that he was a police officer. The man shouted 'if you open this bloody door, I'll shoot the first one in'. Inspector Beavis kicked the door open and found the man facing him with a rifle and bayonet fixed. The man shut the door. Constable Drew then took a running kick at the door and both officers rushed in. The man was still holding the rifle and pointing it at the officers, but Inspector Beavis knocked the rifle up, and punched the man on the jaw, knocking him back. Constable Drew seized the rifle and the man was arrested. Both officers also received a monetary award from the Bow Street Fund.

KING'S POLICE MEDAL
LG. 1/1/43

Carpenter	Reginald	WR Police Constable	21275 T
Grant	George Sidney	Police Constable	115985 T
Lindsell	Charles	Police Constable	114269 T
Salter	Percy Henry	Police Constable	119391 T

At about 3.15 am on 21st May 1942 a Canadian soldier stationed in Surrey, stole a Thomson machine gun and a revolver from the armoury at his depot, and then held up the picket at the transport park, and stole a lorry, and headed for London. Cordons were set up across the main road at Bagshot and also at Egham, but the man drove straight through both of them. Constables Lindsell and Salter were directed to set up a road block at Staines Bridge, West London, and with constables Carpenter and Grant the waited. When the lorry approached, constable Lindsell switched on his headlights of his car, blinding the fugitive, causing him to swerve into the kerb. Constables Carpenter and Grant jumped up onto the cab of the lorry and disarmed the soldier before he could use any of the weapons. Constable Lindsell had sat in the car in the middle of the road, knowing that the lorry had already been driven through two cordons. All the officers received a monetary award from the Bow Street Fund.

KING'S POLICE MEDAL
LG. 2/6/43

Court   Dennis Sturgess   Police Constable   124678 X

At about 1.30 am on 8th October 1942 while two women were talking to an American soldier in Coventry Street, London, the soldier suddenly attacked one of them with a knife, and wounded her in the throat. He than ran away with the two women following. Constable Court and other officer gave chase, although not sure of the reason for the chase, and constable Court by going round the block cut off the soldier in Whitcombe Street. During questioning, the soldier suddenly stabbed the constable and ran off, with the constable in pursuit. After a further chase he was again stopped, and again stabbed the constable in the face. Although badly wounded, constable Court chased him again, and tackled him to the ground, whereupon he was arrested. A monetary award was also made from the Bow Street Fund.

GEORGE MEDAL
LG. 21/5/43

Gerrard   Albert William   WR Police Constable   K

Bombs had badly damaged a house and it had immediately caught fire. Gerrard was off duty at the time, and saw by the light of the flames inside the house a hand waving in the wreckage. After moving much debris he succeeded in reaching the waving hand, as he pulled at the man the ceiling above began to move. He propped it up with some joists and continued his rescue, eventually freeing the man. He returned to the hole where the man had been and extricated a woman. It was believed that 2 more women were inside, but they were in fact safe in a shelter.

CARNEGIE HERO FUND
30/6/43

Creedon   Richard M   Police Constable

Sustained injuries while stopping a runaway horse at Old Coulsdon.

ROLL OF HONOUR
- Pc Harry Pickett

Run down by a lorry while standing in the roadway questioning another lorry driver in Banstead.

1944
January   Midget cigar box sized radios will go on sale after the war for £6.
February   Stalingrad presented with the Sword of Honour from King George VI for admiration of the heroes of Stalingrad.
March   London, three women and a man are found guilty under the 1735 Witchcraft Act of pretending to be mediums.
April   UK Government bans all travel abroad.
May   RAF Mosquito aircraft successfully pinpoint and bomb a single target.
June   First V-1 bombs land in England.

July   Hitler escapes an assassination attempt in his HQ conference room.

August   first pipe line PLUTO (pipe line under the ocean) begins to send fuel from the
            Isle of Wight to Cherbourg.

September   First V-2 bomb lands and kills 3.

October   Paris De-Gaulle orders the resistance to disarm.

November   Lights switched on in Piccadilly, the Strand and Fleet Street after 5 years of
            blackout.

December   Germany 20 million people reported homeless after allied bombing.

HITS OF THE YEAR

There goes that song again

Mairzy doats

KING'S POLICE MEDAL

LG. 1/1/44

Page   Tom Alec   War Reserve Police Constable   24505

At 2 am on 7th June 1943 war reserve constable Page was making his way to Finchley Police
Station when he saw a light shining from a house in Lyndhurst Gardens. He went to
investigate, and through a gap in the curtains could see a case on the floor, with someone
standing close by. He knocked on the window, and the light went out. Suspecting that
something was wrong, he climbed into an air raid shelter, woke the occupiers in the
bedroom, and searched the house. The front door was open, and in his torch light he saw a
man at the gate. On approaching him the man, a soldier in uniform, pointed a rifle at him.
Keeping his torch focused on the mans face, he threw his truncheon at his head. The man
ran away and war reserve Page followed and confronted the soldier, who now fired a shot,
hitting the war reserve in the leg. The soldier then struck him in the face with the butt of the
rifle and ran off. The soldier was arrested later in the day.

KING'S POLICE MEDAL

LG. 1/1/44

Salmon   John Charles   Police Constable   123603 H

AT about 3.15 am on 8th February 1943 a fire broke out in a house in Somerford Street,
Bethnal Green. Constable Salmon saw flames coming from the ground floor, and a woman
at a first floor window shouting for help. He kicked open the front door and succeeded in
getting half way up the stairs before being beaten back by flames. He obtained some steps
and managed to reach the first floor window, lifting the woman down to other persons
below, before he dropped to the ground. He was then told of a boy in the bedroom and
tried to go upstairs again without success, he decided to go round the back, and climbed
onto an outhouse roof. He wrapped a cloth round his head, and leaned into the room, but
the smoke was too much, and he almost fell from the roof, being saved by another
constable. After he got to the ground the constable collapsed. The child was found dead
by the Fire Brigade.

KING'S POLICE MEDAL
Award of the Bar
LG. 1/1/44

Cole	James Arthur	Sub Divisional Inspector	116839 P	**Bar**
Price	James	Inspector	104163	
Terry	Leslie Howard	Special Inspector	00114934	

During the afternoon of 12th August 1943 an armed lunatic was defying all attempts to secure his removal to hospital from a house in Barry Road, East Dulwich. Inspector Price arrived on the scene at about 5.40 pm, and his first plan was to engage the man in conversation from the bottom of the stairs whilst another officer tried to get into the first floor window. This did not come off, as the man swung round and fired at the window where the ladder was, and then let the second barrel go just above Inspector Price on the stairs. At this stage the man's sister arrived and was allowed up to speak to him, but he then held her hostage. The Inspector then decided to try a tin of tear gas, which was obtained from the local Home Guard. The capsules had to be heated, and when ready, Inspector Price put them on a tray in the hall. The man however, fired a shotgun, and scattered the pellets, making them useless.

At about 8.30 pm Sub-Divisional Inspector Cole arrived, and further attempts were made to rush the man, without success, as he was firing the shotgun indiscriminately. The army were called in and arrived with tear gas bombs. A diversion was made with the tear gas, and Inspector Cole and Terry rescued the woman from the room in which she had been locked, by getting her through a window. Further gas was released, but it collected in a thick cloud downstairs, and was more danger to the police than the man they were after. During long periods of waiting, the man fired the shotgun at any person moving about downstairs. It was decided to throw a tear gas bomb into the room, and then rush the room from the stairs. The bomb fell on the bed and set it alight. At the same time inspectors Cole and Terry rushed the door, as a shot was fired inside. On entering the room, it was found the man had shot himself. The whole incident lasted for 13 hours. All the officers received a monetary award from the Bow Street Fund.

KING'S POLICE MEDAL
LG. 1/1/44

Salmon	Alfred Charles	Police Constable	117725 M

At about 2.40 pm on 3rd February 1943 constable Salmon challenged a group of men in Abbey Street, SE1, but they ran away whilst he was checking their identity cards. The constable chased one of them as he got into a car and drove away. The constable jumped onto the running board and tried to smash the window with his truncheon. The man swerved from side to side, trying to knock the constable off the car, and eventually drove against a costermonger's barrow, throwing the constable into the road, causing multiple fractures to his left leg and left arm. The constable however, recorded the number of the car, and the man was later arrested. A monetary award was also made from the Bow Street fund.

GEORGE MEDAL
LG. 7/3/44

Robson	James Arthur	Police Sergeant	E

BRITISH EMPIRE MEDAL FOR GALLANTRY

Evans	Stanley Charles	Police Constable	E
Foxton	Stanley George	WR Police Constable	E

During an air raid a bomb caused four adjoining houses to collapse. Robson with two others began searching for trapped persons. They tunnelled into the debris and after 2 hours brought out one man. Hearing sounds further inside they continued tunnelling for another 2 hours. Finally they reached. At one state oxygen had to be released into the tunnel so they could continue work. They found that the woman was pinned beneath a bedstead, but after further efforts she was eventually released.

Constable Foxton later resigned from the police in order to join the Armed Forces.

BRITISH EMPIRE MEDAL FOR GALLANTRY
LG. 24/10/44

Abbs	Robert Henry Charles	WR Police Constable	E

Abbs was regulating traffic when he heard the noise of an approaching flying bomb which seemed about to fall nearby. Some confusion occurred and Abbs took control of the situation shouting to the pedestrians to get down. He then noticed that one woman was still standing up obviously very confused. The bomb was so close that further words would have been wasted, so he pushed her to the ground and threw himself over her to protect her. The bomb fell about thirty yards away and the constable was injured but the woman was unhurt.

BRITISH EMPIRE MEDAL FOR GALLANTRY

Tribe	William James	Sub Div Inspector	106001 B
Holyhead	Rodney Victor	WR Police Constable	01620 B

During an air raid, a bomb made a deep crater which extended across the roadway and fractured a water main sewer and gas main. Water from the broken pipes flooded the crater, overflowed and filled the cellars of the adjoining houses. People were trapped in a building and Inspector Tribe tried to reach them but found his way blocked by debris. Inspector Tribe and constable Holyhead then forced their way through the flood water and entered the adjoining house. Holyhead climbed through a first floor window and along a narrow ledge about ten inches wide, and entered the damaged house. He found two women and a man on the ground floor and realising the impossibility of taken the victims back the way he had come, sought an alternative way out. Meanwhile the Inspector made the perilous journey along the narrow ledge and joined the constable. Tribe and Holyhead then carried the two women and piloted the man through the garden, which was flooded to a depth of four feet, and over the walls to safety. Immediately afterwards Inspector Tribe, in spite of his wet condition went to another incident, Holyhead returned to the house to put out a fire in the grate of an upstairs room to obviate danger from escaping gas. He then helped in the general police work.

Inspector Tribe and constable Holyhead showed courage and great devotion to duty, in addition to the hazard of crossing a narrow ledge the officers were exposed to the grave risk of the whole structure collapsing under their weight and of being projected into the water filled crater.

BRITISH EMPIRE MEDAL FOR GALLANTRY
Kemp   Harold George   Police Constable   10030 E
A flying bomb demolished a house and hearing calls for help coming from the ruins, Kemp commenced to move the debris with help. A hole 9 feet deep was made and Kemp crawled down this hole until he uncovered the head of an unconscious woman who was bleeding badly. He rendered first aid and found that she was pinned down by a settee and a treadle sewing machine. He broke these articles up until he was able to partially free the victim. He then found that the narrowness and slope of the excavation made it impossible for him to move her out unaided, so he grasped her under the shoulders and shielded her from falling debris as far as he could until both were dragged out together by a chain of helpers. After this rescue the constable went into the hole again and widened it with his hands in order to search for further casualties.

BRITISH EMPIRE MEDAL FOR GALLANTRY
Holloway   William James   Inspector   114205 Z
A flying bomb demolished a house and lifted a nine inch slab of concrete which formed the roof of the shelter under the house and left it tilted inside the shelter. A large quantity of debris poured in and trapped the occupants. Inspector Holloway heard cries and with help cleared away debris until there was a hole big enough to allow him to squeeze in between the slab and the wall. He found a woman and a baby whom he handed out to safety, but a little girl was still buried. A piece of wall collapsed and the slab slipped lower and the Inspector realised that nothing could be done without heavy rescue apparatus. He sent for this and then started the rescue of another woman who had been heard calling from a part of the shelter which could be reached more easily from the top. After a hole had been made he lowered himself and found her pinned down by broken masonry. He uncovered her head and arms but before he could complete the rescue he had to call a doctor to give her morphine. The debris caught fire but he remained below with the woman while the fire was being put out. After Holloway had brought out the second woman, he returned to the space under the slab to direct the rescue parties efforts to save the child. They managed to clear her head and shoulders but she died before the slab could be moved.

BRITISH EMPIRE MEDAL FOR GALLANTRY
Meager   William John   Police Sergeant   119598 X
A HE bomb demolished houses, hearing cries Sergeant Meager with help commenced to tunnel through the debris passing back rubble as he went forward. After tunnelling for about an hour he came to a pocket of gas from a broken pipe. This was so bad that the Sergeant was overcome and had to give up work for a few minutes. Eventually another hold had to be made to let in air to drive out the gas. Another hour's work, which included sawing through wooden

joists while lying on his stomach, enables Meager to reach the man who was pinned by fallen masonry. He freed the man's head and shoulders and after further work he was able to release the victim completely and drag him out. During part of the time the work was going on the air raid was still in progress and bombs were dropped in the neighbourhood. Heavy gun fire from the nearby guns increased the risk of the tunnel collapsing.

GEORGE MEDAL
LG. 5/12/44

| Wright | Charles Harry | Police Sergeant | 119728 G |
| Sexton | Archibald Ernest | WR Police Constable | 10416 G |

A flying bomb demolished premises and started a large fire. There was a public shelter in the basement of the burning building. The entrance was blocked by debris. An entry point was found. Wright followed by Sexton dropped into the area. There were two men and a woman in the shelter. It was not possible to rescue them via the way they had come in due to the fire, the rear exit was also blocked. The shelter was slowly flooding and was filled with smoke and debris, electric cables had become detached from the walls. A fuse box exploded in the Sergeant's face causing temporary blindness with severe burns. Wright made the people lie down in the water in an endeavour to assist with breathing, which was made difficult by dense smoke and overpowering heat. After a while the fire abated and an attempt to get them out was made. Sexton assisted by the Sergeant succeeded in climbing over debris and ran to get assistance. They were eventually extricated from the building by means of ladders and ropes.

GEORGE MEDAL
LG. 30/5/44

| Gray | William James | Police Constable | 119381 V |

A bomb fell on a garage causing a big fire. Six employees were trapped in an air raid shelter inside the building and their rescue was almost impossible as the flames had already reached the shelter. A diesel tank nearby was liable to explode at any time. Cox and Gray volunteered to help. On entering Gray found a man who was pinned down by debris, they got to work to release him, eventually the man was freed. They had scarcely got away when the walls of the burning building collapsed and made the rescue of the remaining men impossible.

GEORGE MEDAL
LG. 13/6/44

| Hack | Albert Edward | Police Sergeant | 119029 V |

Bombs caused considerable damage, a first floor flat had collapsed onto the ground floor flat trapping the occupants. At the rear of the building a serious fire was raging in a factory containing much highly inflammable material. Hack managed to get into the flat, he wriggled his way as far as the entrance to the kitchen. There were 3 women and 2 babies trapped under the debris. Hack dealt with escaping gas from a broken pipe, he then cleared the debris away and managed to release the babies. One woman was unconscious, eventually the Sergeant was able to drag her free and also free the other woman. The Sergeant had to come out 3 times as the air inside was stifling. The remaining victim was more difficult to free as she was pinned under broken furniture. He managed to clear the debris and pull her to safety. An air raid was in progress at the time.

KING'S COMMENDATION FOR BRAVE CONDUCT
LG. 7/3/44

Rose	Thomas	WR Police Constable	20695 E

For Civil Defence

KING'S COMMENDATION FOR BRAVE CONDUCT
LG. 30/5/44

Tilly	Percy Edmund Henry Basil	Police Constable	111723 B
Spooner		Police Constable	111537 C
Catchpole		Police Sergeant	114770 P
Edmonds		Police Constable	113621 W
Browning		Police Constable	124161 X
Wright		Police Constable	121716 X

For Civil Defence

KING'S COMMENDATION FOR BRAVE CONDUCT
LG. 13/6/44

McDonald	William Anderson	Inspector	N

'when rescuing a man from drowning.'

CARNEGIE HERO FUND
28/2/44

Warren	Edward F	Police Constable

Sustained injury while stopping a pair of runaway horses.

ROLL OF HONOUR
- Pc Walter Charles Tralau

Fatally injured in an accident while on duty on J division.
- Pc Henry Charles Ernest Howell

Struck by an Army truck while riding a pedal cycle on duty.
- Spc Dennis, 19888H B

Died as a result of injuries received at a bomb explosion during an enemy air raid.
- Wrpc Keller, 14063 L

Killed by a bomb explosion during an enemy air attack.
- Pc Lord, 114296 J

Killed by a bomb explosion during an enemy air attack.
- Pc Moir, 098909 J

Killed by a bomb explosion during an enemy air attack.
- Ps Smith, 107879 L

Killed by a bomb explosion during an enemy air attack.

1945

January	Russian troops discover the horror of Auschwitz concentration camp.
February	Dresden devastated, 130,000 killed in a night and day relentless bombardment by the RAF.
March	Germany, Montgomery bans British troops from fraternising with locals.
April	The partial blackout ends.
May	Germany surrenders.
June	The UN (United Nations) Formed.
July	BBC introduces the Light programme and resumes regional services.
August	Japan surrenders.
September	British troops land and take control of Singapore.
October	RAF Gloucester Meteor flies at record 540 mph.
November	De Gaulle is elected President of France.
December	Palestine terrorists bomb four cities.

HITS OF THE YEAR

Cruising down the river
We'll gather lilacs in the spring

KING'S POLICE MEDAL

LG.

Smith	Supt 105182	K
Pateman	Sub Div Insp 105435	Z
Jenkins	Insp 115644	M
Conelly	Insp 097197	P

KING'S POLICE MEDAL

LG. 14/6/45

Mayger	Herbert George	Police Sergeant	118793 D

At 10.30 pm on 4th January 1945 Sergeant Mayger and a constable went to a block of flats to search for a man who had apparently threatened the manager with a pistol, and then disappeared into the basement. Sergeant Mayger entered the switch room and saw a man lying on a mattress pretending to be asleep. After being asked what he was doing, the man suddenly pulled out an automatic pistol from under him, pointed it at the Sergeant and said 'get out of here or I'll shoot you'. The man got to his feet, but Sergeant Mayger backed out of the door and slammed it shut. The man opened the door a few inches, and pointed the gun out towards the Sergeant threatening him again. The Sergeant hit his hand with his truncheon, and then kicked the door open, and jumped on the man, and after a brief struggle arrested him.

BRITISH EMPIRE MEDAL FOR GALLANTRY

Moseley	Henry	Police Sergeant	01032Q M
Painter	Francis Leslie	Station Sergeant	118545 M
Whife	James Samuel	WR Police Constable	16772 M

Houses were damaged as the result of the enemy action and Painter, Moseley and Whife went to one where people were trapped. The three men, guided by voices, found a woman held down by ceiling joists. Moseley and Whife held up part of the ceiling, while Painter sawed through the joists and released the victim. They then saw a child's hand and legs sticking out from under some debris. Moseley, using a piece of joist as a lever lifted the beams which were holding the child down. After moving debris and bedclothes he was able to free her and pass her out to safety. A child in bed had fallen through to the room below. As there was no way of reaching her from above, the three men went down to the street and crawled through the wreckage. After moving heavy pieces of brickwork they found the girl under the upturned bed with two 6 inch beams across her body. Moseley and Whife were able to lift the bed just enough to enable Painter to crawl underneath and he sawed through the beams and released the girl. They also discovered that a man was trapped in a bed which had buckled when a large piece of brickwork had fallen on the head of it. This brickwork was too big to be moved and Painter had to break it up with a sledgehammer. The top of the bed was then prised up and the man released. The three men then went to give a hand at the adjoining house and helped in the rescue of two more people.

BRITISH EMPIRE MEDAL FOR GALLANTRY

Denyer   James Francis   Police Constable   113499 Y

When houses were demolished by enemy action, constable Martin was thrown to the ground but he at once crossed the road and entered a partly demolished house from which screams were heard. He was joined by Denyer who, in order to make it possible for Martin to work more effectively, braced himself against the wall to hold it up. At the same time he lifted a roof beam which was pressing down on a casualty. This action made it possible for Martin to crawl through the pile and reach a woman and after removing more debris, he succeeded in extricating her. Throughout Denyer had been holding up the wall with his back and taking the weight of the beam. Denyer and Martin remained in the dangerous passage for some time to help in handing out debris removed during the course of the rescue of the other occupants of the house. Both men showed courage and determination without thought for their own safety.

KING'S COMMENDATION FOR BRAVE CONDUCT

LG. 9/1/45

Warren   Edward Francis   Police Constable   110134M MM

'Stopping runaway horses.'

KING'S COMMENDATION FOR BRAVE CONDUCT

Robertson   Police Constable   118272 F

KING'S COMMENDATION FOR BRAVE CONDUCT

LG. 26/6/45

Hamblin   William   Police Constable   110532 D

'When arresting an armed miscreant.'

Kirkup	George Riddle	Police Constable	116971 D

'When stopping runaway horses.'

KING'S COMMENDATION FOR BRAVE CONDUCT

Chandler		Police Sergeant	119086 L
Tucker		Police Constable	116148L
Walter		Special Constable	017631HP

For Civil Defence

KING'S COMMENDATION FOR BRAVE CONDUCT
LG. 17/7/45

Allen	Reginald Arthur	Police Constable	110320 P
Ellis	Leonard Joseph	Police Constable	119159 R
Gray	Alexander	Police Constable	115453 R
Hill	Charles George	Inspector	112381 N

For Civil Defence

KING'S COMMENDATION FOR BRAVE CONDUCT
LG. 18/9/45

Hill-Cottingham	Leslie George	Police Sergeant	118633 K
Dundas	David	Police Constable	117535 K
Dyson	Clarence Leonard	Police Constable	113198 K
Goodge	Edward Raymond	Police Constable	117472 K
Saley	Richard	Station Sergeant	117036 K
Trollope	Arthur	Police Constable	116988 K

For Civil Defence

CARNEGIE HERO FUND
3/8/45

Stratford	Ernest A	Police Constable

Along with two others rescued a number of persons from drowning in the River Dart at Sharpham, Devon following the collision of the steamer in which they were passengers with a motor launch.

ROLL OF HONOUR
- Pc Sharp, K Division, 114844
- Wrpc Howell, V Division, 04369

Killed by an enemy long range rocket explosion.
- Ps Batley, CO SB, 119196

Killed in a flying accident while engaged on special protection duties.
- Pc Edmonds, R Division, 108241

Killed by an enemy long range rocket explosion.

1946

January	First post war bananas arrive in the UK.
February	US Army says it will use German V-2 bombs to test radar's anti-rocket capabilities.
March	UK women can be diplomats but only if they do not marry.
April	A bomb is detonated in St James's Park.
May	China - Civil war erupts between communists and nationalists on the Yangtse River.
June	Morris raise the price of a 2 door saloon to £270 and a four door to £290.
July	Jockey club to install photo finish cameras on all racecourses.
August	British European Airways (BEA) created.
September	9 RAF men who escaped from Stalag Luft III in a glider receive MBE's.
October	MP's approve a memorial to Roosevelt in Grosvenor Square.
November	Ford Prefect and Ford Anglia go on sale for £275 and £229 respectively.
December	Government sets up the tourist board.

HITS OF THE YEAR

A gal in calico

Its a pity to say goodnight

BRITISH EMPIRE MEDAL FOR GALLANTRY

LG. 23/7/46

Barrett   Joseph Charles   Police Constable   118847 F

Police constable Barrett was one of four officers in a patrol car which was chasing a stolen car at 70 mph. Neither of the drivers was aware that the road led down to the river until the stolen car mounted a grass verge and dived over a 30 foot bank turning completely over on the way. The police car was brought to a stand still and without hesitation the four police officers entered the water and waded out to the car which was beginning to settle down. They rescued two of the occupants of the stolen car but the driver plunged into the water. The man was drawn under by the current but reappeared in the middle of the river obviously in great difficulties. Constable Barrett then threw off his overcoat and jacket and swam towards him. The constable was also dragged under by the current, but on coming up again caught hold of the drowning man and succeeded in bringing him safely ashore. Barrett then returned to assist in the rescue of the fourth occupant of the car who was unconscious and wedged inside. Throughout the incident constable Barrett showed outstanding initiative, persistence and disregard for his own safety.

ROLL OF HONOUR

1947

January	UK most popular radio shows 'Radio forfeits', 'Dick Barton' and 'Woman's hour'.
February	Lord Mountbatten appointed Viceroy of India.

March	300 roads are blocked and 15 towns are cut off by snow as appalling weather continues.
April	Private Medical company BUPA formed.
May	Skeletons of a herd of mammoths unearthed at Tucson, Arizona.
June	Fire at a rubber dump in Mitcham, London blots out the sun in the area.
July	Palestine - two British Army Sergeants are kidnapped and hanged.
August	Britain's first atomic reactor starts up at Harwell.
September	Police in Paris foil a plot by Zionist Stern gang to bomb London from the air.
October	31 die in train crash at Croydon.
November	Princess Elizabeth marries Philip Mountbatten.
December	200 Dartmoor inmates stage a protest against prison food.

HITS OF THE YEAR
They say its wonderful
Maybe its because I'm a Londoner

KING'S POLICE MEDAL
LG. 27/6/47

Snelling	Cecil		Police Constable	120693 S

At about 9.45 pm on 13th March 1946 constable Snelling was at home, off duty, when he saw a man pass by the side window of his house. He went into the passageway and challenged the man, and then caught hold of him, and there was a violent struggle. The man managed to free his right arm and suddenly the constable heard a loud explosion, and felt a severe pain in his left hip. He released the man and fell to the floor. The man ran off towards the back garden. Despite the injury, constable Snelling chased and caught the man, who turned and fired two more shots at the constable before making good his escape. Constable Snelling was taken to Redhill hospital, where a bullet was removed from close to the main blood vessels in his thigh. The criminal was later arrested. The suspect was sentenced to 7 years imprisonment.

KING'S POLICE MEDAL
LG. 27/6/47

Rowswell	Bertie	Police Constable	121037
Strange	Norman	Police Constable	114553

At about 10.30 am on 27th December 1946 constables Rowswell and Strange were on patrol in plain clothes in Russell Square, when they saw a man answering the description of a person wanted for murder. Aware that he might be armed, they approached him, and spoke with him. The man drew an automatic pistol and pushed it into constable Strange's stomach, saying 'don't come another inch, or I'll blow your guts in'. He then turned and ran along Upper Woburn Place followed by the constables. The man continued to run and fire the pistol at the chasing officers through several streets. One shot went through constable Strange's jacket. The officers split up, and went each side of a building to try and corner the man. As he came round the corner of the building constable Rowswell was shot in the eye, which later had to be removed. The man was eventually trapped in a block of buildings and surrounded by police. He was then arrested without further injury to anyone, and charged with attempted murder of the police officers, as well as the murder for which he was already wanted.

KING'S POLICE MEDAL
LG. 27/6/47

Watts (nee Law)   Alberta Mary   Woman Police Sergeant   391

Following a series of brutal robberies against women on Tooting Bec Common, it was arranged that observation should be maintained by plain clothes officers. Woman Sergeant Watts volunteered to act as a decoy. At about 6 pm on 24th January 1947, Sergeant Watts walked onto the common, and saw a man standing on the corner of the road. The man followed her onto the common, caught up with and then passed her. She stopped, turned round and began to walk in the opposite direction. Before she had gone very far, she heard footsteps behind her, and suddenly the man leapt on her dragging her to the ground. She struggled fiercely, but was hit and kicked by the assailant, who then snatched her handbag and made off. Sergeant Watts ran after the man, and again struggled with him, as other male colleagues in the vicinity came to her assistance, and the man was arrested.

KING'S POLICE MEDAL
LG. 27/6/47

Deans   William Hosie   Police Sergeant   122419

Early in 1947 information was received that a gang of thieves intended to waylay an official of the bank, steal his keys and rob the bank. Information received indicated that the gang had been watching the bank and the movements of the bank official for some time. It was decided that the raid should be allowed to take place, so that the whole gang could be arrested and that a police officer should impersonate the bank official. Sergeant Deans who was similar in build and looks to the bank official, volunteered. He was fully aware of the likely dangers.

On 21st February 1947 Sergeant Deans, wearing some of the bank official's clothes, locked the bank doors, and started on the journey to the bank official's home. He was followed at first by two men, and then two others joined them. As he was walking along a footpath near Woodside Park railway station, North Finchley, he was suddenly hit from behind by a heavy object, and knocked unconscious to the ground. He was bound and gagged, and the keys stolen. He was then driven in a van to a deserted spot and dumped in the snow. It was some time before he was able to struggle free, and go to a house some distance away, from where he called assistance. As a result of this operation, six men were later arrested and convicted.

KING'S COMMENDATION FOR BRAVE CONDUCT
LG. 20/5/47

Young   James Fuller   Police Constable   112354 A

'For rescuing a woman from drowning.'

KING'S COMMENDATION FOR BRAVE CONDUCT
LG. 5/8/47

Aram   Edward   Police Constable   120935 K
'For rescuing a child from drowning.'

ROLL OF HONOUR
• SDI Oscar Thompson
Killed in a car accident with Allied Control Commission in Germany.
• Pc Leslie Edwin Thompson
• Pc Gilbert Edward Perkins
Killed when their patrol car collided with a tree while responding to an urgent call to a housebreaking in Woodford.

1948

January	Riots in India after the assassination of Gandhi.
February	UK warn Argentina over the Falkland Islands.
March	King Farouk of Egypt lays the foundation stone for the Aswan Dam.
April	In the UK the King and Queen celebrate their silver wedding.
May	Arab forces muster as Israel is born.
June	RAF flies in to beat the Berlin blockade.
July	Worlds first turbine propellor aircraft Vickers Viscount makes its maiden flight.
August	12 die when 70 mph gales hit Britain.
September	Queen Wilhelmina of the Netherlands abdicates in favour of her daughter Juliana.
October	BBC broadcasts from Downing Street for the first time in London.
November	The worst fog in years leaves 4 dead, 3 trains crash, and buses and police vehicles taken off the road.
December	Leading car makers Austin, Morris, Ford, Rootes, Standard and Vauxhall agree to standardise motor parts.

HITS OF THE YEAR
Its magic
On a slow boat to China
Hamlet

DONALD THOMAS - 1948
MURDER OF Pc NATHANIEL EDGAR
At 8pm on 13th February 1948 a woman walking along Broadfields avenue, in North London with her brother heard 3 shots coming from another road, a man then ran past them. The couple found a badly wounded police constable lying in the drive of 112 Wades Hill, they called for help.

The police constable was Nathaniel Edgar; he was 33 and married with two children. He had been patrolling the Winchmore Hill area looking for any break-ins. Seeing a young man acting suspiciously he stopped him to question him, going as far as writing the man's name and address in his note book. The suspect then suddenly pulled out a gun and fired 3 times and fled. The constable had been shot at the base of the spine, the buttock and right thigh. He was able to tell his colleagues what had happened and the information he had in his pocket book. He died an hour later in hospital.

The suspect Donald George Thomas, aged 23, was born and brought up in Edmonton. When he was 16 he was sent to approved school. He had been called up for military service in January 1945 but soon deserted. After two years on the run he gave himself up and was given 160 days detention. On being returned to his unit he absconded again, this by now was October 1947. Now both the police and the army were looking for him.

Police by now had started a hunt for him, and they appealed for help on the radio and in the newspapers. Mr Winkless saw the photograph in the newspaper and contacted the police saying that his wife had fallen for this young man and had run off with him. The woman's picture was then published and was seen by a Mrs Smeed, the landlady of a house converted into bed sits in Stockwell, Clapham. She immediately telephoned the police.

Four police arrived a few minutes later, as the door of the bed sit opened in order to collect the breakfast tray, the police rushed in, Thomas was overpowered and disarmed before he could shoot the Luger pistol.

Bullets taken from the Luger pistol matched those that had been removed from constable Edgar. Donald Thomas was tried at the Old Bailey in April 1948, he was found guilty and sentenced to death. The Home Secretary announced that no executions would be carried out while the House of Commons debated on experimental 5 year suspension of the death penalty. So Donald Thomas was never hanged.

Donald Thomas was released from prison on licence in April 1962.

Four police officers who arrested Thomas in the bed sit all received the King's Police Medal for Gallantry, their citation can be read in the 1949 section.

KING'S POLICE MEDAL
LG. 1/1/48

| Cutt | James Bryce | Police Constable | 125806 G |

At about 4.20 am on 4th September 1947 two cars were seen outside a tailor's shop in Camden Walk, Islington, one of which had been reported stolen. Two men were seen removing goods from the broken shop window display, whilst a third sat in one of the cars. Constable Cutt was the passenger in a police car, and as they approached the scene, the two men dropped the clothing they were carrying, and jumped into the empty car and drove off. The other car was rammed by the police car, but the driver backed off, and constable Cutt jumped onto the car as it was driven away. For over three and a half miles constable Cutt hung onto the car, with the police car following, the driver of the stolen car swerving to try to dislodge the constable. Eventually the car was driven into a police road block, and crashed into a lamp standard, throwing constable Cutt onto the roadway. He received serious bruising, but no broken bones. The car driver was arrested.

KING'S POLICE MEDAL
LG. 8/6/48

| Beale | Thomas | Police Constable | 107247 G |

At about 2.20 pm on 2nd February 1948 the driver of a single horse drawn van was about to mount the van when the horse was startled by a pneumatic drill, and bolted, leaving the driver on the footpath. It galloped along Noel Road, Islington colliding with a lamp standard. Constable Beale was at the junction with Graham Street, and tried to catch the bridle of the horse as it passed but missed. He then jumped on a passing lorry, and as the lorry drew abreast of the horse, jumped onto the horse's neck, pulling the horse to a stop in a short distance. The constable was 55 years old and as a result suffered from shock and nervous debility.

KING'S POLICE MEDAL
14/12/48

| Shepherd | Ralph Donald | Police Sergeant | 123248 T |
| Kay | Harry Patterson | Police Constable | 119571 T |

At about 4 am on 29th May 1948 four officers in a patrol car when they received information about suspects at a factory. Sergeant Shepherd went round the back to investigate, the three others remaining at the front. The Sergeant found a side door open, and through it saw two men standing beside a safe. One was holding an oxyacetylene torch. The man with the burner threw it at the Sergeant and both ran towards the front of the building. As they reached the front, one man turned and pointed a revolver at the Sergeant and threatened ' stand back or I'll shoot you'. He admitted later that he did in fact pull the trigger three times but three of the chambers were empty. Sergeant Shepherd then tripped on some rubbish and the men turned and ran out of the back door. Sergeant Shepherd followed and caught one man as he climbed the fence. The other man went round to the front of the building, where he was confronted by constable Kay. The man fired the revolver, hitting constable Kay in the stomach. The man was overpowered by other constables and arrested after he had stumbled, and dropped the revolver. Although constable Kay was on the danger list for some time, he made a full recovery. Both officers received a monetary award from the Bow Street Fund.

BRITISH EMPIRE MEDAL FOR GALLANTRY
LG. 10/12/48

| Butler | Theobald | Detective Sergeant | 125999 D |
| Barlow | Jack | Detective Constable | 127714 D |

Police Sergeant Butler and constable Barlow went to the third floor flat with a warrant to search the premises for stolen property. As the officers entered the living room a man came out of the bedroom. On being questioned he suddenly stepped backwards and entered the sitting room, made towards the landing door. The officers followed and when the man was half way across the room he swung round and pointed an automatic pistol at them, and he threatened to fire if they advanced further. The officers immediately closed with the man who repeated his threat, and a violent struggle ensued. Suddenly the pistol discharged and the man collapsed with a wound in the head, the bullet having entered his forehead after grazing Sergeant Butler's wrist. The man was taken to hospital. The two police officers knew that he was a dangerous criminal and there is little doubt he intended to use firearm to make good his escape. Both Sergeant Butler and constable Barlow showed great courage and determination in their endeavour to disarm and apprehend him.

KING'S COMMENDATION FOR BRAVE CONDUCT
LG. 14/12/48

Thomas	David Cyril	Police Constable	127161 T
Tween	William	Police Constable	111121 T

'For services in arresting armed and dangerous criminals.'

ROLL OF HONOUR
• Pc Arthur Edward Quemby
Killed when his police motorcycle skidded on an icy road.
• Pc Patrick George Fitzgerald
Died as the result of an accident while on motorcycle patrol.
• Pc Nathaniel Edgar
Shot while questioning a suspect in Winchmore Hill.

1949
One infamous murder took place, the man involved John George Haigh thought that he had got away with murder as there was no body, but he was wrong, see over the page for the story.

January	5 RAF reconnaissance aircraft shot down by the Israelis.
February	WRAF and WRAC incorporated into Britain's armed forces.
March	UK has succeeded in manufacturing plutonium for the first time.
April	Chocolate and sweet rationing ends.
May	Britain's first launderette opens for 6 month trial at 184 Queensway, Bayswater, London.
June	Lord Jersey gives Osterley Park to the nation.
July	HMS Amethyst reaches safety after 140 mile dash under cover of darkness along the Yangtse River.
August	London figures show that juvenile crime rose by 16.7% in 1948.
September	War time propaganda broadcaster 'Tokyo Rose' found guilty of treason in the US, subsequently jailed for 10 years and fined $10,000.
October	Stalin sets up communist German state.
November	HMS Amethyst returns to the UK.
December	Israel Government moves the Capital from Tel Aviv to Jerusalem.

HITS OF THE YEAR
Buttons and bows
Riders in the sky
Baby, its cold outside

JOHN GEORGE HAIGH - ACID BATH MURDERER 1949

As a child he had an uncontrollable urge towards spitefulness, malice and dishonesty. He delighted in punching and tweaking little girls and anyone who was younger and weaker than himself, and when there were no human playmates to torment he would torture insects and small animals. He left school at seventeen without distinction or any qualifications.

By the age of twenty two he started his own estate, insurance and advertising agency, he then moved onto selling cars. This then led to using fictitious letter headings to obtain money on hire-purchase agreements. He became prosperous and on 6th July 1934 he married Miss Beatrice Hamer. Four months later he was imprisoned and his wife left him never to communicate with him again. On his release from prison fifteen months later he moved to Glasgow where he was later imprisoned for four years for fraud.

After his release he renewed his acquaintance of William Donald McSwan, this meeting proved the turning point, Haigh the swindler became Haigh the acid-bath murderer.

Haigh's murder spree began with William McSwan. In a confession by Haigh he said when they went to a rented house in Gloucester Road, in the basement Haigh hit him on the head with a cosh, withdrew a glass of blood from his throat and drank it. William McSwan was dead within five minutes, and was then put into a 40 gallon tank. Haigh then disposed of him with acid washing the sludge down a manhole in the basement. He tried to cover up the disappearance of William to his mother and father whom Haigh had known for some time by writing letters to them purporting to come from William. The following year on two separate occasions Haigh took both of the parents Donald and Amy to the address and there he disposed of them in exactly the same way as their son.

Later on he met the Hendersons when he answered an advertisement for a house for sale. He did not buy the property as they had previously sold it. After they had sold the property the Hendersons moved. Haigh went to visit them at their new property. He took Dr Henderson to his home in Crawley and disposed of him in a store room and put him in a tank of acid, this was done during the morning, in the afternoon he brought up Mrs Henderson on the pretext that her husband had been taken ill. He shot her in the store room and put her in another tank of acid. He said that in each of the last four murders he had drunk a glass of blood as before.

In February 1949 Haigh was living at the Onslow Court Hotel in the West of London and there he became friendly with a fellow resident Mrs Olive Durand-Deacon who was a widow of independent means, whose modest fortune Haigh had already earmarked for himself. On the pretext of marketing false finger nails Haigh lured her to his workshop outside Crawley where he shot her through the neck, removing all of her valuables and put her in a 40 gallon oil drum of sulphuric acid.

Haigh was interviewed several times during an enquiry into the disappearance of Mrs Durand-Deacon. A visit to his Crawley workshop revealed significant clues, not least a .38 Webley revolver and traces of blood sufficient for the police to arrest Haigh. On being questioned Haigh stated that Mrs Durand-Deacon no longer existed, "I've destroyed her with acid, you can't prove murder without a body." He was wrong as a number of significant cases have been proved without a body.

Although he had managed to reduce the flesh and bone to a greasy sludge, he had not taken into account that longer time was needed to destroy plastics. A set of acrylic dentures which had been custom made for Mrs Durand-Deacon were positively identified by her dentist, and her red plastic handbag, with many of its contents, was positively identified by her friends.

The extravagant claim by Haigh that he was a vampire who drank the blood of his victims was seen by all as an unsophisticated ruse to establish a defence of insanity, and an attempt to exchange the hangman's noose for Broadmoor.

John George Haigh was found guilty and was hanged at Wandsworth Prison on 10th August 1949.

KING'S POLICE MEDAL For the arrest of suspect for murder of Pc Edgar

LG. 22/2/49

Moody	William Arthur	Inspector	116590
Hide	Robert Henry	Police Constable	115578
Searle	George Charles Ex War Reserve	Police Constable	14145
Wheeler	Dennis Edward	Police Constable	120288

On 13th February 1948 constable Edgar (see page 151) was shot dead in an Essex lane by a man he was questioning. An extensive search was made for the man responsible, and at 7.40 am on 17th February 1948 war reserve constable Searle was in Stockwell, South London when he was informed by the landlord of a boarding house, that a woman tenant in the house looked like the newspaper photograph of the woman reported to be with the wanted man. War reserve Searle reported immediately to Brixton Police Station, and kept observation. Inspector Moody together with constables Hide and Wheeler arrived. An arrangement was made with the landlady to take breakfast to the two persons in the room, and leave the tray outside on the landing. The officers followed, and hid on the landing and stairs. After the landlady had gone downstairs, the door was opened a few inches by a man, who, on seeing the police slammed the door. Constable Wheeler burst open the door, and followed by Inspector Moody. The man had made for the bed, and had his hand under the pillow when he was jumped on by the police officers. A loaded pistol was taken from him before he could use it, and he was arrested.

KING'S POLICE MEDAL

LG. 23/3/49

Bland	Harold	Detective Sergeant	123436
Baxter	John Malcolm	Detective Constable	128992

At about 3.15 pm on 27th August 1948 information was received at Arbour Square Police Station that a man wanted for questioning about stolen cars was at Eastern Auction Mart, Stepney. Sergeant Bland and Constable Baxter went there, and spoke with the man. Another man was also seen, but he began to drive off when the officers approached, and constable Baxter tried to stop the vehicle, but after hanging onto the car for some distance he was thrown off. The other man was put into the police car, and as they were approaching the police station, the man pulled out an automatic pistol, and in the struggle fired it, the bullet passing through Sergeant Bland's trousers and into the seat of the car. The man was disarmed and arrested.

KING'S COMMENDATION FOR BRAVE CONDUCT

LG. 1/11/49

Godwin   Thomas William   Police Constable   114391

'For stopping a pair of runaway horses.'

ROLL OF HONOUR

- Pc Harry Harding

Died from injuries received in a road accident while on traffic patrol.

- Pc Albert Victor Hawkins

Died from a fractured skull when he fell from his cycle on duty on Ealing Division.

Chapter Seven

THE YEARS OF 1950 - 1959

During the next ten years of this century we see the world in a kind of peace, that is to say the whole world is not involved in just one conflict. There were a couple of wars of note that did take place, one in Korea the other in the Suez Canal Zone.

The death of Stalin brought changes to the Soviet Union, the cold war continued to divide East and West. The USA tested their first hydrogen bomb, and the Soviet Union started the development of their own nuclear capability.

The civil unrest in the USA was beginning. There emerged a young black Baptist minister and civil rights campaigner Martin Luther King, he came to note at the boycott of blacks on the buses in Montgomery and Alabama. The racial integration rights became louder in the Southern States where their voices were being heard within the White House.

The race riots started in London at Notting Hill with several arrests being made. The Munich air disaster with the loss of many of the Manchester United football team 'The Busby Babes'. Russia launches the first satellite into space 'Sputnik 1', followed by a dog then finally a space craft which crashes on the moon.

With regards to the UK we saw the death of King George VI and our new monarch Queen Elizabeth was crowned live on television. One of the worst train crashes happened at Harrow with the loss of over 112 lives. Man conquered Everest, British police were sent to Cyprus to aid the Army with the riots and civil unrest, several gallantry awards were made to the police including two mentioned in this book.

This also seems to be the decade of infamous murders in London, John Reginald Halliday Christie, Christopher Craig and Derek Bentley and Ruth Ellis.

1950

January	British submarine sank in the Thames Estuary 60 feared dead, after accidentally being rammed by a Swedish ship.
February	Record 1,866 candidates standing for the general election.
March	Air crash near Cardiff 80 die, mainly Welsh rugby supporters.
April	The USSR shoot down a US bomber over Soviet occupied Latvia.
May	Petrol rationing ends.
June	North Korea marches into the South.
July	J Sainsbury's first self service store opens in Croydon.
August	Force of British Infantry leave Hong Kong for Korea.
September	A blue moon is visible from the South East of England.
October	28 die when BEA DC-3 Dakota crashes at Mill Hill, London.

November   US F-86 shoots down a MiG-15 in first ever combat between jet fighters over Korea.

December   Eisenhower is appointed head of NATO.

HITS OF THE YEAR
I've got a lovely bunch of coconuts
Music, music, music
Mona Lisa

KING'S COMMENDATION FOR BRAVE CONDUCT
LG. 1/8/50

Taylor	Thomas	Police Constable	133426 A

'For services when attempting to rescue a man from drowning.'

CARNEGIE HERO FUND
29/11/50

Mockendge	Donald	Police Constable

Stopping a runaway horse.

ROYAL HUMANE SOCIETY BRONZE MEDAL

Robson	Police Sergeant	117451 GM BEM

For saving a schoolgirl from drowning in the sea at Kingsgate, Kent.

ROLL OF HONOUR
• Pc George Ronald Cooper
Killed in a collision with a lorry while on motorcycle traffic patrol.
• Pc Robert Gilchrist Martin
Skidded on a wet road while on motorcycle patrol in Hampton.
• Pc Samuel Lock
Accidentally shot while cleaning a police pistol at Wood Green Police Station.
• Ps Thomas Armstrong McFadzean
Died from a fractured skull due to an accidental fall on the pavement while he was on duty on Holborn Division.

1951
January   Chinese launch a heavy assault North of Seoul crossing the 38th parallel.
February   BBC says its test of very high frequency (VHF) transmission has been a success.
March   US, MacArthur threatens invasion of China.
April   US, convicted spies Julius and Ether Rosenberg are sentenced to death.
May   Festival of Britain Pleasure Gardens open at Battersea.
June   Britain gives the USAF permission for an air base at Greenham Common.
July   The Hawker Hunter aircraft makes its maiden flight.
August   Dartmoor designated a national park.

September   Peace treaty finally signed with Japan.
October   90 mph Porsche is the hit of the motor show.
November   British families evacuated from Egypt.
December   Foot print of the alleged Yeti is found on the Himalayas.

HITS OF THE YEAR
Shall we dance
An American in Paris

BRITISH EMPIRE MEDAL FOR GALLANTRY
LG. 25/9/51

| Wheeler | Edmund Jackson | Police Constable | 135398 M |

A man attempting to commit suicide by jumping into the River Thames off London Bridge, constable Wheeler who was directing traffic was told about the incident and dashed to the scene divesting himself of his jacket and helmet as he went. He ran down about 60 steps leading to the water's edge and without hesitation plunged into the river. He swam about 20 yards to a spot indicated by onlookers, dived under the water and after a search found a man in a semi conscious state. With some difficulty Wheeler brought him back to the steps where they were both helped ashore. Although exhausted by his efforts the constable immediately started artificial respiration on the man who later recovered in hospital.

GEORGE MEDAL
LG. 13/3/51

Ashwin	Owen Percival	Police Constable	120372 P
King	Ivan Stanley	Police Constable	132226 P
McCallum	John Kerr	Police Constable	121989 P

Police Constables Ashwin, King and McCallum were in a patrol car when shortly before 1 am they received a message to go to Temple Stores, Biggin Hill as it was suspected that persons were unlawfully on premises. Thomas Temple the Director of the store met the officers on their arrival and he and constable Ashwin entered the premises by the back door, the lights were switched on and Temple locked the door on the inside. The other two officers with two relatives of Temple covered the outside of the store. Ashwin and Temple went upstairs by different staircases and met at the shop office in which through a glass panel they could see two men. One of the men stepped out of the office and raised an automatic pistol and fired a shot in their direction. The shot struck the framework of a showcase. Both men then ran out of the offices to the other side of the building followed by Ashwin and Temple. As he reached that side of the premises the constable saw the second man who was unarmed walking towards him and the constable closed with him. The first man who was at the top of the staircase about 3 yards away thereupon turned and fired at the officer wounding him in the throat. After firing one or two more shots this man then ran downstairs into another department of the stores pursued by Temple, he eventually plunged through a plate glass window into the street. Temple at once returned to help constable Ashwin whom he found lying unconscious on the floor with the second man on top of him striking him in the face. Temple struck the man with the baton he was carrying, forced him into a corner of the room and held him at bay until help arrived. Meanwhile the first man who still held the pistol as he came through the window was tackled by constable McCallum but broke free and ran off down the road. Constable King who had been on the roof preventing any escape through the sky light joined McCallum and with Temple's two relatives they went in pursuit. After a chase of some 400 yards the two police constables had almost caught up with the man when he turned round and pointing the pistol at McCallum who was slightly in front pulled the trigger. Both officers heard a click but the magazine of the weapon was apparently empty. McCallum jumped at the mans right hand and got hold of the pistol while King grasped his left hand. After a violent struggle they succeeded in overpowering the man.

GEORGE MEDAL
LG. 13/3/51

Smith   Leslie Alan   Police Constable   131025 T

Constable Smith was on motorcycle duty at High Street Hounslow when he saw two men in a large saloon car driving towards London at about 40 mph. His suspicions were aroused and he decided to stop and question them. He rode after the car drew level on the off side and signalled the driver to stop. Instead of doing so the driver accelerated and steered the car towards the officer who was forced to brake sharply to avoid a collision. He then continued to pursue the car which reached a speed of about 70 mph. A large lorry coming towards the car pulled across the road to enter a yard, and the car swerving to the off side to avoid it crashed into a tree. Both men got out and the driver made off. As constable Smith went to detain the other, the man drew an automatic pistol from his pocket and pointing it at the officer's stomach threatened to shoot him. Without hesitation constable Smith grabbed the mans wrist, twisted his arm and forced the pistol from his grasp, slipping it into his own pocket. A violent struggle ensued but the man was eventually over powered. Later he escaped and hid on the roof of an outhouse in a yard about 400 yards away. The constable found him, climbed up, brought the man to the ground and took him to the Police Station.

ROYAL HUMANE SOCIETY BRONZE MEDAL
Eales   Police Constable   129041 TA

Bronze medal and certificate for attempting to rescue a woman from drowning in the River Thames.

ROLL OF HONOUR

1952
This year there was one famous murder trial, the murder of a police officer by two young men, their names remain known to this day. Christopher Craig and Derek Bentley and the policeman was constable Sidney Miles. The brief story of this murder is shown over the page.

January	The driver of a bus which killed 23 military cadets in 1951 is fined £20 and loses his licence for 3 years.
February	ID cards in the UK are abolished.
March	The 'Kite Mark' replaces the Utility sign.
April	The USA finally end the Pacific War.
May	Thieves attack three postmen and steal a van carrying registered mail worth over £200,000 in London.
June	Anne Franke's diary is published.
July	London bids farewell to the City's last tram, which runs from Woolwich to New Cross.
August	Floods kill 22 in Lynmouth, Devon.
September	26 spectators are killed when a prototype jet aircraft falls apart at Farnborough air show having just broken the sound barrier.
October	Harrow train disaster - 112 die.
November	Agatha Christie's play 'The Mousetrap' opens in London.
December	Queen gives permission to have the Coronation televised.

HITS OF THE YEAR

I'm singing in the rain
I saw mummy kissing Santa Claus
The greatest show on Earth

CHRISTOPHER CRAIG AND DEREK BENTLEY 1952

Christopher Craig came from a good home, they lived in comfort at 9 Norbury Court Road in Norbury South London. He was born on 19th May 1936, he left school at 15 suffering from dyslexia and on leaving school was still barely able to read or write. To hide this he gave the impression of a hard man taking the role from American gangsters of the 1930's. He started to acquire guns which just after the war were easy to obtain.

Derek Bentley was born in 1933 and lived at Fairview Road, Norbury not far from Craig. He suffered a head injury when the family were bombed twice during the blitz and this was the main cause of his below average intelligence. His main passion was body building and he did some occasional jobs, but it was not long before he was sent to approved school for shop breaking. On his return to Norbury he took up with Christopher Craig.

On Sunday 2nd November 1952 Bentley met up with Craig and two other friends, after a while the two friends went off and Craig and Bentley caught a 109 bus to Croydon. At the time Craig was armed with a revolver, a knuckle-duster and a sheath knife. Bentley had a similar knife on him, and Craig passed him the knuckle-duster.

On arrival in Croydon they got off the bus and walked along Tamworth Road, where they stopped at one stage to look in a sweet shop window. Craig then climbed over a 6 foot high iron gate into the yard of Barlow & Parker a wholesale confectioners, he was soon followed by Bentley. They were seen by a woman across the road who phoned the police at 9.15 pm. A van and police car went to investigate, in the van were Dc Frederick Fairfax, Pc Norman Harrison, Pc Budgen and Pc Pain. The car contained Pc Sidney Miles and Pc James McDonald and they arrived at Tamworth Road at 9.25 pm.

Craig and Bentley had by now climbed a drainpipe and were on the flat roof of the building. When the police arrived they too went up to the roof by means of the drainpipe and from inside the building by the stairs. Fairfax during the altercation was shot in the shoulder, 6 officers arrived armed with officially issued police guns. As the police officers emerged through the roof door a shot rang out and one officer fell dead (Pc Miles). He had been shot through the forehead. Craig had fired the gun, Bentley did not have a gun during this incident. Bentley was apprehended on the roof and Craig whether trying to evade arrest or kill himself jumped from the roof and was badly injured.

Both were charged with the murder of the policeman and appeared at the Old Bailey on 9th December 1952. The jury only took 75 minutes to find both guilty but did recommend mercy on behalf of Bentley. Craig because of his age was ordered to be detained during Her Majesty's pleasure and Bentley (who did not fire the shot) was sentenced to death, he was hanged at Wandsworth Prison on 28th January 1953 after several appeals had been made and refused.

Craig was released from prison in May 1963, he moved to Buckinghamshire and married in 1965. Bentley was finally cleared of the murder and given a posthumous full pardon in 1999.

Several police officers received gallantry awards for this incident, they can be found in the 1953 section of this book.

BRITISH EMPIRE MEDAL FOR GALLANTRY
LG. 29/7/52

Lowndes	Anthony	Police Sergeant	129264

Police Sergeant Lowndes was on duty in plain clothes in a police car when a call was received for assistance at Wandsworth where two police officers had seen a man in the grounds of a private house. The Sergeant went in the car in the direction in which the man had made off, and then left the car ordering the driver to continue to patrol the area while he carried out a search on foot. After searching for a short time he saw a man move from behind a tree, he walked towards him and the man started to walk away. He was quite near the man and he called for him to stop, saying that he was a police officer, whereupon the man turned around and pulled a pistol from his pocket, pointing it at the Sergeant threatened to shoot him. Without hesitation the Sergeant jumped on the man and in the ensuing struggle the pistol fell to the ground. The man then ceased struggling and the Sergeant arrested him. The pistol was found to be an automatic weapon loaded with six rounds in the magazine and one in the chamber with the safety catch off.

BRITISH EMPIRE MEDAL FOR GALLANTRY
LG. 16/12/52

Wells	Albert Frank	Detective Sergeant	113508 M
Foster	John	Police Constable	119258 M
Furner	Maurice	Police Constable	133786 M

A man entered a post office and threatened the counter clerk with a revolver, seized a bundle of postal orders and made off. The alarm was given and the police summoned. Detective

Sergeant Wells and constable Furner searched for the man and when they caught up with him he immediately stepped back a few paces, drew a revolver from his pocket and pointed it at the Sergeant. The weapon was open chambered with what appeared to be a bullet in one of the chambers. Meanwhile constable Furner was trying to get behind the man, but the latter saw him and ran off. The constable and Sergeant pursued him but he dodged into a large block of flats. A few minutes later Wells saw the man coming towards him from the back of the building the Sergeant challenged him and although threatened with a revolver tried to reason with him, at the same time moving closer. Furner also closed in but the man still pointing the revolver at the officers ran into a garage yard. Constable Foster then arrived and with constable Furner entered the yard followed by Sergeant Wells. The man was standing with his back to a wall pointing the revolver at them. He threatened to shoot but the two constables rushed at him together whereupon he threw the weapon at them. There was a violent struggle but the man was overpowered.

BRITISH EMPIRE MEDAL FOR GALLANTRY
LG. 16/12/52

Burke   John Simpson   Police Constable   133173 M

Police constable Burke and another constable went to a flat to arrest a woman, a man answered the door but he refused to give any information, was abusive to the officers and threatened them with violence. Shortly afterwards he left the flat and the officers followed him. They saw him producing a revolver, he pointed it at them and threatened to shoot. Police constable Burke then told the other constable to get assistance while he followed the man as the latter backed away. Burke drew closer and the man again threatened to shoot, but constable Burke tackled him and brought him to the ground. There was a violent struggle but the other constable returned and the man was disarmed and overpowered.

GEORGE MEDAL
LG. 12/2/52

Stone   Frederick Mark   Police Constable   111658 C BEM

A man with a heavy iron bar smashed the window of a jeweller's shop and seized a valuable bracelet, at the same time a car with two men in it drew up by the shop and one of the men got out and threatened by-standers with a heavy instrument. The smash and grab incident was seen by constable Stone who was on duty in plain clothes and was walking on the opposite side of the street. He immediately ran across the road and as he did so he noticed a man threatening people with what appeared to be a stick with a large knob at the end. Constable Stone made straight for the man at the window who turned round and struck him on the arm and body with the iron bar. Stone however caught the man around the legs, throwing him on the ground. Stone was struggling with his opponent when he was attacked by the other man who hit him several times on the head with the weapon, severely wounding him and causing serious bleeding. Inspite of his wounds the constable clung to his prisoner who crawled towards the kerb near where the car was standing, but with the help of other police officers who had now arrived the man was overcome and taken into custody. Although both men were armed, constable Stone did not hesitate in his duty and even when he had been severely wounded in the head he still clung tenaciously to his prisoner, by his courage and determination he secured the arrest of a dangerous criminal.

GEORGE MEDAL
LG. 6/5/52

Bailey	Kenneth Alfred	Police Constable	129295 X
Darby	Sydney	Police Constable	120272 X
Shipton	Alfred Leonard	Inspector	113413 X

Inspector Shipton and police constables Bailey and Darby went to a house in Maida Vale when they were told the man in the first floor bedroom had shot at his wife. During their endeavour to arrest him he fired at them at short range, they were able nevertheless to rescue the woman, ultimately after further shots he tried to escape by the balcony. The officers eventually overpowered him.

GEORGE MEDAL
LG. 6/5/52

McKenzie	James Angus	Police Constable	127944 D

KING'S COMMENDATION FOR BRAVE CONDUCT

Ellar	Walter	Police Constable	130305 D

A man entered a public house in Paddington, fired two shots from an automatic pistol and wounded two men, he was tackled by another man but broke away and ran into the street. Police constable McKenzie and another constable who were on duty in the vicinity heard the shots and ran towards the public house. They reached it in time to see the men struggling in the street. McKenzie who was first on the scene saw the gun in the man's hand, nevertheless immediately made for him. He was almost in reach when the man broke loose and fired a shot, wounding the other man in the left leg. The gunman then ran off followed by McKenzie who caught up with him and after a struggle managed to disarm him and pull him to the ground and he was eventually overcome and arrested.

GEORGE MEDAL
LG. 6/5/52

Edwardes	John Sherrard Maxwell	Police Constable	136329 F

Constable Edwardes was on duty in Kensington High Street when he saw a motor car which had been reported stolen. He signalled the driver to stop, but the car gathered speed and he jumped on the off side running board and tried to open the door but found it locked. By this time the car was travelling very fast and was being swung from side to side in an endeavour to dislodge the officer. The car grazed a stationary car and the constable's left boot struck the refuge, at a junction the car was driven straight across against the traffic lights, the constable drew his truncheon, smashed the windscreen and hit the driver on the knuckles. The car hit a refuge and the lower part of the constable's body was struck, but he managed to retain his hold until the driver suddenly braked hard and succeeded in throwing him into the road. As the car moved off he jumped on again, and it finally crashed head on into the coping and wire fencing surrounding some gardens. The force of the impact threw the constable over the fencing which was about 6 feet high and into bushes on the other side. Inspite of this fall he quickly regained his feet, climbed back over the fence and tackled the driver before he could leave the car. A passing motorist telephoned for assistance, and the prisoner was taken to the police station. Pc Edwardes resigned from the police before the entry appeared in police orders.

KING'S COMMENDATION FOR BRAVE CONDUCT
LG. 12/2/52

Williams	Harold	Police Constable	134235 W
Clarke		Police Sergeant	124262 W

'For services when preventing the escape of an armed man.'

KING'S COMMENDATION FOR BRAVE CONDUCT
LG. 23/9/52

Bowman	John Edward	Police Constable	128435 Z

'For saving two children from serious injury when an accident occurred at a pedestrian crossing.'

KING'S COMMENDATION FOR BRAVE CONDUCT
LG. 16/12/52

Durbery	Ronald Arthur Jesse	Police Constable	130657 B

'For rescuing a woman from drowning.'

QUEEN'S COMMENDATION FOR BRAVE CONDUCT
LG 12/12/52

Sayers		Police Constable	133298

CARNEGIE HERO FUND

Bowman	John Edward	Police Constable	128435 Z

Sustained serious injury while preventing two boys from being run down by a dust cart at Croydon, also received an award of £10 from the fund.

Penrose	Peter John Harold	Police Constable	131829 W

'For services when stopping a runaway horse in Banstead.'

ROLL OF HONOUR
* Pc Sidney George Miles KPFSM

Craig & Bentley incident
* Pc Ronald Victor Saunders

Died from a fractured skull as a result of a motorcycle accident while on duty on Catford Division.

1953

This year also had one famous murderer, John Reginald Haliday Christie, this case was the subject of a film '10 Rillington Place' starring Richard Attenborough as John Christie. See below for the outline of the murders.

January	RAF's first supersonic fighters US designed Sabres arrive at RAF Abingdon.
February	128 die when a car ferry sails with its door open and sinks off Belfast Lough.
March	Police launch hunt for John Christie for murder of his wife, her body is discovered at 10 Rillington Place. Christie is subsequently arrested.
April	The Queen launches the new Royal Yacht Britannia.
May	Police exhume the bodies of Beryl Evans and her baby.
June	Mount Everest is conquered by Edmund Hillary and Sherpa Tensing.
July	Guns fall silent in Korea.
August	In Greece over 1000 reported dead after earthquakes and tidal waves.
September	Jacqueline Bouvier marries Jack Kennedy.
October	Scotland Yard uses television for the first time in its hunt for murder suspect William Pettit.
November	Peers approve plans for commercial television.
December	Jack Hawkins leads an opinion poll as Britain's most popular film star.

HITS OF THE YEAR
I love Paris
Diamonds are a girl's best friend
From here to eternity

JOHN REGINALD HALIDAY CHRISTIE - 1953
John Christie was born on 8th April 1898 in Halifax, his father Ernest was a carpet designer and was a founder member of the Halifax Conservative Party and a leading light in the Primrose League, an organisation promoting purity among the working classes. Christie's mother Mary Hannah was keen on amateur dramatics. John was one of seven children, he was disciplined by his father whom he grew to hate. John Christie had a share of his father's ill temper and meanness and so had very few friends.

At 18 he was called up for service in World War 1 and was sent to France, 2 years later in June 1918 he was gassed and for a short while received a disability pension. On 20th May 1920 he married Ethel Waddington, soon after he was caught stealing money and was jailed for 9 months. He had several more periods in prison, and after a time he wrote to Ethel asking her to go back to him, this she did until her death.

Christie and Ethel lived at 10 Rillington Place, North Kensington, London moving there in 1938, they had a ground floor flat. In 1949 a young couple Timothy Evans, his wife Beryl and their baby daughter Geraldine moved into the top floor flat. For some reason Timothy Evans confessed to killing his wife and disposing of her body down a drain. When the police searched they found not only the body of his wife but that of his baby daughter. Evans was arrested and later convicted of the murders. During the trial Evans changed his story and accused Christie, but as Christie was one of the prosecution witnesses he denied any knowledge, Evans was found guilty and hanged for the murders.

In 1952 Christie killed his wife and buried her under the floorboards of his ground floor flat, in January 1953 he killed 2 prostitutes, in April he killed another. In March 1953 Christie moved out of the flat, the new tenant, a Jamaican, Mr Brown moved in. Over the next few days Mr Brown started to clear the flat of a large amount of rubbish and was then able to start on the decorating. He started peeling away some wallpaper and discovered an alcove, he shone his torch in to see what was behind and that is when the grisly truth emerged. Detectives immediately discovered that 10 Rillington Place concealed not one but several bodies.

One vital witness was needed. A description was circulated of 'John Christie'. Several sightings were reported. On 31st March 1953 Pc Thomas Ledger saw a man leaning over the embankment by Putney Bridge. The hunt for Christie was finally over.

In all Christie, between 1943 and 1953, was known to have murdered at least 8 women and one baby. He was charged, and found guilty of the murders and hanged at Pentonville Prison on 15th July 1953.

On 18th October 1966 Timothy Evans was granted a posthumous pardon for the murder of his wife and child, murders which he did not commit.

John Reginald Haliday Christie became a war reserve police constable in the Metropolitan Police Force, he joined on 1 September 1939 warrant number 07732.

GEORGE CROSS - CRAIG & BENTLEY
LG. 2/1/53

| Fairfax | Frederick William | Detective Constable | 125235 C |

GEORGE MEDAL

| Harrison | Norman | Police Constable | 135799 Z |
| McDonald | James Christie | Police Constable | 127068 Z |

KING'S POLICE & FIRE SERVICE MEDAL
Posthumous

| Miles | Sidney George | Police Constable | 119962 Z |

BRITISH EMPIRE MEDAL FOR GALLANTRY

| Jaggs | Robert James William | Police Constable | 137256 Z |

Shortly after 9 O'clock on the night of 2nd November 1952 2 men (Christopher Craig and Derek Bentley) were seen to climb over the side gate of a warehouse at Tamworth Road, Croydon, and to reach the flat roof of the building about 22 feet above. The alarm was given and Detective Constable Fairfax and Constable Harrison and other officers went to the premises in a police van. At about the same time Constable McDonald and another Constable arrived in a police wireless car. Other police officers took up various positions around the building. When told the suspects had climbed up the drainpipe to the roof Detective Constable Fairfax immediately scaled the drainpipe. Constable McDonald followed him but was unable to negotiate the last six feet and had to return to the ground.

Fairfax reached the top and pulled himself onto the roof. In the moonlight he saw the two men about 15 yards away behind a brick stack. He walked towards them, challenged them and dashed behind a stack, grabbed one of the men and pulled him into the open. The man broke away, his companion then fired at Fairfax and wounded him in the right shoulder. Fairfax fell to the ground but as the two criminals ran past him he got up and closed with one of them and knocked him down. A second shot was then fired at Fairfax but he retained his hold on his man (Bentley), dragged him behind a skylight and searched him. He found a knuckle duster and a dagger which he removed. Constable McDonald meanwhile had made another effort to climb the drainpipe and had almost reached the top. Fairfax helped him onto the roof and called to the gunman to drop his gun, but he refused and made further threats. During this time Constable Harrison had climbed onto the sloping roof nearby and was edging his way along towards the gunman by lying back on the roof with his heels in the guttering, he was seen and a shot was fired at him which struck the roof close to his head he continued his journey, however another shot was fired at him which missed. Harrison then got behind a chimney stack and reached the ground where he joined other officers who entered the building, ran up to the fire escape exit door on the roof and pushed it open. Fairfax warned them that the man with the gun was nearby but Constable Miles jumped from the doorway onto the roof. As he did so the gunman fired and the Constable fell to the ground shot between the eyes. Fairfax immediately left cover to bring in the casualty and a further shot was fired at him. McDonald also came forward and the two officers dragged the shot Constable behind the fire escape exit. Constable Harrison then jumped out onto the roof and standing in the roof doorway threw his truncheon and other things at the gunman who again fired at him. Constable Jaggs then reached the roof by way of the drainpipe and was also fired upon but joined the other Constables. Fairfax, helped by Harrison, pushed his captive through the door and handed him over to the other officers. Detective Constable Fairfax was given a police pistol and he immediately returned to the roof. He jumped through the doorway again called for the gunman to drop his weapon. A further shot was fired at him but he advanced towards the man firing his own pistol as he went. The gunman (Craig) then jumped over the side of the roof to the ground below where he was arrested.

This was the last award of the KPM. It became the Queen's Police Medal and was only awarded posthumously for gallantry.

A small memorial garden with a stone is at the front of Croydon Police Station in memory of Pc Miles.

GEORGE MEDAL - AIR RAID 1940
LG.31/1/53

McDonough   Clarence Lambie   Station Inspector

During an air raid 3 houses were demolished, on hearing the cries of people trapped, he entered the premises and passed several of the injured to safety. Unable to free one elderly occupant, he stayed with him until he was freed. On another occasion a 4 storey building was bombed, he climbed a stair case and operated a stirrup pump while molten lead was actually falling on his shoulders. On arrival of the fire brigade he removed the pump and a moment later the roof collapsed.

GEORGE MEDAL
LG.6/10/53

| Dorsett | George Edward | Police Constable | 129121 J |
| Snitch | Edward Norman | Police Constable | 127219 J |

The manager of a firm at Hackney saw three men acting suspiciously just below his window. He informed the police. Constables Snitch and Dorsett together with another constable went to the scene in a police car. On arrival they saw two men being pursued. The police car chased after the two men who ran across a bombed site, the car was driven across the rough ground as far as possible and while constable Dorsett remained behind Snitch and the other constable jumped out and followed the men who had separated. Constable Snitch was about 5 yards behind one man, he called on him to stop, the man turned round, threatened the constable and then reached under his raincoat with his right hand pulled out a revolver and fired at the officer. The bullet grazed the right side of Snitch's face, and he stumbled and fell to his knees. Constable Dorsett believing Snitch to be shot jumped from the car and ran towards the criminal as he did so Snitch got up and with Dorsett closed with the man who fired two more shots. Dorsett got hold of the man's head while Snitch grasped the weapon and wrenched it away. The revolver was found to contain 3 spent and 3 live cartridges. Although fired at, the two constables persisted in the pursuit of an armed and reckless criminal.

QUEEN'S COMMENDATION FOR BRAVE CONDUCT
LG. 6/10/53

| Baldwin | George Kenneth Frank | Police Constable | 134311 J |

'For services when 2 dangerous criminals were arrested.'

| Gilbert | David Ben | Police Constable | 135453 W |

'For stopping a runaway horse.'

| Williams | Tom | Police Constable | 136214 B |

'For stopping a runaway horse.'

ROLL OF HONOUR
•   Ds Harold John Whatley

Died from a fractured skull received in a motor car accident on duty when his car collided with a lorry at Catford.

1954

January	Flashing direction indicator lights become legal on motor vehicles in Britain.
February	800th episode of the 'Archers' is broadcast, it now has an audience of 10 million.
March	Television licence is to increase from £2 to £3.
April	Independent trials of Polio Vaccine begin.
May	Boeing unveils the new 707 aircraft.

June	In London doctors urge a stricter drink test on drivers rather than tongue twisters and walking in a straight line.
July	Government publishes plans for civil defence in the event of an H-bomb attack.
August	Atomic Energy Authority is established in London.
September	Opening of Kidbrooke school, the LCC's first new comprehensive school.
October	In the UK Emperor Haile Selassie of Ethiopia begins a State Visit.
November	MP's approve the new Highway Code.
December	The old age pension rises by 7/6d to £2 a week.

HITS OF THE YEAR

Fly me to the moon
Rock around the clock
On the water front

BRITISH EMPIRE MEDAL FOR GALLANTRY

13/4/54

Gulliver   John Alan   Police Constable   136881 L

Pc Gulliver was on duty one night when he became suspicious of a parked up vehicle. He went over to speak to the driver and while he was at the driver's window the vehicle started to drive off. The constable called on him to stop, but instead the driver increased his speed and the car drove off and turned into another street. Gulliver clung onto the car by putting his arm through the driver's window and his hand onto the open sunroof. The driver swerved the car to the off side, mounted the pavement and increased its speed to about 30mph. One of the passengers in the car shut the sunroof crushing the constable's fingers and forcing him to let go. He did however manage to remain on the car by putting his arm around the pillar between the front and rear doors. The driver then drove the car along a wall attempting to dislodge the constable. He did manage to hold on to the car even though he was in considerable pain. The car turned sharply and then overturned. Pc Gulliver was thrown over the roof of the car and lost consciousness for a few seconds. When he recovered he saw the driver scramble through the sunroof and run off. Pc Gulliver although still dazed gave chase. After chasing the man through several streets, he finally caught up with him in a back garden and after a struggle arrested the man.

GEORGE MEDAL

28/9/54

Bailey   John Richard Thomas   Detective Constable   128776 W

BRITISH EMPIRE MEDAL FOR GALLANTRY

Nicholls   Cyril Charles   Detective Sergeant   W

After being arrested for being a deserter and suspected criminal, a man broke away from his escort. He pulled a revolver from his pocket and ran. Detective constable Bailey and Detective Sergeant Nichols gave chase; a police dog was released and sent after the man. The man then turned and fired his revolver at the police dog but missed. Detective constable

Bailey was only a few yards from him and was immediately followed by Detective Sergeant Nichols. Bailey had almost caught up the man when he suddenly spun round, pointed the revolver at him and then pulled the trigger, but there was only a click and no explosion. The man then continued running along the road. Bailey threw his truncheon at the man but missed. The man then fired a second time at the police dog but the shot missed. Bailey continued the chase and when only a few yards away was again fired at but the shot missed. The police dog then tackled the man, who again fired the revolver, but the dog was jumping about and the shot missed its target. Detective constable Bailey had in the mean time caught up the them and although being threatened by him with the revolver closed with the man and threw him to the ground. Within a few seconds Detective Sergeant Nichols arrived and assisted in making the arrest.

GEORGE MEDAL
28/9/54

Bocking	Leonard Geoffrey	Police Constable	131524 D
Sinclair	George Alexander	Police Constable	132862 D

Police were called to a jeweller's shop. When the arrived, they found the door locked but all the lights were on. Three of the officers that arrived ran down a passage way at the side of an adjoining premises while another remained at the shop entrance to prevent anyone leaving. On arrival constable's Bocking and Sinclair went into the work room at the back of the jeweller's shop and discovered two men lying in a pool of blood. One of the men appeared to be dead and the other was unconscious with his hands tied behind him with a tie. Constable Sinclair started to search the premises and Bocking went to the yard at the rear. When Bocking reached the basement area he looked down and noticed a man crouching in a doorway. He shouted to him as he made his way down the steps, he then saw the man bring his right arm from under his raincoat that he was carrying. As Bocking approached the man he saw that he was holding a pistol. Bocking immediately jumped onto him and grabbed his right wrist in an attempt to get the pistol from him. By the time constable Sinclair had come to the back of the shop and hearing a noise from the basement area he looked down and saw constable Bocking struggling with the man from behind and trying to prevent him from moving his arms and hands. Constable Sinclair could see the pistol which was by now being waved from side to side in front of the man. A violent struggle was taking place. He then ran down the steps to aid his colleague. Just before he got there the pistol went off, but with total disregard Sinclair grabbed the pistol and after a struggle wrenched it from the man's grip. The man then collapsed, and it transpires that he had shot himself during the struggle. The weapon the man was holding was an automatic pistol in working order, 3 bullets had apparently been fired.

QUEEN'S COMMENDATION FOR BRAVE CONDUCT
28/9/54

Geesing	Peter George	Police Constable	134370 G

'Tackling three men who were acting suspiciously.'

ROLL OF HONOUR
- Pc David Barrett

Collided with a lorry at Hunton Bridge while on an advanced motorcycle course.
- Pc Percy James Claxton

Killed by a gas explosion when called to investigate a suspected suicide in Hampstead.

1955

A crime of passion or pure murder. Ruth Ellis was the last woman to be hanged in the United Kingdom for the murder of her lover David Blakely. See below for highlights of the story.

January	Archaeologists confirm that 'Piltdown man' was indeed a hoax.
February	London Transport announce plans for new tube line from Victoria to Walthamstow.
March	The City of London is to become a 'smokeless zone'.
April	Ruth Ellis charged with the murder of David Blakely and later convicted and hanged.
May	Government declares a State of Emergency as the dock strike deepens.
June	80 die when 3 cars crash at 150 mph on the le mans race track.
July	US Disneyland opens at Anaheim, California.
August	US airman runs amok in Broadstairs Kent, killing 3 and wounding 9.
September	Force of British Commandoes sent to Cyprus amid mounting tension.
October	BBC demonstrates the colour television at Alexandra Palace.
November	State of alert in Cyprus.
December	Cardiff becomes the capital of Wales.

HITS OF THE YEAR
Cherry pink and apple blossom white
Rosemarie

RUTH ELLIS - 1955
CRIME OF PASSION OR PURE MURDER?

Ruth Neilson was born on 9th October 1926 the fourth child of a professional musician Arthur Neilson and his wife Bertha, they had fled to England from Belgium as refugees during the first world war.

In 1941 the family moved to Southward, South London and at 15 yrs Ruth began work as a machine minder in the local OXO factory. She contracted Rheumatic fever and spent a year off work, she was ordered to take up dancing as a convalescent exercise. At 17 she became a photographer's assistant, her work taking her to London Dance halls. She soon met and fell in love with a Canadian soldier, they were to marry but it was soon discovered that he already had a wife and family back home. He went back to Canada and Ruth gave birth to his son on 15th September 1944. While Ruth tried to find work, the bringing up of her son was left to her mother and older married sister Muriel.

Ruth married George Ellis on 8 November 1950, she realised that he could provide her with money, a name for her and her son and the social status which she had longed for. They moved out of London to Southampton. Their relationship quickly fell apart, he could not stop his drinking, they often had violent arguments, and by the time their daughter Georgina was born in 1951 their marriage was over.

Ruth moved back to London with her two children she had to support. She returned to the Court Club now called Carrolls, new clientele were there, young racing drivers from the Steering Wheel club in Brick Street near to Hyde Park Corner. It was here that Ruth met David Blakely. On her birthday in 1953 she was made manageress of the club, she was allowed to live rent free in the flat above the club. One month after their first meeting David Blakely moved in with her.

For two years they were involved in a torrid affair even though he was already engaged to another woman. Although having money of his own he sponged off Ruth and enjoyed free drinks in the club. Eventually his oppressive and juvenile behaviour drove away the club members and caused Ruth eventually to lose her job.

Ruth and David continued their stormy relationship, he broke off his engagement, which Ruth believed was for her sake and possible marriage to her. But a short time after this he arrived home with love bites all over his back, she realised that he was up to his old tricks.

She was again pregnant but he refused marriage even though her divorce to George Ellis was imminent. A few days later he beat her so badly, punching her in the stomach that she miscarried.

At a party hosted by David Blakely's friends, they ran out of beer, he said he would go and get some more, on walking to his car Ruth was waiting for him, she shot him once, he ran but fell down, she walked up to him and emptied the chamber into his back. Several people had witnessed the gunning down of David Blakely in cold blood, Ruth remained at the scene and handed the gun to Pc Thompson and watched while the ambulance took David Blakely to the hospital where he was pronounced dead on arrival.

She appeared before the Central Criminal Court in June 1955, the jury were only out for 23 minutes and returned a verdict of guilty with no recommendation for mercy. Ruth Ellis was hanged at Holloway Prison at 9 am 13th July 1955.

GEORGE MEDAL

14/6/55

Bush	Ethel Violet	Woman Police Sergeant	578 Z
Parrott	Kathleen Flora	Woman Police Constable	1000 Z

Woman police Sergeant Bush and woman police constable Parrott both displayed outstanding gallantry, determination and devotion to duty when they brought about the arrest of a dangerous criminal. They both acted as decoys in the full knowledge that they might be the victims of horrible and violent assault. Both the officers were attacked and seriously injured.

The man who attacked the two women officers was William George Barnett a 29yr labourer. The attack took place on Fairfield Path, Croydon. William George Barnett was sentenced to 10yrs imprisonment.

Wpc Parrott joined the Metropolitan Police on 11th September 1951 and resigned on 9th September 1956.

QUEEN'S COMMENDATION FOR BRAVE CONDUCT
17/5/55

| Tomlinson | David Arthur | Police Constable | 140109 G |

'Attempting to stop a motor car driven in a dangerous manner.'

ROYAL HUMANE SOCIETY BRONZE MEDAL

| Hall | | Police Constable | 135700 B |

For attempting to save a man from asphyxia in a gas filled room.

| Weeks | | Police Constable | 138360 B |

Resuscitation certificate by the society for restoring Pc Hall to consciousness by applying artificial respiration.

ROLL OF HONOUR

1956

January	London report that the import and export of heroin is banned.
February	MP's vote in favour of abolishing the death penalty.
March	British deport Makarios from Cyprus.
April	Prince Rainier of Monaco marries US actress Grace Kelly.
May	Commander 'Buster' Crabb disappears while diving near two Russian cruisers at Portsmouth harbour. His headless body is found in the sea off Chichester in June.
June	Nasser elected President of Egypt.
July	ERNIE (electronic random number indicator equipment) to pick premium bond winners is unveiled.
August	British and French troops sail for Suez.
September	Elvis Presley wins a massive television audience, performed on the Ed Sullivan show and was viewed by 82% of potential 54 million audience.
October	Anglo French forces bombard Suez.
November	Egyptian Government begins expelling British, French and Zionist residents.
December	Government approves television broadcasting between 6 pm and 7 pm.

HITS OF THE YEAR
Heartbreak hotel
Que, sera sear
I'll be home
Around the world in 80 days

GEORGE MEDAL
27/1/56
Burdett

| Keith Trevor | | Police Constable | 130809 L |

BRITISH EMPIRE MEDAL FOR GALLANTRY

Frampton	George Henry	Detective Sergeant	121609 CO C8
Green	Robert Neville	Police Constable	127078 CO B6
Morgan	Wyndham David	Police Constable	133323 B
Lewis	John Atkinson	Police Constable	126283 L

Constable Burdett was on night duty when he saw two men near a parked and unattended car, one of whom was apparently attempting to open the rear door. There was also a third man standing nearby. As the officer walked towards the three men they ran off, he then gave chase. The constable heard a noise coming from behind a wall of a derelict and bombed site. Constable Burdett went to a telephone and called for assistance. Shortly after making the call constable Lewis and other officers arrived by car. On their arrival Lewis and Burdett climbed the wall of the bombed site, and as Burdett was reaching the top of the wall shots were fired from 5 or 6 feet in front of him. Constable Burdett felt a blast hit the right side of his face and at the same time something struck his helmet. He then dropped from the wall and crouched down for a moment.

At this time the man on the other side of the wall then shouted out that he would kill anyone who came over the wall. Constable Burdett started to climb the wall again and as his hands were on top of the wall levering himself up two more shots were fired, the second shot struck the officer's left index finger causing him to fall from the wall. Between the shots being fired Burdett saw a man crouching in the yard about four feet from the wall. On hearing the shot Constable Lewis went to assist his colleague and both officers looked over the wall, they saw a man climbing into the next yard. Burdett was then taken to hospital and in the mean time constable Lewis who by this time had climbed the wall in pursuit of the man and was joined by Detective Sergeant Frampton and constables Green and Morgan. Constable Green shone his torch from the roof of a lean to shed and through a crack in the door noticed movement. He shouted to Detective Sergeant Frampton who was following constable Lewis. They jumped into the yard and pushed back the door. A shot was fired in the direction of Detective Sergeant Frampton. The officer jumped back and the door then shut. He called out to the man to come out but was answered with more threats; another shot was fired from a hole in the top of the door. Frampton and the constables charged the door and broke the bottom part of it, a leg came through the opening and Frampton grabbed it and pulled hard causing the man inside to slip and fall. As the officers broke down the remaining part of the door a pistol fell to ground and after a struggle the man was arrested.

GEORGE MEDAL

1/1/56

Chambers	Albert Eric John	Police Sergeant	125742 CO C8
Karn	George William	Police Constable	129627 P
Wood	David Evans	Police Constable	138970 C

BRITISH EMPIRE MEDAL FOR GALLANTRY

Cameron	Donald	Police Constable	119602 CO B6

Three criminals had joined together, they stole a car and had acquired firearms for use in armed robberies. Armed with revolvers the gang had entered a jewellery shop at Earls Court and held up the owner and his two assistants and had taken about £400 worth of jewellery. They were disturbed and made their escape in a stolen car. Sergeant Chambers and another Sergeant were in a police car driven by constable Cameron when they saw the stolen car with its three occupants coming towards them. Cameron then turned the car and started to give chase, the stolen car at several occasions reached speeds of 70mph, but Cameron managed to keep it in view all the time. At Stanhope Gate the cars were only about 10 to 15 yards apart. At this stage one of the criminals leaned out of the window of the car and fired two shots at the police car. The first shot apparently missed but the second shot made a hole in the centre of the windscreen and caused extensive cracking of the window which blurred the officer's view, and cut Cameron's hands. Sergeant Chambers immediately knocked out some of the broken glass so that they could see where they were going. A further shot was fired at them and then the stolen car collided with another car and the three criminals abandoned it. Two of the men ran off along Curzon Street. Sergeant Chambers and constable Cameron ran after them but due to the heavy traffic and the number of people about the officers lost sight of them. Cameron returned to the police car and maintained wireless communication with headquarters, while the Sergeant continued pursuit. Constable Wood was on his beat in Curzon Street when he saw the criminals abandon their vehicle. He at once ran in pursuit of one of the men of who was at the time holding a revolver. Constable Karn was on motorcycle patrol when he heard shots and soon afterwards saw two men running towards him closely followed by constable Wood and Sergeant Chambers. He crossed the road to intercept the gunman who however turned and fired at the officer from about 3 yards away. Fortunately the bullet missed Karn who then threw his crash helmet at the man which struck him on the back of the head but did not stop him. Karn then retrieved his crash helmet and along with constable Wood and Sergeant Chambers continued the pursuit. Further shots were fired and the gunman after trying to get away firstly in a taxi cab and then a lorry, both of which were blocked in by traffic ran into Charles Street with constables Wood and Karn who finally caught up with him. Wood who at the time was in front tried to close with him but the man then fired at the officer. The shot missed Wood who then grabbed the criminal's jacket, the man then fired again and the shot struck Wood and passed through his right thigh near the groin causing him to fall to the ground. Constable Karn was separated from Wood and the gunman by a line of parked cars, again threw his crash helmet at the man and hit him but did not knock him down. Sergeant Chambers was also hindered by parked cars was running along abreast of the man and seeking his opportunity to get close to him. At least one shot was fired at the Sergeant over the roofs of the parked cars, eventually Sergeant Chambers saw an opening between the cars and ran through and brought the gunman to the ground. But as he did so he was shot through the right forearm, but the Sergeant managed to wrench the revolver away. Constable Karn immediately came to his assistance and together with another officer the man was finally arrested.

BRITISH EMPIRE MEDAL FOR GALLANTRY
18/12/56

Wall	Anthony Gaius	Police Constable	137996 S

Constable Wall was in plain clothes along with another officer when they examined the back of a large unoccupied house which appeared to have been unlawfully entered. Constable Wall made his way to the side of the house where he found a door had been shut but not locked. When he entered he saw two boys run from the kitchen to an inner part of the house. He followed them and called out that he was a police officer. One of the boys made for the stair case and the other ran off to the lounge. Wall then went into the room and saw the boy with a revolver in his hand. As Wall walked up to the boy he pointed the gun at him and then fired from a distance of about 3 feet. The bullet entered the constable's left cheek. Despite the injury and extensive bleeding constable Wall walked towards the boy telling him to drop the revolver but the boy continued to struggle and several of the windows were broken. The constable did manage to get hold of the revolver and arrested the boy. The constable was eventually taken to hospital where it was discovered the bullet had entered his left cheek and exited from his left ear.

GEORGE MEDAL
5/10/56

| Loxley | Norman George | Police Sergeant | 136136 V |
| Oliver | Thomas | Police Constable | 120688 V |

The leading coach of an electric passenger train from Waterloo to Chertsey overturned after colliding at speed with the rear of a freight train from Battersea. The overturned carriage had a number of trapped passengers inside, and an intensive fire ensued. Police Sergeant Loxley was in charge of the crew of a police car on the night of the accident and constable Oliver was the driver. They drove immediately to the scene of the accident, where they found the wreckage burning fiercely. The heat was so intense that the iron bridge supports were red hot. The two officers made their was to the leading coach and when there they saw a man's legs moving beneath the smashed and burning debris of the compartment. They both rushed into the fire to pull him out but found that the victim was pinned tightly. They could not free him and had to leave momentarily from the heat, smoke and flames. At this time the current was still on and the fire was increasing. Constable Oliver once again rushed into the flames and tore at the burning wreckage which was covering the man. Sergeant Loxley was then able to release the trapped man and drag him to safety. Both of the officers risked their lives in effecting the rescue of this man.

GEORGE MEDAL
Posthumous
5/10/56

| Eden | Maurice | Police Sergeant | 136095 |

Attached to the UK Police Unit, Cyprus Police Force.

QUEEN'S POLICE MEDAL
Posthumous

| Demmon | Leonard | Police Sergeant | 138760 |

'A' Division Attached to the UK Police Unit, Cyprus Police Force.

Sergeant Eden along with another member of the United Kingdom Police Unit and two Cypriot Police wardens were taking a political detainee to Nicosia General Hospital for an X-ray examination. Sergeant Eden was in possession of a .38 revolver and the others with sub machine guns. On completion of the X-ray the party were going through the crowded main hall of the hospital when they were attacked by three or more terrorists. The companion of the Sergeant was seriously wounded and fell to the ground. Sergeant Eden with complete disregard for his own safety engaged the terrorists, he shot one dead and after running out of ammunition knocked one other on the head with the butt of his revolver while he was trying to escape. Sergeant Eden returned to his mortally wounded colleague but was again fired on by other terrorists. Sergeant Eden chased the attacker but he managed to escape.

QUEEN'S COMMENDATION FOR BRAVE CONDUCT
1/5/56

Roberts	James Derek	Police Constable	139967 Y

'Dealing with an insane man who was armed with a knife.'

Cooke	Ernest Frank Christopher Darters	Police Sergeant	127363 CO C8

'For services when an armed criminal was pursued and arrested.'

QUEEN'S COMMENDATION FOR BRAVE CONDUCT
20/5/56

Goring	Arthur Harry	Police Constable

'Rescuing a child and attempting to rescue other occupants trapped in a blazing house.'

QUEEN'S COMMENDATION FOR BRAVE CONDUCT
18/12/56

Utley	David Boyd	Police Constable	139144 N

"Scene of a road traffic accident on a pedestrian crossing."

ROLL OF HONOUR
- Ps George Goggins, 121755, H, aged 48

Collided with a lorry while undergoing car driver training near Dunstable.
- Ps Maurice Eden GM, A
- Ps Leonard Demmon QPM, A
- Ps Reginald Tipple, T

Shot during a terrorist incident while attached to the Police in Cyprus.

1957

January	A man upset by the shape of his nose is jailed for 10 years for threatening a plastic surgeon with a gun.
February	The Vulcan bomber enters service with the RAF.
March	Northern Ireland police uncover a plot to attack Royal Naval bases.
April	Singapore granted self government from Britain.
May	GPO announce plans for an automatic trunk dialling by 1959.
June	Benidorm is the new holiday spot on Spain's Costa del Sol.
July	State of Emergency declared in Ireland.

August	The drunkometer is tested in the US, it measures the amount of alcohol on the breath.
September	Asian flu death toll rises in the UK.
October	Russia launch man made satellite into space - Sputnik 1.
November	Russia puts a dog called Laika into space.
December	Elvis Presley is called up and joins the US Army.

HITS OF THE YEAR
All shook up
Love letters in the sand
The Bridge on the River Kwai

BRITISH EMPIRE MEDAL FOR GALLANTRY
8/10/57

Bullard	Brendan Thomas	Police Constable	142335 L
Thompson	Thomas Charles William	Police Constable	132188 H
Kay	John	Police Constable	124266 H

Constables Bullard, Kay and Thompson were on duty in the early hours in a police car driven by Kay when the noticed two men acting suspiciously. Thompson and Bullard left their vehicle to keep observation on them and noticed a large black saloon car unlit containing four men pull up from behind some stationary lorries, it then drove away quickly. The police car followed the saloon car which had been stolen and which drove away at very high speed across Tower Bridge. The pursuit which followed gained speeds varying from 70 to 80 mph through many streets of south east London. During the chase the rear doors of the stolen car were opened and iron bars were brandished by the occupants, the car swerving from side to side. After a dangerous chase of 9 miles the stolen car was stopped. As constables Thompson and Bullard got out of their car they were attacked by four men with iron bars. A violent struggle began during which constables Bullard and Kay were knocked unconscious by blows to their head with iron bars. Thompson was still dazed from a similar blow to the mouth but he managed to assist his seriously injured colleagues. A second police car then arrived and the four men ran away through a courtyard of a nearby block of flats. A search was carried out and later 3 men were arrested. The constables knew they were outnumbered and that the criminals were armed but showed great courage in attempting to make the arrest.

BRITISH EMPIRE MEDAL FOR GALLANTRY
8/10/57

Harris	John Richard	Police Constable	139255 S

Police officers were on plain clothes duty at an underground railway station when they noticed four youths leave the forecourt of the station and loiter in a shop doorway which was near to some parked and unattended cars. In view of their behaviour they were all stopped by the three officers and were questioned. During the search they were found to be in possession of two torches and two pairs of gloves, the officers were not happy with their explanations for being there. They were all told they were being arrested but one of them managed to break free and ran off with constable Harris chasing. After some distance the youth turned and pointed a revolver at Harris who was at this time several yards away from him. The youth then fired at him, the bullet passing to the right of his head. The youth ran across the road, but was soon tackled by constable Harris and after a struggle the constable was able to gain possession of the revolver. With the assistance of a colleague the youth was finally arrested. The revolver was ready for free firing and was loaded with three live shotgun cartridges which had been cut down in length in order to fit.

QUEEN'S COMMENDATION FOR BRAVE CONDUCT
12/2/57

Young	Robert John	Police Constable	139759 C

'Fire broke out on the 4th storey of a building.'

QUEEN'S COMMENDATION FOR BRAVE CONDUCT
7/5/57

Norman	James Winton	Police Constable	133105 J

'Pursuing and trying to arrest a man driving a car containing stolen property.'

QUEEN'S COMMENDATION FOR BRAVE CONDUCT
9/7/57

Claridge	Stanley Richard	Police Constable	139984 E
Edwards	Trevor Leslie	Police Constable	140331 E

'Arrest of a man for house breaking.'

Grove	Frederick Arthur	Police Constable	117080 Y

'For arresting an armed criminal who attempted to rob a jeweller.'

QUEEN'S COMMENDATION FOR BRAVE CONDUCT
26/11/57

Morcock	Leonard Charles	Police Constable	137212 H

'Attempting to arrest 3 criminals in a stolen car.'

ROLL OF HONOUR
• Supt Cornelius Carson

Overcome by fumes rescuing a child from married quarters during a fire at Hackney Police Station.

1958

January	First radar speed checks introduced in London.
February	Munich air disaster - 7 members of Manchester United football team die.
March	Britain's first parking tickets being issued to motorists.
April	3000 anti nuclear protesters set out on a march to Aldermaston.

May	The new high altar of St Paul's is dedicated as the Empire War Memorial.
June	In the UK Yellow no waiting lines come into force.
July	Prince Charles is created 'Prince of Wales' by the Queen.
August	13 arrests made in the fighting between white and black youths at Notting Hill, London.
September	British trawlers defy the 12 mile limit which came into force in Iceland.
October	BOAC launches the first scheduled transatlantic jet service.
November	In Cuba Castro frees 25 people held on a hijacked aircraft.
December	Britain's first 8 mile stretch of motorway the Preston By Pass opens.

HITS OF THE YEAR
Who's sorry now
All I have to do is dream
Magic moments
Gigi

BRITISH EMPIRE MEDAL FOR GALLANTRY
21/10/58

Winter   Stewart John   Police Constable   144111 T

Just after midnight police constable Winter notice a man get out of a jeep and enter a shop. As Winter crossed the road, he heard a sound of glass being smashed and saw the man run back to his jeep. Winter called on the man to stop and flashed his torch at him, but the man drove his jeep straight at him. As it passed he managed to jump onto the bonnet. The man then drove about 150 yards down the road doing all he could to throw the officer off, he even zig zagged to try to dislodge the officer. Winter managed to hold on until the vehicle hit a pedestrian guard rail. The force of the impact threw the officer over the rails, he was being badly shaken and received cuts and abrasions to his shins and left knee, injury to his right foot and elbow. The man abandoned the vehicle and ran off, but despite his injuries the officer gave chase. After some 80 yards he overtook the man, there was a violent struggle but another constable arrived and the man was overcome and arrested.

GEORGE CROSS
21/10/58

Stevens   Henry William   Police Constable   138848 P

Constable Stevens was in plain clothes assigned to a police car in Bromley, Kent along with two other officers. They received a message over the police radio to make their way to a dwelling house where a burglar alarm has been activated. When they arrived at the house two of the officers entered the front door in order to search while constable Stevens went to the rear which was separated from the road by a high fence. As he reached the rear of the house a man jumped over the fence a few yards from him. He immediately shouted that he was a police officer and called out to the man to stop. The man ignored him and ran off the constable chased after him. After a distance of about 75 yards the man turned and pointed a revolver at the officer and threatened to shoot. Stevens continued running towards the man who when the constable was close enough fired the revolver. The bullet struck Stevens in the mouth, it shattered his teeth and part of his jaw bone. But despite these injuries the officer threw himself on the man and managed to wrench the weapon from him and pinned him against some railings. The man eventually stopped struggling and gave the impression he would yield, but he suddenly managed to break away and ran back along the road. Bleeding extensively from the mouth and in a great deal of pain constable Stevens chased the man who after about 40 yards doubled back and tried to pass him. The officer again tackled the gunman but was again unable to stop him from struggling free again, leaving his jacket and coat in the hands of the officer. At this point Stevens was close to collapse but continued the chase but after a short distance collapsed to the ground exhausted. But mainly owing to the jacket and coat which Stevens had managed to retain, the man was later traced and arrested.

QUEEN'S COMMENDATION FOR BRAVE CONDUCT
21/10/58

Hoggard	Phillip	Police Constable	127135 H

'For his services when a basement club was set on fire.'

Vibart	Jasper Peter	Police Sergeant	125169 W
Perkins	John Joseph	Police Constable	129892 CO C8

'For effecting the arrest of an armed criminal.'

ROLL OF HONOUR
- Pc Edgar Gerald Allen

Crashed on a police motorcycle while pursuing a speeding car at Chiswick.
- Pc Raymond Henry Summers, 144871 N

Stabbed while breaking up a gang fight in Seven Sisters Road, Holloway.
- Pc Royston Ernest Adams

Died from a fractured skull received in a accident on duty on Ealing Division.
- Pc Royston William Hird

Fatally injured when his patrol car crashed into a trolley-bus standard at Colindale.

1959

January	Castro takes control of Cuba.
February	Unemployment in the UK stands at 620,728.
March	Dalai Lama flees China.
April	Hovercraft moves from the drawing board to reality.
May	UK Jodrell bank radio telescope transmits a radio message to the US via the moon.
June	Debenhams launch a £33.8 million bid for Harrods.
July	Crime rate in London rose by 21% in a year.
August	Mini motor car is launched in the UK.
September	Soviet Lunik II space craft crashed into the moon, first man made object to reach our nearest neighbour in space.

October   Labour promises to abolish purchase tax if elected.

November   M1 motorway opened.

December   Oven ready turkeys popular this Christmas.

HITS OF THE YEAR

Livin doll

What do you want to make those eyes at me for

Ben Hur - 11 awards

MURDER OF DC RAYMOND WILLIAM PURDY
GUENTHER PODOLA - 1959

Guenther Podola was born on 8th February 1929 in Berlin. The only child of a banker, he was a studious piano playing boy but his life was irrevocably changed by the second world war. In his early teens he spent his time in the lawless bombed City. He became a member of Hitler's youth. After the war in 1952 with his parents dead he emigrated to Canada. He was there for six years before being deported after being jailed for theft and burglary. In May 1959 he came to London.

He turned to burglary and he broke into the flat of an American woman. Items were taken. He wrote to her later claiming to be a private detective and said that certain items that had been stolen would be returned to her on the payment of £500. She received further demands from Podola but this time her phone was tapped, the call being traced to a phone box at South Kensington Underground. She heard a scuffle and another man spoke on the phone, it was Dc Purdy.

Dc Purdy was 40, a married man with three children. He had driven from Chelsea with another Ds to apprehend the caller. They hauled Podola out of the phone box but as they went upstairs he broke loose and ran down Sydney Place and into a block of flats at Onslow Square. He hid behind a pillar in the hall but was soon spotted by the two detectives, both of whom were in plain clothes and unarmed. Podola was briefly questioned but not searched. Ds John Sandford crossed the hall to summon the caretaker to enlist some assistance before going to the police car to summon further assistance from police officers. There was no answer to the bell so he called out to Purdy across the hallway. Purdy momentarily distracted, turned his head towards the other detective, Podola pulled out a gun and shot Purdy through the heart and fled outside.

Podola was identified by fingerprints on the marble ledge of the hallway. 2 days after the shooting, Purdy's widow said that the address book which had been returned to her with Purdy's personal possessions was not his, it belonged to Podola. A photograph was sent to London from Canada to aid in the apprehension of Podola. He was eventually tracked down to a hotel room. The door to the room was charged by police and Podola was overpowered and arrested.

His trial began at the Old Bailey on 10th September, he was eventually found guilty and was sentenced to death.

Guenther Podola was the last man to be hanged for the killing of a policeman, and was executed at Wandsworth Prison on 5th November 1959.

Ds Purdy's widow received a pension of £546 a year.

GEORGE MEDAL
Award of the Bar
19/6/59

Dorsett   George Edward   Police Constable   129121 J **Bar**

After a tour of night duty constable Dorsett was at home asleep when he was woken by an explosion, the noise of glass breaking and someone screaming out. When he looked out of his window he saw a youth standing in the road pointing a shotgun at a man. Dorsett ran outside, and saw the youth on the opposite side of the road with the gun still in his hand and he was still shouting and making threats. Dorsett started to walk towards the youth who still had his finger on the trigger and was now pointing the weapon at him. Dorsett told him he was a police officer and told him to put down the gun. The youth was refusing to do this and threatened to shoot the constable, but Dorsett kept walking towards him. He managed to knock the gun aside and with the assistance of another man who came forward was able to disarm the youth. If the youth had fired the weapon while the constable was walking towards him he would have no doubt have either killed or seriously injured him.

QUEEN'S COMMENDATION FOR BRAVE CONDUCT
Berry   Robert Beavis   Police Constable   134345 J
'Showed great courage and determination in arresting a man armed with a rifle'.

ROLL OF HONOUR
• Dc Raymond Purdy, B
Murdered arresting suspect see above.
• Pc Melvyn Davies
Died in hospital following an injury received when his motorcycle was in collision with a car while on duty at Kilburn Division.

Chapter Eight

THE YEARS OF 1960 - 1969

This was the decade of the swinging sixties, of flower power, drugs and massive demonstrations against the Vietnam war. Technology advanced beyond belief, some even said that it could never happen, but it did.

In the 1960's many of Africa's nations received their independence from France, Britain and Belgium, some of this brought about through unrest and bloodshed.

The civil rights battle in the United States of America was escalating, but by the death of Dr Martin Luther King the USA had made more progress in a few years than in the whole of the preceding generation. The civil rights act which was started by President J F Kennedy was completed by his successor L B Johnson.

The space race was on between the USSR and the USA, the 1960's started with the first man into orbit, and by the end of 1969 the first man had actually walked on the moon.

The Kennedy clan in America saw one of their worst decades, one of them, President J F Kennedy, and then Senator Bobby Kennedy being assassinated.

The Berlin wall is built and separates families in the East and West of Berlin. Another war criminal is executed for atrocities carried out during the second world war. The world itself came close to a nuclear war when the USA invaded Cuba, known as the 'bay of pigs'. The Vietnam War was escalating, with no end in sight.

In 1965 Britain bid farewell to one of its great leaders, Sir Winston Churchill who died aged 90. Over 300,000 paid their last respects to him, and a state funeral was held.

There were many disasters during this decade Aberfan, Ronan Point, Torrey Canyon, Biafra to name just a few. Some of these we will remember for a long time, if not by personal recollection, by history itself.

Timothy Evans was granted a posthumous pardon for the murder of his wife and baby daughter, these murders having been committed by John Christie in 1953. The great train robbery took place in 1963, the moors murders in 1965 and in the USA, Sharon Tate along with her friends was murdered by Charles Manson's 'family'. The Metropolitan police also lost officers, one particular sad case was the crew of a Q car Fox-trot one one in Shepherds Bush in 1966.

But remember this, not only did man conquer space and land on the moon but England won the World cup beating Germany 4 - 2.

1960

January	BBC want a second television channel.
February	Britain to fund a supersonic aircraft.
March	Police kill 56 at Sharpeville massacre in South Africa.

April   Film Ben Hur wins a record 10 Oscars.

May   Russia shoots down US U-2 aircraft claiming it was spying.

June   Plans to introduce colour television are shelved indefinitely.

July   Kremlin says that nuclear war is not inevitable.

August   East Germans close the border with West Berlin.

September 344 tickets are issued in central London on the first day of parking tickets and traffic wardens.

October   Southern England hit by the worst flooding since 1953.

November   Worlds first hover-scooter is demonstrated.

December   Richard Baer the last commandant of Auschwitz is arrested.

HITS OF THE YEAR
Cathy's clown

Please don't tease

The girl of my best friend

BRITISH EMPIRE MEDAL FOR GALLANTRY
29/11/60

Young   Thomas   Police Constable   147547 T

Police constable Young was on duty in uniform but was at the time wearing a civilian rain coat over his uniform while at a cinema car park. He noticed a man go over to the rear of a car and syphon petrol from the tank into a large can which he then put into the boot of another car. The man then got into this vehicle, constable Young stepped into the head lights of the car, he opened his raincoat to show his uniform and called out that he was a police officer and requested the man to stop. The man immediately drove his vehicle straight at the officer who threw himself onto the bonnet of the car and managed to get a hold of the luggage rack. The man then drove the car for several miles at reckless speeds, he moved from side to side, mounted the pavement and braked sharply and accelerated all in an effort to dislodge the officer. At one stage while trying to dislodge the officer the car drove around a roundabout four times, it was also driven over a hump back bridge at an estimated speed of 70 mph. The journey went on for about 35 minutes with constable Young continually calling on the man to stop and shouted to pedestrians to call for police assistance. While the vehicle was driving along he also tried to cover the windscreen to obscure the drivers view. It was not until the car ran out of petrol that it finally stopped, the man jumped out and ran away. Constable Young was badly shaken and bruised, but despite this he gave chase and after about 250 yards he overtook the man who kicked him and aimed a blow at his head. The officer then drew his truncheon and after a short struggle managed to overpower the man and arrest him.

QUEEN'S COMMENDATION FOR BRAVE CONDUCT
11/10/60

Cameron   Alan Roderick   Police Sergeant   129342

Strood   Peter Edward   Police Sergeant   139476

'Arresting a violent man armed with a revolver.'

ROLL OF HONOUR

- Pc Ronald Alan Addison

Died from a heart attack suffered when chasing 2 youths in the Pentonville Road.

- Pc Terrence Daniel Furnell

An observer in a patrol car which crashed while on its way to an emergency call.

- Pc Edward Roy Dorney

Struck by a train when his dog picked up the scent of a burglar along a railway line in Peckham.

- Pc Leslie Vincent

Struck by a motor car after he was thrown off a car which had driven off after he had been questioning the driver about stolen property in Woolwich.

- Pc Leslie Meehan, R

Killed after being thrown off a car which drove off whilst he was attempting to question the driver.

1961

January	J F Kennedy is sworn in as the youngest ever US President.
February	Postmaster General announces it plans to build a 507 ft GPO tower in central London.
March	E-Type Jaguar which can reach 150 mph will cost £2,196.
April	Soviet Union put the first man into space.
May	Post Office install first pay on answer phones at phone boxes with pips when coins are needed.
June	Dr Ramsey takes office as the 100th Archbishop of Canterbury.
July	Kuwait, British troops land in anticipation of an attack by Iraq.
August	A man is murdered and his girlfriend raped by a savage killer on the A6 (Hanratty murder case).
September	First Mothercare shop opens in Kingston.
October	The last steam train runs on the underground.
November	Stalingrad is re named Volgograd.
December	South East of England plunged into darkness by an electrician's error.

HITS OF THE YEAR

Wooden heart

You don't know

West side story

BRITISH EMPIRE MEDAL FOR GALLANTRY

24/11/61

Findlay	David Jones	Police Sergeant	124887 J

Police had been informed that a man had gone berserk with a shotgun. Sergeant Findlay made his way to the address and when he arrived was informed that a youth aged 19 had a gun and that he had locked himself in the house along with his younger brother.

Sergeant Findlay tried to open the door to the flat but could not as it had been bolted. He looked through the letter box and saw the muzzle of a 12 bore shotgun pointing at him. He called out to the youth to put the gun down and to open the door, he repeated the request several times while still looking through the letter box. Eventually the youth put the gun down against the wall of the hallway and heard the bolts of the door being opened. He then saw the youth reach for the gun and pick it up and put his finger onto the trigger. Sergeant Findlay without any hesitation opened the door and entered. He went up to the youth who was holding the gun in his right hand, he seized the gun and pushed the youth into an adjoining room. It was found out that the gun was in fact loaded with a cartridge in the breech.

GEORGE MEDAL
24/11/61

Cox	Charles Edward	Police Constable	132059 K

QUEEN'S POLICE MEDAL

Pawsey	Phillip	Inspector	129523 K

Posthumous

Hutchins	Frederick George	Police Sergeant	122805

Posthumous

BRITISH EMPIRE MEDAL FOR GALLANTRY

England	Leslie Charles	Police Constable	139637 K

While a man was being interviewed at a police station he produced an automatic pistol. He covered the officers and backed out of the office and ran down the stairs. Constables Cox and England saw the man run into the charge room, then cross the main entrance where he turned and pointed the gun at them. The man then left the station and ran into a recreation ground. Constable Cox along with other officers ran after him but he had disappeared into the park. Constable Cox entered the park. Constable England who was now on his motorcycle then drove up and was told the gunman had gone down the road. Constable England then drove off in the direction indicated. Cox was now joined by a Sergeant and together they ran into a road where they saw the gunman walking along the footway. The Sergeant who at this time was in front jumped onto the man's back and flung his arms around him, but he was thrown off and was then shot in the abdomen. The gunman backed away but Cox jumped forward in order to tackle him. The man fired his gun again, this time hitting the constable in the stomach. Constable England reached the road in time to witness the shooting of the Sergeant. He immediately rode in pursuit of the gunman and managed to get within 20 feet of him when the man again turned and fired a shot which fortunately missed. At this time an Inspector in a police wireless car tried to stop the gunman but he was shot at point blank range. The man then ran off with constable England in close pursuit, but he crossed some waste ground, he then entered the rear of a house and escaped. The man later shot himself in a telephone box. The Inspector and the Sergeant both sadly died of their wounds, constable Cox was severely injured.

ROLL OF HONOUR

- Insp Phillip Pawsey, QPM, K
- Ps Frederick George Hutchins, QPM, K

See above entry.

- Dc Peter George Bridgwood

Killed in a road accident on duty on Tooting Division.

1962

January	Smallpox outbreak in Britain.
February	US astronaut John Glenn orbits the earth.
March	300 year skull discovered underneath 10 Downing Street.
April	First push button controlled Panda crossing introduced in the UK.
May	Last trolley buses taken out of service in the UK.
June	First edition of Police 5 shown on television.
July	The first hovercraft enters service.
August	Mariner II space craft launched by the US to Venus.
September	Fierce street battles in London between the Fascists and the East Enders.
October	Amnesty International is created to investigate human rights abuses.
November	An agreement to build Concorde is signed by Britain and France.
December	60 deaths attributed to Smog in London.

HITS OF THE YEAR

Stranger on the shore

I remember you

Rock a-hula baby

Lawrence of Arabia - 7 awards

BRITISH EMPIRE MEDAL FOR GALLANTRY

26/6/62

Rees   Hubert Melville   Detective Chief Inspector 123357 A

A man had entered the premises of his firm at about 9 am, he was shot in the face with a sawn off shotgun and received severe injuries. Detective Chief Inspector Rees was the officer in charge of the investigation and as a result of enquiries decided to interview one employee of the firm. At 10 pm on the same day Chief Inspector Rees, who was with 3 other officers, knocked onto the door of a ground floor room occupied by the same employee. The room was in total darkness but the officers heard a voice, the voice told them to go away. A movement was then heard and the light was switched on and a key was turned in the lock. Chief Inspector Rees then pushed open the door and was confronted by a man pointing a sawn off double barrelled shotgun at him. Chief Inspector Rees rushed at the man forcing the gun behind his back and at the same time the other officers ran into the room and helped him overpower the man and disarm him. The gun was found to be loaded in both barrels and the safety catch was off.

BRITISH EMPIRE MEDAL FOR GALLANTRY

18/12/62

Watt   Thomas Forbes   Police Constable   149418 G

Constable Watt along with 3 other officers were all off duty in plain clothes, they were passing the entrance of a social club at about midnight. A man with blood over his face came out of the doorway. Constable Watt identified himself as a police officer and started to question him. The man then grabbed at the officer and held onto his coat and started to punch him. A second man then joined in the struggle and slashed Watt about the face with a razor. By this time a large hostile crowd had gathered, constable Watt was now bleeding heavily from the face but managed to hold onto his captive who was now struggling violently. Constable Watt eventually had to let the man go. The officer then heard a shout and when he looked round he saw an angry crowd running towards them. The officer ducked his head down as he received kicks and punches on his head and body from some of the crowd, he managed to hold onto the man who had first attacked him. By this time Watt's jacket had almost been torn off and the man managed to break free and run off. The constable chased him for about 400 yards and with the assistance of two uniformed officers arrested him. The constable eventually went to hospital where he needed 60 stitches to his head and face.

Later on Thomas Watt transferred to Glasgow City Police.

QUEEN'S COMMENDATION FOR BRAVE CONDUCT

Wharton   Arthur John   Police Constable   142267 CO C4
Woodrow   Robert Alfred   Police Constable   144886 G

'For pursuing and arresting an armed criminal.'

ROLL OF HONOUR

• Pc Roderick Mackay Munro

An observer in a patrol car which crashed into a tree at Catford.

1963

January   BBC ends its ban on mentioning politics, royalty, religion and sex in its comedy shows.

February   First successful kidney transplant undertaken at the Leeds General Infirmary.

March   Alcatraz jail in the US is to close.

April   129 feared dead as US submarine Thresher sinks in the Atlantic.

May   1000 arrested on a civil rights march in Alabama US.

June   Russia puts the first woman in space.

July   UK Government proposes the creation of the Ministry of Defence.

August   Great Train Robbery nets £1,000,000 - see page 203.

September   New Zealand doctors give first successful blood transfusion to an unborn baby.

October   Beatle mania takes hold in the UK.

November   The detective who arrested Anne Franke during World War II is suspended from duty.

December   Frank Sinatra jnr is freed after his father pays $240,000 ransom.

HITS OF THE YEAR
She loves you
From me to you
Tom Jones

THE GREAT TRAIN ROBBERY - 1963
This is one robbery where the criminals have somehow become celebrities.

On 8th August 1963 the Glasgow to London night mail train was stopped by a fake signal in Buckinghamshire. Men wearing balaclavas uncoupled the engine and high value cargo coach from the rest of the train. They climbed aboard the engine and beat the driver who had tried to resist. They forced him to drive on another mile to Bridego Bridge. Once there the robbers broke into the van with the high value cargo. They threatened the Post Office workers inside with axe handles and formed a human chain and unloaded £2.5 million in old used bank notes which were destined for destruction at the Mint. This took the robbers 30 minutes to do, they then drove off in a convoy of vehicles. They escaped before they could be detected but left some bags of money behind on the train.

Buckinghamshire police called for the assistance of Scotland Yard. It was apparent that this was the work of professional thieves, probably from London. The large convoy of vehicles had probably gone to ground locally. The police concentrated their search on lonely buildings in the local area and told the radio station this in the hope that it would make the thieves panic.

The ruse worked, a local shepherd reported strange goings on at a farm and when police arrived they found mail bags, tinned food, sleeping bags and other evidence that this was where the robbers had flown from.

The first robber was arrested in Brighton, the finger then pointed at the Wisley gang from South London who specialised in stopping trains. All but four of the criminals were arrested and brought to trial, together with the solicitor who had helped them to acquire the farm. The inside man from the railway or the Post Office was never caught. It was years before one gang member was captured, he was caught when his money had run out and he returned to England.

Only a small quantity of the money was ever recovered.

Ronald Biggs who escaped from prison after serving only a short time, made his way to South America. He returned to the United Kingdom in the year 2001. By this time he was very ill and had run out of money. As soon as he arrived back at the airport he was arrested and returned to prison to finish his sentence.

BRITISH EMPIRE MEDAL FOR GALLANTRY
19/4/63

Bartholomew	Norman Eric	Police Constable	129634 L
Thomas	Richard Willis	Police Constable	133620 L

Constable Thomas along with constable Bartholomew made their way to a building site in Camberwell where a 165 foot high block of flats was under construction. Near the building attached at intervals of about 12 feet was a builder's hoist of a lattice girder construction. This hoist was about 200 feet high. When the officers arrived they saw a man on the scaffolding, he was 6 floors up and was throwing planks of wood and other debris and loose objects at people in the road. The scene had been lit by search lights by the London Fire Brigade. Thomas and Bartholomew entered the building and climbed the partially constructed stairway to the top floor. When they reached this level there was a loading platform of scaffolding and planks which extended 8 feet from the building along side a girder 12 inches wide and 12 feet long. The man was clinging to the hoist some feet above this panel. Constable Thomas then walked out to the end of the girder, holding onto a scaffolding pole, and tried to persuade the man to come down. Constable Bartholomew followed and sat astride the girder to support Thomas. The man refused to come off the hoist, he suddenly collapsed and fell. Thomas immediately leaned out and managed to grab hold of the man's raincoat and hold him in mid air. Bartholomew put his legs around the steel tie and held Thomas around his waist to support him. Between them both they managed to pull the man onto the loading platform and into the building.

BRITISH EMPIRE MEDAL FOR GALLANTRY
23/4/63

Laurence	John Michael	Special Police Constable	024117H E

Police had been called to a gas holder station at the Kennington Oval where a boy had managed to climb to the top of the tallest gas holder and was threatening to jump. The boy was sitting on the upper most girders some 130 feet above the ground. At this time the gas holder was almost full to capacity and its top was 15 feet higher than the girder which the boy was sitting on. Special constable Laurence realizing the danger immediately made his way to the steel ladder which ran up the side of the gas holder and started to climb to the top from where he saw the boy hanging on by one hand to the lattice work. Laurence walked along a narrow girder which projected from the top of the dome and lowered himself to the girder from which the boy was hanging on. The boy was by then holding on by one hand and his legs were dangling below. Laurence stretched himself to his limit along the girder and with one hand managed to reach down and grasp the boy's arm. Meanwhile a turntable ladder from the London Fire Brigade had arrived and was put into position and extended, but it was found to be about 50 feet too short. The fire brigade officers therefore climbed on to the top of the gas holder and two of them got onto the girder and were able to support constable Laurence while he passed ropes around the boy. In order to do this Laurence had to have both his arms free, so he gripped the girder with his legs. The boy was then swung across a 10 foot gap between the girder and the gas holder where the fire brigade officers then lowered him to the ground by a rope. He was found to be unconscious and was subsequently taken to hospital. Constable Laurence had spent some 25 minutes in a very precarious position while on the girder.

BRITISH EMPIRE MEDAL FOR GALLANTRY
28/5/63

Huntley	Robert	Detective Inspector	127480 B
Russell	John George	Police Constable	148534 B

Detective Inspector Huntley and police constable Russell along with other officers made their way to a gaming club in order to arrest a man who had fired a gun in another club a few hours earlier. It was strongly believed that the man would not hesitate to use the gun in order to resist arrest. On their arrival constable Russell entered the gaming room which led off the front room by the way of two steps and a small archway. He was followed closely by Detective Inspector Huntley. Huntley then approached the suspect who was at the time sitting at a table with several other men, the man then produced a revolver which he pointed at the officers and threatened to shoot. Both officers immediately rushed the man and while Russell threw himself across the table and grabbed the man's right wrist, Huntley grasped the mans right arm, both officers then tried to disarm him. A furious struggle began in which the gunman tried to point the revolver at the officers. Russell managed to force down the man's arms. With the assistance of other police officers the man was eventually overpowered and disarmed. The revolver was found to contain 3 spent cartridges and 3 live rounds of ammunition.

BRITISH EMPIRE MEDAL FOR GALLANTRY
1/10/63

Mackey	Leslie John	Special Police Sergeant	132946 S
Keylock	Frank Victor	Detective Constable	137232 S

A man had climbed onto the roof of a building, he was in possession of an axe and was refusing to come down. When police arrived they saw a man running over the various roof levels, he was brandishing an axe and was shouting that he would kill the first person who came near him. The man then started to throw down tiles, slates and coping stones and pieces of wood which he was chopping from roof ladders and duck boards. When Mackey and Keylock arrived they volunteered to go onto the roof to try to get the man down. Both officers inched their way across the apex of the roof and spotted the man on top of the roof nearby. The man began to shout threats and broke off a centre ridge tile and threw the pieces at the officers. Mackey and Keylock were able to fend off the missiles with improvised shields. At last the officers came face to face with the man who then struck at the safety shields with the axe. Both officers then rushed at the man and eventually managed to overcome him. At the time a high wind was blowing which made this operation even more hazardous.

ROYAL HUMANE SOCIETY BRONZE MEDAL

Marr	Police Constable	150285 B

Awarded a bronze medal and certificate by the Royal Humane Society.

ROLL OF HONOUR
* Pc Brian Bernared Joseph Holden

Died from multiple injuries sustained in a road accident on duty on Ealing Division.

1964

January	First ticket collecting machines are installed on the underground.
February	UK Government announces plans for a fleet of 5 Polaris submarines.
March	Radio Caroline begins transmissions from a ship in the North Sea.
April	BBC2 goes on the air, its first programme 'Playschool'.

May	Mods and Rockers battle on the beaches of Brighton.
June	Nelson Mandela sentenced to life for treason in South Africa.
July	President L B Johnson signs the Civil Rights Act of the US.
August	US steps up action against Vietnam.
September	Opening of the Forth road bridge, Europe's longest bridge.
October	Nikita Khruschev deposed by Leonid Brezhnev while on holiday in his villa at the Black Sea.
November	South Vietnam launch major attacks on the US base at Bien Hoa.
December	Gangland shooting in the East End of London, the Kray brothers likely suspects.

HITS OF THE YEAR

I love you because
I won't forget you
Its over
My Fair Lady

REGGIE AND RONNIE KRAY - 1964

They were born within an hour of each other on 24th October 1933, their mother was Violet and father Charlie. They had an elder brother Charlie. They all lived and were brought up in a house which was very poor even by East End standards at Hoxton.

Throughout their childhood Violet doted on them, always ensuring they were treated equally. Although identical in appearance they each had differing characters and from an early age these began to emerge, Reggie being slightly brighter and more outgoing. Each twin would place close attention to every move the other made. They were fiercely loyal to each other and also the greatest of rivals.

Shortly before the out beak of World War II the family moved from Hoxton to Vallance Road, in Bethnal Green. During the destruction of the Blitz, the boys discovered the thrill and excitement of fighting. They fought rival gangs of boys and very quickly gained a reputation as the toughest of scrappers. They also gained the practical experience of out witting the Police. Their father went on the run when he received his call up papers, but would occasionally return home to see his family, and the boys would do their best to fool the police who would from time to time visit and search the house for him.

Their eldest brother Charlie had joined the Royal Navy and was soon established as a forces boxer, and while home on leave he started to teach the twins a few tricks or two. In 1948 Reggie won the London's schoolboys' boxing championship and turned professional at 16, he won all 7 of his fights and Ronnie was not far behind him.

The twins were unable to confine their violence to the ring, in 1950 they beat up a 16 year old fellow East Ender in a Hackney alley. Two witnesses had seen the fight and named the Krays as the attackers. Reggie and Ronnie were remanded in custody for trial at the Old Bailey. The witnesses were told of the dangers of telling what they had seen and as a result when the case came up it was dismissed for lack of evidence. The twins had learned the power of threats backed by violence and intimidation.

British Empire Medal
– Reverse.

George Cross
– Reverse.

Queen's Police Medal for
Gallantry – Obverse.

George Medal
– Reverse.

George Medal
– Obverse.

Queen's Gallantry Medal
– Obverse.

Police Constable Francis Stubbs awarded the KPM in 1919 for the arrest of an army deserter.

Class photograph showing Constable Francis Stubbs later KPM, 5th from the left on the back row.

From left to right – Constable Ernest Jacobi KPM, Constable John Bertram KPM, Sergeant Frederick Muggeridge KPM, Constable Walter Raymond KPM.

Police Constable Walter Ernest Raymond awarded the KPM in 1931 for saving the life of a woman apparently intending to jump and commit suicide.

Police Constable Keith Giles BEM for arrest of armed criminal see 1972.

From left to right – Sergeant Arthur Garner GM, Sergeant Brian Parsons BEM, Constable Keith Giles BEM – after receiving their award from the Bow Street Fund.

Carnegie Hero Fund Medal
– Obverse.

Carnegie Hero Fund Medal
– Reverse.

Binney Memorial Medal.

Royal Humane Society Medal
– Obverse.

Royal Humane Society
Stanhope Medal – Obverse.

Sergeant David Pengelly receiving his Commissioner's High Commendation from Sir Peter Imbert in 1988.

Sergeant David Pengelly with the crew of serial 502 after receiving their gallantry awards at Buckingham Palace.

Phillip Rainsford, Queen's Gallantry Medal Awarded 1991. Phillip joined the Metropolitan Police in 1984 after two years as a police cadet. He served for ten years on Greenwich division before moving to Croydon. He is still a serving officer.

In 1951 the twin were again charged with another assault, due possibly to a little provocation when Ronnie was pushed and told to move along by a police constable, he hit him and ran off. Ronnie was later arrested, but due to the intervention of a priest nothing more serious than probation was given out.

They enlisted for National Service but this lasted only a short time, serving a stint in the guardroom for striking a NCO. After the army they started to drink in night clubs. One particular club had a lot of problems with damage and rowdy behaviour, and the manager later resigned, Reggie and Ronnie stepped in with an offer to rent the hall for £5 a week. Needless to say the trouble stopped when they took over and before long the hall was making itself pay. This then became their base of operations.

One Maltese gang appeared and demanded protection money, the twins went after them with knives, word then started to circulate about the new arrivals in the east end underworld. The twins then began to operate protection rackets themselves.

In 1955 it appeared that their break had finally arrived. The joint bosses of London's underworld were two men called Billy Hill and Jack Corner (known as Jack Spot), who between them had overseen the West End's drinking, gambling, prostitution and protection rackets for more than 10 years. They had broken up after being badly cut up in a fight. Spot decided he needed some extra muscle so he called on the Krays.

This was the news the Krays had been waiting for, they immediately embarked on a large scale preparation for a gang war with Spot's enemies, they collected weapons and made their base at Vallance Road.

They sought a confrontation in a social club in Clerkenwell Road which was the head quarters for a gang of Italians. They arrived shortly after 10, Ronnie entered alone and challenged the men there to a fight, a bottle was thrown at his head, in response to this he pulled out a Mauser and fired 3 shots into a wall, no one reacted so he walked out. Ronnie had by now made the point.

In 1956 he beat a man to an inch of death, Ronnie received 3 years for Grievous Bodily Harm. Meanwhile Reggie had free rein to manage the twins business interests even though the separation from Ronnie was a great emotional blow to Reggie. He opened a legitimate club the 'Double R' on the Bow Road which soon became an East End premier night spot.

Isolated from his family and friends in Wandsworth Prison, Ronnie's mind began to collapse with amazing speed. Just after Christmas 1957 he heard that his favourite aunt had died. After spending the night in a straitjacket the next morning he was certified insane. His condition rapidly improved once he was transferred to a psychiatric hospital. Ronnie escaped with the assistance of his brother and moved to Suffolk. He remained at large long enough for his certificate of insanity to expire, he was then taken back to Wandsworth Prison to complete his sentence.

After his release in 1958 they opened a more profitable venture 'Esmeralda's Barn' a successful casino in Wilton Place, Belgravia. They managed to pay off the owner with £1000, they were now earning over £1,600 a week from the tables. Over the next few years their income grew and grew and eventually they had a tidy sum of money.

Reggie married Frances Shea, the wedding was celebrated in typical Kray style with Rolls Royces, David Bailey was the official photographer, and lots of celebrities attended.

Over the years Ronnie's bouts of depression deepened, he would have sudden bouts of pathological violence, it did not take much to set him off.

In 1966 the twins sprang Frank 'the mad axeman' Mitchell, an old friend from Dartmoor Prison where he was on an outside working party. Everything ran to plan, he was driven to a flat in Barking before the prison authorities noticed he was missing. While in the flat Mitchell wrote to the Times newspaper. For the Krays it was a time of crisis, if he escaped from the flat he could wreak havoc on their organisation implicating them in his escape. The Krays told him they were taking him to the countryside, he got into a van and was never seen again.

In the summer of 1967 Reggie's life fell apart, barely 2 months after the wedding Frances moved back with her parents, her mental condition had deteriorated; she was receiving treatment for depression. In June she committed suicide. His wife's death had shattered him and changed him forever.

Ronnie despite his preference for boys, was the hard man, Reggie with his taste for women was soft, Ronnie had killed a man Reggie had not. As the problems with Jack 'the hat' McVitie grew, Ronnie began to talk of killing him himself, Reggie was left with no choice if his brother was planning once again to prove his superiority in the field of violence then he had to get his blow in first, and in October 1967 he finally did.

Reggie Kray stabbed Jack 'the hat' McVitie to death because he had insulted and challenged the Krays in public.

The trial for the Krays began in January 1969 at the Old Bailey and in March they were found guilty and sentenced to life imprisonment.

Ronald Kray died in 1995 and his brother Reginald released from prison suffering from cancer died in 2001.

BRITISH EMPIRE MEDAL FOR GALLANTRY
14/8/64

Hobbs	Roy Albert	Police Constable	150142 C
Stamper	Roy	Police Constable	152104 C

At about midnight constables Hobbs and Stamper saw a man run out of a house. The woman shouted out that the man had a gun. Both officers then ran after the man and when they were about 25 yards away they shouted out to the man to stop. The man glanced at the officers over his left shoulder and then pulled out a gun. The man continued to run and a member of the public put out his foot and tripped him. As the man lay on the pavement he fired at Hobbs but fortunately the shot missed. After this shot had been fired both constables leapt on the gunman and managed to disarm and arrest him.

GEORGE MEDAL
14/8/64

Cleland	Margaret Shaw	Woman Police Constable	1793 E

Woman Police Constable Cleland had been called to a house where a man was sitting on a railing at the corner of the roof holding in his arms his baby son aged 22 months. When she arrived she made her way to the roof top through an adjacent house, there she joined other officers. The roof was about 43 feet high and was protected by a low parapet surrounded by a single iron railing which was about 2 feet above the top of the parapet. A gully about 12 inches wide ran between the steeply pitched slate roof and the low parapet. When she was on the roof the man was seen sitting astride the railings on the corner of the roof, he was holding the child in his right arm. The guard rail was not secure and there was imminent danger of the man over balancing and falling to the ground with the child. It has been decided that a woman officer might have a better chance of success in persuading the man away from the edge, and Cleland despite the danger made her way along the gully towards the man. When she was about 6 feet from him he made it clear that if she came any closer he would throw himself and the child into the street below. For about an hour or so she talked to him and tried to persuade him to either hand over the child or come away from the railings. While this was going on other officers tried to reason with the man but as soon as they went towards him he stood up as though he was about to throw himself off the roof. After a time the boy began to cry and Cleland persuaded the man the child needed warmer clothing, and he agreed that she should place a coat around the baby. While she was making the suggestion she had slowly edged forward and was now only about 4 feet away from him. She realized that this was probably the only opportunity she would have to reach the baby, she went to place the coat around the child's shoulders, she caused the man to disengage his left arm from the child in order to help her. Cleland then jumped forward, grabbed the child firmly and gripped the man's coat by the right elbow. She then threw herself backwards wrenching the child from the man's grip, at the same time pulling the man towards the roof. The violence of her action had caused her to lose her balance and fall backwards with the baby in her arms, but she managed to throw herself sideways onto the pitched roof. The man sat motionless, he had been taken completely by surprise, he was grabbed by ambulance attendants and was secured, he was then taken to hospital.

QUEEN'S COMMENDATION FOR BRAVE CONDUCT
21/4/64

| Couzens | William Edwin Alfred | Police Constable | 145346 C |

'Arresting an armed criminal.'

Crayden	Bert	Police Constable	129233 G
Garvey	Denis	Police Constable	146481 G
O'Callaghan	Denis	Police Constable	145417 G

'Arresting an intruder armed with a shot gun.'

Dibell	John	Police Sergeant	144207 X
Pitcher	John	Police Constable	146692 X
Stevens		Police Constable	144962 X

'Arresting an armed and mentally deranged man.'

QUEEN'S COMMENDATION FOR BRAVE CONDUCT
18/8/64

| Duneclift | Peter Charles | Police Constable | 151430 F |

'Attempting to rescue 2 children from a burning house.'

QUEEN'S COMMENDATION FOR BRAVE CONDUCT
13/11/64

Powell	Bernard James	Police Constable	151015 S
Sargent	Edwin Rex	Police Constable	151909 S

'For tackling a criminal who used a bottle of corrosive liquid to effect his escape.'

ROLL OF HONOUR
- Dc John Bell Maughan

Killed when a car collided with a police car in which he was the observer in Thornton Heath.
- Pc David Alyn Jones

Killed in an accident while under instruction on a light weight motorcycle course.
- Pc George Ernest White

Killed when as an observer in a patrol car crashed while escorting heart technicians urgently to hospital.

1965

January	Stanley Matthews is the first ever professional footballer to be knighted.
February	American aeroplanes bomb North Vietnam.
March	Goldie the Eagle flies to freedom from London Zoo.
April	Home Secretary announces that incitement of racial hatred is to be outlawed.
May	Scotland Yard appeals for world help to catch 3 great train robbers still at large.
June	First US astronaut takes a walk in space.
July	Start of the TV soap Coronation Street.
August	US space capsule Gemini V splashes down after 8 days in space.
September	EMI begins selling LP records through 3000 grocers for 12/6d each.
October	2 arrested for Moors Murders - Ian Brady and Myra Hindley.
November	Housewife to probe television sex and violence - Mary Whitehouse.
December	2 Gemini space craft achieve the first rendezvous in space.

HITS OF THE YEAR
Tears
A walk in the black forest
The sound of music

BRITISH EMPIRE MEDAL FOR GALLANTRY
29/6/65

Crossingham	Cyril Charles	Police Constable	132504 Z

QUEEN'S COMMENDATION FOR BRAVE CONDUCT

Caines	Arthur Ernest Edward	Police Constable	149228 Z
Graham	Kenneth David	Police Constable	144878 Z

A man had become mentally ill, and during this had assaulted his wife and children and then gone berserk brandishing a carving knife in each hand and was threatening anyone who came near him. When the police arrived they tried to reason with the man who was by now standing in the doorway. He made a charge at the officers, and threatened to kill them and his children. He then rushed back into the house and slammed the front door and bolted it. It was thought that there were 3 children still in the house and the officers tried to gain access from the back of the property. Constable Crossingham stayed near the front door, he tried unsuccessfully to open it through a broken window, he eventually managed to kick the door open. He grabbed a dustbin lid to act as a shield and advanced on the man who was in the small lobby and still brandishing the knives. The man kicked at the dustbin lid knocking it to one side and then he lunged at Crossingham with one of the knives, which struck the officer near his right breast pocket and was deflected into his arm pit. Crossingham fell backwards dropping the dustbin lid and was pulled away by another officer. At the same time 2 constables rushed at the man, knocked him off balance and forced him into the corner of the room. After a violent struggle and with the help of Crossingham and other officers the man was eventually disarmed.

BRITISH EMPIRE MEDAL FOR GALLANTRY
29/6/65

Lane	John Kenneth	Station Sergeant	139457 C
Everett	Thomas	Police Constable	149455 C

QUEEN'S COMMENDATION FOR BRAVE CONDUCT

Akrigg	John Laurence	Police Constable	152747 C
Herrington	Jeffery	Police Constable	152250 C

A robbery had been committed by three men one of them carrying an automatic pistol in the West End of London. They then made off in a stolen Jaguar car. A passing motorist followed them and he picked up constable Everett while on route. The 2 vehicles reached Piccadilly and the driver of the Jaguar lost control of the car which then mounted a pavement knocking down a pedestrian, and finally stopping at the traffic lights at Piccadilly Circus. The three occupants of the vehicle then ran off. Constable Everett then ran after one man down Lower Regent Street while Sergeant Lane who was also on duty in the vicinity joined in the chase. The gunman threatened a taxi driver and private motorist in an attempt to escape. As the police officers closed the gap the gunman then turned and threatened them with the gun, but Lane continued running at him and knocked him to the ground and fell over him. The other officer went to his aid and the gunman who had struggled so violently throughout was finally disarmed and arrested.

QUEEN'S COMMENDATION FOR BRAVE CONDUCT
29/1/65

Cocks	Thomas Michael Greig	Police Constable	151799 D

'Arresting a youth although threatened with a firearm.'

Douglas	Peter	Police Constable	153384 C

'For aiding when a man was shot and fatally wounded.'

Whyte	William	Police Constable	150135 N

'Stopping a runaway horse and cart in a busy thoroughfare.'

QUEEN'S COMMENDATION FOR BRAVE CONDUCT
10/8/65

Caulfield-Kerney	Shaun Graeham	Police Constable	151356 J
Pearce	Michael John	Police Constable	151267 J

'Apprehending a man who was in danger of falling from a roof.'

QUEEN'S COMMENDATION FOR BRAVE CONDUCT
19/10/65

Naish	Philip Henry	Police Constable	148972 D
Webster	Bruce Ian	Police Constable	150877 B

'Attempting to rescue the occupants of a burning house.'

ROLL OF HONOUR
• Pc Dennis Edward Cowell

Drowned after a police launch capsized towing a disabled customs vehicle.

• Pc Eric McLaughlan

Killed on duty when his moped was in collision with a van at Stratford.

1966

There was one murder case in August this year which involved the Metropolitan Police, it was the murder in cold blood of three unarmed plain clothed police officers, the crew of a Q car. The murders were reported as the Shepherd Bush Murders, the car's call sign being Fox-trot one one.

January	Nehru's daughter Indira Gandhi takes over as Prime Minister of India.
February	Freddie Laker forms an airline for cut price tours.
March	A man and his dog 'Pickles' find the missing World Cup.
April	British Airports Authority (BAA) is formed.
May	Moors Murderers sentenced to life imprisonment.
June	UK Barclays bank introduces the Barclaycard, the first British credit card.
July	31 arrested during anti-Vietnam war protests in London.
August	3 Policemen killed in London Street - see over the page for the full story.
September	In Japan 174 feared dead during a typhoon.
October	Pardon granted to Timothy Evans, hanged for the murder of his wife and baby. These murders were in fact carried out by John Reginald Haliday Christie in 1953.
November	NASA releases close up photographs of the moon taken by Orbiter 2.
December	280 feared drowned in Greece when a ferry sinks during a storm.

HITS OF THE YEAR
Distant Drums
Strangers in the night
Spanish Flea
A man for all seasons

JOHN DUDDY, JOHN WITNEY AND HARRY ROBERTS - 1966
SHEPHERD BUSH MURDERS - FOX-TROT ONE ONE
This was the murder of three police officers, on duty at the time in plain clothes, driving an unmarked police car, they were also unarmed.

At about 3.15pm on 16th August 1966 Sergeant Christopher Head, Detective Constable David Wombwell and Police constable Geoffrey Fox, all were attached to Shepherds Bush Police Station. They were patrolling the division in the Q car. In Braybrook street they saw a battered blue Standard Vanguard estate van parked up with three occupants inside.

Wormwood Scrubs Prison wall abuts directly into Braybrook Street and escape attempts were sometimes made with the support of a getaway car.

Sergeant Head and detective constable Wombwell walked over to the vehicle and Sergeant Head asked whether Witney owned the vehicle and why it was there and noticed there was no road fund licence. Sergeant Head asked for his driving licence and insurance certificate and noticing that the latter had run out left constable Wombwell to take Witney's name and address. Harry Roberts sitting in the passenger seat of the van shot and killed Sergeant Head without warning. Roberts was trying to shoot his way out of a possible arrest.

Detective constable Wombwell ran back to the Q car to take cover but Roberts ran after him and shot him through the head, at the same time Roberts shouted something at petty criminal Duddy who was in the back of the van. Duddy ran over to the Q car and shot constable Fox through the window as he tried to start up and pull away.

The two murderers got back into the van which Witney had reversed rapidly down a side street and out onto Wulfstan Street then drove off at speed. Fortunately a witness believing the car could have been used in a prison escape took down the number of the car.

This led to Witney's speedy arrest, and the discovery of the van at a railway arch lock up at Vauxhall. Witney admitted that Roberts and Duddy had been with him and had shot the policemen. Duddy was traced to Scotland, by information given by his brother, but Harry Roberts was at large for a further 90 days.

A £1000 reward was offered, the atrocious murders led to massive public sympathy for the police and many calls for the restoration of the recently abolished death penalty.

GEORGE MEDAL
11/2/66

Bowerman	Kenneth John	Police Constable	149991 N
Brown	Terrence Victor	Police Constable	146588 G
MacLeod	Alasdair Cameron F	Police Constable	147781 G
Whitham	Douglas	Police Constable	146421 Y

BRITISH EMPIRE MEDAL FOR GALLANTRY

Robson	Allen	Detective Sergeant	137559 X
Eyles	Roy Gordon	Detective Sergeant	137109 L
Gibbins	Patrick Glanville	Detective Sergeant	135699 RCS

Information has been received by the police that a dangerous escaped criminal would be at a certain address. Police officers in plain clothes were dispatched to the vicinity in order to effect the arrest. Constables Whitham and Brown saw the man and his wife drive up in a car which they then left and entered a shop. Several officers then entered the shop and discovered the man and his wife on a flat roof over the front of the shop premises. The officers called upon them to give themselves up, they moved to the roof of the next shop where the woman tripped over a wall. A constable grabbed her as she fell whereupon the man turned and fired a gun at the officers. A second shot was then fired followed by another all in the direction of the police in the street below. Constable Whitham had taken up a position in a doorway of an adjoining shop and as the man and his wife emerged and started to run towards their car he struck the man with a broom which he had picked up. Although hit the man staggered but kept running, he again fired the gun this time at Whitham and other officers who were following him. At this time constable Macleod rushed the man and brought him down in a tackle, but the man broke loose and fired his gun again. The woman had reached the car but was overtaken by Sergeant Gibbins, who managed to pin her against the side of the car. The man then approached from the other side of the car and fired 2 shots over the roof in the direction of Gibbins. The man then got into the car, at this time constable Brown had picked up the broom which had been used earlier and broke the glass of the driver's window and attempted to strike the man was shot at. The man then dived through the window into the street where constable Bowerman grabbed him and hit him with a truncheon, but he was struck with the pistol barrel over the eye, the man then ran off. The man was pursued by other officers and overtaken by Sergeant Eyles who managed to tackle him. The man again turned and fired at Eyles from about 2 feet and broke away. Eyles and other officers continued to chase and Sergeant Robson caught up with the man and tackled him but he kicked his way clear and jumped over a fence into a back garden. He was finally caught, disarmed and arrested.

GEORGE MEDAL

15/2/66

Wheelhouse	Michael James	Police Constable	145028 CO B12
Woodmore	Peter Alan	Detective Sergeant	136604 CO C8

BRITISH EMPIRE MEDAL FOR GALLANTRY

Porter	Arthur William	Police Sergeant	136801 CO A2
Oliver	Roger Keith	Detective Constable	148235 L
Birkhead	Derek Edwin	Police Constable	138204 V

QUEEN'S COMMENDATION FOR BRAVE CONDUCT

Cross	Roger Victor	Police Constable	139546 T
Wetherell	John Michael	Police Constable	153026 B
Whiteford	Angus Cochrane	Police Constable	147748

Police had been alerted and were on the lookout for an escaped and dangerous criminal who was travelling to London in a stolen car. Police cars and motorcyclists were alerted and warned that the man was in possession of a gun. The stolen car had been seen and pursued in several places but had succeeded in evading the police until about 10 pm when it was seen in Parliament Square. A police motorcyclist immediately gave chase and was soon joined by constable Wheelhouse also on a motorcycle in the vicinity of the Tate Gallery. Wheelhouse tried to stop the car by driving alongside its off side but the car was being driven across the crown of the road which forced the motorcycle into oncoming traffic. The car then accelerated along the Embankment. As the chase continued the speed reached around 90 mph, but the two officers kept the vehicle in view. They were joined by another motorcycle and a police car in which was Sergeant Porter and constable Oliver. The stolen vehicle continued along the Embankment where constable Birkhead in another police car tried to stop the car but then joined the chase. While driving along there was some congestion as a result of an accident and the road was blocked by a private car. The stolen car immediately reversed violently back and tried to ram its way through the traffic. Birkhead manoeuvred his police vehicle behind it and the driver of the private car quickly summing up what was going on drove his car against the near side of the stolen car forcing it to stop. The driver of the private car opened his door and pressed his feet against the near side door of the stolen car to prevent any one from getting out. Constable Wheelhouse followed by the two other officers had already run to the offside of the car and tried to force the door open while the car was still trying to move forwards and backwards. But as the car was forced to stop the driver fired his gun through the closed window, the bullet embedding itself in Wheelhouse's right elbow. The criminal then jumped from the car and again fired, he then ran off chased by the officers on foot. After a short distance the man fired again at the officers, shattering the rear window of a parked car. Leading the chase was Sergeant Porter and constables Oliver and Birkhead, as they rounded a corner they saw the criminal climbing over a low wall, he jumped down and fired again at the officers as they continued to chase him. After gaining access to a large garden which was now in complete darkness, the man then climbed into the basement area of the house. A police dog which had been brought to the scene was then released into the basement, where it located the criminal and barked, whereupon it was shot through the heart and killed instantly. The police and members of the public kept the man pinned down by throwing milk bottles and other objects at hand for some 15 to 20 minutes, during this time several shots were fired by the criminal. The criminal then climbed onto the roof of an outhouse just below the window of which 2 constables had taken up their positions. They struck at him with a truncheon and torch, the blow caused the man to stagger and at this time a number of officers ran towards him, but he quickly recovered and fired a further 2 shots. One of these shots hit a constable. The officers were then forced to retire, but the criminal was now trapped on the roof with a 6 foot high railing to scale if he wanted to reach the pavement. He tried but fell onto the adjoining area of the other side of the roof. Sergeant Woodmore climbing onto the railings called out to him to surrender, and as the man turned on him with the gun in his hand the Sergeant dived about 10 feet down onto him. Crashing him to the ground, the Sergeant grabbed the gun and other officers immediately followed and the man was overpowered and arrested after a violent struggle.

BRITISH EMPIRE MEDAL FOR GALLANTRY
20/5/66

Barrett	John Henry	Police Constable	144071 J

Constable Barrett was keeping observation on a car of which the number plates were known to be false. He saw a man unlock the car and get in. The constable then ran over to the car and told the man that he wanted to speak to him. The man then started the engine and drove the car at the officer, the officer was forced to jump onto the bonnet to avoid being run over. For the next 5 minutes the driver tried to swerve the car from side to side, he braked and accelerated sharply in several attempts to dislodge the officer. Barrett was only able to maintain his position by holding onto the rain channels on either side of the car. The car was deliberately driven at vehicles parked at the side of the road, swerving away at the last minute. But during this time there were two collisions. During this the driver was also banging the officers fingers in order to try to loosen his grip, and kept shouting at him to get off or be knocked off. Barrett however clung on and finally the man braked suddenly and jumped from the car which continued its journey. The driverless car continued down an incline with the officer still on the bonnet. He was thrown from it when the car hit a small road side tree and stopped. The officer landed on his head and shoulders and was dazed. Barrett went after the man but lost him when he ran into a side street. Knowing that the man must be nearby and possibly hiding he kept watch until assistance arrived and the man was soon found and arrested.

BRITISH EMPIRE MEDAL FOR GALLANTRY
12/8/66

Clement	Henry	Detective Sergeant	142526 RCS
Bartlett	Dennis Mead Boyse	Temp. Detective Con.	151332 B

The police were called to a hotel in order to question 2 men suspected of having stolen property from the hotel 3 weeks earlier. One of the men was recognized as having been committed on bail to stand trial, but had failed to surrender. On being confronted with this he drew a plastic squeeze container from his pocket, Sergeant Clement realising that it could contain some form of noxious substance shouted to other officers present to hold the suspect while he and constable Bartlett closed with the man holding the container. The second man broke away and jumped onto a bed and squirted household ammonia at the police officers from a similar container. Some of the substance went into Sergeant Clements eyes and temporarily blinded him. Constable Bartlett was forced to fight on alone. Ammonia was also squirted into his eyes and he was also struck on the head with a small axe, hit with a stool and kicked viciously until he lost consciousness. The two men then broke out of the room and ran off. A chase began in which Sergeant Clements who by now had recovered his sight took part along with police reinforcements. The two men were cornered at a hotel next door. Ammonia was again squirted at the officers, the axe which was used against constable Bartlett was also thrown at them. One of the men was finally overpowered after he had been knocked to the ground by a heavy ashtray thrown by Sergeant Clements. The other man had made his way to a window and was brandishing the axe which he had retrieved; he then smashed the window with the table and climbed onto the window sill. He was now confronted by other police officers so he jumped back into the room and rushed at Sergeant Clements and other officers threatening to kill them. Sergeant Clements ducked an axe blow, closed on him and with the help of other officers finally overpowered him.

BRITISH EMPIRE MEDAL FOR GALLANTRY
12/8/66

Carney	Brian	Temp. Detective Con.	152839 Q

Constable Carney along with another officer had received information as to the location of a man who they knew was carrying a loaded firearm. They saw the man along with two others running away through a narrow foot passage. After a chase which was unsuccessful the officers made their way back to the underground station in order to search a train that was standing at one of the platforms. Inside the train they saw the man with the two others. As the officers approached the man pulled a pistol out and pointed it at constable Carney and threatened to shoot him. The officer quickly grabbed his arm and after a short struggle wrestled the pistol from his grip. It was later found to be loaded. The man was then arrested and taken from the station. When outside on the forecourt the police officers were attacked by a group of young men and in the course of the struggle the criminal broke free from constable Carney and escaped. He was later seen on the roof of some flats above some shops, after a short struggle the man was finally arrested.

BRITISH EMPIRE MEDAL FOR GALLANTRY
11/10/66

Jones	Stuart	Police Constable	153273 E

Constable Jones had seen a man peering into parked cars and tampering with their door handles, the constable caught hold of his arm and told him that he was being arrested. The man struggled free and ran off. The officer gave chase but the man got into a waiting car which then drove off. As the car drove off Jones flung himself across the bonnet of the car and caught hold of the aerial mast. After a short distance another officer threw his truncheon at the windscreen and shattered it. The car was being swerved from side to side in an effort to dislodge the constable, but Jones managed to pull himself into a sitting position by supporting himself by holding onto the windscreen frame. He managed to put both feet through the broken windscreen and kicked at both men. The men eventually caught hold of the officer's feet and threw him off the moving car. Jones hit the road feet first and escaped with just an ankle injury. Both men were subsequently arrested.

BRITISH EMPIRE MEDAL FOR GALLANTRY
11/10/66

Dawson	John Anthony	Police Constable	150106 V
Heaton	Derek	Police Constable	144855 V

While off duty at home, constable Dawson became suspicious at the behaviour of two youths who had called at his house. He had watched them go to another house further along the road, he followed them but was unable to see what they were in fact doing. He telephoned for police assistance from a private house, and then remained at the street corner near where two post office engineers were working. Dawson told these men what he had seen and asked for their help if the need should arise. Shortly afterwards the two youths approached, Dawson went over to them and announced himself as a police officer, whereupon both youths tried to run away. The two post office engineers chased after them and detained one of them, while the officer struggled with the other one. During the course of the struggle the youth drew what appeared to be a Luger pistol from his pocket and threatened constable Dawson with it. Despite this Dawson continued to grapple with the youth who eventually managed to break free and run away. The officer gave chase. During the chase at least twice the youth turned and fired at the constable, the shots passing his face but he carried on with the chase. Constable Heaton who had arrived on the scene on a motorcycle in response to a radio call joined in the chase and took the lead. He knew the youth was armed, and a shot was in fact fired at him. But in spite of this he went on after the youth until the latter stopped, faced towards the officer and levelled the gun at him. The constable ordered the youth to drop the gun, the youth finally obeyed and after a brief struggle the youth was arrested.

BRITISH EMPIRE MEDAL FOR GALLANTRY
2/12/66

| Chorlton | John | Police Constable | 152620 C |

A fire quickly took hold of a three storey house, and smoke had completely obscured the lower part of the building. Constable Chorlton who was off duty at the time saw the smoke coming from the windows of the house and heard screams for help from a man and a woman who by now had climbed out of a window and were standing on the ledge above the ground floor bay window. The constable reached the ledge by climbing up a drain pipe but was unable to see anything through the thick smoke until his arm was grabbed. The constable then lowered the two people one after the other by their wrists to those who had arrived below. The constable then heard screams for help from the floor above, and although he was coughing and his eyes were watering he managed to edge along the window above the front door, broke the glass and climbed into the house. Once inside the smoke was so thick he could not see anything and returned to the window and called for a torch which was then thrown up to him. But even with the torch he was still unable to see through the smoke. Nevertheless he persisted in his efforts to reach the floor above, and made his way towards the sound of crying. By this time he found that he could not breathe and turned back to the window for some air. As he did so he fell over something, and was so overcome by the smoke that he could not get up again. He was eventually rescued by firemen wearing breathing apparatus, and was given artificial respiration before being taken to hospital.

BRITISH EMPIRE MEDAL FOR GALLANTRY
6/12/66

| Connell | William Cyril | Detective Constable | 150810 D |
| Packman | Ernest Arthur | Detective Constable | 151589 CO C10 |

Constables Connell and Packman were in plain clothes in a basement club at about 1.25 am. They had arrested a youth who was wanted by the police. But on reaching the landing at the top of the stairs which led down to the club the youth attempted to escape. Packman caught hold of the youth and in the following struggle they both fell to the floor. The youth then managed to free his right arm and managed to pull a .22 revolver from the waist band of his trousers. when constable Connell saw this he shouted a warning and dived at the youth. A shot was then fired at the constables and the struggle continued. As Connell tried once again to grab the gun another shot was fired and the officer staggered to his feet with his forehead bleeding, but despite this he tried once again to join in the struggle for the gun. The youth then again aimed at him and constable Packman tried to divert his aim by slamming him against the wall. The youth did however manage to fire a third shot, and this time Connell fell backwards to the bottom of the stairs. Packman and the youth then fell together down the stairs and landed partially on Connell. During the violent struggle between them the youth was overpowered and arrested.

GEORGE MEDAL
5/4/66

Rose   Michael John   Police Sergeant   142495 CO D3

Police Sergeant Rose was in charge of a Q car, responding to an emergency call along with other officers attended a house where they disturbed 2 youths who had broken into the premises. One of the youths ran off but Sergeant Rose gave chase and was about 15 yards behind. The youth produced a pistol and pointed it at Rose and threatened to shoot him. Nevertheless the Sergeant still went on as the criminal took aim and fired. Fortunately the shot went over the officer's head, but still undeterred he continued the chase until the youth entered a block of flats. The officer carried out a search but without success. He then telephoned for assistance. Later on, a .22 cartridge case was found near to the spot where the shooting had taken place. Although the Sergeant narrowly escaped being shot, he did not hesitate risking injury in an effort to arrest this armed criminal.

QUEEN'S COMMENDATION FOR BRAVE CONDUCT
15/2/66

Bowen   Richard William   Police Constable   147957 D

'Rescue of a mentally disturbed woman who was in danger of falling from a roof.'

QUEEN'S COMMENDATION FOR BRAVE CONDUCT
12/8/66

Cawdell   Edward Roy   Police Constable   153948 C

'Rescue of a man from an overturned van which had crashed and caught fire.'

Davies   Gareth   Police Constable   154356 S

'Arresting a violent and desperate criminal.'

Douglas   Herbert Leonard   Police Constable   133062 H

'Disarming a man in possession of a loaded shot gun.'

QUEEN'S COMMENDATION FOR BRAVE CONDUCT
6/12/66

Manley	Donald	Police Constable	151154 Y

'For services when a woman climbed scaffolding to the top of a church steeple and was in danger of losing her life.'

ROLL OF HONOUR
- Pc Geoffrey Fox, 135999 F, 41yrs old
- Ds Christopher Tippett Head, 146521 F, 30 yrs old
- Dc Stanley Bertram Wombwell, 152227 F, 25 yrs old

Crew of police vehicle call sign Foxtrot one one.
- Pc Sidney Seager

A traffic patrol motorcyclist, killed when an articulated lorry overturned and fell on him.
- Pc John London

Died from a fractured skull received in a road accident on duty on L Division.
- Pc Kenneth Charles Wilkinson

Died as a result of multiple injuries received in a motorcycle accident on duty on J Division.

1967

January	BBC television begins its acclaimed adaptation of the 'Forsyth Saga'.
February	US launch major attack on the Viet Cong headquarters.
March	Police begin trial of helicopters.
April	US more that 200,000 protest against the Vietnam War.
May	Pop group the Rolling Stones in court on drugs charges.
June	Israel triumphs in the 6 day war.
July	Minister of Transport says the 70 mph speed limit is to stay.
August	£8 million Deptford tunnel under the River Thames opens.
September	Liner Queen Mary arrives at the end of her last cruise.
October	Liner Queen Mary leaves for her last resting place at Long Beach, California.
November	All horse racing in the UK is suspended due to the foot and mouth epidemic.
December	World's first heart transplant takes place in Cape Town.

HITS OF THE YEAR
Release me
The last waltz
All you need is love
In the heat of the night

BRITISH EMPIRE MEDAL FOR GALLANTRY
14/2/67

Lock	Victor John	Temp. Detective Con.	137721 Y
Von	Charles Browne	Temp. Detective Con.	147061 Y

A police car which was escorting a wages car was rammed, the occupants were savagely attacked by about 10 men wearing masks, these men were armed with iron bars and other weapons. The robbers then made off with over £32,000 in cash. Constables Lock and Von who were patrolling in a police wireless van heard the call for assistance and went to the location in order to search for the robbers. While making their way they decided to stop and question a man, but as they approached him he drew a revolver from the belt of his trousers, he pointed the gun at Lock and threatened to shoot him. Both officers then moved towards the man, he then pointed the gun at chest level, the officers heard it click as the trigger was pulled. Both officers dropped to the ground and the gunman ran off with the gun still in his hand. The constables both ran after him keeping their distance, the chase continued with the man still brandishing the revolver. At one point the man stopped and turned he again threatened to shoot the officers. Eventually however the man began to tire and was seen to throw the gun away. Lock and Von both closed in on the man and he was overpowered. When the gun was recovered it was found to be loaded in 5 of its 6 chambers.

BRITISH EMPIRE MEDAL FOR GALLANTRY
14/2/67

Wheeler	Brian Edwin	Police Constable	146443 G
Nield	William Arthur	Police Constable	146015 G

A shop window had been smashed and the goods that were on display had been stolen. On hearing this, constables Wheeler and Nield went to the scene by car and managed to obtain descriptions of the suspects. They began to search the area in the car, and after about half an hour they came upon a man and a woman who fitted the descriptions they had been given. Constable Nield got out of the car and questioned the man. The man while making out to produce a receipt from his pocket without warning slashed the face of officer Wheeler who by now had been joined by Nield. Wheeler's face had been slashed from mouth to ear with a barber's razor. Both of the officers grabbed the man who was powerfully built and struggled to overpower him. The following struggle lasted over 10 minutes and was extremely violent, subsequently further injuries were inflicted on both of the officers with the razor. It was not until police reinforcements arrived that he was finally overpowered and arrested.

GEORGE MEDAL
10/2/67

Scott	Laurence	Police Sergeant	129404 Y

BRITISH EMPIRE MEDAL FOR GALLANTRY

Davies	Frank	Detective Sergeant	128352 N
Eist	Alexander Anthony	Detective Sergeant	133266 Y

A series of house break-ins were being investigated by Sergeant Davies and Scott and they established that the thieves were using a car hired in an assumed name. The car had been seen parked outside a house and the officers decided to enter the house. Sergeant Eist and other officers were called in to help. With Sergeants Scott and Eist covering the side of the house Sergeant Davies knocked at the front door. Davies was talking to the woman who had opened the door Sergeant Scott was now watching through the letter box of a basement door and saw a man emerge from a room, he called out to the man that he was a police officer and asked him to open the door. The man then returned to his room and later came out carrying a rifle and ran across the passageway and ran into the back garden. Scott kicked the door open and followed him to the end of the garden. The man sat on a wall and was pointing the rifle at Scott and was threatening to shoot if he came any closer. Davies and Eist then joined Sergeant Scott and Eist and at once recognized the man as an escapee from prison. The man was in fact well know to all three officers as a vicious and callous criminal. The man then jumped down from the wall and made off across the next garden with Sergeants Scott and Eist in direct pursuit and Sergeant Davies attempting to cut him off at the rear. After a short distance the gunman stopped and aimed the rifle at Scott and Eist in turn, again he threatened to shoot them. He then backed away from the officers but still levelled the gun at them. The officers threw flower pots at the man who turned and ran away. At the end of the garden he again stopped put the rifle to his shoulder, aimed deliberately at Sergeant Scott who was nearest to him and said he would shoot if he came any closer. But despite the threats Scott and Eist together closed in on the man. With the assistance of Sergeant Davies who had joined the struggle, he was soon disarmed and overpowered. The rifle was found to be loaded with three .22 bullets and a fourth in the breech ready for firing. Following the arrest Sergeant Davies went to the car parked outside the house, he met and challenged a caller to the house who struck out at the officer, a violent struggle began in the course of which the two men fell together some 8 feet into the basement area. On hearing the noise another police officer came from the house and helped Sergeant Davies to overpower and arrest the second man.

BRITISH EMPIRE MEDAL FOR GALLANTRY

31/3/67

McDowell   Gordon George   Inspector   139515 X

Police had been called to a house where a youth had armed himself with a shot gun and was threatening to shoot his younger brother. On arrival police found that all the doors were locked and that the youth was sitting in the dining room with the shotgun at his side. Police told him to come out but he ignored them and walked out of the room with the gun. Officers then found a key and managed to enter the house but the youth had locked himself in his bedroom. They once again appealed to him to hand over the gun and come out but he again refused and once again threatened to shoot his brother. At this time Inspector McDowell and a Superintendent arrived and they in turn tried to reason with the youth but he only shouted out threats to kill the first person who came through the door. Soon afterwards a shot was heard from the bedroom, Inspector McDowell immediately burst open the door and was followed in by a constable where they found the youth standing on a conservatory roof outside the bedroom window and pointing the gun at them. On entering the room both the officers ducked below the bed, the youth moved further along the conservatory roof, and as he did so, Inspector McDowell went onto the conservatory roof where despite being warned by a police officer standing in the garden that the gun had been reloaded, closed with the youth and grabbed the barrel. Another officer who had entered the room then managed to grab hold of the youth around the neck. A struggle ensued during which the gun was wrenched from the inspector's grasp and was once again pointed at him. The Inspector caught hold of the barrel and managed to turn it away so that the gun was across his stomach. At this time the gun went off but fortunately no injury or damage was done. The youth was then disarmed and arrested.

BRITISH EMPIRE MEDAL FOR GALLANTRY
3/10/67
Manns   Leslie Victor   Police Constable   134935 T
Two boys were behaving suspiciously outside a house, both were aged about 15 years. Police were informed and soon after Manns and another constable arrived. On arrival constable Manns went to the rear of the house while the other constable stayed at the front door. He rang the door bell but got no reply. He then walked along the side of the house and saw one of the youths in a down stairs room carrying a rifle. He then called out a warning to Manns and told him to return to the front of the house in order to cut off any escape by the two intruders. Constable Manns then tried to enter the rear door but as he did so the two youths ran out from another door. He shouted out to them to stop and began to chase after them. After a short distance one of the youths suddenly stopped raised the rifle and took aim at the officer. The officer then drew his truncheon and told him not to be foolish. Manns then jumped towards the boy who then shot him from point blank range hitting him in the forehead. Manns then fell to the ground and both the youths then made good their escape. Manns was taken to hospital where a pellet was removed from his head just above the right eye.

GEORGE CROSS
23/5/67
Gledhill   Anthony John   Police Constable   144670 P

GEORGE MEDAL
McFall   Terence Frederick   Police Constable   146605 P
Constables Gledhill and McFall were in a police car McFall, was the wireless operator, a message was received over the radio that the occupants of a motor car had been seen acting suspiciously at Creek Side, Deptford. As the two officers reached the area the car in question drove past them. The two officers immediately gave chase, the other vehicle was being driven recklessly through the streets of south London travelling on the wrong side of the road and against traffic through a one way system. Constable Gledhill showed considerable skill in following the vehicle at high speed and keeping up with the bandit vehicle. The ensuing chase covered a distance of 5 miles at speeds of up to 80 mph. During the chase the bandit vehicle tried to ambush the police vehicle and no less than 15 shots were fired at the police car by the occupants of the bandit vehicle who were using a sawn off shotgun and revolvers. Pellets from the shotgun struck the windscreen of the police vehicle several times. At a road junction the escaping vehicle then crashed into a lorry and 5 men left the car, a group of 3, one armed with a pistol ran into the yard of a transport contractor. The officers then followed the group of 3 and as the police vehicle arrived at the yard gates the men ran towards the car and the one with the pistol held it to Gledhill's head and ordered

the officers to get out of the car or be shot. Both officers then got out of the police car, the man with the gun then got into the driver's seat, it was obvious his intention was to make a getaway. Gledhill was then backing away across the road and the man then reversed away from the gates towards him still pointing the revolver at him. When the driver stopped to put the car into a forward gear he momentarily turned his head away and Gledhill immediately grabbed hold of the gun hand and as the vehicle moved off he managed to hold onto the car window with his left hand. At this time McFall had run along the road to a group of men to get the lorry driven across the road to block it, he heard constable Gledhill shout. He then ran back to the police car and saw him holding onto the car window. McFall then saw the car gather speed and was now dragging Gledhill along the road. It was at this time that the front offside tyre burst, causing the car to veer across the road and crash into parked cars, Gledhill was then thrown under one of them. McFall then opened the front passenger door and as the driver was still holding the pistol he began hitting him about the legs and body with his truncheon. Gledhill by this time had returned to his feet and as he went to the driver's door it was flung open knocking him to the ground. The man then got out of the car and started to back away from the officers, he warned them not to move and at the same time fired a shot. The constables then heard the gun click and both rushed the man as McFall struck him with his truncheon and Gledhill grabbed the man's right hand and took the gun from him. There was a violent struggle and the gunman fell to the ground trying desperately to reach the inside of his jacket. It was at this point that other officers arrived, the man was finally subdued, a further gun, an automatic pistol, was found in the pocket of his overalls. Both Gledhill and McFall received injuries and had to be treated in hospital.

Terence McFall retired from the police and is now living in Canada, he has written a book on the incident called Papa One. The incident involved the criminal John McVicar.

QUEEN'S COMMENDATION FOR BRAVE CONDUCT
31/3/67

Barker	Leonard	Superintendent	137201 X

'Arresting a youth armed with a loaded shot gun.'

QUEEN'S COMMENDATION FOR BRAVE CONDUCT
3/10/67

Jordan	Albert Charles George	Police Constable	141949 P
Marlow	Frederick Charles	Police Constable	134483 P

'Armed youths who stole a motor car.'

ROLL OF HONOUR

- Pc Desmond Morgan Acerman   139481 R

In the early afternoon of 11th February Pc Acerman was on duty and while following suspects was struck by a passing motor vehicle and received fatal injuries.

- Pc James Brian May

Killed when he was run down by a lorry while directing traffic at a road junction.

- Ps David Edward Westney

Instructor killed when two training machines collided at Hendon driving school.

• Pc Paul Robert Cherry

Radio operator in a patrol car which crashed while answering an emergency call in Bromley.

1968

January	Escaped great train robber Charles Wilson arrested in Canada.
February	UK Home Office launch anti theft campaign - watch out there's a thief about.
March	300 arrested, 90 police hurt, many seriously, as police try to prevent demonstrators storming the US Embassy in Grosvenor Square.
April	US oil tycoon Robert McCullough buys London Bridge for £1 million.
May	Ronan Point disaster, tower block corner flats collapse after a gas explosion.
June	James Earl Ray wanted by the FBI for the murder of Martin Luther King is arrested in London.
July	Queen opens the Hayward Gallery on the South Bank.
August	Tanks from the USSR and 4 other Eastern bloc states cross the Czech border.
September	First part of the £80 million Victoria Line is opened between Walthamstow and Highbury.
October	John Lennon and his girlfriend Yoko Ono are arrested on drugs charges.
November	Richard Nixon elected President of the US.
December	Apollo 8 orbits the moon with crew of 3.

HITS OF THE YEAR

I pretend

Wonderful world

Those were the days

Oliver

BRITISH EMPIRE MEDAL FOR GALLANTRY

14/5/68

Robb   John Anthony Grant   Police Constable   156097 L

A message had been received that a man was threatening to jump off the roof of a building. Constable Robb went to the building, the man was standing on a narrow ledge around a dome about 90 feet above the ground. He was shouting that he was going to jump. Robb stepped onto the ledge of the north side of the dome to the right of the man and he started to talk to the man. The man then moved away and threatened to jump if the officer came any closer. The man by now was on the outermost part of the ledge, and Robb started to edge towards the man. The man was by now above some spiked railings. The officer was talking to the man who was continuously threatening to jump. When the man saw a turntable ladder was being raised towards him he became very excited and made further threats to jump, but when the ladder was halfway up he became limp and fell forward in a dive like position. Robb immediately stepped towards him and managed to pull him back towards the dome. The man at first struggled violently and the constable while being held by other officers who had arrived had to use considerable force in order to restrain him and keep him from the edge. The man finally collapsed and Robb who was still supported by other officers had to hold him to prevent him from falling to the ground. The turntable ladder eventually reached the ledge and the man was lowered to safety.

BRITISH EMPIRE MEDAL FOR GALLANTRY
14/5/68

Cox	Terence Michael	Police Constable	154177 J

While investigating shooting a forest keeper was fired at several times by a youth. Police were called and shortly afterwards constable Cox arrived and followed the youth into the forest. During the chase that followed the youth fired several times at Cox in fact a total of 6 times despite this the officer continued the chase until he was about 6 yards behind him. Cox then sprang at the youth, caught hold of the rifle and in the struggle both fell to the ground. Another constable then arrived, the youth then drew a sheath knife, but he was disarmed, overpowered and taken into custody.

BRITISH EMPIRE MEDAL FOR GALLANTRY
6/9/68

Page	Terence John	Special Police Sergeant	143633 C
Rich	Anthony Paul	Police Constable	154809 C
Ross	John David	Police Constable	155629 C

Having arrested two men for being in possession of dangerous drugs constables Ross and Rich were on the way to the police station. On the way they had to restrain one of the men several times and on arrival he was taken into the charge room by constable Ross. When the man was questioned he put his hand in his pocket and pulled out a pistol and threatened to shoot. Constable Ross ran from the room in order to get assistance. On hearing a lot of shouting, constable Rich looked into the charge room and saw a man pointing the weapon. He then threw his truncheon at him. The man still holding the gun and covering the officer then backed out of the room. In the meantime constable Ross had informed Sergeant Page of what had happened and together they followed the man up some stairs to the first floor which had two exits. Constable Rich made his way by an alternative route, Sergeant Page and constable Ross then entered the room. The man then took aim and warned the officers that he would shoot if they came any closer. He then threatened to kill them both if he was not let out. Sergeant Page then signalled to Ross and both officers then drew their truncheons. At this time constable Rich who was still guarding the other exit did the same. After a short time the man then appeared to relax and the officers saw him lower the gun. Page immediately shouted and the three officers rushed forward and jumped on the man who was then disarmed and placed into a detention room.

BRITISH EMPIRE MEDAL FOR GALLANTRY
23/12/68

Pulley	Frank	Police Constable	151157 B

Constable Pulley was with two other constables who were patrolling in a car when they noticed two men, one a known criminal looking at shops. The officers then decided to question the men. Constable Pulley stopped on of the man and told him that he was a police officer and asked him to return with him to the other officers. Pulley then started to question the man who suddenly rammed his knee into the officer's groin and then tried to run off. The officer was in great pain but managed to grab hold of the man whereupon the man took a gun from his right hand pocket, kicked the officer in the shin and threatened to shoot him if he was not released. At this time Pulley shouted to his colleagues who on seeing him threatened with a gun ran towards him. Pulley threw himself at the man and managed to knock the gun from his hand, and although in considerable pain managed to subdue the man after a violent struggle. The man was then arrested.

QUEEN'S COMMENDATION FOR BRAVE CONDUCT
14/5/68

Mitchell	Ian Donald Thornton	Police Constable	146241 L
Young	Reginald James	Police Constable	156380 L

'Arresting a man from the roof of a building.'

Price	Royston Nickel	Police Constable	129169 J

'Assisting in the arrest of an armed youth.'

QUEEN'S COMMENDATION FOR BRAVE CONDUCT
10/9/68

Burns	David Johnston	Police Constable	152215 F

'For services when the jib and counter balance of a large crane collapsed and trapped two workmen.'

QUEEN'S COMMENDATION FOR BRAVE CONDUCT
18/10/68

Jacobs	Peter David	Police Constable	149420 B

'Arresting a man armed with a firearm.'

QUEEN'S COMMENDATION FOR BRAVE CONDUCT
24/12/68

Allan	Thomas	Police Constable	143301 B
Cunliffe	William Christopher	Police Constable	151906 B

'Arresting a criminal armed with a loaded firearm.'

Hurley	Dermot Edward	Police Constable	157692 F

'Rescuing people from a burning building.'

ROYAL HUMANE SOCIETY BRONZE MEDAL

Morgan	Police Sergeant	143116
Dalmasio	Police Constable	141356
Beasley	Police Constable	146399
Skinner	Police Constable	145137

For the rescue of a man from a dangerous height 94 ft above the ground at a building site.

ROLL OF HONOUR
•   Pc George Arthur Dale, V
Killed in a car accident while on duty.

1969

January	Police battle with 4000 demonstrators trying to take over South Africa House in London.
February	Boeing 747 airliner, largest commercial aircraft, makes its maiden flight.
March	Golda Meir is elected as Prime Minister of Israel.
April	First flight of Britain's Concorde.
May	In Belfast Ian Paisley is released under a wide ranging amnesty.
June	High grade oil has been discovered on the borders of British and Norwegian sectors of the North Sea.
July	Man sets foot on the moon, Neil Armstrong and Buzz Aldrin walk on the moon.
August	Sharon Tate and her friends are butchered by Charles Manson's 'family'.
September	Gaddafi seizes power in Tripoli while the Libyan monarch King Idris is in Turkey.
October	The seven sided 50p coin comes into circulation.
November	Anti apartheid protesters battle with police at a Springbok match in the UK.
December	in the UK 294 people have died of the flu in a week.

HITS OF THE YEAR
My way
Gentle on my mind
Midnight cowboy

BRITISH EMPIRE MEDAL FOR GALLANTRY
15/7/69

Lawson	Peter Laidlaw	Police Sergeant	136029 Z
Arnold	Clive Lester	Police Constable	156617 Z

A man became abusive to his estranged wife when he arrived at her home and she refused to go back with him. He took her by the neck and threatened to kill her, the children and any others that helped her. The eldest daughter went to a neighbour's home and shortly after the man went there and demanded his daughter return. He threatened to shoot the three occupants one of whom then telephoned the police. Sergeant Lawson and constable Arnold made their way to the house and heard screams coming from inside, and after repeated knocking the door was finally opened by the man who then threatened to kill the officers if they entered. Arnold managed to force the door open and on gaining access to the house saw the man standing in a room holding his wife in front of him with his left arm around her neck, in his right hand he held a pair of long bladed scissors with the points at the woman's neck. Both of the officers then threw themselves at the man and after a struggle he released his wife, he then appeared to go berserk. He still had hold of the scissors in his right hand and he made a sweep with his arm and brought the scissors towards his left side. Arnold at this time was able to parry this and further blows but was only able to reduce their force. It was at this time that Sergeant Lawson was stabbed, he collapsed and fell unconscious to the floor. Arnold continued to struggle with the man until other officers came to his assistance and the man was finally overpowered and arrested.

BRITISH EMPIRE MEDAL FOR GALLANTRY

15/7/69

Ryland	Leonard Joseph	Detective Sergeant	147034 R

A man believed to have been involved in a number of serious crimes with the use of a firearm was to be picked up by a car from a block of maisonettes. Sergeant Ryland along with 2 other officers who were nondescript undercover officers were in a police car parked outside the address. The officers saw a car driven by a youth enter the road and turn around and then stop. A man ran from the building and got into the car which then started to drive off. The three police officers then left their vehicle and ran towards the car shouting that they were police, at which time the car stopped. As Ryland went towards the passenger side of the car he saw the man draw a revolver from the waist band of his trousers. Ryland then opened the passenger side of the car and saw the man point the gun at him. He immediately grabbed the gun around the chamber and forced the muzzle away from himself at the same time he grappled with the man who was now face to face with him and was threatening to kill him. At this time the other officers tried to force the man to drop the gun but it was suddenly fired and the youth fell from the car screaming. Then the man forced the gun towards Sergeant Ryland's stomach and pulled the trigger but the hammer struck Ryland's left hand between the thumb and the forefinger this prevented the gun from firing. The three officers then managed to force the gun away and after a violent struggle and with the assistance of other officers who had by then arrived arrest the man.

GEORGE MEDAL

8/8/69

Williams	Phillip John Dixon	Police Constable	143516 CO C11
Wharton	John Stuart Northmore	Police Constable	146281 CO C8

BRITISH EMPIRE MEDAL FOR GALLANTRY

Jenkins	Reginald Alfred	Temp. Detective Con.	138662 CO C11
Marshall	James William	Detective Inspector	136034 CO C12
O'Brien	Patrick Lawrence	Detective Sergeant	136595 CO C8
Adams	Raymond Charles	Detective Constable	151794 CO C8

Police had kept observation on four men for several weeks as they had reason to believe that an attempt was to be made to rob a bank. Constable Jenkins who was riding a motorcycle saw a car containing four men which he recognized as the vehicle used by the suspects. Jenkins then followed the car and saw three men leave it and walk towards the bank. Jenkins informed the other officers by radio as the attacked appeared to be imminent. He then positioned himself near a parked car. The three men then crossed the road towards him as a police car stopped nearby. The car's occupants Sergeant O'Brien and another officer, as the car pulled up Jenkins then heard a shot fired and the three men running towards him. The first two men were armed with shotguns and the third with a pistol. Sergeant O'Brien then jumped from his car and saw that the men were armed and ran after them. One of the men then turned towards O'Brien and pointed his weapon at him and threatened to shoot. O'Brien however continued to go forward. Constable Williams on a motorcycle saw the three men running towards him and rode his motorcycle towards one of them but missed him. But when Williams back was turned one of the three men aimed his shotgun at the officer and fired, Williams turned his machine round and accelerated towards another of the men who ran round the back of a parked car and pointed his pistol at Williams as he rode towards him. Williams then collided with the man who fell to the ground with the officer landing on top of him. The man then got to his feet and again pointed his pistol at Williams who was only 2 or 3 feet from him. The man then threatened to shoot the officer. Williams jumped at the man a shot was fired and a struggle ensued. Sergeant O'Brien and another officer joined in the struggle and the gunman was then overpowered and finally arrested. In the meantime Jenkins tried to run down the first man with his motorcycle but missed, he tried again but was knocked from his machine by a car. He saw the third man coming towards him and was pointing a shotgun. When Jenkins went towards him he then turned and ran off. The first gunman had made off being chased by Detective Chief Inspector Marshall who was in charge of the operation, along with Sergeant Adams. The man was trying to escape. He was pushing members of the public aside and was also pointing the shotgun at them. While the chase was going on he turned and pointed the gun at Marshall, who at this time was slightly ahead of Adams and he threatened to shoot, but the officers continued the chase and eventually the man disappeared out of sight into a garden. As two officers approached the place the man suddenly emerged pointing the weapon at them and was also shouting that he would shoot. Both officers then approached him from different angles in order to widen the angle of fire. At this point the man momentarily lowered the barrel of the gun and both officers immediately sprang towards him. Marshall hit him with his truncheon while Adams grabbed the gun away from him. After a struggle the man was overpowered, searched and arrested. Sergeant Wharton had heard the shots fired and saw the third man running along the road, he was carrying a shotgun. Wharton shouted at him to stop but he pointed the weapon at him and shouted, he then ran off and was chased by the officer who saw him run into a block of flats. Wharton lost sight of the man, but he eventually saw him on a top floor corridor with the shotgun on the floor behind him. On hearing his name being called the man turned and went for the gun. Wharton grabbed hold of him and after a violent struggle succeeded in detaining him until assistance arrived.

BRITISH EMPIRE MEDAL FOR GALLANTRY
9/12/69

| Honey | Richard | Police Constable | 158150 Y |
| Lennox | William Buchanan | Police Constable | 148776 Y |

A man was threatening to jump from the parapet of a bridge. Constables Honey, Lennon and fireman Novak were among those were were called to the scene. The man was standing outside the parapet on a ledge about 8 inches wide, he was threatening to jump to the roadway below which was a distance of about 92 feet. Several attempts had been made to talk the man down who at this time was in a very distressed condition. They tried to talk him back over the parapet back onto the bridge. The parapet of the bridge is surmounted by an open work metal balustrade topped by a metal spindle with revolving spikes. The man was now showing signs of physical and mental deterioration and made an attempt to jump from the bridge, but two people on the bridge managed to lean through the balustrade and grabbed the man by his clothing, but he struggled free. At this point constable Honey climbed over the balustrade onto the ledge of the parapet and grabbed hold of the man putting his arm across his chest and pushing him backwards against the side of the bridge. He was immediately followed by constable Lennox who supported him in this unstable position. At the same time fireman Novak climbed over the balustrade at the other side of the man and put his right arm across him. The man by now was struggling violently and kicking out and the officers had great difficulty in retaining their foothold on the parapet and their handhold on their balustrade, both of which were wet and slippery. During the rescue both the rescuers lost their foothold on more than one occasion. And at one point Honey's legs were kicked from under him and as he slipped Lennox caught hold of his right wrist and held him until he regained his balance. Finally a rope was provided and while Lennox supported Honey with a firm hold on his wrist, Honey and fireman Novak each used his free hand and teeth to tie the man. When all the rescuers were satisfied that he was now secure he was moved a few feet along the ledge to a place where he could be hauled over the railings to safety.

Fireman Novak also received the BEM for Gallantry.

QUEEN'S COMMENDATION FOR BRAVE CONDUCT
25/2/69

Cross	Howard Robert	Police Constable	146336 J

'Arresting a criminal armed with a loaded shot gun.'

Harness	John	Police Constable	151044 D
Morse	Dennis Charles	Police Constable	150213 D

'Arresting a man armed with a loaded automatic pistol.'

QUEEN'S COMMENDATION FOR BRAVE CONDUCT
13/5/69

Kellett	Robert	Police Constable	152138 G

'Arresting a man armed with a loaded shot gun.'

Perry	Roger Charles	Police Constable	153052 D
Steele	Henry MacFarlane	Police Constable	149723 D

'Arresting a violent criminal armed with a pistol.'

QUEEN'S COMMENDATION FOR BRAVE CONDUCT
15/7/69

Bulger	Stuart Guest	Police Constable	156242 M

'Arresting a youth armed with a pistol.'

Grant	Terence	Detective Sergeant	149446 R
Harrison	Tordiff	Detective Sergeant	145015 R

'Arresting an armed man.'

Huse	Henry James	Police Sergeant	141547 C

'Arresting a man armed with a pistol.'

QUEEN'S COMMENDATION FOR BRAVE CONDUCT
8/8/69

Dick	Stuart John	Police Sergeant	147983 CO C8

'For services when armed men attempted to rob a bank.'

Sallabank	Lawrence Phillip	Detective Inspector	139142 Q
Lowe	Bernard John	Police Sergeant	142705 B

'Arresting a criminal armed with a gas gun.'

QUEEN'S COMMENDATION FOR BRAVE CONDUCT
9/12/69

Aldred	Thomas	Police Constable	145343 W
Allison	Robert	Police Constable	143075 W

'Arresting two armed criminals.'

Jackson	William Frederick	Police Constable	137053 V
Clarabut	David Louis	Police Constable	147158 V

'Arresting a man armed with a loaded revolver.'

Leeder	Paul	Police Constable	155843 V
Redpath	David	Police Constable	143843 M

'Arresting an armed criminal.'

ROLL OF HONOUR
• Pc Michael John Davies, V
Stabbed while off duty after identifying himself to warn a man who had accosted him.
• Pc Ronald Reginald Pell
Killed in a road accident while on duty as an observer in a police car.
• Pc David John Prior, L
Died as a result of injuries received in a road accident on duty.

Chapter Nine

THE YEARS OF 1970 - 1979

International terrorists were active during this decade, kidnappings in the Middle East started and the death toll rose. The murder of Israeli athletes during the Olympic games by Arabs, and there was increasing activity by the IRA after the 'Bloody Sunday' shootings.

The United States was greatly involved in the Vietnam War, the difference with this war was how the reality reached all of us by the television pictures of the bombings of Hanoi and the My Lai massacre, and the unforgettable picture which appeared in nearly every newspaper of the young girl running from a village which had been devastated by a Napalm raid. These pictures helped turn public opinion against the war, not only in America but elsewhere. After the conflict ended a world wide problem began with the Vietnamese refugees, namely the boat people.

The United States was also hit with the 'Watergate' scandal, which rocked the heart of the White House resulting in the resignation of President Nixon.

Car bombings and IRA activity was rife on mainland Britain with high profile bombs at the Old Bailey, Tower of London, Whitehall and even the Houses of Parliament. Such incidents included the murder of Airey Neave by car bomb while he was driving out of the underground car park at the House of Commons. One notable incident was the Balcombe Street Siege when 4 IRA suspects took the occupants of a house hostage after being chased by police, this siege lasted 6 days before they surrendered, see 1975.

Papa India was the call sign of the BEA Trident jet that crashed at Heathrow Airport, the UK's worst aircraft accident. There was the Grunwick dispute and one of the worst droughts to hit England.

We saw the Vietnam war; a civil war break out in Pakistan, Idi Amin took over Uganda, and terrorism hits the Olympic games. The Yom Kippur war when Egypt and Syria invade Israel, IRA bombing in the UK, riots in South Africa and a revolution in Iran. This was certainly an eventful decade.

But on the lighter side we also saw a man drive a vehicle on the moon, I hope he didn't speed. Princess Anne married Captain Mark Phillips, and in the mid 70s to the delight and amusement of some, streaking came to England, one famous occasion was a streaker jumping over the wicket at the Lords Cricket ground.

1970

January	First jumbo jet lands at Heathrow airport.
February	'Anastasia' loses her 50 year fight to prove she is the daughter of Tsar Nicholas II.
March	In the UK the quarantine period for cats and dogs is extended to one year as an anti-rabies move.
April	President Nixon sends in US troops to Cambodia.

May	England soccer captain Bobby Moore is accused of theft of jewellery.
June	Election victory for Edward Heath.
July	The Aswan Dam is completed.
August	Coronation Street is 1000 episodes old.
September	Arab terrorists blow up a hijacked aircraft in Jordan.
October	790 couples are married in a mass ceremony by Sun Myung Moon of the Unification Church.
November	NASA puts a satellite into orbit which it claims can detect missile launches anywhere in the world.
December	MP's reject a move to keep British Summer Time in winter.

HITS OF THE YEAR

Yellow river

The wonder of you

In the summertime

Patton

BRITISH EMPIRE MEDAL FOR GALLANTRY
AWARD OF THE BAR

13/2/70

Gibbins   Patrick Glanville   Detective Sergeant   135699 B **BEM**

Three men were seen to go to a parked car as two employees were returning from a bank with cash. One of the man got into the driver's seat while the other two took a bucket from the car along with something wrapped in a cloth. They then moved down an alleyway. The man in the car was soon arrested and he was found to be in possession of a metal bar and a plastic container containing ammonia. Sergeant Gibbins who was accompanied by another officer had driven his car to an alleyway where he saw the other men standing against a rear wall, one of whom held an iron bar, the other a bucket in one hand and an iron bar in the other. One of the men aimed blows at the Sergeant with the iron bar but the officer managed to avoid it and swung the car door at him knocking him off his feet and this caused him to drop the bucket from which the ammonia spilt. The other man, in the meantime, attacked the Sergeant with an iron bar but again the officer managed to avoid the blows and succeeded in knocking him down with his fists. The first man by this time had managed to get to his feet and struck the Sergeant a vicious blow to the head with one of the iron bars and then ran off. The Sergeant had sustained an injury which was by now bleeding heavily and blood was flowing freely down his face and over his clothing. Nonetheless the Sergeant continued to pursue the man, who managed to escape by climbing over a fence and crossing a railway line. He was however later arrested.

BRITISH EMPIRE MEDAL FOR GALLANTRY

12/5/70

Miller   John   Police Constable   159351 D

The constable saw 4 youths carrying haversacks in a private road. He stopped the first youth and asked him what he was up to and what was in his bag. The youth the dropped the haversack and ran off. The other youths also ran off. The constable managed to chase and catch one youth but he managed to break away and ran off. The officer again gave chase after the youth who then pulled a pistol from his pocket. He then pointed it at the constable and threatened to shoot. The police officer was by this time about 10 feet away and walked towards the youth who once again ran away. And while the youth was running away he managed to point the pistol at Miller and fired. The constable despite this continued the chase through a number of streets and finally caught the youth behind some parked cars. He was then arrested.

BRITISH EMPIRE MEDAL FOR GALLANTRY
Greaves   Police Constable   161321 N

BRITISH EMPIRE MEDAL FOR GALLANTRY
11/12/70
Griffiths   John Malcolm   Police Constable   160133 C
Constable Griffiths was with another officer and on patrol in a police vehicle. They received a message over the radio that suspects were believed to be on premises nearby. The officers then drove to the area, when they arrived Griffiths went to an alleyway running parallel to the rear of the houses. The other officer went to the front. As Griffiths entered the alleyway he saw a man carrying a holdall. The constable stopped him and told him that he was a police officer and produced his warrant card. The man suddenly pulled a sawn off double barrelled shotgun from the bag and threatened the constable. Griffiths immediately knocked the gun from his hand as the man ran away down the alley. Griffiths gave chase and the man turned around and then threw an open knife at him. The man still not deterred took an iron bar from the inside of his left sleeve and started to hit out at Griffiths about the chest and stomach. A violent struggle ensued but the man managed to get away from the constable. As Griffiths approached him again he was again violently assaulted with the iron bar but eventually managed to overpower the man and finally arrest him.

BRITISH EMPIRE MEDAL FOR GALLANTRY
15/12/70
Shacklock   Ronald   Police Constable   152669 C
Constable Shacklock was on duty In the West End of London at about 2 am when he was approached by a man who said he had been robbed by 3 men who were believed to be still nearby in a passageway. One of the suspects was standing in the centre of the passageway and the others were standing against a wall a few feet away. As the constable walked towards them one of them started to back off lifting the front of his overcoat and putting his left hand into his hip pocket. The officer undeterred continued to walk slowly towards the man and when he was a short distance away the man pulled his left hand from his pocket and pointed a pistol directly towards the officer. Constable Shacklock did not hesitate but immediately drew his truncheon; he then jumped at the man and struck him on the left wrist. The officer then summoned assistance on his radio and when other officers arrived the man was arrested.

BRITISH EMPIRE MEDAL FOR GALLANTRY
15/12/70

| Jones | Russell | Police Constable | 157087 C |

Constable Jones along with 2 other officers were on duty in a police car and were crossing Waterloo Bridge when their attention was drawn to a large crowd looking over the side of the bridge. They stopped their car and Jones got out and ran to the railings. He looked over and saw a woman struggling in the water. Jones without hesitation stripped to his under clothes, climbed onto the parapet and jumped into the river a distance of about 50 feet. When he came to the surface he could not see the woman so he dived down and felt around in the water until he touched some clothing and then finally the woman's body. He pulled at the woman and surfaced, he then supported her on her back swimming in small circles. A life belt was thrown to the constable from a passing pleasure boat. The constable was unable to put it over the woman's head, he managed to place the rope under the woman's arms this then enabled the people on the boat to pull her on board. Finally Jones was helped on board in an exhausted and shocked condition. The constable was in danger of being taken below the surface by the eddies and under tows set up by the bridge buttresses, but there was no doubt that his gallant actions saved the life of this woman.

QUEEN'S COMMENDATION FOR BRAVE CONDUCT
17/2/70

| Lewis | Nigel John | Police Constable | 157316 C |
| Morris | Stanley | Police Constable | 157894 C |

'Arresting two armed men.'

| Parker | Hugh Hamilton | Police Constable | 151590 B |
| Tucker | Derek | Police Constable | 155264 B |

'Arresting a man armed with a loaded pistol.'

QUEEN'S COMMENDATION FOR BRAVE CONDUCT
12/5/70

| Price | David Henry | Police Constable | 151258 E |
| Tarling | Michael Ronald | Police Constable | 157341 E |

'Arresting a criminal armed with a loaded pistol.'

QUEEN'S COMMENDATION FOR BRAVE CONDUCT
29/9/70

| Barnes | Barrie Keith | Police Constable | 151353 |

'Arresting an armed man who had broken into a house.'

| Munroe | Brian Roderick | Police Constable | 155190 |

'For arresting a thief armed with a gun.'

ROYAL HUMANE SOCIETY BRONZE MEDAL

Davey	Police Constable	148644

DISMISSAL

Pc Z Division found guilty at the Central Criminal Court (Old Bailey) of Manslaughter.

ROLL OF HONOUR

1971

January	Charles Manson is convicted of the Sharon Tate murders in the USA.
February	Idi Amin promotes himself to General and President of Uganda.
March	In the UK 1.5 million workers stage a one day strike to protest at the Industrial Relations Bill.
April	The City of London gives the go ahead for the building of the £17 million Barbican Arts Centre.
May	The Daily Sketch, Britain's oldest tabloid newspaper closes down.
June	UK Opportunity Knocks is the most popular TV show watched by 6.6 million.
July	First heart and lung transplant carried out in South Africa.
August	Riots flare in Ulster after internment starts.
September	In London, thieves tunnel into a branch of Lloyds bank and steal £500,000.
October	In London, the crowds greeting the Japanese Emperor Hirohito were completely silent.
November	NASA says Mariner 9 has gone into orbit around Mars.
December	In London the Jordanian Ambassador escapes a machine gun attack on his car by Black September Guerrillas.

HITS OF THE YEAR

Chirpy, chirpy cheep cheep
My sweet lord
Maggie May
The French Connection

BRITISH EMPIRE MEDAL FOR GALLANTRY

27/4/71

Reynolds	Anthony	Police Constable	152692 Z
Burch	Colin Peter	Police Constable	160602 Z

A man had gone berserk and shot two people. Constables Reynolds and Burch who were both in police cars made their way to the address and were informed that the man had escaped from the address from the back and had driven off in his car. Both the officers gave chase in their cars, constable Reynolds overtook the car and managed to box it in between his car and a police van which had arrived to assist. Constable Reynolds then got out of his car and walked towards the man who was sitting in the driver's seat pointing the gun directly at the officer's face. Constable Reynolds grabbed at the gun but the man had by now transferred it to his left hand as was threatening to shoot the officer in the head. As the officer was unable to grab the man's left wrist he had to let go, he warned other officers in the vicinity that the man was armed with a gun. At this time constable Burch ran over to the car door, and grabbed the barrel of the gun. A violent struggle began for the gun but constable Burch was able to get the gun away, the man was then overpowered and arrested.

BRITISH EMPIRE MEDAL FOR GALLANTRY
26/4/71

Mogford	John	Police Constable	151092 M
Black	George	Police Constable	154802 M
Turnbull	Ronald	Police Constable	155707 M

All three constables were in plain clothes keeping observation on a lock up garage which had a stolen car parked inside. Three men then arrived at the garage and started to tamper with the padlock of the garage. The three officers went over to the three men and informed them that they were police officers. One of the men struck out at constable Turnbull and pulled a gun from his right hand coat pocket. Constable Turnbull knocked the gun from his hand. But in the struggle that followed the man regained possession of the gun, but he was pinned to the ground by Turnbull with the gun beneath him thus preventing its use. While this was going on, constables Mogford and Black were struggling with the other two men, one of whom managed to break free and run away, constable Mogford gave chase and managed to catch him. He sat astride him on the ground. Constable Black pulled down the third man whereupon he was punched in the cheek stunning him. This man then went over to constable Turnbull and felled the officer with a heavy blow to the head. Constable Black had in the meantime recovered and managed to arm himself with a chair and went after the assailant who way by now making his way over to constable Mogford. The man was hit on the head and shoulders by the chair knocking him to the ground. Black then went to assist Mogford but he was grabbed from behind and a scuffle ensued. All three men broke free and ran away, but were being chased by Black and Mogford. Constable Mogford then caught one of the men who drew a gun from his pocket and fired it in Mogford's face rendering him unconscious. Undeterred by this Black continued the pursuit, chasing the three men for a considerable distance. He saw them force a woman driver from her car, which they then got into and drove towards the constable. He took out his truncheon and threw it through the driver's open window and hit one man on the side of the head. Despite this, the three men made good their escape. The three criminals were eventually arrested and convicted.

John Michael Mogford retired from the force and died Sunday 19th December 1993.

BRITISH EMPIRE MEDAL FOR GALLANTRY
27/4/71

Williams	Wesley	Police Constable	151742 N

Constable Williams was with another officer in plain clothes, they had gone in a police car to keep observation on a car which had earlier been reported stolen. Two men approached the vehicle within a few minutes and got into it. Constable Williams drove the police car along side the stolen car and stopped. The other officer got out of the car and spoke to the occupants of the stolen car which was then immediately driven forward onto the pavement in an attempt to escape. The car became jammed between a lamppost and a wall, constable Williams went over to the car to try to detain the driver. But as he passed behind the car it was reversed clear of the wall and he had to jump back in order to avoid being run over. As the car reversed into the road Williams broke the passenger window with his truncheon. Constable Williams was about 15 yards in front of the car and the driver drove forwards straight at the officer. Constable Williams then threw his truncheon at the windscreen but it missed and hit the bonnet instead. The officer then heard the car accelerate and as it neared him he put both hands on the front of the bonnet. The impact threw the officer into the air and he landed on the bonnet. The car was now being driven at speed and Williams knew that if he rolled off the car it would run over him. At first he managed to hold onto the windscreen wipers, but he managed to get hold of the guttering running around the edge of the bonnet and also above the driver's door. He then tried to lie across the windscreen to try to block the driver's view and cause him to stop, but the driver continued to drive at high speed, the driver then braked and accelerated in an attempt to dislodge the officer. The car eventually collided with another car at a junction but did not stop. Williams then managed to wedge his feet through the window he had broken and on three occasions he could feel the passenger trying to push his feet out. Finally the car struck a van and the officer was thrown into the road. The driver got out of the car, Williams had now got to his feet and closed in on him. Williams after a struggle managed to get the driver to the ground and arrest him.

BRITISH EMPIRE MEDAL FOR GALLANTRY
25/10/71

Donnelly	James	Police Constable	150956 P
Whitehead	John Philip	Police Constable	146329 P

On 10th February 1971 constables Donnelly and Whitehead were sent to the scene of a fire and when they arrived found that the first floor landing was engulfed in flames and smoke, and that a child was trapped in the first floor bedroom. They both made determined efforts to enter the burning room, but each time they were beaten back down the stairs by the intense heat and choking smoke. Donnelly had obtained a blanket and soaked it in water, he then rushed up the stairs followed by Whitehead who was also covered by a wet blanket. Once inside the bedroom they were unable to see because of the thick smoke, constable Donnelly heard a whimper and eventually touched the child, he picked up the child and wrapped it in the blanket, both officers then ran down the burning staircase and out into the garden. Constable Donnelly immediately gave the child artificial respiration and continued until resuscitation was taken over by the fire brigade officer who used oxygen equipment.

BRITISH EMPIRE MEDAL FOR GALLANTRY
21/12/71

Butcher	Peter Edmond	Police Constable	152822 A

Information had been received that the occupants of a Rover motor car had been concerned in a shooting incident. Constable Butcher along with two other officers went to Parliament Square in a police car in order to keep observation. The Rover was seen travelling south at great speed.

The police car gave chase for some time, the Rover was finally forced to stop by another police car which managed to block its path. Constable Butcher ran to the rear side door of the Rover and as he opened the car door he saw that the passenger was holding an automatic pistol. Without any hesitation the officer grabbed the man's arm and in the struggle that followed the man threatened to shoot and tried to point the gun at the officer. Constable Butcher struck the man's hand several times knocking the gun away, he eventually managed to pin the man's arms down and the pistol fell to the floor. With the assistance of other officers the man who was by now struggling violently was taken from the car and handcuffed. Later the pistol was found to be loaded and cocked with 5 rounds in the magazine and one in the breech.

BRITISH EMPIRE MEDAL FOR GALLANTRY
21/12/71

Knight   Malcolm John   Police Constable   160246 F

Constable Knight was on plain clothes duty when he saw three men run into an alley. As he approached the men he had reason to believe that they may be responsible for the robbery of a taxi driver at gun point. The men then rushed past him, one of them produced a gun. Knight immediately grabbed the wrist of the man holding the gun whereupon his accomplices grappled with him. During the violent struggle that ensued he was struck on the back of the head by the gun and kicked and punched repeatedly. Knight fell but managed to get up and gave chase, he brought one man to the ground. The man's accomplices returned and there was a further struggle during which the men pinned the officer down on the ground. The constable was attacked and hit with a rock and severely bitten, and was again threatened with the gun. The constable continued with the struggle until he was knocked unconscious.

BRITISH EMPIRE MEDAL FOR GALLANTRY
21/12/71

Marsh   Peter   Inspector   145913 L

A call for assistance had been made and in answering the call Inspector Marsh and two other officers made their way to a house where a man who was in an excitable state was believed to have a pistol and a bomb. One of the officers attempted to get into the back of the house Inspector Marsh tried to talk to the man who had now appeared at the ground floor bay window which he then broke with the barrel of a Luger pistol, he then threatened to shoot the Inspector and his men if they did not go away. The Inspector then ordered the other officers away while he continued to reason with the man. The man broke more windows glass and picked up a parcel which he said was a bomb. Inspector Marsh then offered to shake hands with the man in the hope of pulling him though the window, but he was not able to get a firm grip, finally with the arrival of a police motorcyclist which diverted the man's attention the Inspector was able to break a side window, disarm the man and snatch the parcel. He then kicked the front door open and arrested the man. The gun was found to be unloaded, but a clip containing 2 bullets was later found in the house. The parcel did not contain a bomb, but at the time the Inspector was not to know that.

BRITISH EMPIRE MEDAL FOR GALLANTRY
21/12/71

| Phillips | Rodney | Police Constable | 157174 B |

Constable Phillips was on patrol in a police car when he received a message that there was a search going on for two suspected criminals in the area. He then drove to the area and saw a man running towards him. From the information received he concluded that his was one of the men the police were looking for. He then called on the man to stop, but the man ignored him and ran past. The officer gave chase but he was unable to overtake him but did manage to strike out at him and hit his left shoulder. The man then turned and Phillips then saw the man had a gun in his hand. The officer struck at the gun with his truncheon but the man managed to avoid the blows and ran off. In the following chase the constable managed to strike the man again so that he fell, but he got up and threatened to shoot. Despite the constable's truncheon being broken and the fact that he was dazed by a blow from the butt of the gun, the officer continued to give chase and struggled with his assailant. During the following struggle the officer was repeatedly struck about the face but did not lose his grip until other officers arrived on scene and restrained the man and arrested him. Subsequent examination revealed that the gun was unloaded.

BRITISH EMPIRE MEDAL FOR GALLANTRY
21/12/71

| Price | John Dilwyn | Police Constable | 141486 N |

Constable Price along with another officer made their way to a building in Camden Passage, N1 where the occupant had reported that someone had tried to break in. The occupant's son had seen a neighbour climb over the back fence and made towards the house. While the officers were on the roof of the house where the attempted burglary had taken place they saw a man climbing over a roof towards the end of the building. Constable Price went down to the street where he was joined by two other constables. They went to the neighbour's house which they found was open. The house was in complete darkness, while constable Price went to get a torch the other two officers entered and saw a man standing quite still in the dark passageway. He told them he was the owner and then went up the stairs threatening to shoot them. Constable Price returned and while the other officers searched the first floor he went to the second floor and found a man with a shotgun. The man again threatened to shoot, the officer then stepped forward and knocked the barrel away and tried to seize it but was struck violently over the head with the weapon. Despite his head injury the constable grappled with the man and seized the gun and finally managed to force him back and press the barrel release on the stock. At this point the other two officers arrived, restrained the man and arrested him. Constable Price later required stitches to his head wound.

BRITISH EMPIRE MEDAL FOR GALLANTRY
21/12/71

| Dench | Robert Graham | Police Constable | 160132 X |
| Bowcock | Peter John | Police Constable | 162077 X |

While patrolling in a panda car constable Bowcock saw a car being driven recklessly. While both the vehicles were held up by traffic lights the officer left his car to speak to the driver of the other car. The man drove off against the red traffic light and the constable gave chase. The driver of the car later abandoned the vehicle and with the constable in pursuit ran across fields and waste land to the River Brent into which he jumped to hide in a sewer outlet. The man hid in the pipe and when the officer called to him he disappeared from sight further down the pipe. At this time constable Dench arrived with other officers including a dog handler with a dog. The dog was sent into the sewer but came out and refused to go back. In the meantime a manhole had been discovered and opened to reveal an inspection chamber in which the man's hat was seen to float. Constables Dench and Bowcock immediately entered the inspection chamber with a search lamp and made their way over a four feet deep mud trap and along the slimy sewer pipe for a distance of about 75 yards. They came upon a man lying unconscious face down in the water. By now the officers were choking with fumes and sewer gas, but they succeeded in rolling the man onto his back and dragged him back along the pipe to the manhole entrance, where another officer lifted him out and administered artificial respiration. But for the courage of constables Dench and Bowcock, the man would have died through inhalation of water and marsh gas fumes.

BRITISH EMPIRE MEDAL FOR GALLANTRY
Peacock

QUEEN'S COMMENDATION FOR BRAVE CONDUCT
27/4/71

Clunes	Ronald	Police Constable	130934 R

'When a mentally deranged man ran amok with an axe.'

Wood	Michael Victor	Police Constable	155007 M

'Man armed with a knife resisted arrest.'

Waddell	Douglas Robin	Police Constable	156464 V

'Arresting a man armed with an offensive weapon.'

Douglas (Kip) Waddell joined the Metropolitan police on 6 September 1966 and retired 5 September 1996. He served on several divisions including V Division and Hendon Training School. He also had the occasion to serve in Anguilla for 3 months.

QUEEN'S COMMENDATION FOR BRAVE CONDUCT
26/10/71

Healing	Terence Eric	Police Constable	151078 X
MacRae	Kenneth Allan	Police Constable	158687 X
Tomlin	Geoffrey Clive	Police Constable	155578 X

'Arresting an armed man.'

Loughead	Thomas Alphonsus Joseph	Police Constable	R

'Arresting two violent and dangerous criminals.'

QUEEN'S COMMENDATION FOR BRAVE CONDUCT
21/12/71

Seprini	Anthony John	Police Constable	162077 Z

'Arresting and restraining a man who had a firearm.'

QUEEN'S COMMENDATION FOR BRAVE CONDUCT
24/12/71

Phillips	Police Constable	143047 Y
Hickson	Police Constable	159645 N
Jordan	Police Constable	156696 T
Baldwin	Police Constable	159421
Ewan		

CARNEGIE HERO FUND
25/4/71

Choules	Alan	Police Constable	**Posthumous**

Lost his life while attempting to rescue a boy from drowning in the River Thames, near Staines, Middlesex. He was also awarded the Royal Humane Society 'In Memoriam' with a certificate going to Mrs Choules.

ROLL OF HONOUR
- Pc Douglas Frederick Beckerson

Fell through a glass roof at Baker Street Station while pursuing a drunken youth who was running amok and smashing glass with an iron bar.
- Pc Michael Eaton De Lisle Ince

Killed in a collision between two police cars answering an emergency call.
- Tdc Alan Choules

Drowned while off duty after saving the life of a boy after a boat capsized in the River Thames at Staines.
- Pc Robert Beazer

Killed when his Panda car crashed on an emergency call to a 4 year old savaged by a dog.

1972

January	Parachute Regiment soldiers shoot Derry Marchers - Bloody Sunday.
February	The IRA bombs the Parachute Regiment HQ at Aldershot, 7 die.
March	Prime Minister Edward Heath imposes direct rule for Ulster, 100,000 in Belfast Protestants protest.
April	In London Police seize arms in raids on 40 East End homes in a big operation against organised crime.
May	Bomb disposal experts parachute onto the Liner QE2 in mid Atlantic after a warning of 6 bombs on board.
June	BEA Trident crashes in a field near Staines, London. All 118 on board die, 2 rescued alive but die later.

July	A sniper kills the 100th British Soldier in Northern Ireland.
August	General Idi Amin, dictator of Uganda to expel 50,000 Asians to the UK.
September	Israeli Olympic team murdered inside the Olympic village.
October	Access credit cards introduced into the UK.
November	In Vietnam the first US B-52 bomber is shot down.
December	Andes plane crash victims survive by eating the dead.

HITS OF THE YEAR
Amazing Grace
Mouldy old dough
Puppy love
The God Father

GEORGE MEDAL
10/4/72

Garner	Arthur Howard	Police Sergeant	149740 T

BRITISH EMPIRE MEDAL FOR GALLANTRY

Giles	Keith Victor	Police Constable	142485 T
Parsons	Brian	Police Sergeant	136380 T

Police were called to a square in Shepperton in order to arrest a man who had previously escaped from a police officer. The wanted man's car arrived shortly afterwards and pulled up behind a parked vehicle. The police car which was driven by Sergeant Parson followed the car into the square and stopped immediately behind it. Parsons went to the driver's door of the Zephyr car and found that it was locked. Sergeant Garner, who was already in the square, also approached the car and as he did so the man reversed it into the police car and accelerated forward, turned the car and drove at speed at the officer. As the car passed the Sergeant he smashed the windscreen of the driver's side with his truncheon, but the car continued on and struck another vehicle and came to a stop. Meanwhile constable Giles arrived in another car and had driven it across the path of the man's vehicle. Garner ran to the car and saw that the man was holding a shotgun. He then smashed the rest of the windscreen and called to the man to give himself up. The man refused, the Sergeant tried without success to put him out of the car and when Parsons went to assist, the man then pointed the gun at Sergeant Garner and fired, but the officer managed to throw himself down and escaped injury. The man then left the car and pointed the gun at constable Giles who threw his truncheon at the man. Garner seeing the gun aimed at the constable also threw his truncheon. The man then ran off pursued by the police vehicles. As the car with Sergeant Garner drew level with the man a gun was again pointed at him and the man threatened to shoot and kill him. Sergeant Parsons and the constable had by now left their car and were walking towards the man calling on him to surrender. But the man then ran into the driveway of a house, stood with his back to the door and levelled the gun at the officers, they spread in an arc and closed on the man. Sergeant Garner lunged forward and caught the barrel of the gun and pushed it down while at the same time Sergeant Parsons and constable Giles closed in. a violent struggle took place and the man was eventually overpowered and disarmed. The gun was later found to contain one live cartridge in one barrel and one spent in the other.

All three officers also received a monetary award from the Bow Street Fund.

Keith Giles was 37yrs of age when he received this award, he joined the Metropolitan Police on 5th December 1955 and retired on 4th December 1985 having completed 30 years service, he is now living happily in retirement in Spain.

BRITISH EMPIRE MEDAL FOR GALLANTRY
29/6/72

Dixon	Ernest	Police Constable	139820 S

While on patrol in a panda car constable Dixon's attention was drawn to a crowd gathered outside a bank. A bystander told him that three men armed with sawn off shotguns were attempting to rob the bank. Without any hesitation the constable entered the bank and with a complete disregard for his safety grabbed the gun held by one of the gunmen guarding the entrance. A violent struggle began during which the man managed to wrench the gun free. Dixon believing that the man would fire the gun crouched down, he then saw the other two men running towards him carrying shotguns and a bag of money. He tried to tackle one of the men in order to get his gun. The gunman struck the officer with the gun with such force that he was knocked to the floor. As the robbers ran from the bank to escape in a stolen car the constable who was still dazed and now bleeding kicked one of them. Constable Dixon managed to radio a message to the local police station. He was taken to Barnett hospital where he received several stitches to his wounds.

QUEEN'S COMMENDATION FOR BRAVE CONDUCT
10/4/72

Millett	Kenneth James	Police Constable	156542 B
Ross	Michael Bradley	Police Constable	159561 B

'Arresting an armed man.'

QUEEN'S COMMENDATION FOR BRAVE CONDUCT
29/6/72

Baker	Cecil John Pole	Police Sergeant	140800 CO C8
Birch	Nicholas John	Police Sergeant	147022 CO C8
Broughton	Alan Frederick	Police Sergeant	151241 CO C8
Davies	Kenneth Lynn	Inspector	143640 CO C8
Snooks	Frederick Albert	Police Constable	142430 CO C8

'Arrest and disarming of 2 escaped convicts.'

Ferguson	Joseph Peter	Police Constable	148646
Piper	Jeffrey Alan	Police Constable	148646
Dadds			154791

'Arresting 2 armed men.'

| McKay | Albert | Lately Police Constable | 138516 J |

'Attempting to rescue a woman from a blazing room.'

| Mackin | Peter Harold | Police Constable | 161924 G |
| Summerfield | David Victor | Police Constable | 158797 G |

'Assisting 5 people to escape from a burning flat.'

| Offord | Harold David | Police Constable | 150113 X |

'Rescuing a man trapped in an upturned blazing car.'

QUEEN'S COMMENDATION FOR BRAVE CONDUCT
30/6/72

| Peacock | | Police Constable | 154952 J |

QUEEN'S COMMENDATION FOR BRAVE CONDUCT
15/8/72

| Hobday | Peter John | Police Constable | 139443 M |
| Willmott | Barry Joseph Sidney | Lately Police Constable | 154007 M |

'Arresting two youths armed with knives.'

ROLL OF HONOUR
- Pc Douglas John Price

Killed by a motorcycle landing on him during training for a police motorcycle display.
- Pc George William Higgs

Pc William Randall.

Killed in a traffic car crash on an urgent hospital escort.
- Dc David Eric Dench

Killed when a van driven by a drunk driver collided with his unmarked car from which he had just alighted at East Dulwich.

1973

January	Peace treaty brings Vietnam war to an end.
February	2 Pakistanis holding dummy pistols are shot dead by police, see page 240.
March	IRA bombs London, car bombs at the Old Bailey and Whitehall.
April	VAT introduced in the UK.
May	US Senate begins hearings on Watergate.
June	The Greek Government abolishes the Monarchy and proclaims a Republic.
July	Kidnap of Paul Getty III grandson of Paul Getty the Oil tycoon.
August	Princess Anne first member of the Royal Family to visit Russia.
September	World's deepest undersea rescue, two Britons rescued from inside the mini sub Pisces III.
October	IRA terrorists hijack a helicopter and force the pilot to land in a prison exercise yard and snatch 3 IRA leaders to freedom.

November   Princess Anne marries Captain Mark Phillips.
December   Britain goes on a three day week.

HITS OF THE YEAR
Eye level
Tie a yellow ribbon
The Sting - 7 awards

BRITISH EMPIRE MEDAL FOR GALLANTRY
14/5/73

Arnold   Ronald James   Police Constable   155589 Q

An emergency call has been received and constable Arnold was one of a number of officers who went to a house where a man had gone berserk and stabbed to death three of his family and seriously injured a fourth. The man had barricaded himself in an upstairs room and had placed large pieces of furniture against the door. After several attempts to persuade him to leave quietly it was quite apparent that it was impossible to reason with the man while he was in such a violent state. After several hours had passed it was decided to force him to leave the room with the use of CS gas. Constable Arnold with other officers wearing gas masks stationed themselves on the landing outside the man's room. A canister of CS gas was then fired into the room, constable Arnold began immediately to chop down the door with an axe. The man suddenly burst from the room brandishing two knives and he lunged at the officers. Constable Arnold, who throughout the whole siege had been positioned in the front of the bedroom door in a position of greatest danger. He immediately tackled the man and another officer grabbed the man's legs. Arnold fell over backwards with the man on top of him and together they tumbled down the stairs, the man was still holding the two knives, he continually lunged at the officers in a violent frenzy, during the struggle constable Arnold received a stab wound to his hand and injuries to his right leg. By this time his gas mask had become dislodged and he was now suffering from the effects of the CS gas. With the assistance of other officers the man was finally disarmed and arrested.

BRITISH EMPIRE MEDAL FOR GALLANTRY
25/6/73

Clabby   Kim   Police Constable   160185 F

A vehicle displaying false number plates was being kept under observation by constable Clabby and another officer. The driver then approached the vehicle, he was then challenged by both of the officers but before he could be questioned by them he sprayed fluid at them which temporarily blinded them. The fluid had a lesser effect on constable Clabby, so he quickly recovered and chased the man and gained on him sufficiently to strike him with his truncheon. The man stumbled but continued to run, he had only gone a few yards when he turned and fired a shot at the constable from a long barrelled pistol. Despite this the constable continued the chase, the man turned again and fired and after a short distance fired a further two shots. The officer managed to duck between two parked cars and after a few seconds was chasing after the man again who fired a further shot, he then got into another car. He started the car and drove it at the constable, but he managed to jump aside throwing his truncheon at the windscreen. The car made off at high speed, the man was eventually arrested some time later.

BRITISH EMPIRE MEDAL FOR GALLANTRY
17/12/73

Biddle	William Geoffrey	Major	Explosives Officer
Hawkins	Richard Vernon Hawkins	Captain	Explosives Officer
Gurney	Peter Edwin Spencer		Explosives Officer GM

A suspect car was parked near two buildings which had a wide area of glass in their walls, and housed a large number of staff. Major Biddle and Mr Gurney went to the scene. They quickly realised the seriousness of the situation, they entered the vehicle and immediately recognized the smell of explosives. They noticed a cord protruding from underneath the passenger seat which they knew was the detonating cord and this was traced to the rear seat which was lifted up and found to be packed with explosives. Both of then knew that they were dealing with a very large bomb. They ensured that the immediate area was evacuated and that the staff in the surrounding buildings were warned before they began the dangerous task of rendering the device safe. They found that the initiatory system of the bomb was in a wooden box under the front seat. Mr Gurney severed the detonator cord and together they moved the back seat containing the explosive as far as possible from the initiatory system. They both suspected that there might be a second such system and immediately unpacked the squab and separated the bags of explosives in order to reduce the effects of any explosion. They did not find a second system so they returned to the car where they cut the lead connecting the detonator to the wooden box. When the box was eventually opened it was found to contain a device based on an alarm clock which would have exploded the bomb at about 3 pm. The vehicle was finally declared safe after being searched for further explosives and none being found. During the morning Major Biddle and Mr. Gurney with other colleagues were extremely busy attending to further suspect car bombs, these turned out to be false alarms. At about 2 p.m. that afternoon an anonymous call to a newspaper had warned that other car bombs had been planted. Mr. Gurney with Captain Hawkins went to deal with one of them. They immediately approached the car and gained access. Again they were met by the distinct smell of explosives and rapidly located the detonating cord in a position like the one they found previously. The bomb was similar to the earlier one and having cut the detonation cord, they removed the rear seat squab, Captain Hawkins carefully dismantled the explosive charge and made certain it contained no secondary means of detonation, while Mr. Gurney made the initiatory device safe. This was again found to be based on an alarm clock which would have caused the bomb to explode at about 2.50 p.m.. Together the officers searched the car for any further explosives and finally declared it safe.

BRITISH EMPIRE MEDAL FOR GALLANTRY
26/6/73

Rumble	David Robert	Police Constable	159746 H

A motorist had reported that a robbery was taking place outside a nearby bank, a police officer who was near the scene saw a security van being driven towards him. He saw that the driver was wearing civilian clothes, he immediately broadcast this, alerting other police units in the area. Constable Rumble was in a panda vehicle nearby he quickly collected the officer and pursued the van. The police vehicle was able to draw alongside the van with the assistance of the driver of a commercial van which was moving slowly ahead, the security van was forced to stop. Two men then jumped out of the security van and one of them was carrying a sawn off shotgun. Rumble ran after this man who then turned and pointed the gun at the officer. Rumble pushed the gun away with his truncheon and the man ran off. The officer caught up with him again, hitting him with his truncheon and managed to knock him to the ground. The officer then leapt on the man and the shotgun fell out of his hand, but it was picked up by the other robber who then raised it and attempted to strike the officer. The constable managed to parry the blow and the gun struck his arm. He was knocked to his knees but the officer managed to gain control of the gun. He made sure that the gun was unloaded, he then continued to chase the first man, and after some distance he caught up with him and finally arrested him.

GEORGE MEDAL
17/12/73

Slimon	Peter	Police Constable	161720 V

A traffic blockage had been caused by a van parked at right angles across the road. Constable Slimon went over to deal with the obstruction and he noticed that the alarm signal from a nearby bank was sounding. He ran across the road and as he reached the bank a number of bystanders warned him that there were armed robbers inside. At the time of the incident the officer was on his way to a protection post therefore he was armed, he drew his revolver from his pocket. At the opening of the bank he saw a man with a shotgun which he had aimed at a number of people. The constable acted within the regulations and shouted out "I am armed". At this point the man shouted a warning to his accomplices and turned towards the officer and raised his revolver. At the same time the constable saw another of the robbers at the far end of the bank aim a shotgun at him and in self defence constable Slimon fired his revolver at the man precisely the same time as he discharged the shotgun at the officer. The constable received wounds to both his hands and arms and in the chest and was thrown from the doorway to the footpath as the result of the blast. He managed to struggle to his feet and even though his left arm was useless and bleeding heavily he kept the revolver in his injured right hand and again moved towards the bank door. The three men ran out of the bank at this moment each was carrying a case and one had a pistol pointing in the constable's direction. The officer fired at this man but was unable to fire again as he was losing the use of his right hand. Although badly wounded and incapable of using his revolver constable Slimon courageously pursued the robbers and saw them escape in a van. It was at this point that other officers arrived and the constable was taken to hospital where he was treated for shot gun wounds and was detained. Two of the robbers were wounded, one of them fatally.

QUEEN'S COMMENDATION FOR BRAVE CONDUCT
20/2/73

Harfield	James Edward	Police Constable	160651 Z
Jackson	Ernest Percival	Lately Police Constable	128513 Z

'Disarming and arresting a mentally deranged man.'

Murrock   Stanley Alexander   Police Constable   154519 R
'Arresting and disarming a youth who was firing an air rifle at a house.'

Pearce   Peter Edward   Police Constable   158229 G
Wiles   Peter Michael   Police Constable   157255 G
'Arresting 2 violent criminals.'

Roach   Lawrence Thornton   Inspector   146346 S
Webb   Ronald Philip Norman   Police Constable   140608 E
Wilkinson   Victor Legender Herbert   Chief Superintendent   135760 E
'Arresting a bank robber who threatened to cause a bomb explosion.'

QUEEN'S COMMENDATION FOR BRAVE CONDUCT
14/5/73
Davies   Michael   Police Sergeant   150047 Q
'Assisting in arresting and disarming a man who was mentally disturbed.'

QUEEN'S COMMENDATION FOR BRAVE CONDUCT
25/6/73
Atkinson   Francis Dwight   Police Constable   157317 H
'Assisting with the arrest of a robber following a bank raid.'

Babbidge   Terrence   Police Sergeant   151544 CO C12
'Pursuing and arresting an armed man.'

Collins   William Albert   Police Constable   161919 B
Dinsdale   Thomas Michael   Police Constable   160534 X
'Arresting an armed man who was causing a disturbance.'

QUEEN'S COMMENDATION FOR BRAVE CONDUCT
9/10/73
Binning   Forrest John   Lately Police Constable   150723 H
Castle   David John   Lately Police Constable   159025 H
Duffus   Gordon James   Police Sergeant   152232 H
'Disarming and arresting 2 violent criminals.'

QUEEN'S COMMENDATION FOR BRAVE CONDUCT
Crojier   Ronald   Police Constable   157753 K
Turner   William Bertram Cranstoun Lately Police Constable   161933 G
'Rescuing a mentally disturbed boy from the roof of a house.'

QUEEN'S COMMENDATION FOR BRAVE CONDUCT
Jewell   Martin Clive   Police Constable   158115 R

'Leading to the arrest of the driver who had caused him bodily harm by wanton and dangerous driving.'

QUEEN'S COMMENDATION FOR BRAVE CONDUCT
17/12/73

Holleyman	Charles Frank	Police Constable	160298 C

'Leading to the arrest of a driver who had caused him bodily harm by dangerous driving.'

CARNEGIE HERO FUND
Posthumous
26/7/73

Will	Stewart	Police Sergeant

Lost his life in an attempt to rescue a girl who had been swept out to sea by high waves at North Berwick.

ROYAL HUMANE SOCIETY BRONZE MEDAL
6/11/73

Slessor	Police Constable	154140

ROLL OF HONOUR
* Pc Michael Whiting - QPM
* Ps Stuart Will

Drowned on holiday in Scotland attempting the rescue of a girl in difficulties in rough seas.

1974
HM The Queen authorised the issue of a new Medal for Gallantry, it was to be called the Queen's Gallantry Medal. The date of institution was 20 June 1974.

January	Dr Christian Barnard performs the first heart transplant.
February	Great train robber Ronald Biggs is arrested in Brazil.
March	Kidnap attempt on HRH Princess Anne in the Mall - see page 254.
April	Heiress Patty Hearst becomes a bank robber after being kidnapped by the Revolutionary Symbionese Liberation Army.
May	Mass hysteria grips London at a concert by David Cassidy.
June	Huge explosion at Flixborough, Humberside 28 die.
July	Bomb explosion at the Tower of London kills 1 and injures 41.
August	Richard Nixon becomes the first US President to resign from office.
September	First transmission of Ceefax and Teletext information service on BBC-TV.
October	London, bombs in Pall Mall and Marble Arch.
November	Police hunt for Lord Lucan after the family nanny is found murdered.
December	Labour MP and former Minister John Stonehouse is arrested in Australia after going missing in the US. His clothes were found on a Miami beach.

HITS OF THE YEAR
She
Seasons in the sun
Tiger feet
The Godfather Part II

BRITISH EMPIRE MEDAL FOR GALLANTRY
17/6/74
Griffiths   William Ian   Police Constable   157404 CO C13
A telephone call had been received and constable Griffiths along with another officer went to a shop where they saw a man and a woman who were already wanted for seriously assaulting a police officer. His colleague went to the back of the shop to call for a car to take the couple to the police station for questioning, Griffiths stood between them and the closed door to prevent their escape. The woman managed to push the constable violently and the man then immediately stabbed him in the left side of the neck with a pair of sharply pointed scissors. The constable staggered from the blow and was stabbed twice more, once on the left temple and once over the left ear. The attack was so violent that it bent the scissors and the officer fell to the floor. Regardless of the intense pain he was in he jammed his feet against the shop door to prevent it from being opened. The couple then kicked the fallen officer violently on the legs and body until they were able to open the door enough and make their way out. As the woman tried to leave the shop the constable grabbed hold of her ankle but the man managed to pull her free, they both then ran off. The other officer by this time had run back into the shop and the two officers chased after the couple, constable Griffiths by this time was bleeding heavily from the wound in his neck. The other officer managed to catch the woman and left her in the custody of constable Griffiths who although weak from the loss of blood, managed to hold her until another police officer arrived. The man had managed to escape but was eventually arrested by other officers. The constable's condition was so critical that he was driven to the hospital and was unconscious on arrival. He was finally discharged 3 days later.

BRITISH EMPIRE MEDAL FOR GALLANTRY
18/6/74
Wolfenden   David Andrew   Police Constable   161177 C
A young man had climbed onto the outside ledge on the fifth floor of a department store. Constable Wolfenden immediately ran to the store and saw the man who appeared to be in a very distressed state. The officer then ran up to the fifth floor and went out onto the ledge as he feared the man would jump. The ledge only had a guard rail around it. The constable then climbed out onto the ledge, but when the man saw him he moved away to a point where the guard rail ended and the ledge narrowed to about 3 feet. The constable followed and seeing the man brace himself to jump grabbed his clothing, both men fell struggling on to the ledge and were in imminent danger of falling to the pavement about 100 feet below. There was a struggle but the officer managed to retain his hold on the man. In the mean time 3 other officers had also seen the man and ran to help constable Wolfenden. They saw the

constable out on the ledge where he was still trying to restrain the man who was now fighting violently. Eventually all four officers managed to drag the man back along the ledge where they passed him to safety though a window.

BRITISH EMPIRE MEDAL FOR GALLANTRY
22/4/74

Conley	Stanley	Police Constable	144798 CO A8
Burrows	George	Police Constable	141634 CO A8
Smith	James	Detective Constable	151399 CO C11

Constable Burrows and constable Conley were engaged on special duty for which they were both armed with revolvers and were patrolling in a police vehicle. They heard an emergency message come out over the police radio that a number of armed and masked men had entered the office of the Indian High Commission and were holding several members of staff as hostages. The constables immediately drove to the location. As there were already a number of other police officers at the front of the building they decided to go to a side door, when there they both entered. They quickly ran upstairs to the reception area both drawing their revolvers as they ran and stopped at a set of swing doors through which they could hear shouting and screaming. The two officers pushed open the swing doors, they saw a masked man partially hidden by a large pillar who pointed a revolver at both of them and threatened to kill them. Dropping to the ground the officers let the doors swing shut in front of them, constable Burrows pushed open one door slightly while constable Conley called out to the man that they were armed police officers and that he should put the gun down. The man continued to point the weapon at him. Constable Conley fired a single shot through the gap. Both officers shouted several times that they were armed and called upon the man to throw down his gun but he merely ducked out of sight behind the pillar. The officers then saw another masked man with a knife in one hand and a gun in the other run towards several people lying on the floor threatening that he would kill them. Constable Burrows called upon him to stop but he turned slightly and pointed the gun at the officers, firmly convinced that the lives of the hostages were in danger both officers fired at the man and he fell to the floor. Constable Conley then approached the man who was behind the pillar by crawling into the room on his stomach, he made use of furniture as a shield and with constable Burrows providing covering fire from the doorway he reached a position from which the man was completely exposed. All this time the man continued to point the weapon at constable Burrows in the doorway until constable Conley shouted 'drop that gun'. The man spun round pointing the gun directly at the officer who fired one shot which hit the man in the chest and he fell to the floor. Both men were killed. While constables Conley and Burrows went to the side door constable Smith who had also answered the emergency call arrived at the front entrance. Shortly after his arrival a window was smashed from the inside and through it he saw a masked man with a pistol in one hand and a knife in the other. Constable Smith immediately shouted to the man that he was a police officer and ordered him to drop the weapons, but the man pointed the pistol at him, the officer then heard shots from within the building. Assisted by other officers who had just arrived he cleared a number of pedestrians from outside the building and had the traffic stopped. Hearing further shots and screams coming from the High Commission he saw members of the staff struggling with a masked man. Constable Smith climbed through the smashed window armed only with his truncheon and went to their assistance. He hit the masked man with his truncheon, he was then able to arrest him and search him for any weapons. It was later found that the guns the raiders had been using were imitations although police officers could not possible have known this. Knives a sword and a pump full of acid which had also been taken into the building were however capable of inflicting lethal injuries upon the officers and the hostages.

After this date - the BEM was no longer awarded. It was replaced by the Queen's Gallantry Medal.

GEORGE CROSS - KIDNAP ATTEMPT ON PRINCESS ANN
27/9/74

Beaton	James Wallace	Inspector	151319 A

GEORGE MEDAL

Hills	Michael John	Police Constable	164382 A

QUEEN'S GALLANTRY MEDAL

Edmonds	Peter Roy	Police Constable	162760 G

On Wednesday 20th March 1974 at about 8 pm, HRH the Princess Anne and her husband Captain Mark Phillips were returning to Buckingham Palace after an official royal engagement. Their car was being driven by Mr Callender and they were accompanied by Princess Anne's personal protection police officer Inspector Beaton, also in the car was her Lady in Waiting. As the royal car approached the junction of the Mall and Marlborough Road a white car swerved in front of it, Mr Callender was forced to stop suddenly. The driver of the white car left the vehicle and went over to the royal car. Inspector Beaton who was seated in the front passenger seat got out of the car to see what was wrong. As the Inspector walked towards the man, the man pointed a revolver at him and fired, wounding him in the shoulder. But despite the wound the Inspector drew his pistol and fired at the man but the shot missed. Inspector Beaton was not able to fire the gun again as it had jammed, and as he moved to the near side of the car he tried to clear the stoppage, the gunman told him to drop his weapon or he would shoot the Princess. As the officer was not able to clear the blockage he placed his gun on the ground. At this stage the gunman was trying to open the rear offside door of the car and was demanding that Princess Anne went with him. Princess Anne and Captain Phillips were at this time struggling to keep the door closed, the Lady in Waiting managed to get out by the rear near side door, Inspector Beaton then entered the same way. He then leant across to shield Princess Ann with his body. Captain Phillips managed to close the door and the Inspector on seeing that the man was about to fire into the back of the car put his hand to the window directly in the line of fire in order to absorb the impact of the bullet. The gunman then fired, this shattered the window and the officer was wounded in the right hand by the bullet and the broken glass. But despite his wounds Inspector Beaton asked Captain Phillips to release his grip on the door so that he might kick it open violently so as to throw the man off balance, but before he could do this the man opened the door and fired at the officer again wounding him in the stomach. The Inspector then fell from the offside door and collapsed unconscious at the gunman's feet. Mr Callander in the meantime had tried to get out of the car but the gunman had put his gun to his head and told him not to move. Nonetheless he got out of the car at the first opportunity and grabbed the man's arms in an attempt to remove the gun. Despite being threatened by the gunman Mr Callander clung onto the man's arms until he was shot in the chest. In the meantime Mr McConnell was in a taxi in the Mall when he heard shots. A royal car appeared to be involved so he told the taxi driver to stop. He ran back to the scene where he found the gunman shouting at the occupants of the car. He saw the gun in the man's hand, he went up to him in a placatory manor and asked him to hand over the gun. He was told to get back, but when Mr McConnell continued to walk towards the man he took aim and fired a shot wounding him in the chest. McConnell staggered away and collapsed. Constable Hills was on duty at St James's Palace when he heard the noise and he saw the car stationary in the Mall. On thinking that there had been an accident he reported on his radio and went over to the car, when he got there he saw a man trying to pull someone from the back of the car and touched his arm.

The man then spun around, moved a few feet away and pointed the gun at the officer. As the constable moved forwards to take the gun the man shot him in the stomach and then returned to the rear of the car. Constable Hills staggered away and using his radio sent a clear and concise message to Cannon Row Police Station reporting the seriousness of the situation and calling for assistance. As he walked around the back of the car he saw Inspector Beaton's discarded gun, he picked it up returned to the offside of the car intending to shoot the gunman, but he felt very faint and did not use the weapon as he was not sure of his aim. He was then assisted to the side of the road where he collapsed.

Also driving along the Mall was Mr Martin, he saw the situation and he drove his motor car into the gunman's car so as to prevent any possible escape. He then went to the Royal car to render assistance but the gunman pushed the gun into his ribs, at this point constable Hills intervened and was shot and it was Mr Martin who assisted in moving him to the side of the road. Mr Russell was also driving along the Mall when he saw the gunman attempting to open the door of the Royal car, he too stopped and as he ran back he heard shots. When he arrived at the car he saw the man with the gun in his hand and a police constable being assisted to the side of the road. With disregard to the obvious danger and seeing that the gunman was holding Princess Anne by the forearm and trying to wrestle her from the car Mr Russell ran up and punched him on the back of the head. The man immediately turned and fired at him, the shot fortunately missed. Mr Russell in the meantime tried to get the constable's truncheon but on hearing more commotion he returned to the Royal car from which the gunman was still trying to drag Princess Anne with one hand while still pointing the gun at her with the other, threatening to shoot her if she refused to come. The Princess was still refusing and in trying to delay the gunman was trying to distract his attention by engaging him in conversation, Captain Phillips managed to keep a firm hold around her wrist and was trying to pull her back into the car. Mr Russell now ran around to the other side of the car and saw that Princess Anne had managed to break free from the gunman and was about to leave by the near side door. She was almost out of the car when the gunman came up behind Mr Russell and once again tried to reach the Princess. Captain Phillips promptly pulled her back into the car and Mr Russell punched the man in the face. It was at this point that other officers began to arrive. The gunman then ran off. Constable Edmonds was one of the first to arrive on scene and he saw the gunman running away with the gun still in his hand. Constable Edmonds gave chase shouting at the gunman to stop, but the man continued to run away, he again pointed the gun directly at the officer, but completely undeterred the constable charged the man and knocked him to the ground, other officers who had also given chase immediately threw themselves on the man who was then disarmed.

The wounded men were all taken to hospital where bullets were removed from Inspector Beaton, Mr Callander and Mr McConnell. Constable Hills received treatment for his wound but no attempt has been made to remove the bullet from his liver.

All the individuals involved in the kidnap attempt on Princess Anne displayed outstanding courage and a complete disregard for their personal safety when they each faced this dangerous armed man who did not hesitate to use his weapon. It is entirely due to their actions as well as to the calmness bravery and presence of mind shown by both Princess Anne and by Captain Mark Phillips in circumstances of great peril that the attack was unsuccessful.

James Beaton later became the Queen's Police Officer and has since retired from the force.

QUEEN'S POLICE MEDAL
Posthumous
11/10/74

Whiting   Michael Anthony   Police Constable   162273 C

The constable was on duty in the West End of London in a police car along with another officer. They were behind a Jaguar car which was waiting at traffic lights. It moved off quickly and turned off sharply when the lights turned to green. The officer's suspicions were aroused and they decided to stop the car. The car then went the wrong way around roundabout and continued at speed swerving from side to side and from lane to lane, until it eventually stopped at some traffic lights. Constable Whiting got out of the police vehicle and opened the front passenger door of the Jaguar in order to speak to the occupants. The car moved off and constable Whiting began running alongside it holding onto the door and to the roof. The other officer ran to his assistance and tried to take out the ignition key but could not. Both officers were now running alongside the car as it collided with a van. The driver made no attempt to stop the car but put his foot down hard onto the accelerator, trying to push the van out of the way. The van veered to the right and the Jaguar shot forward. Whiting had his feet inside the car; he could have jumped off but continued to hang on. As the Jaguar sped away the occupants of the car tried to dislodge the officer but he continued to hold on. Eventually he was thrown from the car as it collided with another car and landed on the roadway. His skull had been fractured and he sadly died the same day.

QUEEN'S GALLANTRY MEDAL
3/10/74

Wordsworth   Alan   Police Sergeant   144872 D

Sergeant Wordsworth along with another officer went to the assistance of a police officer who had made a call over his radio. He was keeping watch at a hotel when an armed man who had previously shot and wounded a shop assistant was hiding. When the Sergeant and his colleague who were both armed arrived at the hotel the door to the man's room was quietly unlocked. They both drew their weapons as they were aware the man inside had already shot someone. Sergeant Wordsworth then took the lead. The man in question was in fact inside the room holding a revolver in his right hand which he then pointed at the Sergeant and told them to get out. Sergeant Wordsworth pointed his gun at the man and ordered him to drop his gun or he would be shot, whereupon the man extended his arm in a threatening manner so that his gun was now closer to the officer. The Sergeant repeated the warning and the man lowered his gun. The officer who was with the Sergeant rushed past and grabbed the gun as the man put it down. Two other officers who had also arrived entered the room and seized and overpowered the man. The man's weapon was subsequently found to be loaded with 6 rounds and was cocked ready for firing.

QUEEN'S GALLANTRY MEDAL
16/12/74

Chaffey	Godfrey Henry	Police Constable	149404 D
Gage	Barry Neil	Police Constable	157051 CO B8
Pointer	Alan Kenyon	Police Constable	158061 D

Shortly after a restaurant had closed for business one man entered the door which was shut but not locked, it was about 1 am in the morning. He took a handbag containing some cash, jewellery and cheques, these being the property of the proprietor. The man's accomplice remained at the wheel of the getaway car which was stolen. The owner of the restaurant was in the street at the time and saw the man enter and then leave the property and instantly recognized his wife's handbag. He then challenged the man and chased him, where upon the man shot at the restaurateur and the shots were heard by constables Chaffey and Gage who were on duty nearby in a police car. As they approached they heard shouting, then they saw the stolen car turn into the road in front of them at slow speed. It was driving without lights and the passenger door was wide open. They noticed a man running after the car. Constable Gage opened his door intending to stop the man who, when he saw him, immediately slowed and pointed the gun at the officer and threatened to shoot him. The man then ran up to the open door of the car and got inside. Constable Chaffey joined his colleague and together they ran towards the stolen car, and as they did so the gunman again pointed the gun at them and threatened to shoot. The constables ducked and the car then drove off. Chaffey ran a short distance after the car and then returned to the police car. The officers then chased after the stolen vehicle in their police car. As the chase started Chaffey gave the commentary over the radio. When the car was within 10 yards of the getaway car the gunman put his right arm out of the passenger window and shot at the officers. Constable Gage had swerved so the shot did not hit them. Meanwhile constable Pointer who was in a police van with another officer had heard about the robbery over the police radio, they saw the stolen car turn at a road junction and immediately followed it. Constable Pointer tried several times to try to overtake the car but was not able to, eventually the stolen car crashed into a pile of sand by some road works and stopped. The police van then pulled up close to the rear of the stolen car. Constable Pointer and his colleague then got out of the car and started to chase the gunman and his accomplice who both ran in different directions. Constable Pointer chased the gunman who was still in possession of the stolen handbag, as the constable closed on him the man turned, shouted and attempted to fire his gun. Constable Pointer managed to knock the pistol away and grabbed the man around the neck. The man was eventually overcome and arrested. His accomplice was also caught and arrested by other officers one of whom was constable Chaffey.

QUEEN'S GALLANTRY MEDAL
17/12/74

Humm	Frank Henry	Police Constable	148251 Y
Usher	Gordon	Police Constable	148358 Y

Constable Humm along with another officer were called to a block of flats where there was some kind of domestic dispute taking place. The man who opened the door had a brief word with the officers but then suddenly pulled out a carving knife, and without any warning stabbed constable Humm in the left side of his neck and pushed him to the ground. The man then started to attack the second officer, he tried to grapple with the assailant and parry the blows but was stabbed repeatedly in the head and face and received serious wounds which were bleeding heavily. Constable Humm realised that his fellow officer had been gravely injured. He quickly got to his feet and despite his own injury went over to the officer with his truncheon drawn. He hit the man with the truncheon but it had no effect. To save his colleague from further injury he grabbed the man and grappled with him at close quarters. At the same time, shouting to the injured officer to get away. The officer was not able to escape and eventually the three men tumbled down the stairs onto the landing below. The other police officer managed to break away from the man who was still fighting, but he collapsed on reaching the police car. Constable Humm continued the violent struggle with the man who as they rolled further down the stairs dropped the knife. The man then broke away and ran out of the entrance to the flats closely followed by constable Humm. Knowing that the other police officer's life was in danger if he did not receive immediate medical attention, the officer wisely summoned assistance on the car radio and rendered first aid. Constable Usher was patrolling in a panda car when he heard of the incident on his radio, and having been informed that one officer had been seriously injured was well aware of the danger. By skilful use of his local knowledge, constable Usher anticipated the man's avenue of escape and found him walking along the footway. Usher stopped the car and approached the man and began to question him. The man immediately pulled a knife from his sleeve and made threats to the officer. The officer then grasped his right hand and a violent struggle took place. Constable Usher could not get a firm grip on the man's clothing which was slippery with blood. The man was then able to break away he then ran off still holding the knife. The officer ran after him at the same time calling for assistance over his personal radio. The officer then saw the man enter a house. The man stood in the doorway facing the constable and brandishing the knife, after he had made threats to the officer the man then slammed the door. Constable Usher immediately kicked the door open and saw the man enter the kitchen at the rear of the house. Again the man slammed the door shut, on opening the door the constable found himself facing the man who was still armed with the knife. When other officers arrived at the scene constable Usher rushed the man and managed to overpower him, but only after another violent struggle.

QUEEN'S GALLANTRY MEDAL
17/12/74

Young John Raymond Police Constable 160617 P

Constable Young along with another officer were on duty in plain clothes in the early hours of the morning, in an unmarked police van. They noticed three men in a car who were acting suspiciously. The officers then decided to follow the car which then accelerated away once the occupants realised that they were being followed. The officers continued to follow for some time until the men abandoned their vehicle and ran off. Constable Young chased one of the men into a school playground. He shone his torch on the man and shouted out "stop police", the man stopped and turned around and the constable saw that he was armed with a double barrelled shot gun. The man then fired at the officer from a distance of about 15 yards and wounded him in the left leg. Constable Young then took cover behind a nearby pile of sand and the man then ran away once more. Despite his wounds the officer took up the chase again shining his torch onto the offender. The gunman still running turned and fired another shot at the officer but fortunately it missed. The officer then switched off his torch and continued to follow the man until he lost sight of him. All three of the men escaped but the gunman was subsequently caught and arrested.

QUEEN'S COMMENDATION FOR BRAVE CONDUCT
23/4/74

Dover Police Sergeant 131369 V

QUEEN'S COMMENDATION FOR BRAVE CONDUCT
18/6/74

Mackaness	Paul Andrew John	Police Constable	160987 H
Monti	Frank Renate	Police Constable	161650 H

"Arresting a man who has attempted to commit an armed robbery."

QUEEN'S COMMENDATION FOR BRAVE CONDUCT
18/6/74

Smith	Frank	Police Constable	138735 X
Wright	Alan Thomas	Police Constable	138350 X

"Disarming and arresting a mentally disturbed man who was armed with a loaded shotgun."

QUEEN'S COMMENDATION FOR BRAVE CONDUCT
3/10/74

Brown	Ian	Police Sergeant	155697 CO C8
Crampton	Ian Richard	Police Sergeant	155096 CO C8
Kirby	Colin Edward	Police Constable	150744 CO C8
Mills	Guy Samuel	Police Sergeant	150177 CO C8
Street	Roger Robin	Police Sergeant	152202 CO C8

"Disarming and arresting 2 armed criminals who attempted to rob a security van."

| Kerr | David McMorrin | Police Constable | 148607 F |
| Riley | Brian Douglas | Inspector | 148740 B |

"Arresting an armed woman who entered the public gallery of a Magistrates Court during a trial and attempted to bring about the release of the prisoner in the dock."

| O'Rourke | Brian Anthony Michael | Police Constable | 155901 B |

"Arresting an extremely dangerous and violent man who was armed with a pistol."

| Shadrack | Michael John | Inspector | 154829 F |

"Disarming and arresting an armed man who had previously shot and wounded a shop assistant during an attempt to rob a jeweller."

| Ward | Robert | Police Constable | 161056 N |

"Arresting a mentally disturbed man armed with a pistol."

QUEEN'S COMMENDATION FOR BRAVE CONDUCT
17/12/74

| Beer | James Anthony Roy | Police Constable | 157029 D |

"Arrest of an armed criminal who had fired his weapon at two Police Officers."

Dixon	George	Police Constable	158223 X
Hammond	Derrick Oswald	Police Constable	143664 X
O'Driscoll	Walter	Police Constable	142757 X

"Tackling and arresting an armed man who had robbed a bank."

ROYAL HUMANE SOCIETY BRONZE MEDAL

| Woodhams | Police Constable | 159911 F |
| Lambert | Police Constable | 155137 W |

ROLL OF HONOUR
- Tdc Vernon Rupert Weatherstone

Died when he was involved in a collision while driving a CID car.
- Inspector David George Gisbourne

Collapsed 2 days after being involved in policing disorder in Red Lion Square on 15 June which substantially contributed to his subsequent death.

1975

January	Heiress Lesley Whittle is kidnapped from her Shropshire home.
February	Metropolitan policeman Stephen Tibble shot dead by the IRA, see 1976.
March	Charlie Chaplin is knighted.
April	Cambodia falls to the communists, US Embassy falls.
May	Evel Knievel suffers spinal injuries while attempting to jump 13 buses in his car.
June	Suez Canal re opens for International maritime traffic.

July	Ancient 'Terracotta' army of 6,000 life size warriors discovered near the city of Xian in China.
August	London has its hottest day for 35 years of 32c.
September	Beirut is torn apart by Civil War.
October	Bomb goes off outside Green Park underground station, 1 dies and 20 injured.
November	Monarchy returns to Spain with King Juan Carlos.
December	Balcombe Street siege, London - see below for brief summary, and 1977 for awards made to police officers.

HITS OF THE YEAR
Bye bye baby
Sailing
Bohemian Rhapsody
One flew over the cuckoos nest

BALCOMBE STREET SIEGE - 1975
This Balcombe street siege started in December 1975 when 4 IRA terrorists in an attempt to escape from police burst into the house of John and Sheila Matthews in Balcombe Street, London, and held them hostage. The four terrorists were ultimately responsible for three murders one of which was an explosives officer for the Metropolitan Police, Capt. Roger Goad, who was awarded a posthumous George Cross in 1976.

Police were on the offensive against IRA attacks at hotels and restaurants. After 3 days of police attention a policeman who was patrolling Mount Street saw 4 men in a car approach Scott's restaurant which had previously been bombed, killing one person and injuring a further 15. The officer saw what he believed to be a rifle in the car and relayed the information over his personal radio when a volley of shots were fired from the car at the restaurant windows.

Details of the car and the occupants were circulated to all police units. It was then spotted in Carlos Place and a number of police cars took up the chase. The car and occupants drove into a cul de sac and decamped from the vehicle firing wildly as they ran. They saw an opening at a block of flats, they ran up the first flight of steps, knocked on a door and forced their way into the home of Mr and Mrs Matthews an elderly couple, threatening them with guns.

Police immediately surrounded the area. The terrorists were at a disadvantage as they had not planned on being caught up in a siege. It was fortunate for the police because earlier in the year they had dealt with another siege ('Spaghetti House Siege'), and this had given the police a little experience with dealing with such events.

The break through came on 12th December when the terrorists agreed to allow a telephone back into the flat, they had thrown the last one out 2 days earlier. With contact re-established negotiations progressed.

The gunmen realised their situation was hopeless but were afraid that Scotland Yard marksmen would shoot them if they walked out. Mrs Matthews was released first and after a few more hours the siege was finally over. No one was injured and the 2 elderly occupants were taken to hospital for a check up. The 4 IRA men were taken in pairs away from the scene.

QUEEN'S GALLANTRY MEDAL
LG. 17/3/75

Brady	David	Police Constable	142226 Y
David	Ryan Kenneth	Police Constable	156799 Y
Peffer	Michael Thomas	Police Sergeant	147798 Y

A robbery had taken place at a sub post office by four men armed with sawn off shot guns, they made off with postal stock and cash and escaped in a stolen car. Later they were seen by a police patrol car, the occupants were not aware that a robbery had been committed, but just decided to stop the car due to the manner in which it was being driven. They gave a running commentary over the radio as they chased after the vehicle for several miles and eventually lost sight of it. Constable David who was in another police car heard the commentary and as a result recognized the stolen car as it approached him, he then drove his police car across the road to block it. The driver however managed to get past him. The constable then reversed his car and continued the pursuit. The passenger in the stolen car fired at constable David and his colleague striking the windscreen of the patrol car but they continued the chase. Another police vehicle was by now ahead of these two vehicles and had been place across the road to form a road block. When the robbers car reached the road block it turned sharply into a cul-de-sac. As it was stopping, still being followed by the police, the occupants fired 2 shots at the police officers who were manning the road block but neither officer was hit. Constable David grappled with one of the gunmen in order to gain possession of his weapon, while the other gunman who had been beating the officer on the arm with the gun began loading his shotgun. The constable had no choice but to release his grip but did manage to pull one of the unarmed members of the gang from the car and arrest him. At the same time other police officers ran towards the car and managed to arrest another armed robber. Sergeant Peffer arrived on the scene knowing that armed police officers had been requested, he decided to try to talk the armed criminals remaining in the car into giving up, and so avoid the possibility of a gun battle. He accordingly approached the gunmen's car and spoke to one of the occupants who was very abusive and threatened to kill him. The officer then indicated that he was unarmed and despite having two guns pointed at him continued to talk the occupants into surrendering. One of the men then began to reverse the car still keeping his shotgun pointed at the Sergeant. Constable Brady was one of a number of officers who had arrived on scene, he threw his truncheon in an unsuccessful attempt to stop the vehicle. The vehicle then collided with a metal post and shattered the rear window. Brady immediately ran to one of the police cars, reversed it and rammed it into the stolen car, whilst another constable driving a police van assisted in the ramming of the car from another direction. One gunman fired a shot at constable Brady, causing slight wounds to his face and left hand. Then Sergeant Peffer with other officers rushed the car and after a violent struggle overcame the two armed men who were then arrested.

QUEEN'S COMMENDATION FOR BRAVE CONDUCT
18/3/75

Coburn	Steven Ronald	Police Constable	164356 N
Collett	Raymond Leonard	Police Constable	151812 Y

| Fitzsimons | Antony Wright | Police Constable | 156154 N |
| Graham | Charles Hamish | Police Constable | 162904 Y |

"Arrest of four armed criminals who had robbed a sub post office and driven away in a stolen car."

QUEEN'S COMMENDATION FOR BRAVE CONDUCT
6/6/75

| Deeming | George Thomas | Police Constable | 148014 G |
| Gatland | Victor Raymond | Police Constable | 156931 G |

"Leading to the eventual arrest of four armed man who had robbed a security van."

Mann	Graham Finlay	Police Constable	157386 Q
Todd	Lindsay Cameron	Police Sergeant	151928 X
Bowen			145345
Harrison			161621

"Arresting 2 members of an armed gang who had attempted to rob a bank."

ROYAL HUMANE SOCIETY BRONZE MEDAL

| Parker | | Police Sergeant | 156478 P |

For attempting to rescue a man from the BBC TV transmitter at Crystal Palace.

ROLL OF HONOUR
- Pc Stephen Tibble QPM, F Division

Shot dead by the IRA while chasing a suspect while off duty.
- Expo Roger Goad - GC BEM

Killed when a bomb he was defusing in a shop doorway in Kensington exploded.

1976

January	Hurricane force winds up to 105 mph cause havoc across the UK, 22 die.
February	Post Office announce the end of Saturday and Sunday collections.
March	Tube driver is shot dead chasing a gunman moments after a bomb goes off on a train near West Ham underground. See police gallantry for Pc Kiff.
April	26 arrested after clashes break out at a National Front march in Bradford.
May	Cab driver George Davis is released from jail serving 1 year of a 17 year sentence.
June	Britain and Iceland sign an agreement to end the 3rd Cod war.
July	Israeli commandos free 100 hostages at Entebe.
August	Race riots break out at Notting hill, London. 68 arrested, 36 buildings looted, 35 police cars damaged, 350 police injured, several being stabbed.
September	Riot at Hull jail ends after 65 hours £1 million damage caused.
October	Building Society put up mortgage interest rate to 12.25%.
November	Vietnam and US begin their first formal talks since the Vietnam War.
December	Sex Pistols run riot on the ITV chat show 'Today' the presenter of which is suspended.

HITS OF THE YEAR
Save your kisses for me
Dancing queen
Don't go breaking my heart
Rocky

QUEEN'S POLICE MEDAL
Posthumous
17/6/76

| Tibble | Stephen Andrew | Police Constable | 165956 F |

On Wednesday 26th February 1975 an officer engaged in plain clothes duty and on an observation saw a male acting suspiciously. The officer stopped him and started to question him. While this was taking place the suspect suddenly ran off and the officer then gave chase. At the same time the officer summoned help over his radio. As the suspect was being chased he was seen by a witness to take what appeared to be a gun from out of his pocket. Two other officers also in plain clothes then joined in the chase and at the same time, constable Tibble who was off duty in plain clothes was on his motorcycle also gave chase. He managed to overtake the suspect, got off his motorcycle and faced the man in an attempt to arrest him. As constable Tibble approached the man he shot the officer 3 times at the range of about 6 feet, constable Tibble fell to the ground mortally wounded.

GEORGE CROSS
Posthumous
1/10/76

| Goad | Roger Philip | Explosives Officer | CO C7 BEM |

On Friday 29th August 1975 a telephone call had been received at the office of a national newspaper stating that a bomb had been left in a shop doorway. This information was immediately passed onto the police and two police officers patrolling the area went to the scene. On arrival the officer saw a plastic bag in the shop doorway. One of the approached and examined the bag and saw a wrist watch attached to the top of the contents by adhesive tape. It appeared almost certainly to be a bomb, the officers raised the alarm. The street was subsequently taped off and cleared of all pedestrians and the occupants of the surrounding building were warned to keep to the rear of the premises and away from all windows. Captain Goad had returned to London after having dealt with a suspect parcel, and he accepted the call to deal with this device. When he arrived he was briefed by a senior police officer while they walked towards the shop. At some distance to the bomb the police officer stopped and Captain Goad walked towards the shop alone and entered the shop doorway. He was seen to bend over the bomb and was in the process of defusing it when it exploded. Captain Goad was killed instantly by the force of the explosion.

GEORGE MEDAL
27/7/76

| Clements | David Michael | Police Constable | 162876 E |

Members of the public informed constable Clements that three armed men were robbing a bank nearby. Constable Clements who was driving a panda car immediately went to the front entrance of the bank where he was confronted by the robbers as they were leaving. He was threatened with their weapons and one of the raiders fired several shots in the direction of his panda car and struck the officer in the face causing him to stumble. The constable quickly returned to his vehicle to pursue the gang but due to a faulty radio he was not able to summon any assistance. Nevertheless he chased the gang's car which was travelling at times against one way traffic. When it came to a road junction one of the raiders fired a shot through the rear window of the car. The bullet shattered the windscreen of the police car and hit constable Clements in the right shoulder, this caused him to momentarily lose control of the car and he crashed into a rubbish skip in the road. The constable recovered and pushed out the glass from the shattered windscreen and although in great pain from his wounded shoulder he pulled away and continued the pursuit of the bandit car for a further mile until he finally lost them.

GEORGE MEDAL

6/12/76

Biddle   Geoffrey William   Explosives Officer   CO C7 MBE

Shortly after midnight on Sunday 9th November 1975 a man and his wife returned to their car, bearing in mind police warnings to be cautious of explosives attached to stationary vehicles they looked under the car and saw a duffel bag jammed underneath below the passenger's seat. They did not interfere with the bag but called the police. Major Biddle was called for and attended the scene which had been sealed to traffic and was clear of pedestrians. After an initial examination it was decided that the residents of the nearby houses should be evacuated before the bag was examined. There was only a small amount of ground clearance underneath the car and Major Biddle could see the tightly wedged object was securely closed by a cord. He could not touch the bag so he tackled the inspection by lying in the gutter but because of the background noise he was not able to decide whether or not the bomb was actually ticking. He used his torch and saw a small piece of plastic covered wiring and came to the conclusion that the device was not only a time bomb but was also fitted with some kind of sophisticated anti handling trap. Major Biddle slowly pivoted the device so the opening was facing where he was lying in the gutter, he had to do this gently so that the pressure contact between the bag and the vehicle remained unbroken. When the bag was eventually close enough he managed to cut the cord, open the bag and this then enabled him to disarm the device sufficiently to pull it from under the car and render it safe. The bomb would have exploded if the bag had been removed or if the car had been subjected to any movement, this would include occupants getting into the car.

Major Biddle has over a period been involved in defusing other terrorist explosive devices. On Saturday the 5th January 1974 following a day of bomb activity he was called to some premises where the area had been evacuated following the discovery of a suspicious object. The suspect device had been placed among several plastic bags in a poorly lit position it was seen to contain a clock, batteries and explosives. Major Biddle eventually defused the bomb by cutting the wiring to the batteries and removed the detonator he then managed to reach the clock, the setting of which showed that the device was probably within seconds of exploding at the time it was disarmed. In the early hours of the following day Sunday 6th January 1974 Major Biddle was called to the basement at the front of a house where a suitcase had been left on the doorstep. He noticed that the street lighting had been deliberately extinguished and the area was in complete darkness. The suitcase was bound tightly with rope and due to the lack of room in which to work Major Biddle was obliged to move it from its original position. When the case was opened it was found to contain explosives a battery and a clock. The bomb was made safe by disconnecting the wire to the battery and removing the detonator. If this bomb had exploded considerable damage and injury would have been caused. Major Biddle also defused a bomb contained in a haversack and left at the rear of some premises on Sunday 19th May 1974.

GEORGE MEDAL
7/12/76

Henderson   Donald Victor   Explosives Officer   CO C7

Two women walking past a block of flats notice a black holdall wedged between the railings against a window of a restaurant on the ground floor. It was Monday 13th October 1975 shortly after 9 pm. The women had spoken to the night porter of the flats and he immediately called the police. Two police officers in a patrol car arrived and examined the holdall and saw what appeared to be batteries and several sticks of explosives. The officers immediately informed information room and set about evacuating about 55 diners from the restaurant and the also cleared the street. By the time this had been done and the street was cordoned off Major Henderson had quickly reached the area. On arrival Major Henderson was briefed as to the contents of the bag he immediately went to the device, he then opened the holdall and inspected the inside. It was at once evident that he was now dealing with an extremely large high explosive bomb which posed a very real danger to both him and the nearby residents who were still inside their flats. A decision was made to attempt to neutralize the device and he completed this both quickly and successfully. When the timing device was examined the modified pocket watch showed that only two minutes remained before it would have detonated. The device contained 25 lbs of high explosive with heavy metal coach screws which on the detonation of the bomb would have been shot out at high speed, through the restaurant window thereby causing very heavy loss of life or serious injury to the diners inside, 20 of whom were seated at the table immediately inside the window against which the bomb had been placed. In defusing this bomb within minutes of its detonation Major Henderson's achievement in preserving this device intact was invaluable.

QUEEN'S GALLANTRY MEDAL
17/2/76

Breslin   William John   Chief Inspector   139484 P

A police patrol car stopped and questioned a man who was carrying a large holdall type bag, as one of the crew of the police car opened the door to get out the suspect fired a gun. The windows were shattered and the policeman was wounded in the right arm. Further shots were then fired and the second policeman was seriously wounded in the stomach, while a third collapsed in the driving seat and was held there only by the seat belts. The driver was sadly found to be dead on arrival at hospital. The gunman made off into the darkness and escaped. Six days later on Friday 12th July 1974 the gunman stopped a private car and forced the driver at gun point to drive him though South East London. During this journey he fired a sawn off shotgun at a passing car. Eventually the car stopped in the Brockley area and the gunman got out. Police were informed and units under the command of Chief Inspector Breslin were sent to the area. The Chief Inspector along with other units approached the house where it was believed the gunman was thought to be, they then heard two explosions which they thought were shot gun blasts. However it was discovered that these were in fact detonation devices in a nearby garden. The gunman emerged from one of the houses and was waving a sawn off shotgun. Breslin walked towards the man and told him to put the gun down, the man still brandishing the gun. Chief Inspector Breslin continued to walk towards the man and repeated his request for the man to put down the gun. He noticed that is was a short barrelled gun and he had no doubt it was a sawn off shotgun. He once again told the man to hand over the weapon, and at this time the man surrendered and broke the gun open showing that is was still loaded with two live cartridges.

Chief Inspector Breslin acted with great courage, he already knew that the suspect had fired a gun at a passing car, shot a policeman and that he was armed with a sawn off shot gun. If the weapon had been fired his chances of escaping serious injury were negligible, nevertheless he remained cool, resolutely approached the gunman and arrested him.

QUEEN'S GALLANTRY MEDAL
Award of the Bar
7/12/76

David   Ryan Kenneth   Police Constable   156799 Y QGM

In the early hours of Saturday 6th December 1975 a young man was in a distressed state of mind and had climbed over the railings of a bridge and threatened to jump 57 feet onto the road below. Police and the fire brigade were called to the scene and the man was now seen standing in the middle of the bridge on the two foot wide and unprotected ledge which ran the whole length of the brigade. On arrival several officers tried to gain the man's confidence but without success. Constable David climbed over the railings onto the ledge but the man moved away. In the meantime the fire brigade had prepared a noose with the intention of dropping it over the man. The young man was aware of what was happening and made an attempt to jump from the bridge. At this point constable David released his own hold on the bridge and quickly moved forward and seized the youth forcing him back against the railings. The man then began to struggle violently in an attempt to break free and at times his legs were over the ledge. Other police officers that had arrived climbed down onto the ledge and stood behind David holding his clothing. To those looking at the incident it appeared that all three were in danger of falling to their deaths. With the help of a fireman who had also climbed over the railings and moved to join them the youth was then manhandled back over the railing to safety despite his continued struggles. In the end constable David was completely exhausted in his efforts.

BRITISH EMPIRE MEDAL FOR GALLANTRY
28/5/76

Matthews	R G	Police Constable	A

QUEEN'S COMMENDATION FOR BRAVE CONDUCT
17/2/76

Muggleton	Alan Charles	Police Constable	152528 K

"Leading to the arrest of an armed man who had stabbed his wife."

QUEEN'S COMMENDATION FOR BRAVE CONDUCT
27/7/76

Baker	Donald Edwin	Police Sergeant	154550 A

"Leading to the arrest of an armed man who had entered a restaurant and threatened the manager."

Barnes	Dennis	Police Sergeant	135908 CO C8
Fox	Francis Stanley	Police Constable	131809 CO C8
Hunter	Randolph Stewart	Police Constable	129238 CO C8

"Tackling and arresting a gang of armed robbers."

Birse	Graham Keith	Police Constable	161989 E
Bransgrove	Arthur James	Police Constable	146946 E

"Rescue of a mentally disturbed woman who had climbed from an attic window onto a sloping roof and was threatening to jump."

Godley	John Arthur	Police Constable	CO B8

"Leading to the arrest of a drunken driver who had caused him grievous bodily harm."

Gowan	David John	Police Constable 157464 J

"Leading to the arrest of an armed man who had robbed a jeweller's shop."

Haxell	Geoffrey Arthur	Police Sergeant	158639 R
Hunter	Norman Robert Caven	Police Sergeant	151325 R
Jardin	Alan	Police Constable	153200 R
Jenkins	Anthony Ernest	Police Constable	141823 R
Jones	Ronald David	Police Constable	157521 R
McDonald	John David	Police Constable	144377 R
Stephenson	Peter William	Police Constable	150485 P

"Leading to the arrest of a man who had entered a bank, demanded money and threatened to explode a bomb."

Warrilow	Eva	Woman Police Constable 3116 E

"Tackling an armed man who was resisting arrest."

QUEEN'S COMMENDATION FOR BRAVE CONDUCT
17/2/76
Findlay   Harley James   Police Sergeant
"Attempting to arrest an armed and dangerous man who had shot and wounded him and his two colleagues."

QUEEN'S COMMENDATION FOR BRAVE CONDUCT
7/12/76
Williams   David John   Inspector   148961
"Leading to the rescue of a mentally disturbed youth who threatened to jump from a bridge."

Bundock   Albert Masterton   Commander   129039 QPM
Smith   Thomas   Chief Inspector   136974
"Leading to the arrest of a robber who had threatened to blow up a bank."

Clements   Stephen Frederick   Police Constable
Nightingale   Gordon Eric   Police Constable   147217
"Rescuing a mentally disturbed man who threatened to jump from the roof of a four storey building."

CARNEGIE HERO FUND
30/1/76
White   Raymond J   Police Constable
Sustained serious injury as a result of attempting to rescue a drowning child from a frozen lake at St Paul's Cray, Kent.

ROLL OF HONOUR

1977
January   Seven IRA bombs go off in the West End of London.
February   Silver Jubilee of Queen Elizabeth II's reign.
March   2 Jumbo jets collide on the ground in the Canary Islands killing 574.
April   In London the National Front marchers clash with Anti-Nazi's.
May   Ex police pornography squad Chief Wallace Virgo is found guilty of taking bribes from Soho vice kings.
June   Beacons lit across the UK to begin jubilee festivities.
July   New York, looting and vandalism is rife as the City is blacked out by a massive power failure.
August   Space shuttle makes its first flight gliding from the back of a NASA jumbo jet.
September   George Davis, the subject of a campaign in 1975 to free him from prison, is arrested while committing a bank raid.
October   Police in Yorkshire appeal for help in finding a vicious murderer of women known as the 'Yorkshire Ripper'.

November   UK firemen strike for 30% wage increase.
December   Start of the exodus of the Vietnamese boat people.

HITS OF THE YEAR
Don't give up on us now
Don't cry for me Argentina
Mull of Kintyre
Annie Hall

GEORGE MEDAL - BALCOMBE STREET
7/10/77

Dowswell	Henry	Inspector	146207 CO C8
McVeigh	Murtach Phillip	Police Sergeant	161180 D
Purnell	John Francis	Inspector	155332 A

QUEEN'S GALLANTRY MEDAL

Claiden	Andrew Stephen	Police Constable	161806 C
Court	Barry Charles	Police Constable	159944 CO A8
Fenton	Robert	Police Constable	156820 CO C8
Knight	Stephen Philip	Police Constable	159687 CO C8
Mansfield	William	Police Sergeant	153148 Q

QUEEN'S COMMENDATION FOR BRAVE CONDUCT

Chadburn	Ian Michael	Police Constable	154779 D11
Wells	James Robert	Inspector	147725 D11
Wilson	Peter James	Police Constable	146667 C8

On Saturday the 6th December 1975 several shots had been fired from a passing car into a restaurant, and Inspector Purnell and Sergeant McVeigh who were unarmed and on plain clothes duty in the vicinity went quickly towards the scene. They saw the car and as Sergeant McVeigh broadcast a report Inspector Purnell hailed a passing taxi and asked the driver to follow the vehicle. A chase followed and as the taxi got close to the car it turned into a side turning, began to slow and stopped. The Inspector told the taxi driver to stop about 20 yards from the car and both officers then got out. The driver saw four men running away pursued by the two officers. He heard shots and stopped his cab to broadcast the description of what was taking place to police through the cab radio system. After leaving the taxi the officers had seen the men first walk then run up the road. As the men ran they fired shots at both of the officers who pursued them for some distance. At one point the gunman dropped a bag and as Inspector Purnell ran past the bag he saw that it contained weapons. Police cars then began to appear, the men fired at them and then turned round and ran back towards Inspector Purnell and Sergeant McVeigh. The gunmen split into two pairs, and as they approached Inspector Purnell armed himself with a gun barrel from the bag. Both officers then had to take cover as the men were shooting as they ran. Three men were seen to run down some steps into a side street and the fourth took another direction. Having instructed Sergeant

McVeigh to broadcast details over his radio Inspector Purnell followed the direction which the single running man had taken. He chased the man for some way but he eluded him, managed to join up with the other three gunmen and they entered a block of flats where they forced their way into a flat and held the occupants hostage. Meanwhile the first police vehicle to arrive at the scene was a transit van driven by constable Court with constables Knight and Claiden among the passengers. They had been alerted by the radio of the incident and saw the suspects running along the road pursued by Inspector Purnell and Sergeant McVeigh. Constable Court drove his vehicle past the men stopping about 5 yards in from of them to cut off their escape. As soon as the van stopped, constable Court heard a bang and knew that one of the men was shooting at him, at the same time constables Knight and Claiden who were armed left the van and began to return the fire. Constable Court realised that bullets were entering his van and for the safety of the remaining unarmed officers who were still in the vehicle and had taken cover on the floor he began to move away to avoid injury to them. As he did this he could see the men running away but firing their weapons at constables Knight and Claiden who were pursuing them. As they gave chase the two officers saw the gunmen fire on a second police vehicle when it arrived at the scene. In the second vehicle were Inspector Dowswell, Sergeant Mansfield and constable Fenton who were in plain clothes and unarmed. They had received a radio message of the incident and heard shots being fired as they approached. When they arrived they saw the four men standing by a gate, the siren of the police car was sounding, the men broke up into two pairs, ran past the car firing as they went. Inspector Dowswell and Sergeant Mansfield and constable Fenton all left the car and pursued the men until they reached the top of the steps where the gunmen had turned off. One of the gunmen deliberately stopped and fired a shot at them. Inspector Dowswell then ran on and with constable Knight continued to follow three of the men until they entered the block of flats.

GEORGE MEDAL
5/12/77

Kiff   Raymond Peter   Police Constable   164442 K

On Monday 15th March 1976 at about 4.45 pm, a terrorist bomb had exploded in the leading carriage of a Metropolitan line train, a number of the passengers were injured. After the explosion a man was seen to jump from the damaged coach onto the track. Mr. Stephens who was the driver of the train was seen to get out of the driver's cab. He then moved towards the front to the train where he waved his arms to signal to oncoming trains on another track to stop, as he did this he came face to face with the man who then raised a gun and shot Mr. Stephens who fell mortally wounded. At the station when the explosion happened was Mr. Chalk, he saw the debris and thought it was a bomb. His immediate thoughts were for those who may have been injured and he then ran through the station and onto the line. He saw some of the injured and promised that he would help, he then went into the carriage where the explosion had taken place to see if anyone was trapped inside. He then saw the gunman who was covered in blood with his clothes torn. When he was near the man, he noticed that he was reloading a gun which he immediately pointed at him, telling the man that he wanted to help the injured Mr. Clark continued to move forward and walked within 3 feet of the gun in his effort to reach the injured. He was shot in the chest when he was about 4 feet past the gunman. The gunman appeared undecided as to which way to go and it was at this time that the constable arrived. He had heard the explosion and driven immediately onto a road parallel to the railway. He noticed the man standing near the front of the train and was warned that he was armed and had already shot a man. The gunman then fired a shot at the officer but it missed. The constable immediately gave a clear account of the events over his radio and got back into his car and reversed to a point some 50 yards up the road. He again left the car and saw the man walking towards him along the track. The gunman then took deliberate aim and fired at the constable but he continued his commentary. The gunman then made for the nearest station during which time he threatened one more person. He climbed onto the platform down the exit stairs and into the street. In the meantime constable Kiff, who had heard the constable's commentary, had arrived at the station and had been told that the gunman was coming down the track, he cleared the platform, jumped onto the track but failed to find the man. He then heard some shots in the vicinity of the booking hall, and so he ran down the stairs, where he saw a man lying on the path holding a revolver with both hands. The constable then went to tackle the man who got up and went along the road still brandishing the weapon. The officer followed the man who kept turning and threatening him, so he crossed the road and followed from there. The gunman turned into a factory yard, constable Kiff ran to the shelter of a van parked opposite the entrance where he saw through the driver's window that although the man was semi prone on his back he appeared to be aiming at a target within the yard. The constable immediately left the cover of the van and ran towards the gunman's back, jumped on him striking him with his truncheon, and at the same time disarmed him. The gunman was arrested and it was discovered that he had shot himself in the chest.

QUEEN'S GALLANTRY MEDAL
23/6/77

| Allport | John | Police Constable | 149904 AD |

Information had been received that a car had been stolen locally, and on Friday 21st November 1975 a patrol car in the area received the message over the radio. Later on they saw the car and followed it until it stopped. However as they left their police vehicle to question the occupants the car drove off at high speed and a chase started. The police car was sounding its siren so that those in the stolen car were in no doubt that they were being pursued by the police. The stolen car then turned back along the route and as it did the rear window was smashed and a shotgun was fired at the police car, then a second and third burst all of which struck the car but fortunately no one was injured. Constable Allport was off duty at the time and was travelling in his private car with his two children when he was overtaken at high speed by the two vehicles. He immediately took up the chase and followed the cars. Soon afterwards the stolen car approached a left hand bend near the entrance to a RAF station where it struck a vehicle coming in the opposite direction. It then lost control, swerved across the road and collided with the railings of the camp. Constable Allport stopped his car close to the rear of the stolen car to prevent it being driven away. He saw three men scramble from the car and chased one of them into the grounds of the RAF station where he caught and held him. As he and the man struggled on the ground a second man armed with a sawn off shotgun ordered the officer to release his prisoner. The constable refused and the gunman shot him in the lower part of his legs. Despite his wounds constable Allport still held onto the man, but he eventually had to let the man go when he struggled free, the man escaped.

QUEEN'S GALLANTRY MEDAL
24/6/77

Kinniburgh   William   Police Constable   157989 M

On Monday 12th April 1976 at about 11 pm, as one of the crew of a radio controlled police vehicle constable Kinniburgh was on duty in plain clothes. They received details of a car which had been stolen from the neighbourhood. They then saw the stolen car being driven towards them. They immediately turned their car around and followed the vehicle for about ¾ of a mile to a junction where it stopped at some traffic lights. Their car was positioned in front of the stolen car to block its escape and the three occupants were then questioned. Constable Kinniburgh leant into the car as he recognized the driver and removed the ignition keys. As he did so he noticed that one of the men sitting in the back of the car had produced a pistol. The constable's attention was momentarily distracted by what he had seen and the driver managed to struggle free and escape. One of the other officers struggled with the man with the gun who quickly freed himself and fired at the officer who was fortunately uninjured. The man who had fired the pistol then ran off and was chased by constable Kinniburgh and after about 20 yards he stopped and threatened the officer who tried to reason with him. But the man ran off still pursued by the constable. During the following chase the man continually turned and pointed the gun at the constable. Shortly afterwards constable Kinniburgh was overtaken by a police car which stopped. As the crew started to leave the car they were also threatened by the gunman. As the man approached them he was followed by Kinniburgh who again called on him to give himself up. The gunman hesitated for a short time and when he realised that he was outnumbered he gave himself up quietly and was arrested.

QUEEN'S GALLANTRY MEDAL
5/12/77

Wright   Norman Adrian Robert   Police Constable   138229 CO B8

On Monday 9th May 1977 a man had entered the office of the Chilean Embassy and produced a pistol and had threatened a member of the staff. A woman employee was slow to obey his orders so he fired a shot at the desk and covered her with the weapon and ordered the rest of the staff to leave the room. As the staff hesitated he fired the pistol again. Constable Wright a uniformed police motorcyclist was on duty nearby and was approached by 2 of the woman's colleagues, the constable sent one to warn police officers in the vicinity and then returned with the other to the Embassy. On his arrival at the office he saw a gunman standing with his back to the wall and the weapon trained on a woman. As he entered he was immediately threatened with the gun, but he managed to engage the man in conversation at the same time removing his crash helmet which he could use as a weapon if the opportunity arose. The constable managed to put himself between the gunman and the woman and also gradually eased himself to within 5 feet of the man, and at the first opportunity when the man's attention was distracted grappled with him. In the course of the struggle the gunman was thrown over a desk and the officer lost grip of him. The gunman then crossed the room, turned to face the officer and again threatened to shoot. Constable Wright once more managed to get within 4 or 5 feet of the man again calling on him to surrender his weapon, he also told him that the premises had been surrounded by police, at this point the man still holding the gun put his hands over his head, the officer immediately jumped on the gunman, he was then disarmed and detained until other officers arrived. The weapon it was discovered contained 4 live cartridges.

QUEEN'S COMMENDATION FOR BRAVE CONDUCT
24/6/77

Bannister	Jack	Police Constable	156618 Q
Spinks	John Frederick	Police Sergeant	147924 Q
Turner	Michael	Police Constable	167925 Q

'Tackling and arresting three armed bank robbers.'

Brooks	Anthony	Police Constable	164197 S

'Leading to the arrest of a burglar who was armed with a knife and had attacked him.'

Maloney	Denis Michael	Police Constable	158848 Q
Quinnell	Leonard Henry	Police Constable	156338 D
Wood	David Anthony	Police Constable	160907 CO A2

'Leading to the arrest of three armed criminals.'

Day	Martin	Police Constable	163868 B8

'Leading to the rescue of a mentally sick man, from a high bridge which spanned a busy main road.'

QUEEN'S COMMENDATION FOR BRAVE CONDUCT
6/12/77

Wheal	David	Police Constable	146984 K

'Leading to the arrest of an armed terrorist following the explosion of a bomb on an underground train.'

FINED
W Division, Pc fined 3 days pay (£22.81) for being absent without leave.

ROLL OF HONOUR
• Pc Derek James Bottomley
Passenger in a police car on an advanced driving course in collision with a lorry.
• Pc Alan Michael Baxter
Killed when his police car crashed while chasing a suspect car in Croydon.

- Pc Richard Kenrick Hamilton

Crashed in his Panda car while answering an emergency call in Balham.

- Pc John Alfred Clarke

Killed in a motorcycle accident while on duty on P Division.

1978

January	Arab gunman murders the PLO London representative in a West End basement office.
February	Anna Ford starts work as ITN's first woman news reader.
March	Super tanker Amoco Cadiz spills oil off the coast of Brittany as she splits in two.
April	BBC begins permanent radio broadcasting from the House of Commons.
May	David Berkowitz is charged with 6 'son of Sam' murders in the US.
June	MP Jeremy Thorpe is interviewed by detectives investigating a plot to kill male model Norman Scott.
July	First test tube baby is born.
August	An Arab terrorist and an air hostess die in a machine gun and grenade attack at Heathrow Airport.
September	Bulgarian defector is killed after being stabbed with a poisoned umbrella tip.
October	Ex Sex Pistol guitarist Sid Vicious is arrested and charged with the murder of his girlfriend Nancy Spungen.
November	913 members of the Peoples' Temple commit suicide en mass by cyanide.
December	Millions march in Iran against the Shah.

HITS OF THE YEAR

Rivers of Babylon
You're the one that I want
Summer nights
The deer hunter

QUEEN'S COMMENDATION FOR BRAVE CONDUCT

4/7/78

Baldry	Robert James	Police Sergeant	153092 E
Clark	Brian Malcolm	Police Constable	160681 R

'Disarming and over powering a man armed with a pistol and knives who threatened them while resisting arrest.'

Bazire	Paul Leon	Police Constable	164837 CO B8
Gardiner	Richard Thomas	Police Constable	163292 Y

'Leading to the arrest of a gang of armed robbers.'

ROLL OF HONOUR

- Pc Patrick Alan Croake

Traffic motorcyclist killed after colliding with an elderly pedestrian in the Mall.

- Ds Stuart Arthur Pinder

Killed on duty in a car accident on V Division.

1979

January   Shah of Iran is driven into exile by supporters of the Ayatollah Khomeni.

February   Over 1000 schools close owing to a heating oil shortage caused by a lorry drivers' strike.

March   Idi Amin flees Uganda as his regime crumbles.

April   The Vietnamese reveal the 'Pol Pots' mass graves.

May   Margaret Thatcher becomes Britain's first woman Prime Minister.

June   Brezhnev and Carter (USSR & USA) sign the SALT treaty.

July   New regime in Phnom Pehn accuses Pol Pot of 3 million murders.

August   2 charged in Dublin of the murder of Lord Mountbatten.

September   The Yorkshire ripper claims his 12th victim.

October   The Government is to outlaw 'insider trading' in the UK.

November   Frantic followers of Ayatollah Khomeni take 100 hostages from the US Embassy in Teheran.

December   Soviet troops move into Afghanistan.

HITS OF THE YEAR

Bright eyes

I don't like Mondays

We don't talk anymore

Kramer v Kramer

GEORGE MEDAL

11/9/79

Pawley   Bernard Ernest Walter   Police Constable   148500

On Saturday 11th March 1978 at about midday constable Pawley and a colleague went over to a man they had been given reason to suspect kept firearms in his home. The man admitted to them that he possessed firearms but said that he held certificates that allowed him to do so. He agreed that the officers might search his home. Up to this time the man had behaved rationally. But when the officers were unhappy and asked him to accompany them to the police station to clear up another charge he then produced a gun and said he would kill them and then himself. At that time constable Pawley tried to reason with the man who was now pointing a weapon at the head of the officer. The man then immediately turned the gun on him from a distance of about 3 feet. The constable was sufficiently close to see that the weapon was not an imitation and continued to reason with him but he again pointed the gun at the other constable. Realising from the man's attitude that he meant to carry out this threat and fearing for his colleague's life constable Pawley jumped on him and gripped his wrist to push the weapon away. He was not successful and the man was strong and powerful turned and grappled for the gun. He then moved the gun at arms length until he could point it at the constable's chest and fired. The officer felt a terrific impact as the bullet passed into his body. He was still holding the man and called on his colleague to go and get some assistance. As the other officer ran from the room the gunman fired in his direction but fortunately missed the officer. He then ran past constable Pawley who struck him hoping to knock him off balance. The man was intent on stopping the other officer and as constable Pawley collapsed on the floor he heard another shot. The constable by now was on his hands and knees and had great difficulty in breathing. The gunman then returned and fired a random shot then began to reload the gun. At this time constable Pawley saw an air gun lying close to him on the floor, and convinced that his colleague was at least wounded made up his mind that he would make one last effort to ensure that the gunman was at least incapacitated so that he would not be a danger to anyone else. Summoning a maximum effort constable Pawley got to his feet, faced the man who was still in the process of reloading his gun and took him by surprise. The constable at once hit him with the air gun using it as a club and knocked the gun from the man's hand. During the struggle that followed the man managed to grasp the air gun but the officer was able to fight him off. As the constable pushed the gunman away he struck him about the head and neck until he collapsed. Pawley tried to drag the assailant out of the flats where it would be safe for anyone to approach but he could not as he was too weak. He left the room to look for his colleague, and as he did so he fell down the stairs. He managed to reach the street and called for help before he collapsed on the pavement. Constable Pawley's colleague was uninjured, he had quickly summoned assistance and appeared on the scene with other officers who then surrounded the premises. When they eventually entered the flat the man was found dead with a self inflicted shot wound to the chest. Constable Pawley sustained serious chest and internal injuries.

QUEEN'S GALLANTRY MEDAL
16/2/79

Heyes	Gordon	Police Constable	153030 BEM

In the late evening of Sunday 14th November 1976 a man armed with a loaded double barrelled sawn off shot gun entered a petrol station and demanded money from the till. The cashier who was on duty handed over a small amount of cash, the man was not satisfied with the amount and demanded to enter the showroom. Once the gunman was inside he again threatened the cashier, but when he found out the man did not have any keys to the safe he released the safety catch on the gun and fired a shot which narrowly missed the cashier. A large hole had been blasted in the office door. Two customers who had seen the man noticed the gun as he left and immediately summoned help. When they left they heard the noise of a gun being fired. They reported what they had seen to an officer on duty nearby in a police vehicle. And as a result constable Heyes was among the first officers to arrive on the scene. He noticed a man who had left the garage office and ordered him to stop. The man tried to escape by jumping over a small fence leading into a side street. The constable gave chase followed by other officers. The gunman then stopped, turned, deliberately aimed the shotgun and fired at the officer who fell to the ground injured in the right thigh. Despite his injury constable Heyes got up and continued the pursuit until he was able to tackle the man and brought him down, and with the assistance of other officers the man was arrested.

Gordon Heyes during his career in the police served on H and P divisions, also with the SPG and Central Drugs Squad.

QUEEN'S GALLANTRY MEDAL
11/9/79

Grove   Brian Errol   Police Constable   150814

On Sunday 14th April 1974 constable Grove along with another officer was on plain clothes duty in a police observation van. As they were driving along their vehicle was overtaken by an estate car with 2 men inside being driven in such a manner that the officers were suspicious, so they decided to keep the vehicle under surveillance. They saw the car stop outside an office block where one of the occupants of the car left it carrying an oxygen cylinder, the other then drove the car away. The man carrying the cylinder was then joined by another man who has been waiting nearby. The officers then noticed the men were wearing headgear which concealed their facial features and realised they were about to raid the premises. The officers then made a call on the radio for assistance at the same time as two more men were seen to join the suspects, who then hurled the oxygen cylinder to break open the front doors and then they disappeared inside. At this point constable Grove left the vehicle and faced the men as they left the building. Two attaché cases containing large sums of money were stolen from security guards. The constable had armed himself with a metal bar, he struck at one of the men who was carrying a case, and as he did so the man swung the case and struck the officer on the head knocking him to the ground. He then saw three armed men run past and as he attempted to get up a fourth man stood over him and pointed a gun and fired. The four men than ran off with constable Grove in pursuit. The constable was again fired at and threw himself behind a wall and at sometime during this he was wounded by pellets in his right leg. But despite the injury he got up and continued the chase. He came close to one of the robbers who turned and aimed a gun at him. He took cover behind a van and saw the men run over to the car which the constables had seen earlier. Three of the men clambered into the vehicle, the man who had aimed the gun struggled to enter the rear door and was pulled inside by his accomplices. Constable Grove then ran after the car and attempted to get hold of the man's legs as he was trailed along but the car was driven away too quickly.

QUEEN'S GALLANTRY MEDAL
11/9/79

Martin   David Bert   Inspector   154601

On Sunday 2nd July 1978 Inspector Martin was in uniform and on duty along with other officers at a theatre where a group of foreign students were holding a political meeting. The Inspector noticed a small group of about 60 students march towards the theatre where they were attending a meeting and distributing leaflets. He went and spoke to the group and while they were talking he heard shouts coming from behind and saw another group of 10 or 12 men some were wearing crash helmets and were carrying lengths of wood coming out of the theatre. He then turned towards these men and noticed as he did so that they had disposed of their weapons presumably by passing them back to those behind them. The Inspector then spoke to one of those who had come from the theatre in order to prevent a confrontation between the two groups, and he asked them to return to the

278

theatre. At the same time the first group of students began to approach those from the theatre and the two groups were by then only a few feet apart. The man who had been asked to return to the theatre re appeared with a fire extinguisher from which he sprayed liquid at the rival group. Inspector Martin had become separated from the small group of constables under his command and the two factions were now shouting at one another and the atmosphere became hostile and threatened to turn into an affray. The Inspector grabbed the man with the fire extinguisher and warned him that he would be arrested for having an offensive weapon in a public place. The man then struggled and backed towards the theatre followed by the Inspector. Others now joined in trying to free the man and at this point someone shouted a warning that a man was armed. As they struggled Inspector Martin saw a gun. The man eventually broke free and struck the officer with his fist fracturing a bone in his left cheek. While members of the crowd forcibly held the Inspector who was now unable to defend himself or take any other action, the man produced a gun, pointed it at the officer's head and threatened to kill him. The gunman then turned and ran through a swing door. At this time the Inspector managed to break free and pursued him and eventually came face to face with the gunman. The gunman again threatened to shoot the officer who once again tried to reason with him. The man was by now acting in a hysterical manner. The pair of them were no more than 3 feet apart and the gun was now pointing directly at the inspector's face, the Inspector was in no doubt that the man was desperate enough to use the gun, but he continued to face him edging him back towards the main hall where scuffles were still taking place between the police and various other groups. The officer patiently bided his time till he saw the man aim the gun slightly away from him, he then seized the opportunity to slam the door back and caught hold of the man's right arm, a violent struggle followed during which the Inspector felt the gun pushed into his back as the man twisted to try to get free. All the time the man was continuing to struggle and threaten the officer and two shots were actually fired. One police officer eventually managed to go to Inspector Martin's assistance and between the two of them they were able to restrain and arrest the gunman, although they were surrounded by a small group of men who attacked them and tried to set the man free.

QUEEN'S COMMENDATION FOR BRAVE CONDUCT
16/2/79

Hatch	Anthony Morris	Police Constable	155484
Rowell	Charles Edward	Police Constable	156773
Tierney	Michael Robert	Police Constable	164042

'Leading to the arrest of a burglar who threatened them with a hand grenade.'

QUEEN'S COMMENDATION FOR BRAVE CONDUCT
11/9/79

Baker	John	Police Constable	154390
Price	Michael William	Police Constable	153791

'Tackling a gang of armed criminals following a robbery.'

Brady	David	Police Constable	142276
Marvin	Drummond Gordon	Inspector	149017

'Over powering and detaining an armed and dangerous robber.'

Scott	Eric Bowyer	Police Constable	165323

'Leading to the arrest of an armed burglar.'

ROLL OF HONOUR

•   Pc Kevin Kelliher

Crew member in a police van which crashed while in pursuit of a stolen car in Stepney.

•   Ps Roger Edward Coyne

Killed on duty in a moped accident when knocked down by a drunken driver in Camden.

Chapter Ten

THE YEARS OF 1980 - 1989

It is now only 20 years to the end of one millennium and the start of another. This decade brought us 'Glasnost and perestroika' (openness and reconstruction) according to the Russian Government. The UK had its first woman Prime Minister Mrs Margaret Thatcher.

Although Nuclear Energy had only been a short time in the making, we have harnessed this energy to make weapons and power. We saw in the mid 80's the world's worst nuclear disaster in its short history and a word we will remember for a long time 'Chernobyl'.

The Government in Poland was threatened by unrest mainly due to rises in meat prices. It would appear that the people had just about had enough of the high cost of living and so workers occupied the Lenin ship yard at Gdansk and after a short time 'Solidarity' was born with its leader a man called Lech Walesa.

We in England had our fair share of news including The Iranian Embassy siege in which a police constable was taken hostage along with many Embassy workers, see 1980. Prince Charles married Lady Diana Spencer at St Paul's Cathedral. Riots break out throughout the country including London where they break out in Brixton, but the main talking event of the decade must be the Falklands War. Although it did not last long, 3 months in all, we will never forget the live news coverage that reached our televisions. The IRA again were active with bombings in Hyde Park and Harrods department store.

A few more notable disasters included the Herald of Free Enterprise ferry sinking as it left Zeebrugge, the space shuttle Challenger exploding a few seconds into its flight and Pan-Am flight 106 exploding over the Scottish town of Lockerbie.

We saw some history in the making, the Mary Rose, the flag ship of King Henry VIII was finally raised from the seabed in the Solent, and is still being restored to this day. The first woman cosmonaut Svetlana Savitskaya walked in space and one of the biggest pop concerts took place, Live Aid.

Finally, there was a memorable winter Olympics in 1988, when an eagle flew, yes Eddie 'the Eagle' Edwards the British participant who took part in the Ski jumping. He may not have won a medal or even come near to the top of his sport but he did get a mention in the closing speech.

1980

January	Mrs Gandhi wins the General Election in India.
February	The 6d coin is no longer legal tender.
March	Robert Runcie is enthroned as the new Archbishop of Canterbury.
April	3 gunmen seize 20 hostages at the Iranian Embassy in London, they demand the release of 91 Arabs in Iran - see entry for Pc Trevor Lock page 283.

May	Mount St Helen's volcano erupts in North West United States.
June	English soccer fans riot in Turin, UEFA fine the FA £8,000 for the riots.
July	Fire causes huge damage to Alexandra Palace in North London.
August	56 Iranians are arrested during protests outside the US Embassy in London.
September	Creation of the union 'Solidarity' in Poland, Lech Walesa is the leader.
October	British Leyland introduce their new model, the Mini Metro.
November	A team of London detectives go to Yorkshire to assist the county's police in catching the 'Ripper'.
December	IRA bomber Gerard Tuite and 2 others escape from Brixton Prison.

HITS OF THE YEAR

Women in Love
Crying
Ordinary people

QUEEN'S COMMENDATION FOR BRAVE CONDUCT

28/3/80

Batten	Peter John	Police Sergeant	150758
Wilson	Robert Melvyn	Police Constable	164138

'Arresting an armed and violent man following an attempted robbery.'

Field	Michael Edward	Police Constable	160726

'Disarming a man who had threatened him and fired 2 shots at him following a high speed car chase.'

Green	Michael John	Police Constable	160416

'Disarming and detaining a man who had threatened to shoot him following an attempted robbery at a Sub Post Office.'

QUEEN'S COMMENDATION FOR BRAVE CONDUCT

3/10/80

Farley	Stephen Farley	Police Constable	164517

'Leading to the disarming of a violent and mentally sick man who had made an unsuccessful suicide bid and then threatened to shoot the Police Officers who were called to the scene.'

Hughes	Robert	Police Constable	167275

'Rescue of a badly injured man who was trapped beneath an underground train following a suicide attempt.' The man was suffering from a mental illness and was continually trying to touch the live rail, this happened at Bethnal Green Underground Station.

Humphries	Robin	Police Constable	166966

'Disarming and arrest of a man who threatened him with a loaded revolver.'

ROYAL HUMANE SOCIETY BRONZE MEDAL

24/10/80

Robertson   Chief Inspector   149646 Y

Has been awarded a Bronze medal and certificate for the attempted rescue of a suicidal young man from a high building.

ROLL OF HONOUR

• Pc Francis Joseph O'Neill QGM, 165256 L, aged 31

Stabbed while making an arrest, suspect attempting to obtain drugs from a chemist's shop in Lambeth.

• Pc Alan Edward Smith

Killed on duty in a motorcycle accident on Wandsworth Division.

• Pc James Ralph Barber Snowdon

Killed on duty in a motorcycle accident at Brent.

1981

January	Yorkshire police charge a long distance lorry driver, Peter Sutcliffe, with the Yorkshire Ripper murders.
February	Announcement made that Prince Charles is to marry Lady Diana Spencer.
March	Assassination attempt made on President Ronald Reagan.
April	Brixton riots in London, 213 arrested 201 police injured.
May	Assassination attempt made on Pope John Paul in St Peter's Square.
June	Marcus Sergeant fires 6 blank rounds at the Queen in the Mall during the Trooping of the Colour, he is subsequently jailed for 5 years.
July	Riots break out in several UK cities.
August	Moira Stuart is appointed at the BBC's first black woman news reader.
September	UK garages begin selling petrol in litres.
October	Royal Marine Chief Lt General Sir Steuart Pringle is injured when a bomb goes off under his car.
November	The space shuttle Colombia is launched, becoming the first spacecraft to be used more than once.
December	In the UK a colour TV licence rises by £12 to £46.

HITS OF THE YEAR

Stand and deliver

Under pressure

Imagine

GEORGE MEDAL - IRANIAN EMBASSY SIEGE

13/4/81

Lock   Trevor James   Police Constable   154904

On Thursday 30th April 1980 Constable Lock was on armed duty outside the front entrance of the Iranian Embassy. He had occasion to go into the entry hall and was about to return outside when he was confronted by a man who produced a machine pistol. Constable Lock immediately tried to close the door, a struggle began during which the officer was slightly injured by flying glass and overpowered. Six terrorists then burst into the Embassy firing their weapons at the walls and ceiling and 26 people were then taken hostage. Although searched, constable Lock managed to conceal the fact that he was armed, and kept his revolver hidden for the duration of the siege. Throughout the following five days and nights Constable Lock was on self appointed duty with very little sleep, food or drink, he managed to remained cool and calm, and as a result he gradually built up a rapport with the terrorists. This had a calming effect on the terrorists and his fellow hostages. On more than one occasion but for his intervention the hostages' lives might have been lost. He was also continually called upon to negotiate with the authorities outside the Embassy and to investigate unusual sounds and disturbances that the terrorists heard. On the final day of the siege the atmosphere inside the building was extremely tense. The gunmen placed another deadline by which their terms were to be met. During the morning one of the hostages was killed and his body was placed outside the Embassy. After this, the situation became even more strained, but the constable continued to try to persuade the terrorists to surrender. The leader became more and more agitated and constantly made calls on the field telephone. Finally in an attempt by the authorities to distract the terrorists attention from the imminent rescue assault, Constable Lock, along with the terrorist leader, was called to the telephone on the pretext to discuss the arrangements for meeting the deadline. As the gunman was talking Constable Lock heard breaking glass and a loud explosion and realising that the operation had begun, he shoulder charged the terrorist leader as the man dropped the telephone and moved towards him. The gunman was caught off balance and his weapon fell to the floor. During the short fierce struggle that followed Constable Lock managed to overpower the terrorist and for the first time drew his own revolver and covered the man. However an explosive device thrown into the room threw the two men apart, but the officer managed to recapture the man and hold him until the rescuers arrived and took over. Constable Lock displayed gallantry and devotion to duty of an extremely high order when, in spite of the long strain of the ordeal of his capture, he tackled and overpowered this dangerous and armed man who had already caused the death of one hostage.

QUEEN'S COMMENDATION FOR BRAVE CONDUCT
13/2/81

| Bathgate | Edward Kelly | Inspector | 150856 |

'Leading to the arrest of an armed man who attempted to rob the branch office of a Building Society.'

QUEEN'S COMMENDATION FOR BRAVE CONDUCT
2/10/81

| Adams | Michael Brian | Police Constable | 159526 |

'Leading to the rescue of a badly injured man who had attempted to commit suicide and was trapped beneath an underground train.'

Graves	John	Police Constable	172353
Tyson	Richard Edward	Police Constable	172955

'Pursuing and arresting an armed and dangerous man and his accomplice following a fatal shooting incident.'

ROLL OF HONOUR
- Kenneth Howorth - explosives officer GM

Killed while defusing a terrorist bomb at a Wimpy bar in Oxford Street.
- Pc David Ian Luke

Collapsed at the swimming pool while on duty training on his fourth day of training at Hendon Police College.
- Pc Daniel Clarke

Traffic motorcyclist killed at Holloway while en-route to escort an abnormal load.

1982

January	Aircraft crashes in the frozen River Potomac in Washington US, 78 die on the aircraft and a further 6 on the bridge.
February	De Lorean cars go into receivership.
March	The Government in London gives the go ahead to satellite television.
April	Argentina invade the Falkland Islands - start of the Falklands War.
May	Argentina Cruiser General Belgrano is sunk by a torpedo fired from a British submarine.
June	Argentina surrenders - end of the Falklands War.
July	Michael Fagan enters the bedroom of HM the Queen at Buckingham Palace.
August	Israelis drive the PLO out of Beirut.
September	Lindy and Michael Chamberlain who claim a Dingo killed their baby in Australia, go on trial for murder, Lindy is later jailed for life.
October	Mary Rose, the flag ship of Henry VIII is raised from the sea bed in the Solent.
November	Channel 4 goes on air in the UK.
December	The border between Spain and Gibraltar is reopened after 13 years.

HITS OF THE YEAR
Come on Eileen
Fame
Eye of the tiger
Gandhi - 8 awards

QUEEN'S GALLANTRY MEDAL
12/3/82

Olds	Philip Michael	Police Constable	16221

In the late evening of Tuesday 23rd December 1980, two men wearing masks and armed, entered an off licence and threatened the staff. They demanded money and one of the men fired a bullet into the wall. After unsuccessfully trying to open the till the two gunmen still wearing their masks ran out of the premises. Constable Olds who was in uniform and on duty in a patrol car arrived on scene. He noticed that both men were armed and realised immediately what had gone on at the off licence. With disregard to his own safety, he unhesitatingly drew his truncheon and ran towards the men. When the men saw the constable one of the gunmen stopped running and walked slowly backwards towards the officer. The officer at once knew that he was the more dangerous of the two men and concentrated on him. In spite of the danger he continued to move towards the armed man with his only means of defence a wooden truncheon held out in front of him. As he approached the gunman he raised his weapon above his head, adopted the classical shooting stance and took deliberate aim. At this point both men were only about 5 yards apart. The officer realised what was likely to happen continued to move forwards warning the man not to use the weapon. The gunman ignored the officer and fired the gun, the bullet struck constable Olds below the left shoulder entering the left lung and severing the spinal cord before lodging in the small of his back. The officer collapsed to the ground where he was kicked in the face by one of the men as they both ran from the scene.

As a result of the injuries he received at this incident Constable Olds was paralysed from the mid chest downwards and was confined to a wheelchair. Constable Olds later became an instructor at Hendon for new recruits, he died in 1986.

QUEEN'S COMMENDATION FOR BRAVE CONDUCT
12/3/82

Baker	Paul Gerald	Police Constable	165104

'Attempting to detain 3 violent men who deliberately caused him grievous bodily harm when their getaway vehicle drove off at speed from the scene of a robbery.'

QUEEN'S COMMENDATION FOR BRAVE CONDUCT
12/3/82

Dennis	Steven George	Police Constable	165313

'Leading to the rescue of an emotionally disturbed man who was trying to commit suicide by jumping from a builder's scaffold to the ground 60 feet below.'

Forster	Peter	Inspector	163689
Freeland			
Gorman			

'Arresting and restraining a disturbed and violent man armed with 2 knives who had forcibly entered a house and held one of the occupant's hostage.'

Kearns	Janet Marjory	Woman Police Constable	3323

'Overpowering and arresting an armed man who attempted to rob a bank.'

Lamb	Mark Stephen Peter	Police Constable	168284

'Confronting an armed and violent man following a car and foot pursuit during which he was constantly threatened by a firearm.'

ROYAL HUMANE SOCIETY BRONZE MEDAL
26/2/82
Dealman   Woman Police Constable   991E
Awarded a Bronze medal and certificate for the rescue of a girl from a high building.

ROYAL HUMANE SOCIETY BRONZE MEDAL
30/3/82
Young   Inspector   152424
Awarded a Bronze medal and certificate for the rescue of a mentally disturbed woman from a high building.

ROLL OF HONOUR
• Pc Robert Benjamin Mercer
Radio operator in a police car which crashed while pursuing a stolen car at Northolt.

1983

January	In London police open fire on Stephen Waldorf believing him to be escaped prisoner David Martin.
February	Dennis Andrew Nilsen, former Metropolitan policeman and civil servant is arrested for the murder of up to 16 people (see page 270).
March	In London the 13 members of OPEC all agree to cut oil prices for the first time in the organisation's 23 year history.
April	The £1 coin comes into circulation.
May	First wheel clamps introduced in the Boroughs of Kensington & Chelsea and Westminster.
June	752 have been arrested in 4 days of protests outside Upper Heyford USAF base.
July	UK fossil remains of a previously unknown species of carnivorous dinosaur are found in a Surrey clay pit.
August	Radio Caroline returns to the air 3 years after its previous ship sank in the North Sea.
September	Soviets shoot down a Korean airliner. All 269 on board die.
October	In Blackpool the Home Secretary Leon Brittan says 'child or police murderers face a minimum to 20 years in jail.'
November	Mother Teresa of Calcutta receives the Order of Merit (OM) from HM the Queen.
December	IRA place a car bomb outside Harrods - many killed including 3 police officers.

HITS OF THE YEAR
Karma Chameleon
Uptown girl
Every breath you take
Terms of endearment

DENNIS ANDREW NILSEN - 1983
SERIAL KILLER OF 16 MALES

Dennis Nilsen was born on 23rd November 1945, the second of three children to Betty Whyte and Olav Nilsen a Norwegian soldier. They eventually divorced and in 1949 she went with the children to stay with her parents in Aberdeen.

In 1951 Dennis's grandfather Andrew Whyte died suddenly at the age of 61, Dennis was deeply affected by his death as he idolised him.

In 1961 Nilsen enlisted into the Army Catering Corps at the age of 15 in order to escape from home. He was trained at Aldershot for the next three years. In 1964 he was posted of Osnabruck, Germany as a cook. During this time he began to drink heavily and discover his homosexuality. He decided to resign from the Army in 1972. In November 1973 he joined the Metropolitan Police and on completing his training at the Police College at Hendon was posted to Willesden Police Station. It was not long before he resigned from the police in December 1973.

In February 1983 the residents of the flats at 23 Cranley Gardens, North London were annoyed to find that their lavatories were not flushing properly. Five days later a representative from the drain clearage firm Dyno-Rod opened up a manhole to the side of the house to check for blockages. When Mike Cattran aimed his torch into the dark hole he saw a whitish sludge flecked with red. When he descended the 12 feet to the water line he discovered lumps of rotting meat some with hair attached floating in the slime.

Police made a fuller inspection of the manhole on the following morning, although most of the flesh had been mysteriously removed during the night, they did however remove fragments of flesh and bone which was later to be identified as that of human origin.

Among the residents of the premises in the attic flat was Dennis Nilsen. When he returned from work in the evening of 8th February he was met by three detectives. Cutting to the chase, the senior detective, Detective Chief Inspector Peter Jay confronted Nilsen and told him not to mess about and asked where the rest of the body was. Nilsen answered 'in two plastic bags in the wardrobe'. He was arrested and taken to Muswell Hill Police Station. He then admitted to a total of 15 or 16 murders since 1978.

On 24th October 1983 the trial of Dennis Nilsen opened at the Number One court of the Old Bailey. Although Nilsen had been co-operative throughout the investigation the main thrust of the defence was a plea of manslaughter on the grounds of diminished responsibility. On 4th November a day and a half after the jury had retired they returned with a majority of 10 to 2 on 6 counts of murder and 2 of attempted murder.

Nilsen was sentenced to imprisonment for a term of not less than 25 years. He was taken to Wormwood scrubbs Prison then to Parkhurst and finally to Albany Prison on the Isle of Wight.

GEORGE MEDAL
Posthumous
12/8/83

Howorth   Kenneth Robert   Explosives Officer

On Monday 26th October 1981 an anonymous telephone warning had been received notifying that 3 bombs had been placed in various parts of a crowded area and that they would explode within half an hour. About 25 minutes later the police found two suspicious packages in the basement toilets of a restaurant. The building and nearby shops were evacuated, and in the mean time Mr Howorth the officer tasked to deal with the device arrived at the scene. By now about 54 minutes had gone by between the original phone call and Mr Howorth entering the restaurant. A brief description was given to him by the police officers who had first arrived and seen the object. It was clear that Mr Howorth was aware that the connected packages were probably time elapsed fully armed explosive devices. But nevertheless he immediately entered the confined toilet area and 3 minutes later there was an explosion under the pavement which was lifted about 4 feet away from the restaurant by the force. Mr Howorth was killed instantly.

This restaurant was the Wimpy Bar in Oxford Street.

GEORGE MEDAL
Award of the Bar
12/8/83

Gurney   Peter Edwin Spencer   Explosives Officer   GM MBE

On Monday 26th October 1981 an anonymous phone call warning that 3 bombs were due to go off in a busy shopping thoroughfare. One of the bombs had already exploded killing the explosives officer Mr. Kenneth Howorth, who was on scene trying to disarm it. Mr. Gurney had arrived at the scene shortly afterwards to examine the damage to the building and had also seen the badly injured body of his colleague. He immediately was summoned to a large store nearby where another device had been discovered in the toilets. With the knowledge that an explosives expert had already been killed he went at once to the site where at very close range he examined the bomb which had been placed on the top of the cistern. Knowing the nature of his dead colleague's injuries and the method he normally employed, Mr Gurney concluded that there was a strong possibility that the charge contained a further initiating system. It was also evident that there was little time left before the timing device set off the detonating sequence, and it was more likely that the bomb contained some kind of anti handling device. In the face of these risks Mr Gurney successfully neutralized the device approximately 54 minutes after it had been placed into its position.

Mr. Gurney originally won the George Medal for Bomb disposal operations in Northern Ireland LG. 24/7/73.

QUEEN'S GALLANTRY MEDAL
Posthumous
15/4/83

O'Neill   Francis Joseph   Police Constable   165256

On Saturday 25th October 1980 constable O'Neill along with another officer answered a call to a chemists where it was believed that a man was attempting to obtain drugs by means of a forged prescription. When the suspect returned to the shop to collect the drugs constable O'Neill who was in plain clothes approached the man and identified himself. The man immediately stabbed the officer in the chest. The man then quickly fled towards the front door of the shop in an attempt to escape. In spite of his serious wound constable O'Neill immediately gave chase but as the man reached the shop door he managed to grab him and brought him down to the ground with a running tackle. A short and violent struggle followed, the officer was by now weak from his injuries and collapsed, the attacker made his escape.

Constable O'Neill, whom it was subsequently established had been stabbed in the heart, died shortly afterwards.

QUEEN'S GALLANTRY MEDAL
12/8/83

Henley	Malcolm Jonathan	Police Constable	173428 P

It was about 9.40 am on Wednesday 30th September 1981 the crew of a security vehicle was collecting cash from a bank, the custodian Mr Clements had just picked up a bag containing a large amount of money and was walking back to the security van when he was suddenly confronted by a man. The man threatened him with a hand gun, grabbed the cash bag and ran into an adjoining car park. Constable Henley was off duty at the time and in plain clothes, he was shopping with his wife when he witnessed the incident. Without any hesitation he immediately gave chase and was fired upon by the fleeing raider. He managed to swerve and the bullets passed through his clothing without injuring him. Undeterred he continued to pursue, closely followed by Mr Clements. The gunman then turned and fired 2 more shots one of which hit Mr Clements in the lower chest. But despite his serious injury Mr Clements managed to keep up with the chase. The robber had now made his way towards the car driven by his accomplice, but before he could get into it he was grabbed from behind by constable Henley and pulled away. The gunman still holding the gun was brought down and disarmed by constable Henley aided by Mr Clements. The criminal's car which had been stolen was twice driven at the crowd in an attempt by his accomplice to free the gunman. With the assistance of members of the public at the scene the man was also restrained and both criminals were arrested by constable Henley.

Malcolm Henley has since retired from the police force having completed 30 years service.

QUEEN'S COMMENDATION FOR BRAVE CONDUCT
4/4/83

Evans	Helen Jane	Woman Police Constable	4080

'Leading to the rescue of a deranged woman who had scaled a builders scaffolding tower and threatened to jump to her death.'

Seeds	Angela	Woman Police Constable	3682

'Leading to the capture and arrest of an armed and dangerous man who had stabbed and fatally injured her colleague in an attempt to evade arrest.'

QUEEN'S COMMENDATION FOR BRAVE CONDUCT
11/8/83

Jones	Peter Robert	Police Constable	171879

'Pursuit of 2 armed criminals following a bank robbery.'

QUEEN'S COMMENDATION FOR BRAVE CONDUCT
12/8/83

Olds	David	Police Constable	177060

'Attempting to detain a violent man who armed with a knife attacked and stabbed another Police Constable in an effort to evade arrest.'

Simister	Richard Michael	Police Constable	155491

'Leading to the arrest of an armed raider who had attacked a security guard during an attempted robbery.'

Wannell	Clifford Andrew	Police Constable	174569

'Tackling and disarming a criminal who threatened him with a sawn off shotgun following an armed robbery.'

Forman	Police Constable	181948

Formerly from the City of London Police Force.

QUEEN'S COMMENDATION FOR BRAVE CONDUCT
5/12/83

Cockayne	Christopher	Lately Police Constable	175088
Coles	John	Police Constable	168948

'Leading to the arrest of an armed and dangerous criminal following a robbery at a Post Office'.

Meldrum	Alan	Police Constable	156007

'Pursuing and attempting to detain an armed robber who had previously fired his weapon in order to evade arrest'.

QUEEN'S COMMENDATION FOR BRAVE CONDUCT

Hine	Police Constable	159731

ROYAL HUMANE SOCIETY BRONZE MEDAL
6/5/83

Haggerty	Woman Police Constable	6176

Awarded a Bronze Medal and certificate on Parchment for the rescue of a mentally disturbed woman from a high building.

FINE
2/9/83

A police constable fined 5 days pay (£119.60) fine to be extended over 5 weeks, through lack of care lost a personal radio.

ROLL OF HONOUR
- Wpc Jane Arbuthnot, 6021 B
- Ps Noel Lane, 170099 B
- Insp Stephen Dodd, 159449 B
- Queenie, Police Dog

IRA car bomb at Harrods - the officers were originally put forward for the QPM but no award was made.
- Pc Stephen Walker

Killed in a car while chasing two suspected car thieves across a road at Ashford.
- Pc Mark Simpkins

Area car observer killed in a crash while answering a call to a bank alarm in Chingford.
- Pc Gordon Cornish

Killed on advanced motorcycle training after a collision with a lorry in Cambridgeshire.
- Pc Frank Bellenie

Patrolling home beat officer killed by a car which mounted the pavement at Hillingdon.

1984

January	In the UK at least 6 die in hurricane force winds.
February	First un-tethered space walk from the Shuttle Challenger.
March	Stephen Waldorf, shot in error in 1982, receives £120,000 compensation from the Metropolitan Police.
April	UK expels Libyans after the killing of Wpc Yvonne Fletcher outside their Embassy.
May	Riot police battle with miners at the Orgreave Coking Plant in Yorkshire.
June	In London 720 are arrested when fighting breaks out outside Parliament during a mass lobby by striking miners.
July	Bolt of lightning sets York Minster alight.
August	Over 900,000 Filipinos march against the Government of President Marcos.
September	22 die from salmonella type food poisoning at a hospital in Wakefield within 10 days.
October	IRA bombs the Tory Conference Headquarters in Brighton.
November	Hundreds flee from smoke filled tunnels when fire breaks out at Oxford Circus underground station.
December	Fatal gas leak at Bhopal India kills at least 2,000.

HITS OF THE YEAR
Do they know its Christmas
I just called to say I love you
Two tribes
Amadeus - 8 awards

MURDER OF WPC YVONNE FLETCHER OUTSIDE
THE LIBYAN PEOPLES BUREAU, ST JAMES'S SQUARE

In April 1984 a day like any other, another aid serial for a demonstration outside an Embassy in Central London.

Yvonne Fletcher had always wanted to be a police officer, she had tried in vain to join but was only 5' 2½" tall, and the limit for a female officer had always been 5'4". The time had to come though when the height restrictions were to end, so Yvonne became Britain's tiniest bobby.

On Tuesday 17th April 1984, thirty police officers were on duty outside the Embassy policing a demonstration. Barriers had been put up to prevent the demonstrators getting too close to the building. The demonstrators were very vocal, and were trying to be heard above the loud music which was coming from the building. Suddenly gunfire came from the building; a smoking gun was seen jutting out of a first floor window. The crowds outside dived for cover, but one of the bullets had hit Yvonne in the back and she fell to the ground fatally wounded.

The picture that springs to mind is her hat lying upside down in the street where she fell. She was buried with full police honours, the Metropolitan Police Flag covered her coffin, her hat had been retrieved by one of her colleagues from the street, and that now lay in the centre of her coffin.

To this date those responsible for her murderer have never been brought to justice.

QUEEN'S COMMENDATION FOR BRAVE CONDUCT
10/8/84

Keenan	Stephen Morgan	Police Constable	174000
Sexton-Munns	Alan	Police Constable	148154
Sloman	David Glyndwr	Police Sergeant	168493

'Leading to the arrest of 2 armed criminals'.

Kelly	David James	Police Sergeant

'Leading to the arrest of a gunman who was intending to rob an armoured security vehicle'.

MARGARET WHEATLEY CROSS - RSPCA
10/8/84

The commissioner has pleasure in notifying the award.

Gordon	Police Constable	167927

Is awarded the Margaret Wheatley Cross RSPCA's highest award for gallantry together with the posthumous award of their animal plaque for intelligence and courage for the late Metropolitan Police Dog 'Queenie' resulting from the Harrods incident on Saturday 17th December 1983.

ROLL OF HONOUR
• Wpc Yvonne Fletcher C

Shot while on duty outside the Libyan Embassy, St James's Square, London.

- Pc Stephen Jones, 181200, NH

On Thursday 2 February 1984 whilst on duty, the officer attempted to stop 2 motor vehicles which were racing each other along Seven Sisters Road. As a result of his actions he was hit by one of the speeding cars driven by a drunken driver, and died of his injuries in hospital on 6 February 1984.

- Pc Grant Clifford Sunnucks

Area car driver killed in a crash pursuing a stolen car in North London.

- Pc Ronald Ian Leeow

Collapsed and died from a heart attack following a struggle with a violent prisoner at Barnet.

1985

January	8 die when a gas explosion wrecks a block of flats in Putney, South London.
February	Terry Waite the special envoy of the Archbishop of Canterbury wins freedom for 4 Britons held hostage in Libya.
March	Mikhail Gorbachev is the new Soviet leader.
April	London, Government plans to ban alcohol from 'problem' football grounds in England and Wales.
May	40 soccer fans die as fire sweeps the stands at the Bradford stadium.
June	The corpse of the 'Angel of Death' Joseph Mengele is discovered in Brazil.
July	Live Aid concert rocks the world, one concert at Wembley the other in Philadelphia, they raise over £40 million.
August	Fire on a holiday jet from Manchester when the pilot aborts the take off, 54 die, but over 80 survive.
September	The wreck of the liner Titanic is finally found and filmed by Dr Robert Ballard.
October	Broadwater Farm Riots (see 1988 for citations).
November	The new technique of 'genetic fingerprinting' is used for the first time in the UK to prove a paternity case.
December	The compact disc starts to catch on 2 years after its launch.

HITS OF THE YEAR

The power of love
Dancing in the street
Out of Africa - 7 awards

BROADWATER FARM RIOT

This was the second time that a police constable had been murdered while on duty during a riot. The first being Pc Robert Culley who died during the Coldbath Riots on 13th May 1833, he was stabbed and died of his injuries, and the second Pc Keith Blakelock who was murdered by a mob during the Broadwater Farm riots.

In its time Broadwater Farm was a prize winning housing development in Tottenham, North London.

On 5th October 1985 four police officers went to search the home of Mrs Cynthia Jarrett, her son had been arrested and was at Tottenham Police station for having given a false name when found in a car with an altered tax disc. The visit to her address caused an element of panic, and Cynthia Jarrett did have a heart condition. She collapsed and died of a heart attack despite the efforts to resuscitate her.

The next day Sunday 6th October a small crowd started to demonstrate outside the police station and broke its windows. Later two home beat officers attached to the Broadwater Farm estate were attacked and seriously injured by a brick throwing crowd. One had his spleen ruptured by a paving slab which was dropped onto him while he was on the ground helpless.

While driving past the Broadwater Farm estate an Inspector had his car windows broken by youths riding a motorcycle. A station van which was responding to an emergency call on the estate was surrounded and attacked by a mob with bars, knives and machetes and severely damaged.

By the time the first support groups of police arrived barriers had been put up, and due to the fears that booby traps may have been set, the police officers had to endure prolonged attacks from rioters. Some of the long shields they were carrying were damaged by gunfire which had been directed at the police lines.

Pc Keith Blakelock was a former community constable known as a home beat, and was one of the officers called to the Broadwater Farm riot, he was issued with his riot gear, and formed part of serial 502 along with 10 other constables and Sergeant Pengelly.

This was the most traumatic of all the London riots in the 1980's even more so than the 1981 riot in Brixton, South London. The police who were on duty during the riots had to endure petrol bombs, stones, concrete blocks and vehicles which had been set alight to form barricades. And if that was not enough, the rioters were also firing revolvers and shotguns at police and news crews. The police had to make several charges at the rioting mob and their only protection was a shield, a helmet and a baton.

During the evenings events one constable was shot in the stomach with a revolver round, and three more officers together with a television news crew came under fire from shotguns and a barrage of concrete blocks which were being hurled from the upper storeys of the estate.

It was apparent that the situation was not calming down, so police reinforcements were urgently called for and had to come from all corners of the Metropolitan Police area. Needless to say it took some time for them to arrive. These reinforcements included some police marksmen.

Serial 502 led by Sergeant Pengelly were sent to assist the London Fire Brigade, who were trying to put out a fire in a newsagents shop on the first floor of Tangmere Building, but had been driven off by the rioting youths and a barrage of missiles. But the serial was beaten back and as they retreated in order to regroup Pc Keith Blakelock slipped and fell. He was immediately surrounded by masked and balaclavaed rioters who were armed with sticks, knives and a machete. They began to attack the fallen officer.

Pc Coombes on seeing the plight of Pc Blakelock tried to run back to his assistance but was felled by a tremendous blow to the face which broke his jaw and left him unconscious on the ground. Ps Pengelly along with Pc Pandaya saw the situation that the fallen officers were in, and raced back to the killers who were slashing wildly at Pc Blakelock but despite being hit by missiles of rocks and risking serious personal injury themselves the officers frightened the murderous youths off.

Pc Maxwell Roberts went to help Pc Blakelock to his feet and tried to urge him to run. Pc Blakelock at this time was covered in blood, and a wooden handled knife was sticking out of his neck, he only managed a few steps before he collapsed.

Pc Blakelock was taken to the North Middlesex Hospital but sadly was dead on arrival. He had 40 separate wounds, several being blows to the head with a machete. A very severe cut which had smashed the right side of his jaw bone, which led all to believe that the frenzied mob intended to decapitate him and put his head on a pole in the estate as a trophy.

When news of the death of Pc Blakelock spread throughout the mob, and the rain started, the violence slowly died out, without the police having to use plastic bullets which had been authorised by the Commissioner Sir Kenneth Newman.

During the infamous Broadwater Farm riot, over 200 police officers were injured. Firearms had been used in a riot against the police, but the police did not fire back.

Pc Blakelock was born in 1945, he joined the Metropolitan Police on 14th November 1980. He was only 40 when he was murdered. He was married with three children.

ROLL OF HONOUR
•   Pc John William Fordham
Stabbed while on surveillance duty on a suspected bullion receiver at West Kingsdown, Kent.
•   Pc Keith Blakelock QGM 176050
Stabbed to death during the Broadwater Farm Riot.

1986
January	Space shuttle Challenger explodes 72 seconds after blast off, all 7 astronauts die.
February	Police and pickets clash at Wapping outside Rupert Murdoch's printing plant.
March	A woman dies in a fire which damages the South wing of Hampton Court Palace.
April	Nuclear incident at Chernobyl power station in Russia. The reactor is on fire.
May	Fear of meltdown at Chernobyl reactor.
June	Patrick Magee gets 8 life sentences for the Brighton and other bombings.
July	London estate agent Suzy Lamplugh is reported missing.
August	Manchester United and West Ham fans fight a pitched battle aboard a cross channel ferry.
September	Desmond Tutu is enthroned as Archbishop of Cape Town.
October	Angry crowd surrounds Notting Hill Police Station after a black man dies in police custody.
November	UK police search Saddleworth moor for 2 missing children after Myra Hindley breaks her long silence.
December	Experimental aircraft Voyager lands safely after flying round the world on one tank of fuel.

HITS OF THE YEAR
Don't leave me this way
Every loser wins
Platoon

QUEEN'S COMMENDATION FOR BRAVE CONDUCT
10/1/86

O'Rourke	Stephen John	Police Constable	171462

'Confronting two armed men following an attempted robbery of a security vehicle.'

Horswood	Stephen David	Police Constable	181388
Jones	Stephen Richard	Police Constable	173889

'Leading to the arrest of two armed men who had robbed the Branch office of a Building Society.'

Priddle	Michael	Inspector	149293

'Pacifying and arresting a man armed with a shotgun.'

Sowden	Anthony	Detective Constable	167731

'Tackling and restraining a criminal who was armed with a pistol.'

QUEEN'S COMMENDATION FOR BRAVE CONDUCT
14/3/86

Coleridge	John William	Detective Constable	162758

'Tackling an armed criminal during an attempted bank robbery.'

ROLL OF HONOUR
- Pc Martin Bickersteth Bell, 180057, W

On Thursday 3 July 1986 Pc Bell whilst on duty went to the aid of his colleagues who were pursuing a vehicle they believed to have been stolen. The suspect vehicle failed to give way at a road junction and drove into Pc Bell's police vehicle causing it to collide with a telegraph pole. Pc Bell was pronounced dead on arrival at Queen Mary's Hospital.

- Pc Wayne Darrell Spooner

Killed in a road traffic accident while on duty on Hackney Division.

1987

January	Terry Waite the Archbishop of Canterbury's special envoy is kidnapped in Beirut.
February	Old Bailey jury clears Cynthia Payne of running a brothel in the 'sex on the stairs' case.
March	Car ferry the 'Herald of Free Enterprise' capsizes after leaving Zeebrugge with its bow door still open.
April	It is revealed that 2 of the Queen Mother's cousins have been in a mental hospital since 1941.
May	19yr Mathias Rust lands his light aircraft in Moscow's Red Square, he is later sent to a labour camp for 4 years for violating Soviet airspace.
June	Princess Anne is given the title of 'Princess Royal'.
July	In West Germany 30 die when a tanker lorry crashes into a restaurant in a small town and bursts into flames.

August	Gunman Michael Ryan goes on the rampage and kills 14 and wounds 15 in Hungerford.
September	A search begins for a possible Soviet mole at GCHQ following a series of leaks.
October	Storm of the century hits England, hurricane force winds cause massive damage, and several deaths.
November	Kings Cross underground fire, 30 die in the inferno.
December	In Palermo Italy, 338 are convicted in the biggest ever Mafia trial.

HITS OF THE YEAR
China in your hand
Nothing's gonna stop us now
The last Emperor - 9 awards

BINNEY MEDAL
23/1/87
The Commissioner has pleasure in notifying the grant of the following award.
Martin   G F   Scenes of Crime Officer
Awarded a Binney Memorial Award Certificate of Merit for his actions in a case of attempted armed robbery.

QUEEN'S COMMENDATION FOR BRAVE CONDUCT
13/2/87
Henderson   John Martin   Police Constable   178385
'Pursuing a man armed with a revolver who had attempted to rob a branch office of a building society.'

Hyde   David   Inspector   156207
Saunders   Graham   Police Constable   171501
'Leading to the arrest of a youth armed with a semiautomatic shotgun.'

QUEEN'S COMMENDATION FOR BRAVE CONDUCT
6/8/87
Skinner   John   Police Constable   151284
'Tackling and disarming a criminal who had threatened him with a pistol.'

ROLL OF HONOUR
• Pc Ronan Konrad Aidan McCloskey QK
Killed while clinging to a car which drove off after he attempted to administer a breath test to the driver in Kilburn.

1988
January	An appeal by 6 Irishmen convicted of the Birmingham pub bombing in 1975 is rejected at the Old Bailey.

February	In Israel, Jewish settlers on the West Bank kill 2 Palestinians.
March	Prince of Wales narrowly escapes death after an avalanche at Klosters, a friend of his, Major Hugh Lindsay, is killed.
April	The British passport will be replaced with a European one.
May	BBC broadcasts controversial Falklands film 'Tumbledown' despite MOD concern.
June	In Australia the British Government fails to stop the publication of 'Spy Catcher' by the ex-MI5 agent Peter Wright.
July	Over 150 die in an Oil Rig fire on board the Piper Alpha in the North Sea.
August	Anglican Bishops vote for the ordination of women.
September	The Cuban Ambassador and one of his Envoys are expelled following a shooting incident in Bayswater, London.
October	The Government announces plans to end a suspect's right to silence.
November	In London, Police clash with students demonstrating against Government plans to bring in Student Loans.
December	Lockerbie disaster, PAN-AM 747 blows up over Lockerbie in Scotland, all 259 die and many in the houses of Lockerbie.

HITS OF THE YEAR

The only way is up
I should be so lucky
Mistletoe and wine
Rain man

GEORGE MEDAL - BROADWATER FARM
22/8/88

Pengelly	David Hugh	Police Sergeant	172906

QUEEN'S GALLANTRY MEDAL

Blakelock	Keith	Police Constable	176050

Posthumous

Pandya	Ricky	Police Constable	180556
Roberts	Maxwell	Police Constable	182977
Tappy	Alan	Police Constable	164681
Coombes	Richard	Police Constable	161950
Shepherd	Michael	Police Constable	183289
Martin	Stephen	Police Constable	182979
Milne	Kenneth	Police Constable	172341
Clark	Robin	Police Constable	181475
Barton	Miles	Police Constable	174863
Howells	Martin	Police Constable	183253

On Sunday 6th October 1985 a serious breakdown of law and order took place in North London at Tottenham. A riot involving youths throwing petrol bombs, arson, burglary and the use of firearms against the police. Shortly before 10 p.m. a supermarket on the first floor block of flats was looted and a fire started. A team of fire officers escorted by Sergeant Pengelly and constables Barton, Blakelock, Clark, Coombes, Howells, Martin, Milne, Panday, Roberts, Shepherd and Tappy made their way to the supermarket. The police officers took up a defensive position around the fire officers to allow them to begin to extinguish the fire. Within a few minutes a large group of youths appeared and started to attack the officers with petrol bombs, bricks and other missiles. Sergeant Pengelly ordered a withdrawal, the firemen were placed in the middle of the group for maximum protection. During their retreat down a stair way the mob hacked at the shields held by the police with machetes, swords, knives on poles and similar weapons. When the police and fire officers reached the ground they became open to attack from all directions from a crowd of some 300 youths. They had no alternative but to split up and try to fight their way back through the crowd to safety. Constables Blakelock and Coombes fell or were knocked to the ground, a mob of youths set upon constable Blakelock and brutally attacked him. Sergeant Pengelly sought to beat off with his truncheon those around constable Blakelock. The other police instead of seeking safety joined Sergeant Pengelly and managed to drive back the heavily armed youths and drag their severely injured colleague away, or turn to constable Coombes who had been attacked and was lying on the ground nearby. He was protected by shields, the advancing mob was fought off and the officer was eventually dragged to safety. Sergeant Pengelly with total disregard for his own safety was the first to drive back the heavily armed youths from around constable Blakelock. All the officers involved displayed outstanding bravery and devotion to duty when they were faced by this hostile mob.

Pc Miles Barton received another award, a testimonial on vellum from The Royal Humane Society in 1996.

Pc Coombes has since retired from the police force. Pc Shepherd transferred to a County force, Pc Pandaya left the police force his whereabouts are unknown and Pc Howells retired on ill health as a result of injuries he received during the riot.

QUEEN'S GALLANTRY MEDAL
23/8/88

Proctor	Martin Stephen	Police Constable	172140

On Sunday 26th April 1987 a woman was threatening to jump in front of a train at an underground station. An emergency call was made to the police. Constable Proctor along with another officer arrived at the station and made their way down to the platform where the woman was now about 30 yards inside the tunnel. Both constables tried to engage the woman in conversation but this proved to be fruitless. The other constable then left the scene to arrange for the current to be turned off and to stop any trains for approaching. Shortly after constable Proctor heard and saw the head lights of a train approaching the tunnel. Now the woman appeared unsure whether to run or remain where she was. Constable Proctor immediately leapt from the platform onto the track and ran towards her. As he reached the woman he pushed her away, a short struggle began, the constable picked her up and ran towards the platform. At this time the train was very close but constable Proctor managed to lift the woman onto the platform before seeking refuge himself. The train eventually stopped at the mouth of the tunnel.

QUEEN'S COMMENDATION FOR BRAVE CONDUCT

23/8/88

Broughton	John Leslie	Police Constable	164026
Long	Timothy John	Police Constable	175727

Leading to the rescue of a woman who was trapped by heat, flames and smoke during a severe fire in a flat in an apartment block.'

FINE

5/1/88

A Police Sergeant fined 2 days pay (£88.94) for being uncivil towards members of the public.

1989

January	40 die when a British Midlands aircraft crashes on the M1 Motorway.
February	The Guardian Angels, a group of New York subway vigilantes, arrive to set up a London branch.
March	5 die at a rail crash in Putney, South London.
April	Hillsborough disaster, fans crushed at football stadium, up to 94 die.
May	In Beirut, a 74 year Briton, Jackie Mann is abducted.
June	Pro-democracy supporters die in Tiananmen Square in China.
July	Ken Dodd the British comedian is acquitted of defrauding the Inland Revenue.
August	Pleasure boat, the Marchioness, sinks on the River Thames, 60 die.
September	A bomb explodes at Deal in Kent, killing 10 Royal Marine Bandsmen and injuring 22 others.
October	Police in London take over as Ambulance crews strike.
November	Berlin wall comes down, East and West no longer divided.
December	Dictator Nicolae Ceausescu is ousted in Rumania - he is shot by a firing squad.

HITS OF THE YEAR

Ride on time
Swing the mood
Too many broken hearts
Driving Miss Daisy

QUEEN'S GALLANTRY MEDAL

2/3/89

Pickford	Derek Charles	Explosives Officer	
Chipperfield	Michael Andrew	Police Constable	152604

On Saturday 22nd June 1985 a group of 5 terrorists had been arrested in a flat in Glasgow. On examination of documents found in the flat the police were led to believe that a bomb had been left armed and fitted with a timing device and anti disturbance fuses and it had been concealed in a room of the Rubens Hotel, in London. The Rubens hotel is situated opposite Buckingham Palace, London. The hotel and the immediate area was evacuated, Mr.

Pickford organized a search and led the search of a room suspected to contain the bomb. A lot of the furniture and fittings were of a size, shape and the weight that made a search by one man virtually impossible. To have done this would have greatly increased the chances of the bomb being triggered. Constable Chipperfield immediately volunteered to assist, the two officers then carried out a meticulous search of the room. They began in the bathroom and removed the bath panels, carpet and floorboards and all other fittings. After about 2½ hours of painstaking work, constable Chipperfield having unsecured a bedside cabinet from the wall, located the device in the base of the cabinet. At this point all other persons other than Mr. Pickford left the hotel. Mr. Pickford then X-rayed the bomb and found that the anti disturbance mechanisms had been used and would cause the bomb to detonate if it was moved from the contact with the wall or if it were tilted more than 5 degrees. Following a careful study of the device Mr. Pickford proceeded to render the bomb safe.

QUEEN'S GALLANTRY MEDAL
2/3/89

Thomas   Ian Wynford   Police Sergeant   170634

On Monday 26th January 1987 while Sergeant Thomas was employed on motorcycle traffic duties, he noticed a motorcycle with a pillion passenger being driven erratically. He decided to stop the vehicle. As he switched on the blue light and siren the motorcycle accelerated away rapidly. A chase then developed through old dockyard property, a building development and down a flight of steps. The speed of the chase at times neared 80 mph but the Sergeant managed to stay in close pursuit. The motorcycle eventually collided with a pavement obstruction. Both the rider and the passenger were thrown to the ground. At this point Sergeant Thomas dismounted his machine and restrained the rider by placing him in a head lock. The passenger in the meantime walked over to the Sergeant, he had a pistol in his outstretched arm. The weapon was then pointed directly at the officer. Sergeant Thomas tried to deflect the gun away, as he made the gesture the weapon was fired. The bullet struck the Sergeant's wrist before exiting at the elbow. The officer tackled the gunman to the ground and a fight developed for the possession of the firearm. During the struggle the weapon was fired a second time. Mr. Burnett who had been riding his motorcycle nearby heard the shots and witnessed Sergeant Thomas struggling with the gunman. Mr. Burnett ran to the scene and the rider of the motorcycle tried to make his escape. Mr. Burnett shoulder charged him into a corrugated door and a violent struggle took place. Soon afterwards a police officer arrived and assisted the Sergeant to disarm the gunman and Mr. Burnett to restrain the rider. It was subsequently determined that the rider of the motorcycle was in fact an escaped prisoner.

QUEEN'S COMMENDATION FOR BRAVE CONDUCT
10/8/89

Sulaiman   John   Police Sergeant   171974
Till   John William Alfred   Police Constable   171525

'Rescuing a mentally disturbed man, who was threatening to commit suicide and had to be restrained by force from jumping from the ledge of a high bridge.'

ROLL OF HONOUR
- Pc Paul Michael Breen, 188335 MS

On 25 December 1989 the officer was on duty in a military Landrover ambulance which, whilst responding to an emergency call, was involved in an accident, whereby he sustained fatal injuries.
- Pc Mark Peers

Drowned while searching for a submerged car during underwater search unit training.

Chapter Eleven

THE YEARS OF 1990 - 1999

The 1990's was a very interesting decade. I remember watching the television to see in the distance a small figure walking along a dusty track. It was Nelson Mandela, he had just been released from prison after serving 27 years of a life sentence for sabotage and plotting to overthrow the South African Government. Ironically within four years he was sworn in as the new South African President.

We saw the Soviet Union as a strong race and a hard line country, but with the end of the cold war and 'glasnost' the world seemed a little safer. During this decade we saw unrest in the Soviet Union. The crowds in Red Square jeering the leader Mikhail Gorbachev and within a year Boris Yeltsin would topple the leader in a coup. Several regions would break away from the mother nation and form their own independent states, this only brought hardship and the entry into their countries of the Soviet Army, especially in Chechnya.

The ongoing trouble in Beirut was calming down, the terrorists finally releasing the last three hostages, Brian Keenan after 1597 days, John McCarthy after 5 years and Terry Wait after nearly five years captive. It was a great day seeing them all come home to their loved ones.

There was one major war in this decade which affected us, the Gulf War. Iraq invades Kuwait and the world reacts and watches. Operation Desert Storm begins, and thankfully after 4 days the war is over. Sadly the threat from Iraq still lingers even into the next century.

Mrs Thatcher, the Prime Minister of Great Britain, is ousted by her own faithful, John Major becomes the new Prime Minister, but by 1997 the nation had had enough of Conservative rule and Tony Blair leads in the Labour Party after a landslide victory.

The channel tunnellers finally come face to face after eight years of digging. A dream which began over 200 years ago has now become a reality, travel between France and Great Britain without having to cross by ferry. HM The Queen and President Mitterand cut the red white and blue ribbons to open the new train service.

Violence escalates in Yugoslavia, the UN do their best but are unable to stop the war, the ethnic cleansing and the mass of refugees. The death camps of Serbia are shown on television to the horror of the world. The mass killings are reported, the mass graves and the killing of the innocents by bombing the market in Sarajevo. The United States allows NATO to use their troops to help resolve the situation. A biblical scale of refugees flee the fighting and again to this day peace is not yet guaranteed.

Hopes rise and fall in the Middle East, the world seems to want to do what it can to secure peace between the Israel and Palestine. But it may well be well into the next decade before peace arrives. Terrorism hits home in the USA with the FBI building in Oklahoma being bombed. The IRA in the UK are still active with bombings in Warrington, Docklands London, Manchester and Omagh.

Hong Kong returns to Chinese rule after nearly 200 years of British sovereignty. Most of the UK is plunged into darkness with a total eclipse of the sun. Prince Charles and Diana separate and finally divorce. Princess Anne divorces and remarries her former equerry Cdr. Timothy Laurence. Prince Edward marries Sophie Rhys-Jones. The Queen calls in the tax man as she decides it's time she paid taxes just like all her subjects. But the sad end to the decade was the death of Diana Princess of Wales and Dodi Fayed in a car accident in Paris in 1997. The whole world seems to have been affected by her death.

1990

January	Gale force winds kill 46 and injury many more when storms hit the UK.
February	Nelson Mandela is released from prison in South Africa.
March	The Poll tax riots take place in Trafalgar Square, London.
April	Iraqi super gun is seized in Britain.
May	In London a booby trapped mini bus explodes killing an Army Sergeant.
June	IRA bomb explodes at the Carlton Club, St James's London.
July	British Airways pilot is sucked halfway out of his cockpit after the windscreen blows out.
August	Brian Keenan is freed from Beirut after 1597 days capture.
September	IRA gunmen attack and badly injure Air Chief Marshall Sir Peter Terry, a former Governor of Gibraltar.
October	The Berlin wall comes down and Germany is one nation again, 45 years after the end of the Second World War.
November	Conservatives join forces to oust Mrs Thatcher as their leader.
December	Channel tunnellers finally meet - English and French engineers cut through.

HITS OF THE YEAR
Nothing compares 2 U
Sacrifice
Dances with wolves

QUEEN'S COMMENDATION FOR BRAVE CONDUCT
23/10/90

Bailey	Kevin Christopher	Police Constable	173248 DR

'Pursuing and arresting an armed robber who, curing the chase fired his weapon at the officer before he was overpowered'.

Waterhouse	Timothy Phillip	Inspector	173291 HH

'Pursuing an armed man on foot, despite being threatened with a sawn-off shot gun and fired at, until the man took refuge in a flat before surrendering to police.'

ROYAL HUMANE SOCIETY BRONZE MEDAL

Austin	Samuel	Police Constable	183845 CB

For the rescue of a woman who had attempted to jump off scaffolding and who during the incident suffered an epileptic fit.

ROLL OF HONOUR
- Pc Laurence Peter Brown, 177296, G

Whilst on duty on 28th August having responded to an emergency telephone call the officer approached a suspect who discharged a sawn off shotgun at him causing fatal injuries.
- Pc Ashley Day, 187063, X

On 21st February the officer was on duty as a radio operator in an area car which whilst responding to an emergency call, was in an accident whereby he sustained fatal injuries.

1991

January	Desert Storm launches the 'Gulf War', it lasts just 100 hours.
February	IRA fires mortars at Downing Street.
March	Dr George Carey is formally elected as the new Archbishop of Canterbury.
April	Kurds flee from Saddam Hussain's brutal regime.
May	Britain's first woman astronaut Helen Sharman returns to earth on Soyuz TM-12.
June	The British Army will lose half of its manpower in Government cuts.
July	Milwaukee US, police claim serial killer Jeffrey Dahmer aged 31 cut up 18 victims and ate parts of their bodies.
August	President Gorbachev is toppled by Boris Yeltsin in Russia.
September	The all male Magic Circle finally lifts its ban on women.
October	In Texas a 35 yr man kills 22 in a restaurant.
November	Terry Waite is released from Beirut.
December	Business Empire of Robert Maxwell collapses.

HITS OF THE YEAR

Everything I do I do it for you
I'm too sexy
The silence of the lambs

QUEEN'S GALLANTRY MEDAL

26/9/91

Hadaway	David	Police Sergeant	157520 RG
Rainsford	Philip	Police Constable	182549 RG
Healy	John Andrew	Police Constable	178821 SO16

On Friday 13th March 1987 a security van was making its usual collections and deliveries of cash from various parts of the South East of London. While it was on its way to a warehouse, a motorcycle and rider following the van drew the crew's suspicions. When the van arrived at the warehouse the guard notified the security manager and the police were subsequently called. When two police officers arrived the suspect who had been seen signalling to an accomplice entering the warehouse was arrested and detained after a struggle. Sergeant Hadaway also responded to the call for assistance and arrived on scene as the suspect was being arrested and detained. The Sergeant was notified of the second suspect who was within the warehouse and he made his way to the building. Sergeant Hadaway located the second suspect and called on him to stop. The suspect then drew a revolver and ordered the Sergeant to keep back. It was at this time that constables Healey and Rainsford arrived and entered the warehouse. The suspect then made for the exit and the constables followed led by Sergeant Hadaway. As the suspect reached the exit he turned and faced the Sergeant who at this time was about 10 feet away, the gunman then pointed the gun at the ground and pulled the trigger twice. But for some reason the gun did not go off. Sergeant Hadaway then moved forward and the suspect drew a second revolver and fired another 2 shots at the ground. The Sergeant notified all the officers on his radio that the robber was armed and dangerous. The man then fled the store and entered a car park. He was followed by the three officers. The gunman then tried to hijack a van in order to make his escape this failed, the gunman then ran across the car park still being chased by the officers. In the chase that followed constable Rainsford overtook his colleagues and closed on the suspect who then turned and shot the constable in the leg. Sergeant Hadaway continued with the chase and as he approached the suspect he managed to hit him with his truncheon in the hope that the man would drop the gun. The suspect then turned and at close range shot the Sergeant in the leg. He fell to the ground grievously wounded. Constable Rainsford despite his injury had continued the chase until he came upon the badly wounded Sergeant, he too then fell to the ground, unable to pursue the suspect any further. The chase was however continued by constable Healey, during which the suspect fired several times at the officer. The suspect managed to steal a vehicle at gunpoint and made good his escape. When constable Healey returned to his injured colleagues he discovered that there were two bullet holes in his uniform and upon further examination found a bullet had grazed his hip. The gunman was apprehended some time later and both he and the first suspect were subsequently tried and convicted of a number of serious offences.

Philip Rainsford is a serving police officer in South London. David Hadaway has since retired from the Police Force.

STANHOPE MEDAL OF THE ROYAL HUMANE SOCIETY
Moore   Lesley Allison   Woman Police Constable
At Bury Street, London, SW1 on 16th January 1990 at 11.52 am, a workman who was erecting a protective corrugated iron roof covering to the scaffolding frame stood on a sheet of metal not properly attached and fell onto a sloping room of a building and ended up on the flat roof of a 4th floor dormer window. There was no safe means of approach so the emergency services were called. A police ambulance arrived crewed by Pc Payne and Wpc Moore. They were taken to the roof and shown the location of the injured workman 2 floors below. Pc Payne went to summon assistance and Wpc Moore went to a flat on the 5th floor, climbed out of the dormer window in the kitchen. She was still on the floor above the workman. Dormer windows in these flats are not directly above one another and she therefore had to traverse a precipitous and dangerous gap which increased the difficulty of

her task. There was a railing at the bottom of the sloping roof but, due to the dilapidated state of the building it could easily have given way. Wpc Moore sought the assistance of a scaffolder who, by holding her hand, was able to swing her across the gap and enable her to jump down to the top of the dormer window.

In very confined conditions, Wpc Moore gave first aid and resuscitation to the injured workman, being restricted for space and completely unprotected. She had to turn the injured man over to give him resuscitation and he responded when she encouraged him to breathe. Wpc Moore removed her tunic to make a pillow and her pullover to keep him warm. The temperature was 12c and there were winds up to 43 mph. She kept up support for more than an hour. The injured workman could not be moved until planking and ladders were laid and had to be completed by the Fire Brigade with specialised equipment. Sadly the workman died later in hospital.

There were 6 cases for the 1991 award to be considered, from Australia, Canada, New Zealand, New South Wales, Liverpool and the Royal Humane Society. HRH Princess Alexandra subsequently confirmed the award to Wpc Moore.

ROLL OF HONOUR
* Pc Robert Chenery Gladwell, 191252, D Division
On 16 December 1990 the officer received a blow to the head whilst making an arrest. On 4 January 1991 he collapsed at his home and died on 6 January 1991.
* Ps Alan Derek King, 160284, JC
Stabbed while chasing a suspect.
* Dc James Morrison QGM, 181754, HD
Stabbed while attempting an arrest.

1992
January	Allison Halford, Britain's most senior policewoman, is suspended for misconduct.
February	In London a terrorist bomb attack at London Bridge Station injures 28.
March	Buckingham Palace confirms that the Duchess of York is seeking a divorce.
April	Euro Disney in Paris opens at a cost of £6.4 million.
May	Los Angeles is hit by race riots after several of the police are acquitted of the beating of Rodney King.
June	A bomb blast in London's Victoria Street causes extensive damage.
July	John Smith takes over as the new leader of the Labour Party.
August	Serbian death camps stun the world.
September	Heritage Minister David Mellor resigns after a sex scandal.
October	Fully loaded El Al Boeing 747 cargo plane crashes into a crowded housing estate in Amsterdam.
November	Windsor Castle is badly damaged by fire.
December	President Bush sends in heavily armed Marines to Somalia for humanitarian aid mission, they meet no opposition but the world's press when they land on the beaches.

HITS OF THE YEAR
The days of our lives
Tears in heaven
Why
Unforgiven

GEORGE MEDAL
14/5/92

Knapp	Alan James	Detective Sergeant	165747
Thomas	Stephen Andrew	Detective Sergeant	160738

On Wednesday 14th December 1988 at about 5 pm, an attempted robbery took place by 4 men at a post office. Three of the men were seen to be armed as they entered the premises. Detective Sergeants Knapp and Thomas positioned themselves close enough to observe what was taking place inside. Several customers could be seen lying on the floor while some had backed away from the counter area as an alarm was activated by a member of the staff. The police officers shouted a warning to members of the public to stay back and to take cover. The two officers then drew their service revolvers and donned their high visibility caps, Sergeant Thomas saw an elderly man inadvertently walk into the firing line. As he pushed the man to the ground three robbers then emerged from the post office and fired indiscriminately at both of the officers. Both of the officers were not able to return fire immediately for fear of injuring members of the public. As the robbers fled the officers then opened fire, each discharging all six rounds of ammunition. As both Sergeants crouched low to re load their weapons the fourth man emerged firing at the officers in a bid to escape. Sergeant Knapp fell to the ground, he had been shot in the hand, Sergeant Thomas ran towards the officer as he saw two robbers head in their direction. As he gave chase he felt a sudden pain in his side, he too had been shot. Now aware that he had a bullet wound to his leg he continued to pursue the robbers before falling to the ground severely injured. Detective Sergeants Knapp and Thomas displayed conspicuous gallantry and total disregard for their own safety during an attempt by four dangerous men to raid a post office, three of whom were known to be armed. The officers had to take up positions without any safe cover and had been unable to exchange fire immediately with the robbers for reasons of public safety, and exposed themselves to considerable risk and were shot and severely injured. All four suspects were later arrested and subsequently convicted of a number of serious crimes.

QUEEN'S COMMENDATION FOR BRAVE CONDUCT
15/5/92

Knapp	Alan James	Detective Sergeant	165747

'Pursuing an armed robber, following an attempted hold up of a security van. During the chase the gunman stopped turned and shot at the officer to escape arrest. Detective Sergeant Knapp later apprehended and arrested the gunman after knocking him off his motorcycle during a second chase.'

This award was made for an incident which happened back in 1988.

Phelan   Patrick Richard   Detective Constable   165560

'Pursuing 2 robbers, one armed with a hand gun who turned and threatened the officer, as both men made their escape following a raid on a post office. Assisted by other officers constable Phelan continued the search, arresting and detaining the men who were found hiding close by.'

ROLL OF HONOUR

1993

January	Princess Margaret is admitted to hospital suffering from pneumonia.
February	2 boys are charged with the murder of Jamie Bulger, subsequently found guilty.
March	IRA plants a bomb in Warrington which kills 1 and injures many.
April	Blaze ends the Waco siege in Texas after the FBI storm the building, cult leader David Koresh and many of his followers die.
May	Businessman Asil Nadir jumps £3.5 million bail and flees to North Cyprus.
June	Police announce an anti terrorist cordon which will surround the City.
July	Andrew Lloyd-Webber's 'Sunset Boulevard' is a hit in London.
August	Severe flooding hits mid West US, at least 50 die and 38,000 are homeless.
September	Israeli Prime Minister Yitzhak Rabin and the PLO leader Yassir Arafat shake hands for the first time at the White House.
October	Russia, Boris Yeltsin crushes the hard-liners rebellion.
November	Germany, France and Belgium inaugurate the Euro-cops, a joint military unit they hope will become the core of a future European Army.
December	Northern Ireland peace pact is signed in London.

HITS OF THE YEAR

Can't help falling in love
That's the way love goes
All that she wants
Schindlers List

QUEEN'S GALLANTRY MEDAL

2/7/93

Simpson   Neil   Police Constable   183007

On Thursday 13th April 1989 at about 9 am, constable Simpson was with other officers who were detailed to drive to the back of a parade of shops where a raid on a post office was believed to be about to take place. The suspects were known to the police and were likely to be armed. Constable Simpson and a colleague were therefore issued with firearms. The suspects had made their way to the back of the post office where they attempted to gain entry by ramming the doors. The attempt failed and the police officers moved in. Three men were seen to get into a vehicle, this was known to the officers as having been stolen. As the suspects fled constable Simpson and his colleague took up the chase at high speed. During the subsequent chase the officers were able to see that at least one of the occupants from the stolen car was in possession of a shotgun. The chase finally ended near a footbridge crossing a railway line. The three robbers fled across the bridge and ran though a narrow alley closely followed by constable Simpson and a colleague. The officers shouted several warnings to the men to stop and that they were armed police officers. When they neared the end of the alley constable Simpson saw the three men approach another vehicle, and as the officer shouted another warning to the men, they turned around and two of the suspects raised their hands and pointed their weapons at the officer. A number of shots were fired at constable Simpson, who although adopting a crouched position, was without cover. The officer then managed to return fire and one of the suspects fell to the ground. As the officer turned his weapon towards the second armed suspect he received a shot in the ankle causing him to stumble and fall to the ground. He continued to fire his weapon as he was determined not to let the suspects escape. He was forced to fire from a sitting position. At this point the constables colleague took up the challenge and upon firing his weapon, the second armed suspect fell to the ground. The third man was attempting to enter the car when other police officers arrived and he was arrested. The two wounded robbers subsequently died from their injuries and the third was charged and later convicted of a number of serious offences.

QUEEN'S COMMENDATION FOR BRAVE CONDUCT
2/7/93

Harlow	Paul	Police Constable	171876 SO19

'Assisting a colleague to prevent three highly dangerous and armed men from escaping, following an attempted robbery on a post office. The officer, although armed, came under fire from the robbers who shot and wounded his colleague.'

ROYAL HUMANE SOCIETY BRONZE MEDAL

Brotherton	Christopher	Captain	TO26
Jarvis	Malcolm	Police Sergeant	167866 TO26
Dunster	Geoffrey	Police Constable	156640 TO26

For effecting the rescue by helicopter in extremely hazardous conditions of a man who had been trapped on the roof of a burning building.

ROLL OF HONOUR
- Pc Patrick Dunne, 190636 L

Shot at a disturbance in Clapham.
- Pc Neil Charles Frick

Killed when his surveillance duty motorcycle crashed at Shepherds Bush.
- Dc Thomas Need

Killed when his surveillance duty motorcycle was in collision with a car in Surrey.
- Pc Michael Perry

Panda car crashed answering an emergency call to a man suspected of murder.

1994

January	Torrential rain following the wettest December since 1879 causes havoc across Southern England.
February	A single mortar is fired into a Sarajevo market, it kills 68 and injures over 200.
March	Heathrow Airport is shut for 2 hours after a third IRA mortar attack in 5 days.
April	Rosemary West is jointly charged along with her husband Fred for several murders.
May	Nelson Mandela is sworn in a South Africa's first black President.
June	Millions watch a car chase to capture O J Simpson live on TV in Los Angeles.
July	Car bomb in London damages the Israeli Embassy, 4 are injured.
August	After 25 years of bombing and shooting the IRA announces a complete cease fire after over 3,000 have died in the troubles.
September	Roll on roll off ferry Estonia sinks in the Baltic Sea, over 900 die.
October	HM Queen Elizabeth II makes a historic visit to Russia.
November	Millions chase the jackpot in the UK's first lottery draw.
December	Russian troops cross into Chechnya.

HITS OF THE YEAR

Crazy for you
Park life
Forest Gump

QUEEN'S GALLANTRY MEDAL

1/1/94

Wiltshire	Peter James	Police Sergeant	176074 H

On Thursday 24th October 1991 in the evening a Securicor van crew were delivering money to a building society cash dispensing machine. As the van approached the building it parked directly behind a car near to a bus stop. Mr Spence opened the rear side door of the van and was confronted by a robber who had been waiting at the bus stop. The man was holding a sawn off double barrelled shot gun and ordered Mr Spencer to get back into the vehicle. Mr Spencer then kicked out at the robber, in retaliation the robber fired one barrel hitting Mr Spencer above the knee, he felt a burning sensation but no other ill effects and kicked out again at the robber. The robber fired again, this time almost at point blank range, this time he hit Mr Spencer in the stomach, again there was only a burning sensation with a little stinging. Unknown to the security guard most of the shot in the cartridges had been removed, so the power of the shots was very low. Knowing that his attacker had fired both barrels and despite the fact that the blows were raining on his shoulders and crash helmet Mr Spencer continued to confront the robber who then decided to abandon the raid and ran across the road with Mr Spencer in pursuit. During this attack a second robber had been watching the proceedings brandishing his own shotgun, intent on keeping any assistance at bay. When the first robber attempted to run off Mr Spencer managed to trip him causing the first man to stumble. At this point the second robber fired one barrel of his shotgun into Mr Spencer's leg causing it to buckle beneath him and he fell. Sergeant Wiltshire was off duty and was in his car with his family when he saw the start of the incident. He stopped his car and got out to help when he heard the first two shots being fired. He then saw Mr Spencer shot for the third time and saw the first robber drop his weapon and attempt to escape. Not realising that both barrels had been discharged Sergeant Wiltshire picked up the abandoned gun and began to pursue the fleeing robber. He disregarded the second robber wielding a sawn off shot gun, he then challenged the now unarmed robber who appeared to comply. Sergeant Wiltshire then turned his attention to the second robber, across the road, who now started to point his gun at him. Sergeant Wiltshire told him to stand still. At this time the second robber let go of his weapon which fell beneath his coat as it had been tied to his body. The Sergeant was not able to detain both men so he shouted further instructions to him, he made his lie on the pavement and disarmed him. As he was doing this the first robber ran off and escaped.

Henry Bayly Spencer, a night delivery driver from Securicor Ltd also received the Queen's Gallantry Medal.

QUEEN'S GALLANTRY MEDAL
Posthumous
27/1/94

Morrison	James	Detective Constable	181754 H

On Friday 13th December 1991 at about 9.30pm detective constable Morrison was off duty and attempted to detain a suspected handbag thief. The suspect drew a knife and threatened the officer. The man broke free from the officer and ran into an alleyway. Constable Morrison gave chase throwing off his coat and jacket as he closed with the suspect. The suspect then turned and lunged at the officer with a knife in an attempt to escape. The detective continued to close on the man, who then turned and ran off again, once again the officer gave chase. At this point a woman who was walking through the alley came close to the knife wielding man. Detective constable Morrison placed himself in a position where he was able to maintain the attention of the suspect and he drew him away from the terrified woman. Once the woman had passed the man made off again. The officer again gave chase. During a further confrontation the suspect made a further attempt to stab the officer in the chest. There followed a chase through the streets as the suspect continued to threaten the officer. The man was making good his escape until he turned to find the officer in a breathless state. He then stopped and walked towards the officer, he beckoned to him in a taunting manner. As the officer approached he was stabbed in the chest and fell to the ground seriously injured. He was rushed to hospital but was found to dead on arrival, his assailant has never been caught.

This officer was originally recommended for the George Medal.

QUEEN'S COMMENDATION FOR BRAVE CONDUCT
28/1/94

Hughes	Paul David	Detective Constable	179376
Porter	David William	Detective Constable	167314
Squibb	Jason Paul	Detective Constable	176539

'Challenging and arresting a drugs dealer who, when tackled by Detective constable Squibb pulled a gun and shot and seriously wounded Detective constable Hughes, during a violent struggle with detective constable Squibb the suspect again fired his weapon at detective constable Porter as he was closing in. The gunman broke free and ran off with detective constable Porter now in close pursuit, having discarded his weapon the suspect concealed himself beneath a nearby parked vehicle where he was discovered and arrested by detective constable Porter and another officer'.

QUEEN'S COMMENDATION FOR BRAVE CONDUCT

| Walsh | Christopher Paul | Police Constable | 186076 |

'Pursuing an armed man following a bank robbery. During the chase, the man turned and fired at the officer at close range. He attempted to make his escape by hiding nearby in undergrowth. Constable Walsh on seeing him, undeterred by further threats, approached the armed man who finally surrendered'.

QUEEN'S COMMENDATION FOR BRAVE CONDUCT

1/7/94

Deegan	Edward Richard	Police Sergeant	168717
Nicholls	David	Police Constable	182362
Condie	Mrs	Civilian	

Dealing with a mentally disturbed person armed with a knife and air pistol who had held women hostage at a doctor's surgery. The mentally disturbed person had entered the surgery and taken hostage Mrs Condie and two fellow women employees at the surgery. Mrs Condie managed to raise the alarm. She was twice given the opportunity to escape but decided to remain with her companions, offering herself as hostage if they were released. By remaining on duty she kept the intruders' attention until two policemen arrived in response to her call. Constables Deegan and Nicholls talked the suspect into releasing firstly the two women assistants, and subsequently Mrs Condie herself, offering initially to take their place. The two constables eventually persuaded the suspect to give himself up after five hours of negotiation. Mrs Condie also received the QCBC.

QUEEN'S COMMENDATION FOR BRAVE CONDUCT

Davidson	John Clive	Police Sergeant	181994 Y
Barnett	Helen Francis	Woman Police Constable	7205 Y
Kingdom	Zara Jaqueline	Woman Police Constable	9239 Y
Lawson	Jennifer Jane	Woman Police Constable	7387 Y

'Apprehending a man who became violent when an attempt was made to question him. Following a complaint about an abusive passer-by. Constable Barnett approached the man who assaulted her, knocking her to the ground. Constable Lawson came to her aid but she too was attacked. As constable Lawson lay on the ground, constable Barnett tried a second time to arrest the man and was again violently assaulted and stabbed. As constable Barnett lay on the ground, constable Lawson made another attempt to restrain the man and was also stabbed. At this point constable Kingdom with Sergeant Davidson approached the man and constable Kingdom was also assaulted and cut on the arm and fell to the ground. Constable Kingdom then turned to aid her badly wounded fellow Wpc's, Sergeant Davidson grappled with the violent man, and despite himself being stabbed in the stomach he succeeded eventually in calming the man and getting him to hand over his knife'.

Helen Barnett has since retired from the Police Force, she has written a book of her life as a police constable, entitled Urban Warrior.

ROLL OF HONOUR
- Ps Derek Robertson QGM, 164954, Z

On the morning of 9th February 1994 whilst on duty in uniform the officer attended a call to an armed robbery at a sub-post office in New Addington. He confronted the three suspects as they left the premises and was repeatedly stabbed by one of them. He subsequently died of his wounds later that morning.
- Pc Matthew James Parsonson

Passenger in a police vehicle which crashed on a call for urgent assistance.
- Wpc Gail Doreen Pirnie

Collapsed and died from a heart attack while baton training at the Peel Centre, Hendon.
- Pc Michael Tring

Killed in an accident driving an area car on an emergency call for assistance to his colleagues.

1995

January	Thousands die in the Kobe earthquake in Japan.
February	Jill Phipps an animal rights campaigner dies when she falls under a lorry's wheels which was carrying live calves for export.
March	Nick Leeson financial dealer loses millions and bankrupts Baring Bank.
April	Federal building in Oklahoma is bombed, kills more than 100 including 15 children.
May	In a survey in the UK a large majority of police officers reject the routine arming of police.
June	Hugh Grant is arrested near Sunset Boulevard on lewd conduct charges.
July	A heat wave in Chicago US with temperatures of 106F claims over 300 lives.
August	The pilot of an Argentine jet reports a near miss with a UFO which he alleges flew into the path of his aeroplane.
September	NATO halts the air strikes against the Bosnian Serbs in Sarajevo.
October	Jury finds O J Simpson not guilty of murder.
November	Rosemary West is jailed for life for the murders of 10 women and girls after the bodies are discovered at Cromwell Street.
December	London Head master Philip Lawrence is stabbed to death when he defends a pupil being attacked.

HITS OF THE YEAR
Some might say
All I wanna do
Streets of Philadelphia
Braveheart

QUEEN'S GALLANTRY MEDAL
15/2/95

Kemp	Edward	Police Constable	187988 Y
Kielty	Patrick	Police Constable	189366 Y

On Monday 25th November 1991 at about 5 pm three masked suspects entered a building society as the staff were closing, and locking the cash and valuables away in a safe. The staff were confronted by the three suspects, one of whom was brandishing a sawn off double barrelled shot gun. All the members of staff were put into an office and made to lie on the floor while the contents of the safe were stolen. A member of the public raised the alarm and constable Kemp and Sergeant Kielty who were on patrol nearby responded. When they arrived at the building they made their way to the rear to investigate, and were confronted by the three robbers as they fled the building. The first robber who was the tallest carried a sawn off single barrelled shot gun, which he then levelled at the officers. The second suspect carried a sawn off double barrelled shotgun, and the third man, who was the shortest of the three carried a large holdall which contained the proceeds of the robbery. The two officers took cover behind a parked vehicle until the suspects ran off, they then immediately gave chase. The tallest robber suddenly stopped at a corner and turned to face the pursuing officers. The other two robbers ran up to the gunman as he levelled the shotgun at the officers. He told them to stay back and with the two officers no more than 15 yards away from him fired at them both. The officers momentarily checked their progress and could see that the shortest of the robbers had by then dropped the heavy bag and remained on the corner. He then pulled out a pistol from his waistband and with his two hands levelled the gun at constable Kemp who by now was only a yard or two from him. The constable stopped immediately in front of the man, while Sergeant Keilty joined him. The man shouted at them to stay back or he would shoot. Both the officers then stopped when faced with this very real and dangerous threat. The man with the pistol then turned and began to run away. Sergeant Keilty and constable Kemp then continued to chase on foot. Constable Kemp was able to rugby tackle the suspect from behind, bringing him down onto the pavement. Sergeant Keilty then joined him at once and both the officers began to struggle violently with the suspect but managed to restrain him. The officers were aware of the situation with regards the firearm and managed to prevent him from moving his arms during the struggle. At this time the taller of the suspects with the discharged single barrelled shotgun hovered indecisively about 15 yards away. The suspect who was on the floor managed to shout for help but the constable forced his hand across the suspects mouth to prevent him from shouting out again. The other suspect then turned and ran out of sight. The man was then arrested with the assistance of another officer.

QUEEN'S COMMENDATION FOR BRAVE CONDUCT
15/2/1995

Benedetti	Stephen	Police Constable	189213 W
Jones	Julie	Woman Police Constable	8936 W
Rook	James Robert	Police Constable	171313 W

The occupant of a house notified police of a man in the street with a gun which had been pushed through his letter box. Constables Rook and Jones were on mobile patrol, saw the gunman getting into a parked vehicle. They were aware that he may still be armed, they approached and stopped him. During a subsequent search of his pockets constable Rook found two shotgun cartridges. At this point he tried to arrest the gunman, the man then became violent. A struggle ensued in which the officer was pushed away, this gave the gunman time to draw a sawn off shotgun which he had hidden under his coat. Constable Rook then managed to grab hold of the gun and a violent tug of war commenced. Constable Rook was quickly joined by constable Jones who had been calling for urgent assistance. She too displayed bravery in trying to subdue the extremely strong and violent gunman. A few moments later constable Benedetti arrived to assist his colleagues. As he did so the shotgun was pointed at him. Constable Rook managed to push it to one side and at this point it went off, discharging into the side of constable Benedetti's vehicle a matter of inches from his head. The suspect was still shouting threats and struggling violently. Constable Benedetti joined constables Rook and Jones in attempting to disarm the gunman, but it took the arrival of another two officers, who joined in the struggle, before the gunman was eventually disarmed and restrained.

QUEEN'S COMMENDATION FOR BRAVE CONDUCT
15/2/1995

Castrey	Simon	Police Constable	191045 Z
Jenkinson	John	Police Constable	184011 Z

Constables Castrey and Jenkinson were on mobile patrol when they saw two men in a parked up car. Suspecting the vehicle had been stolen, they called for assistance and began to question the men. Without warning, one of the men who was out of the vehicle, turned away from constable Jenkinson, he instantly swung back and stabbed him in the neck causing the officer to collapse to the ground. The other man in the meantime, ran off. As soon as he realised his colleague was in trouble, constable Castrey turned his attention towards constable Jenkinson. At that point the man came towards him, stabbing him in the face and neck and knocking him to the ground. As constable Castrey fell, the man returned to constable Jenkinson, held the knife close to his face and demanded the keys to the police car. Despite his injuries and in the face of the mans threats, the officer held on to the keys. Constable Castrey, seeing the desperate situation of his colleague, tried to stand up, attempting to draw his truncheon. The man saw this, left constable Jenkinson and returned to attack constable Castrey. In spite of further blows to the head, however, the officer wrestled with the man and succeeded in hitting him with the truncheon, forcing him to run off. Constable Castrey managed to run after him, almost catching the man. Both officers were severely injured in this incident.

QUEEN'S COMMENDATION FOR BRAVE CONDUCT
15/2/1995

Dudley	Martin	Police Constable	175343 P
Hitchings	Julie	Woman Police Sergeant	5503 P

Constable Dudley and Sergeant Hitchings were on patrol with another officer when they spotted two men acting suspiciously. Sergeant Hitchings went to speak to one of the men, constable Dudley went to her assistance when the man became violent. The man stabbed the constable in the arm initially, with a flick knife, before going berserk and stabbing the officer repeatedly. Although constable Dudley realised he had been seriously injured, he nonetheless continued to struggle with his assailant, so preventing him from either escaping or giving help to his accomplice. Sergeant Hitchings had turned to help a third colleague contain the second man, who had also become violent. When she noticed constable Dudley's situation, she returned to help him in his struggle with the knifeman. She managed to prise the knife from the man's grasp and the officers kept him away from his weapon until other police arrived and both suspects were arrested.

Martin Dudley sustained 11 knife wounds requiring some 36 stitches, the main artery in his arm was slashed, both lungs collapsed, one kidney was pierced, and in total he lost 2-3 pints of blood.

The suspect later received a term of 14yrs imprisonment at the Old Bailey for attempted murder.

QUEEN'S COMMENDATION FOR BRAVE CONDUCT
15/2/1995

Goodson	Colin John	Explosives Officer	SO13
Myring	Paul Terence	Explosives Officer	SO13

'For services in respect of courage and professional skill in examining massive booby-trapped improvised explosive devices, making them safe and recovering the constituent parts.'

QUEEN'S COMMENDATION FOR BRAVE CONDUCT
Posthumous
15/2/1995

King	Alan Derek	Police Sergeant	160284 J

Sergeant King was on duty in his police car and at about 1 am he appears to have gone to investigate a man he had seen acing suspiciously near a parked vehicle. The police car double parked alongside the suspect vehicle, and witnesses from the houses opposite describe being woken by shouting and seeing Sergeant King being attacked in a fierce struggle in the roadway by a man connected with the suspect car. He was seen to fall to the ground and the attacker walked away from him towards some nearby flats. Sergeant King then got up and staggered down the road flagging down an approaching car. He was unable to use his radio microphone as the connecting wire had been cut in the struggle. The attacker saw this and ran after Sergeant King shouting that he was going to get him. Catching up with the Sergeant as he was about to get into the car the man was seen to further stab him about the chest causing fatal injuries. The attacker, then joined by an accomplice, moved the police car and drove off in their own vehicle.

QUEEN'S COMMENDATION FOR BRAVE CONDUCT

Buckmaster	Colin	Police Constable	191167 HB

Summers	David	Police Constable	173937 PD
Brown	Bryan	Police Constable	162777 PD
Falkingham	Neil	Police Constable	187619 YT
Phipps	Richard	Police Constable	186228 YT
Heggie	James	Police Constable	175466 AB

ROLL OF HONOUR

• Pc Phillip Walters, 194004 J

During the evening of 18th April whilst on duty in uniform, constable Walters attended a disturbance call at a house in Ilford. He was confronted by three men at the house and in a brave attempt to detain them, struggled with one of the men who drew a gun and shot constable Walters at point blank range in the chest. He later died from his wounds.

• Pc George Pickburn Hammond QPM

Died from complications which followed severe stab wounds he sustained while making an arrest in 1985.

1996

January	Blizzard sweeps across the East coast of the US, New Yorkers have to ski to work.
February	IRA bomb explodes in the Docklands, 2 die. This ends the ceasefire of 17 months.
March	Dunblane massacre, Thomas Hamilton shoots dead 16 young children and a teacher at a local school.
April	In New York Pepsi Cola re launches its image with a new blue can to distinguish it from its rival Coca Cola.
May	In Florida a DC-9 airliner crashes in the Everglades killing 109.
June	IRA bomb blasts the heart of Manchester, over 200 injured.
July	Boeing 747 jumbo jet explodes 45 minutes after take off from JFK airport and plunges into the Atlantic off Long Island, 228 die.
August	Prince and Princess of Wales divorce.
September	IRA terrorist Diarmuid O'Neill is shot dead by police in Hammersmith, London.
October	British Government plans to outlaw the private possession of hand guns following the Dunblane massacre.
November	127 died when a hijacked Ethiopian airlines jet crashes into the Indian Ocean after running out of fuel.
December	Madeline Albright becomes the first woman US Secretary of State.

HITS OF THE YEAR

Design for Life
Champagne supernova
The English patient

QUEEN'S GALLANTRY MEDAL
29/2/96

Boyce	David	Police Constable	186313 W
O'Brien	Mark John	Police Constable	193293 W

Both constables Boyce and O'Brien received a call reporting an armed robbery in progress. O'Brien who was on foot was the first officer to arrive on scene. He was followed shortly after by Boyce who was in a police van. They both joined forces and followed the robbers who had been seen to be armed and who were heading for a stolen van in which they tried to escape. It was at this point that one of the robbers walked towards the police van and fired a shot which hit the windscreen and showered both Boyce and O'Brien with shattered glass. Both officers then left their vehicle and O'Brien ran to warn fellow officers who were at that time arriving to assist. In the meantime the robbers had returned to their vehicle in order to escape. When he noticed this, Boyce got back into the police van and pursued them, he was followed by a police car carrying O'Brien and other officers. The robbers' van crashed a little later on, and further shots were fired at Boyce in the police vehicle. The robbers then hijacked a police car which had also been following them, forcing the occupants out at gunpoint. Boyce had, by then, been rejoined in his van by O'Brien, they rammed the hijacked police car twice knowing full well that the robbers would not hesitate to use their weapons. The robbers did however manage to escape but a further chase followed until they crashed the hijacked police car. The first robber got out of the car and aimed his gun at Boyce, who had by now stopped his van nearby and got out to cover the robbers. At this point armed officers arrived and arrested robber one who gave himself up.

QUEEN'S GALLANTRY MEDAL
Posthumous
1/3/96

Robertson	Derek John	Police Sergeant	164954 Z

On Wednesday 9 February 1994 Sergeant Robertson along with another officer went to investigate a suspected armed robbery at a post office. There being nothing apparently wrong he sent the officer to the front of the premises while he remained at the rear. Seconds later three masked robbers came out of the rear door, one was holding a knife to the Postmaster's throat. The robber then told Sergeant Robertson to stay back, which he did, though he continued describing the scene on his radio. While his two companions ran away (to be arrested shortly afterwards by police arriving at the scene), the armed robber then moved through the garden, with Sergeant Robertson moving with him at a short distance. The robber then pushed his hostage aside and made an attempt to escape. The Sergeant, who was not wearing any protective clothing, stood his ground attempting to prevent the robbers escape and hitting the robber with his truncheon. He was unable to defend himself against the frenzied knife attack by the robber whose escape he was preventing, and fell dying from a series of major stab wounds.

QUEEN'S COMMENDATION FOR BRAVE CONDUCT
1/3/1996

Alston	Phillip David	Police Constable	179615 SO19
Bell	David McKinnon	Police Constable	182276 SO19
Hilton	William Morris	Police Constable	191077 TSG
Oldroyd-Jones	Barry	Police Constable	178366 SO19

After an armed robbery two of the robbers had tried to escape, at first in a stolen van, and then in a hijacked police car. During this incident the robbers had fired shots at two officers who were following them, and had threatened others when hijacking the police car at gunpoint. Eventually the hijacked car crashed and one of the robbers was arrested. At that stage robber 2 made his escape on foot followed closely by Constables Bell (armed) and Hilton (unarmed) who had just arrived. During the chase both Bell and Hilton were fired at and hit by shot gun pellets. The robber also took a passer-by hostage. The two constables followed the robber into residential streets where they lost sight of him. As the constables continued to search for the robber, knowing they could by ambushed, they were joined by fellow constables Oldroyd-Jones and Alston, who were armed and protected by body armour. At that moment robber 2 emerged from his hiding place and fired at constable Oldroyd-Jones hitting him in the legs and causing him to collapse. Constable Hilton moved to help Oldroyd-Jones, putting himself in view of the robbers position and therefore in considerable danger. Constable Alston moved to a forward exposed position to protect his fellow officers and with constable Bell prepared to approach the robber. At this point the robber shot himself.

QUEEN'S COMMENDATION FOR BRAVE CONDUCT
1/3/1996

Haywood-Trimming	Colin Leslie	Superintendent	155030 SO14 MVO

Whist on a Royal tour in Australia, HRH the Prince of Wales was due to present awards in front of a crowd of around 20,000 people in Sydney. Superintendent Haywood-Trimming was seated a short distance behind the place where the Prince of Wales stood awaiting the announcement of the winners. At the time he was seated in deference to Australian Federal Government regulations. As the Prince waited, Superintendent Haywood-Trimming heard a sound which was similar to that of a gun firing, and saw a young man approach the stage at speed with what looked like a gun in his hand. He then heard another shot and saw smoke coming from the barrel of a gun held by the young man. Believing that the life of The Prince of Wales was in danger, Superintendent Haywood-Trimming moved to place himself between the gunman and his target. After pushing The Prince of Wales out of the line of danger he turned to face the gunman ready to tackle him. At this moment further members of the protection team, who were not on the stage, managed to deal with the gunman. Although the attacker's gun was later found to be a starting pistol, Superintendent Haywood-Trimming had no way of knowing this and had to assume it was a real firearm.

QUEEN'S COMMENDATION FOR BRAVE CONDUCT
1/3/1996

Macaskill	John	lately Police Constable	162378 Z
Redford	Peter	Detective Constable	160388 SO8
Stubbs	Michael	Detective Sergeant	167550 SO8
Swinfield	John	Detective Sergeant	179469 SO8

A police surveillance operation was set up after extensive investigations had indicated that there was a likelihood of an armed robbery taking place. The police had planned to arrest the suspects as soon as the robbery started. However at that moment the surveillance team lost sight of the robbers behind a high sided vehicle. Once the police realised that the robbery had in fact taken place, they moved to arrest the robbers who had by then had reached their getaway vehicle. The robbers managed to evade roadblocks and a high speed chase ensued with the four officers, Stubbs, Swinfield Redford and Macaskill in the pursuing police car. During the chase, the police car was fired at on two occasions by a machine gun. On the two occasions, some rounds entered their vehicle, and one bullet injured Stubbs in the left temple. Despite the danger, constable Macaskill, the driver, was urged to continue the chase and only stopped when shots from a heavy calibre Magnum pistol damaged the police car's engine. The robbers were later arrested.

QUEEN'S COMMENDATION FOR BRAVE CONDUCT

Keyte	Andrew	Police Constable	176939 P
Wright	Deborah	Woman Police Constable	8118 P

QUEEN'S COMMENDATION FOR BRAVE CONDUCT

Ritchie	Carl	Police Constable	

Arresting a male who was concerned with fraud at a post office, the officer sustained personal injury. With the assistance of a colleague chased and captured the male.

Carl Ritchie was stabbed in the ribs, the suspect was charged with attempted murder, and the officer was off sick for 8 months.

ROLL OF HONOUR
• Pc Stephen Robert Williams
Motorcyclist killed in a crash on DPG duties in North London.

1997

January	Diana, Princess of Wales walks through a mine field as she attempts to publicise the plight of people killed by anti personnel mines.
February	3 men who were jailed for 18 years for the murder of school boy Carl Bridgewater are freed by the Court of Appeal.
March	'Heavens Gate' cult followers commit mass suicide in the hope they will be transported to a UFO hiding in the tail of the Hale Bopp Comet.
April	IRA bomb threat disrupts the 150th Grand National.

May	Labour wins a landslide victory.
June	William Hague becomes the new leader of the Conservative party.
July	US space shuttle Atlantis docks with the troubled Mir space station to deliver equipment and supplies.
August	Country in mourning at the death of Diana, Princess of Wales.
September	Passenger train crashes into a freight train at Southall London 6 die and over 150 injured.
October	British nanny Louise Woodward is sentenced to life for the murder of baby Matthew Eappen.
November	70, including 60 foreign tourists, are gunned down at Luxor in Egypt by Islamic extremists.
December	The Royal Yacht Britannia is decommissioned, the last in the line of Royal Yachts.

HITS OF THE YEAR

Spice up your life
Candle in the wind
D'you know what I mean
Titanic

QUEEN'S GALLANTRY MEDAL
Award of the Bar

14/6/97

Kielty	Patrick	Police Sergeant	189366 Y QGM

Sergeant Kielty was with a colleague who were on patrol in a police van when they were told that a man had taken a 5 yr old girl hostage at knifepoint and that he had driven off in a hijacked car. Sergeant Kielty and his colleague caught up with the suspect's car as it crashed into a parked van. The man then approached the police van from which the officers had just dismounted, holding the hostage in one arm and making stabbing motions at her with a knife. The man tried to drive away in the police van, but the keys had been removed. It was at this point that the Sergeant tried to reason with the man but he became even more agitated and then ran off down the street still holding and making threats against the child. While he was running down the street he was trying to open car doors. The Sergeant followed him along with the other officer they kept other officers informed of the situation by their radios. The man stopped again and raised the knife as if to stab the young hostage. The Sergeant rushed forward and tackled the man. During the following struggle the Sergeant narrowly missed injury from the knife which had in fact passed between his body and his upper arm. The hostage at this time managed to break free and run to safety. The man also managed to break free and run but he was closely followed by Sergeant Kielty. The man then jumped through a window of a house door, and once he was inside he stabbed one of the occupants and took the other woman as a hostage. He then left the house with the second hostage held at knife point, again he tried to open the car doors parked in the street. Sergeant Kielty knowing that other officers were close to him tried to reason with the kidnapper. In the meantime the kidnapper approached another house and this time tried unsuccessfully to kick in the front door. The man then raised the knife as if to stab the hostage, and at this point Sergeant Kielty rushed forward and grabbed the hand that was holding the knife. He managed to hold his grip while other officers assisted in arresting the kidnapper and releasing the hostage unharmed.

QUEEN'S GALLANTRY MEDAL
13/11/97

Fitzpatrick   Anthony   Police Constable   192777

Constable Fitzpatrick was on mobile patrol along with two colleagues when they became suspicious of a car that was being driven erratically, and which they believed may have been stolen. They stopped the car and started to question the driver, while the passenger stood by the car's passenger door. While the officers were questioning the driver, the passenger became tense and started acting suspiciously, he was attempting to put his hands into concealed pockets. Constable Fitzpatrick told him to stop, but the passenger continued to move his hand whereby the constable moved forward to gain hold of the suspect. As he did so the suspect pushed him away and ran off, constable Fitzpatrick along with another constable chased after him. After a short distance the suspect stopped, turned and faced the constable and his colleague and pointed a small pistol at him and shouted that he was going to kill him. The suspect then walked up the constable Fitzpatrick who then drew his baton and as the suspect got close enough, hit him twice with the baton. The man fired the gun twice once after each baton strike, the second shot hit constable Fitzpatrick in the leg. The man ran off again and was again followed by constable Fitzpatrick, his colleague again was close behind him. While the chase was going on the constable warned his colleague to stay back and he then took the lead role as the suspect stopped. The suspect continued to fire on the constable and on one occasion at least one bullet narrowly missed him. The constable took evasive action when the gun was fired, but he continued the pursuit until the suspect finally disappeared into a housing estate. The constable decided to inform his control room of the whereabouts of the gunman and to report his own injury and seek assistance to stem the bleeding. The armed man was later arrested by armed police officers.

QUEEN'S COMMENDATION FOR BRAVE CONDUCT
14/6/1997

Collins   Stephen Daniel   Police Constable   194306 X

Constable Collins, along with a colleague, was on patrol in a police vehicle when they stopped a car after it was apparently racing with another car. The constables then became suspicious as the replies to their questions became evasive. While his colleague continued to question the driver, constable Collins started a search of the vehicle. Then he turned his attention to the passenger, who had since moved to stand next to the car. Constable Collins began to search the passenger, who was keeping his right hand in his pocket, he asked him to remove his hand. The passenger was reluctant to do so, so constable Collins pulled at his arm. In doing this he managed to pull the passengers hand from his pocket which revealed a gun. Both officers immediately backed away. The suspect then fired twice towards constable Collins, from about five and then 10 - 12 feet. He then started to fumble with the gun. On seeing this constable Collins rushed the suspect and during the ensuing struggle the gun was fired again at the constable. The suspect ran off and was closely followed by the driver of the car and by constable Collins with his colleague. After a short distance constable Collins was asked if he had been hit by a bullet, and in response to his colleague's question he stopped. Realising that he had a bullet wound to his chest, he stopped chasing the suspects who were followed by his colleague. Eventually the gunman was arrested by tracker dogs and armed police.

QUEEN'S COMMENDATION FOR BRAVE CONDUCT

Alan	Neil	Police Constable	183507 YT
Barton	David	Police Constable	183123 YE
Davies	Paul	Police Constable	179027 YE
Dean	Robert	Police Constable	189188 YE
Hooper	Derek	Police Constable	163264 YE
Mabbott	Adrian	Police Constable	192074 YE
Diver	Anthony	Police Constable	184319 KG
Hall	David	Police Constable	187910

ROYAL HUMANE SOCIETY BRONZE MEDAL

Murray	Philip	Police Constable	175268 XH
Woodroffe	Evelyn	Police Constable	195289 XH

For rescuing a man who had been trapped in a burning vehicle following a road traffic accident.

ROLL OF HONOUR

Wpc Nina Mackay, 974, 3 area TSG, aged 25

During the evening of 24th October 1997 whilst on duty constable Mackay attended a house in Forest Gate in support of officers to effect the arrest of a man known to be violent towards police. She was confronted by the man and whilst attempting to detain him she was fatally stabbed.

1998

January	Prime Minister of Japan Ryutaro Hashimoto apologises to British PM for atrocities committed in W.W.II.
February	Details of the Millennium Dome launched.
March	Over 250,000 march in London about concerns for the countryside.
April	Torrential rain and severe floods hit England.
May	Italy declares a state of emergency due to severe flooding and mud slides.
June	100 die and 200 are critically injured in Germany when a high speed train crashes into a concrete bridge.
July	World's largest airport open in Hong Kong.
August	The IRA bomb Omagh, Co. Tyrone, killing 29 and injuring more that 200.

September   Iran today announced it would not assist or encourage the assassination of Salman Rushdie.

October   British police arrest General Pinochet of Chile.

November   10 agricultural ministers from the European Union voted to lift the ban on the sale and export of British beef.

December   President Clinton is impeached for perjury and obstruction of Justice.

HITS OF THE YEAR

My heart will go on
Angel
Shakespeare in love

QUEEN'S COMMENDATION FOR BRAVE CONDUCT

20/11/98

McGlinchey	Kevin William Daniel	Police Constable	179939 MD
Wright	Jonathan Lee	Police Constable	191489 MD

'Arrest of four armed robbers.'

Shepherd	Derek Howard	Police Constable	182902 JI

'Arrest of an armed suspect.'

ROLL OF HONOUR

• Dc Ian Herbert

Killed in a road accident while engaged on a training exercise in Kent.

1999

January   The birth of the single European currency, the Euro.

February   In Austria 30 die in an avalanche at Galtur 2 weeks after 12 die in Chamonix, Mont Blanc, France.

March   Czech Republic, Hungary and Poland all join NATO.

April   Nail bomb attacks in Brick Lane and Brixton in London.

May   Bomb goes off in a Soho Pub kills 3 and injures 73.

June   Royal wedding of Prince Edward to Sophie Rhys-Jones.

July   The Welsh assembly assumes full control.

August   An eclipse of the sun takes place over England, total eclipse in Cornwall.

September   Chauffeur is held to blame for the deaths of Diana, Princess of Wales and Dodi Fayed.

October   Paddington rail crash, 27 die.

November   US, Bill Gates of Microsoft donates $26 million to UNICEF.

December   Boris Yeltsin resigns as Russian leader.

QUEEN'S COMMENDATION FOR BRAVE CONDUCT

22/1/99

McGlinchey	Kevin	Police Constable	179939 MD

| Wright | Jonathan | Police Constable | 191489 MD |
| Shepherd | Derek | Police Constable | 182902 JI |

ROYAL HUMANE SOCIETY BRONZE MEDAL

Banfield	Christopher	Police Constable	185525 DP
Hayward	Andrew	Police Constable	177164
Oliver	Christopher	Police Constable	192069

For their actions in rescuing a man from a burning building block of residential flats despite the risk of an explosion from 2 butane gas cylinders.

ROLL OF HONOUR

•   Pc Kulwant Singh S'dhu, 196278, TW, aged 24

During the late evening of 25 October 1999, whilst on duty Pc Sidhu was pursuing 2 suspects across the roof of a garage in Twickenham. After the suspects had been talked down from the roof, the officer was found to be missing. Following a search by colleagues they found that Pc Sidhu had fallen through the roof receiving fatal injuries.

Chapter 12

THE FINAL YEARS 2000 - 2004

This is the start of a new era, a new millennium. But we have already seen our fair share of troubles and sadness.

Within one year we lost 2 members of our Royal Family, HRH Princess Margaret and one of the best loved royals HM Queen Elizabeth the Queen Mother.

A new terror threat, unleashed on the USA, two aircraft bring down the twin towers of the World Trade Centre in New York, and thousands lose their lives. War is declared on terrorism by the President of America George Bush.

War again takes place in Iraq, this time their leader Saddam Hussain is forced from power and finally captured alive while trying to hide. Many lose their lives in this war both civilians in Iraq and the soldiers sent to free them from this dictator.

2000

ROLL OF HONOUR

2001

ROLL OF HONOUR
- Pc Anthony Ian Haines
Killed while his police car crashed responding to a domestic violence incident at Lewisham.
- Pc Jeremy Scandrett
Killed in a motorcycle accident at Wrotham Kent, while travelling to duty at Lambeth.
- Inspector Alan Douglas Jamieson
Killed in a road accident while cycling to his home in Billericay from duty at Scotland Yard.
- Pc Steven Frank Crawley
Killed in a motorcycle accident at Hounslow while travelling for night duty at Harrow.

2002

ROYAL HUMANE SOCIETY BRONZE MEDAL
29/11/2002
Johnson   Paul   Pc 195365   YR
For saving a man from jumping off a road bridge 150 feet above Archway Road.

ROYAL HUMANE SOCIETY BRONZE MEDAL
POLICE MEDAL ROYAL HUMANE SOCIETY
10/5/02

Brown	Paul	Police Constable	KF

In December 2001 in Dagenham, Pc Paul Brown along with Pc Peter Wilson returning home from a fancy dress party saw a vehicle on fire; the vehicle was suspended over some railings. One occupant had escaped but 2 were still trapped inside. Pc Brown saw the 2 occupants trapped by the passenger door. He tried to open the door without success, so clambered into the vehicle through the broken windscreen. He dragged the first occupant out of the vehicle. By this time the fire was spreading rapidly. After the first male was clear of the car he went back and rescued the second male. By now the car was engulfed in flames. Pc Brown gave mouth to mouth to the first man whose pulse was very weak, his colleague gave him cardiac massage, but sadly they were not able to save him. The other man did however survive.

ROLL OF HONOUR

2003

ROLL OF HONOUR
• Pc Tokunbo Ezobi, LX
Died in a road traffic accident while travelling home to his family after duty on Lambeth Division New Years Eve.

2004

QUEEN'S COMMENDATION FOR BRAVE CONDUCT
2004

Archer	Jeremy	Police Constable	WW
Woodhouse	Nicholas	Police Constable	WW

The officers were involved in a dramatic car chase through Putney in January 2001. When the suspect's vehicle hit heavy traffic the passenger jumped out and ran into an alley, pursued by Pc Archer. The suspect tried to pull a gun from his pocket when he realised he was in a dead end. A violent struggle followed in which Pc Archer found himself staring at a gun pointed at his stomach, but he persisted in trying to restrain the suspect and forced him to drop the gun. The man ran off before he could be handcuffed but Pc Archer caught up with him in a nearby garden, where he was arrested.

Meanwhile Pc Woodhouse was chasing the second suspect down another dead end alley. He saw the suspect enter a garden where a party was taking place. Fearing that the man was armed and a risk to party goers. Pc Woodhouse dragged him back into the alley, where he was handcuffed and arrested.

ROLL OF HONOUR

Appendix 1

Metropolitan Police
Multiple Gallantry Awards

Craig and Bentley incident

Detective Constable Frederick William Fairfax		GC
Police Constable Norman Harrison		GM
Police Constable James Christie McDonald		GM
Police Constable Robert James William Jaggs		BEM
Police Constable Sidney George Miles	**Posthumous**	KPM

Armed escaped prisoner

Inspector Phillip Pawsey	**Posthumous**	QPM
Sergeant Frederick George Hutchins	**Posthumous**	QPM
Police Constable Edward Cox		GM
Police Constable Charles England		BEM

Attempted Kidnap of HRH Princess Ann

Inspector James Wallace Beaton		GC
Police Constable Michael John Hills		GM
Police Constable Peter Roy Edmonds		QGM

Balcombe Street Siege

Inspector Henry Dowswell	GM
Police Sergeant Murtach Phillip McVeigh	GM
Inspector John Francis Purnell	GM
Police Constable Andrew Stephen Claiden	QGM
Police Constable Barry Charles Court	QGM
Police Constable Robert Fenton	QGM
Police Constable Stephen Phillip Knight	QGM
Police Sergeant William Mansfield	QGM
Police Constable Ian Michael Chadburn	QCBC
Inspector James Robert Wells	QCBC
Police Constable Peter James Wilson	QCBC

Broadwater Farm Riot

Police Sergeant David Hugh Pengelly		GM
Police Constable Keith Blakelock	**Posthumous**	QGM
Police Constable Ricky Pandya		QGM
Police Constable Maxwell Roberts		QGM
Police Constable Alan Tappy		QGM
Police Constable Richard Coombes		QGM
Police Constable Michael Shepherd		QGM
Police Constable Stephen Martin		QGM
Police Constable Kenneth Milne		QGM
Police Constable Robin Clark		QGM
Police Constable Miles Barton		QGM
Police Constable Martin Howells		QGM

Appendix 2

Metropolitan Police
Posthumous Gallantry Awards

George Cross

Captain Roger Philip Goad BEM   Explosives Officer

Queen's Police Medal for Gallantry

Temporary Police Sergeant Leonard Demmon (attached to the UK Police Unit, Cyprus)
Police Sergeant Frederick George Hutchins
Inspector Philip Pawsey
Police Constable Stephen Andrew Tibble
Police Constable Michael Anthony Whiting

King's Police Medal for Gallantry

Police Constable Edward George Brown Greenoff
Police Constable Sidney George Miles
Police Constable James Warrender Thompson

George Medal

Kenneth Robert Howorth   Explosives Officer

Queen's Gallantry Medal

Police Constable Keith Blakelock
Police Constable Francis Joseph O'Neill
Detective Constable James Morrison
Police Sergeant Derek Robertson

Appendix 3

Abbreviations

Medals

AM	Albert Medal
A/Ps	Acting Police Sergeant
B	Binney Memorial Medal
BEM	British Empire Medal
C	Carnegie Hero Fund
Capt	Captain
CI	Chief Inspector
Dc	Detective Constable
DCI	Detective Chief Inspector
DI	Detective Inspector
Ds	Detective Sergeant
Expo	Explosives Officer (Civilian or Army)
GC	George Cross
GM	George Medal
Insp	Inspector
KPM	King's Police Medal
LG	London Gazette
Maj	Major
P	Posthumous Award
Pc	Police Constable
Ps	Police Sergeant
RHS	Royal Humane Society
QGM	Queen's Gallantry Medal
QPM	Queen's Police Medal
S Insp	Station Inspector
Supt	Superintendent
Spc	Special Police Constable
S/Ps	Station Sergeant
Sub Div Insp	Sub Divisional Inspector
Wpc	Woman Police Constable
Wps	Woman Police Sergeant
WrPc	War Reserve Police Constable

Departments

CO	Commissioners Office (New Scotland Yard)
CO A2	Police Dogs
CO A8	Public Order
CO B6	Traffic
CO B8	Traffic
CO B12	Traffic
CO C1	Serious Crime Squads
CO C7	Explosives Officers
CO C8	Flying Squad
CO C10	Stolen Motor Vehicle Squad
CO C11	Criminal Intelligence
CO C12	Special branch
CO C13	Anti Terrorist Branch
CO D3	Welfare
CO D11	Police War Duties
DPG	Diplomatic Protection Group
RCS	Regional Crime Squad
SPG	Special Patrol Group
TSG	Territorial Support Group

Appendix 4

Index of Medal Recipients

Key to Awards

AM	Albert Medal	1866
KPM	King's Police Medal	1909
QPM	Queen's Police Medal - Posthumous award	1954
GC	George Cross	1940
GM	George Medal	1940
BEM	British Empire Medal for Gallantry (Civil Division)	1922
QGM	Queen's Gallantry Medal	1974
KC	King's Commendation	1939
QC	Queen's Commendation	1952
RHS	Royal Humane Society Bronze Medal	1774
C	Carnegie Hero Fund	1908
B	Binney Medal	1947
RSPCA	Margaret Wheatley Cross or Society Medal	

Abbott, John	Ps	KPM	Crime	1921
Abbs, Robert H C	Wrpc	BEM	Evacuation	1944
Adams, Michael B	Pc	QC	Rescue	1981
Adams, Raymond C	Dc	BEM	Crime	1969
Adamson, James D	Pc	KPM	Attempted Rescue	1931
Adamson	Pc	RHS	Rescue	1930
Airton, James	Pc	KPM	Rescue	1936
Akrigg, John	Pc	QC	Crime	1965
Aldred, Thomas	Pc	QC	Crime	1969
Alan, Neil	Pc	QC		1997
Allan, Thomas	Pc	QC	Crime	1968
Allen, Joseph	Pc	KPM	Runaway horse	1924
Allen, Reginald A	Pc	KC	Civil defence	1945
Allen, William H	Pc	GM	Rescue	1941
Allison, Bertram	Pc	KPM	Crime	1921
Allison, Robert	Pc	QC	Crime	1969
Allport, John	Pc	QGM	Crime	1977
Almond, Charles F	Spc	GM	Rescue	1941
Alston, Philip D	Pc	QC	Crime	1996
Archer, Herbert	Pc	KPM	Rescue	1917
Archer, Herbert	Pc	C	Rescue	1916
Archer, Jeremy	Pc	QC	Crime	2004
Arnold, Clive L	Pc	BEM	Crime	1969
Arnold, Ronald J	Pc	BEM	Crime	1973

Arram, Edward	Pc	KC	Rescue	1947
Ashwin, Owen P	Pc	GM	Crime	1951
Askew, Arthur	Pc	KPM	Crime	1917
Atkins, Richard H M	Pc	KC	Civil defence	1940
Atkinson, Francis D	Pc	QC	Crime	1973
Austin, Samuel	Pc	RHS	Rescue	1990
Avery	Insp	C	Rescue	1919
Babbidge, Terrence	Ps	QC	Crime	1973
Bacon, Charles	Ps	KPM	Rescue	1930
Bailey, John R T	Dc	GM	Crime	1954
Bailey, Kenneth A	Pc	GM	Crime	1952
Bailey, Kevin C	Pc	QC		1990
Bailey, Ronald T	Ps	KPM	Crime	1939
Baker, Cecil J P	Ps	QC	Crime	1972
Baker, Donald E	Ps	QC	Crime	1976
Baker, Peter G	Pc	QC	Crime	1982
Baker, John	Pc	QC	Crime	1979
Baker, Robert H	Pc	KPM	Crime	1931
Baldry, Robert J	Ps	QC	Crime	1978
Baldwin, George K F	Pc	QC	Crime	1953
Baldwin	Pc	QC		1971
Baldwin, Walter	Pc	KPM	Rescue	1912
Banfield, Christopher	Pc	RHS	Rescue	1999
Bannister, Jack	Pc	QC	Crime	1977
Bannister, John	Ps	KPM	Rescue	1942
Bannister	Ps	C	Rescue	1942
Barclay, Francis H	Pc	RHS	Rescue	1903
Barker, Leonard	Supt	QC	Crime	1967
Barlow, Jack	Dc	BEM	Crime	1948
Barnes, Barrie K	Pc	QC	Crime	1970
Barnes, Dennis	Ps	QC	Crime	1976
Barnes, Douglas M	Pc	KPM	Crime	1942
Barnett, Harold	Pc	C	Runaway horse	1930
Barnett, Helen F	Wpc	QC	Crime	1994
Barrett, Joseph C	Pc	BEM	Crime	1946
Barrett, John H	Pc	BEM	Crime	1966
Barry, Michael	Pc	KPM	Rescue	1912
Bartholomew, Norman	Pc	BEM	Rescue	1963
Bartlett, Dennis M B	Dc	BEM	Crime	1966
Bartlett, Gilbert J A	Insp.	BEM	Rescue	1941
Barton, David	Pc	QC		1997
Barton, James T	Pc	KPM	Crime	1941
Barton, Miles	Pc	QGM	Broadwater Farm Riot	1988
Barwick, Harry C V	Pc	KPM	Rescue	1932
Bass, Harry	Ps	GM	Rescue	1941
Bates, Harry J	Insp.	GM	Rescue	1941
Bathgate, Edward K	Insp	QC	Crime	1981
Batten, Peter J	Ps	QC	Crime	1980
Baxter, John M	Dc	KPM	Crime	1949
Bazire, Paul L	Pc	QC	Crime	1978

Beacham, Henry	Pc	KPM	Crime	1930
Beale, Thomas	Pc	KPM	Runaway horse	1948
Beasley	Pc	RHS	Rescue	1968
Beaton, James W	Insp.	GC	Kidnap attempt	1974
Beavis, Frank G	Insp.	KPM	Crime	1943
Bedwell, Edward M	Wrpc	KC	Civil Defence	1941
Beer, James A R	Pc	QC	Crime	1974
Beesley, Alfred	Ds	KPM	Crime	1924
Bell, David McK	Pc	QC	Crime	1996
Bellamy, Arthur R	Pc	KPM	Attempted rescue	1919
Bellamy, Arthur R	Pc	C	Rescue	1918
Bellinger, James	DI	KPM	Crime	1926
Bence, Alfred	Pc	KPM	Rescue	1918
Benedetti, Stephen	Pc	QC	Crime	1995
Bennett, Frederick E	Sub Div Insp	KC	Civil Defence	1941 P
Bentley, Robert	City Police	KPM	Sidney Street	1911
Berrett, James	Pc	RHS	Rescue	1893
Berry, Robert B	Pc	QC		1959
Bertram, John L	Pc	KPM	Crime	1931
Biddle, Geoffrey W	Major	BEM	Defusing bomb IRA	1973
Biddle, Geoffrey W	Major	GM	Defusing bomb IRA	1976
Biggs, Henry	Pc	RHS	Rescue	1906
Bignal	Wrpc	BEM	Rescue	1941
Binning, Forest J	Pc	QC	Crime	1973
Birch, Nicholas J	Ps	QC	Crime	1972
Bird, Royal	Ps	KPM	Crime	1920
Birkhead, Derek E	Pc	BEM	Crime	1966
Birse, Graham K	Pc	QC	Rescue	1976
Black, George	Pc	BEM	Crime	1971
Blake, Frederick J	Sps	GM	Rescue	1941
Blakelock, Keith	Pc	QGM	Broadwater Farm Riot	1988 P
Bland, Harold	Ds	KPM	Crime	1949
Block, Ralph C	Wrpc	GM	Rescue	1941
Blundell, Frederick G	Pc	KPM	Attempted rescue	1934
Bocking, Leonard G	Pc	GM	Crime	1954
Bond, Harry, L	Pc	BEM	Rescue	1941
Bonner, Richard	Pc	KPM	Crime	1926
Bowcock, Peter J	Pc	BEM	Crime	1971
Bowen, Richard W	Pc	QC	Rescue	1966
Bowen		QC		1975
Bowerman, Kenneth J	Pc	GM	Crime	1966
Bowles, George	Pc	KPM	Rescue	1917
Bowman, John E	Pc	KC	Rescue	1952
Boyce, David	Pc	QGM	Crime	1996
Brady, David	Pc	QGM	Crime	1975
Brady, David	Pc	QC	Crime	1979
Brandon, Henry J B	Pc	GM	Rescue	1941
Bransgrove, Arthur J	Pc	QC	Rescue	1976
Breslin, William J	CI	QGM	Crime	1976
Bridge, William A	Pc	KPM	Crime	1941

Bridle, William H	Pc	GM	Rescue	1941
Brocklehurst, Fred	Pc	KPM	Fire at munitions factory	1918
Brooke, John	Pc	Reward		1830
Brooks, Anthony	Pc	QC	Crime	1977
Brotherton, Christopher	Capt	RHS	Rescue	1993
Broughton, Alan F	Ps	QC	Crime	1972
Broughton, John L	Pc	QC	Rescue	1988
Brown, Frederick	Pc	KPM	Rescue	1915
Brown, Henry	Pc	KPM	Rescue	1915
Brown, Ian	Ps	QC	Crime	1974
Brown, James W	Pc	BEM	Rescue	1941
Brown, Paul	Pc	RHS	Rescue	2002
Brown, Terrence V	Pc	GM	Crime	1966
Browning	Pc	KC		1944
Bryant, Frank	Pc	KPM	Rescue	1919
Bryant, Frank	Pc	C	Rescue	1918
Bryant, William	City Police	KPM	Sidney Street	1911
Buchanan, Thomas	Insp.	KPM	Crime	1921
Bulger, Stuart G	Pc	QC	Crime	1969
Bullard, Brendan T	Pc	BEM	Crime	1957
Bunce, William	Pc	KPM	Crime	1934
Bundock, Albert M	Cmdr	QC	Crime	1976
Burdett, Keith T	Pc	GM	Crime	1956
Burch, Colin P	Pc	BEM	Crime	1971
Burfield, Sidney	Ps	KPM	Rescue	1915
Burfield, Sidney	Ps	C	Rescue	1914
Burgess, Frederick M	Ps	GM	Rescue	1941
Burgoyne, Henry	Pc	GM	Rescue	1941
Burke, John S	Pc	BEM	Crime	1952
Burrows, Charles H	Pc	GM	Rescue	1941
Burrows, George	Pc	BEM	Crime	1974
Bursnall, Matthew	Pc	KPM	Crime	1939
Butcher, Peter E	Pc	BEM	Crime	1971
Burns, David J	Pc	QC	Rescue	1968
Burton, George	Pc	KPM	Rescue	1917
Burton, William	Pc	KPM	Rescue	1921
Bush, Ethel V	Wps	GM	Acted as decoy	1955
Bush, Walter	Pc	KPM	Crime	1923
Butler, Theobald	Ds	BEM	Crime	1948
Byron, Arthur	Pc	RHS	Rescue	1897
Cain, William	DI	KPM	Crime	1933
Caines, Arthur E E	Pc	QC	Crime	1965
Cambers, Arthur	Pc	KPM	Attempted rescue	1911
Cameron, Alan R	Ps	QC	Crime	1960
Cameron, Donald	Pc	BEM	Crime	1956
Cameron, John	Pc	RHS	Rescue	1906
Candlish, William B	Wrpc	KC	Civil Defence	1941 P
Carney, Brian	Dc	BEM	Crime	1966
Carpenter, Harry G P	Pc	KC	Civil Defence	1940
Carpenter, Reginald	Wrpc	KPM	Crime	1943

Carpenter, Walter	Pc	KPM		Runaway horses	1916
Carpenter, Walter	Pc	C		Runaway horses	1915
Carr, Percy	Pc	KPM		Fire on explosives train	1920
Carter, Frederick	Pc	KPM		Crime	1923
Cartwright, W	Pc	RHS		Rescue	1898
Castle, David J	Pc	QC		Crime	1973
Castrey, Simon	Pc	QC		Crime	1995
Catchpole	Ps	KC		Civil defence	1944
Cater, John W	Pc	KPM	C	Tottenham Anarchist Outrage	1910
Caulfield-Kerney, Shaun	Pc	QC		Rescue	1965
Cavalier, Cecil F	Pc	KPM		Crime	1938 MM
Cawdell, Edward R	Pc	QC		Rescue	1966
Chadburn, Ian M	Pc	QC		Balcombe Street Siege	1977
Chaffey, Godfrey, H	Pc	QGM		Crime	1974
Chambers, Albert E J	Ps	GM		Crime	1956
Champs, Frederick H	Pc	KPM		Rescue	1939
Chandler	Ps	KC		Civil defence	1945
Charmichael, Alexander	Pc	KPM		Crime	1939
Chesterman, John W	Pc	KPM		Crime	1938
Chilcott, Charles	Pc	RHS		Rescue	1900
Chipperfield, Michael A	Pc	QGM		Bomb, Rubens Hotel	1989
Choat, Walter C	City Police	KPM		Sidney Street	1911
Chorlton, John	Pc	BEM		Rescue	1966
Choules, Alan	Pc	C		Rescue	1971 P
Christmas, Jesse	Pc	KPM		Rescue	1918
Churchyard, Wallace	Pc	KPM		Crime	1921
Clabby, Kim	Pc	BEM		Crime	1973
Claiden, Andrew S	Pc	QGM		Balcombe Street siege	1977
Clapp, William	Ps	KPM		Runaway horses	1912
Clarabut, David L	Pc	QC		Crime	1969
Claridge, Stanley R	Pc	QC		Crime	1957
Clark, Brian M	Pc	QC		Crime	1978
Clark, Robin	Pc	QGM		Broadwater Farm Riot	1988
Clarke, Albert	Pc	RHS		Rescue	1896
Clarke	Ps	KC		Crime	1952
Clayden, Alfred	Ps	KPM		Crime	1928
Cleland, Margaret S	Wpc	GM		Rescue	1964
Clement, Henry	Ds	BEM		Crime	1966
Clements, David M	Pc	GM		Crime	1976
Clements, Stephen F	Pc	QC		Rescue	1976
Cleverley, Harry	Pc	RHS		Rescue	1901
Clunes, Ronald	Pc	QC		Crime	1971
Coburn, Steven R	Pc	QC		Crime	1975
Cockayne, Christopher	Pc	QC		Crime	1983
Cockburn, Herbert	Pc	KPM		Runaway horse	1933
Cockburn, Herbert	Ps	BEM		Rescue	1941
Cocks, Thomas M G	Pc	QC		Crime	1965
Coker, Frederick G	Insp	GM		Rescue	1941
Cole, James A	Pc	KPM		Rescue	1930
Cole, James A	Insp	KPM		Crime - Bar to Medal	1944

Cole, William	Pc	AM	Explosion Westminster Hall	1885
Coleridge, John W	Dc	QC	Crime	1986
Coles, John	Pc	QC	Crime	1983
Collett, Raymond L	Pc	QC	Crime	1975
Collins, Stephen D	Pc	QC	Crime	1997
Collins, William A	Pc	QC	Crime	1973
Collyer, Sidney	Pc	KPM	Crime	1941
Colvin, George C	Ps	KPM	Crime	1931
Comley, Sidney J	Pc	KC	Civil Defence	1940
Conley, Stanley	Pc	BEM	Crime	1974
Conelly	Insp	KPM		1945
Connell, William C	Dc	BEM	Crime	1966
Cook, Charles	Pc	RHS	Rescue	1916
Cook, Edwin P	Pc	C	Rescue	1927
Cooke, Ernest F C D	Ps	QC	Crime	1956
Coomber, Sidney C	Dc	GM	Rescue	1941
Coombes, Richard	Pc	QGM	Broadwater Farm Riot	1988
Cooper, John	Pc	KPM	Runaway horse	1924
Cosham, Albert E	Pc	KPM	Crime	1939
Coulthart	Pc	RHS	Rescue	1930
Court, Barry C	Pc	QGM	Balcombe Street siege	1977
Court, Dennis S	Pc	KPM	Crime	1943
Couzens, William E A	Pc	QC	Rescue	1964
Cox, Charles E	Pc	GM	Crime	1961
Cox, Terrence M	Pc	BEM	Crime	1968
Cox, William G	Ps	GM	Rescue	1941
Cozens, John	Pc	KPM	Rescue	1924
Crampton, Ian R	Ps	QC	Crime	1974
Crampton, John	Pc	RHS	Rescue	1897
Crayden, Bert	Pc	QC	Crime	1964
Creedon, Richard M	Pc	C	Runaway horse	1943
Crojier, Ronald	Pc	QC	Rescue	1973
Cross, Howard R	Pc	QC	Crime	1969
Cross, Roger V	Pc	QC	Crime	1966
Crossingham, Cyril C	Pc	BEM	Crime	1965
Cummin, Arthur S	Pc	KC	Civil defence	1941
Crump, John H	Pc	GM	Rescue	1941
Cunliffe, William C	Pc	QC	Crime	1968
Cunningham, Alexander	Pc	KPM	Rescue	1927
Cutt, James B	Pc	KPM	Crime	1948
Dadds		QC		1972
Dalby, Charles H A	Pc	KC	Civil defence	1941
Dalmasio	Pc	RHS	Rescue	1968
Darby, Sydney	Pc	GM	Crime	1952
Darke, Gilbert	Pc	KPM	Crime	1920
Davey	Pc	RHS	Rescue	1970
David, Ryan K	Pc	QGM	Crime	1975
David, Ryan K	Pc	QGM	Rescue	1976
Davidson, John C	Ps	QC	Crime	1994
Davies, David	Pc	KPM	Rescue	1919

Davies, David	Pc	C	Rescue	1917
Davies, Frank	Ds	BEM	Crime	1967
Davies, Gareth	Pc	QC	Crime	1966
Davies, Kenneth L	Insp	QC	Crime	1972
Davies, Michael	Ps	QC	Crime	1973
Davies, Paul	Pc	QC		1997
Davies, S	Pc	RHS	Rescue	1902
Davison, Jackson S	Ps	GM	Rescue	1941
Davison, John	Ps	KC	Civil defence	1941
Dawson, John A	Pc	BEM	Crime	1966
Day, George	Pc	KPM	Rescue	1921
Day, Martin	Pc	QC	Rescue	1977
Deacon, Graham	Spc	GM	Rescue	1941
Dealman	Wpc	RHS	Rescue	1982
Dean, George H	Pc	GM	Rescue	1941
Dean, Robert	Pc	QC		1997
Deane, James C		RHS	Rescue	1909
Deans, William H	Ps	KPM	Acting as a decoy	1947
Dednum, Charles	Pc	KPM	Rescue	1918
Deegan, Edward R	Ps	QC	Crime	1994
Deeming, George T	Pc	QC	Crime	1975
Demmon, Leonard	Ps	QPM	Terrorist incident Cyprus	1956 P
Dench, Robert G	Pc	BEM	Crime	1971
Deniham, William	Pc	KPM	Rescue	1911
Dennis, Stephen G	Pc	QC	Rescue	1982
Densham, Alan	Pc	KPM	Runaway horse	1936
Denton, Albert W	Pc	C	Rescue	1930
Denyer, James F	Pc	BEM	Rescue	1945
Dew, John	Pc	KPM	Runaway horse	1916
Dew, John	Pc	C	Runaway horse	1914
Dewhurst, William	Pc	C	Tottenham Anarchist Outrage	1910
Dibell, John	Ps	QC	Crime	1964
Dick, Stuart J	Ps	QC	Crime	1969
Dinsdale, Thomas M	Pc	QC	Crime	1973
Diver, Anthony	Pc	QC		1997
Dixon, Charles	Pc	KPM	Tottenham Anarchist Outrage	1910
Dixon, Ernest	Pc	BEM	Crime	1972
Dixon, George	Pc	QC	Crime	1974
Donnelly, James	Pc	BEM	Rescue	1971
Donovan	Pc	Reward		1858
Dorsett, George E	Pc	GM	Crime	1953
Dorsett, George E	Pc	GM	Crime	1959
Douglas, Herbert L	Pc	QC	Crime	1966
Douglas, Peter	Pc	QC	Crime	1965
Douglas, William E	Sps	GM	Rescue	1941
Dover	Ps	QC		1974
Dowswel, Henry	Insp	GM	Balcombe Street siege	1977
Drabble, Fred	Pc	KPM	Runaway horses	1916
Drabble, Fred	Pc	C	Runaway horses	1914
Drew, Ernest	Pc	KPM	Crime	1943

Dubber, John	Pc	KPM	Crime	1924
Dudley, Martin	Pc	QC	Crime	1995
Duff, James	Pc	KPM	Crime	1923
Duffus, Gordon J	Ps	QC	Crime	1973
Dundas, David	Pc	KC	Civil defence	1945
Duneclift, Peter C	Pc	QC	Rescue	1964
Dunn, Duncan	Pc	KPM	Rescue	1928
Dunn, Duncan	Pc	C	Rescue	1926
Dunster, Geoffrey	Pc	RHS	Rescue	1993
Durbery, Ronald A J	Pc	KC	Rescue	1952
Dyson, Clarence L	Pc	KC	Civil defence	1945
Eagles, Charles	Pc	KPM	Tottenham Anarchist Outrage	1910
Eales	Pc	RHS	Rescue	1951
Eden, Maurice	Ps	GM	Terrorist incident Cyprus	1956 P
Edmonds, Peter R	Pc	QGM	Kidnap attempt	1974
Edmonds	Pc	KC	Civil defence	1944
Edwardes, John S M	Pc	GM	Crime	1952
Edwards, Trevor L	Pc	QC	Crime	1957
Edwards, Walter Rees	Pc	GM	Rescue	1941
Egerton	Ps	Reward	Crime	1857
Eist, Alexander A	Ds	BEM	Crime	1967
Ellar, Walter	Pc	KC	Crime	1952
Elliott, John	Pc	RHS	Rescue	1891
Ellis, Leonard J	Pc	KC	Civil defence	1945
Ellis, Robert	Ds	KPM	Crime	1926
England, Leslie C	Pc	BEM	Crime	1961
English, Albert	Pc	KPM	Crime	1914
Ennor, W	Ps	RHS	Rescue	1903
Entecott	Pc		Advancement Rescue	1875
Evans, Charles	Ps	C	Rescue	1939
Evans, Helen J	Wpc	QC	Rescue	1983
Evans, Stanley C	Pc	BEM	Rescue	1944
Everett, Thomas	Pc	BEM	Crime	1965
Ewan		QC		1971
Eyles, Roy G	Ds	BEM	Crime	1966
Fabian, Robert H	DI	KPM	Defusing a bomb (Fenians)	1940
Fairfax, Frederick W	Dc	GC	Craig & Bentley	1953
Falk, Alan D	Warden	BEM	Rescue	1941
Falkingham, Neil	Pc	QC		1995
Farley, Stephen F	Pc	QC	Crime	1980
Farrance, Thomas	Pc	KPM	Runaway horses	1929
Farrington, W	Pc	RHS	Rescue	1897
Fenton, Robert	Pc	QGM	Balcombe Street siege	1977
Ferguson, Joseph P	Pc	QC	Crime	1972
Field, Michael E	Ps	QC	Crime	1980
Finbow, Leslie E	Pc	GM	Rescue	1941
Findlay, David J	Ps	BEM	Crime	1961
Findlay, Charles J	Ps	QC	Crime	1976
Fisher, George	Pc	KPM	Runaway horse	1925
Fitzpatrick, Anthony	Pc	QGM	Crime	1997

Fitzsimons, Anthony W	Pc	QC	Crime	1975
Flett, James, F J S	Pc	GM	Rescue	1941
Flint, Albert	Pc	KPM	Crime	1924
Forman	Pc	QC		1983
Forster, Peter	Insp	QC	Crime	1982
Foster, George E	Ps	GM	Rescue	1941
Foster, John	Pc	BEM	Crime	1952
Fox, Charles E	Pc	KPM	Rescue	1936
Fox, Francis S	Pc	QC	Crime	1976
Foxton, Stanley G	Wrpc	BEM	Rescue	1944
Frampton, George H	Ds	BEM	Crime	1956
Franklin, Charles F		KC	Civil defence	1940
Freeland, Edward E	Pc	KPM	Rescue	1938
Freeland		QC		1982
Freston, Stanley G	Wrpc	KC	Civil defence	1941
Furner, John	Pc	BEM	Crime	1952
Gage, Barry N	Pc	QGM	Crime	1974
Gahan, Edward R R	Insp	BEM	Work during air raids	1940
Gardiner, Richard T	Pc	QC	Crime	1978
Garner, Arthur H	Ps	GM	Crime	1972
Garvey, Denis	Pc	QC	Crime	1964
Gatland, George	Pc	KPM	Runaway horse	1911
Gatland, Victor R	Pc	QC	Crime	1975
Geer, Edward	Pc	KPM	Runaway horse	1923
Geesing, Peter G	Pc	QC	Crime	1954
George, Ernest W	Insp	KC	Civil defence	1940
Gerrard, Albert W	Wrpc	GM	Rescue	1943
Gibbins, Patrick G	Ds	BEM	Crime	1966
Gibbins, Patrick G	Ds	BEM	Crime	1970
Gibson, Arthur	Insp	KC	Civil defence	1941
Gilbert, David B	Pc	QC	Runaway horse	1953
Gilbert, Ernest F	Wrpc	GM	Rescue	1941
Giles, Keith V	Pc	BEM	Crime	1972
Glasby, Harold	Pc	C	Rescue	1934 P
Gledhill, Anthony J	Pc	GC	Crime	1967
Goad, Roger P	Capt	GC	Defusing bomb IRA	1976 P
Godley, John A	Pc	QC	Crime	1976
Godwin, Thomas W	Pc	KC	Runaway horses	1949
Goff, John A H	Insp	GM	Rescue	1941
Goodge, Edward R	Pc	KC	Civil defence	1945
Goodman, William A	Spc	C	Rescue	1915
Goodson, Colin J	Expo	QC	Crime	1995
Goodwin, Cornelius	Pc	KPM	Rescue	1914
Gordon, Albert V	Wrpc	GM	Rescue	1941
Gordon	Pc	RSPCA	Rescue	1984
Goring, Arthur H	Pc	QC	Rescue	1956
Gorman		QC		1982
Gowan, David J	Pc	QC	Crime	1976
Graham, Charles H	Pc	QC	Crime	1975
Graham, Kenneth D	Pc	QC	Crime	1965

Grant, George, S	Pc	KPM	Crime	1943
Grant, Terrence	Ds	QC	Crime	1969
Graves, John	Pc	QC	Crime	1981
Gravett, Albert	Pc	KPM	Crime	1926
Gray, Alexander	Pc	KC	Civil defence	1945
Gray, William J	Pc	GM	Rescue	1944
Greaves	Pc	BEM		1970
Green, Alfred	Pc	KPM	Rescue	1927
Green, A E H	Pc	RHS	Rescue	1909
Green, Gordon J	Pc	KPM	Rescue	1936
Green, Gordon J	Pc	C	Rescue	1935
Green, Henry	pc	RHS	Rescue	1897
Green, Michael J	Pc	QC	Crime	1980
Green, Percy	Pc	KPM	Runaway horse	1921
Green, Robert N	Pc	BEM	Crime	1956
Green	Pc	C	Rescue	1936
Greenoff, Edward G B	Pc	KPM	Evacuation	1917 P
Grey, Herbert F	Ps	BEM	Rescue	1941
Griffiths, John M	Pc	BEM	Crime	1970
Griffiths, William I	Pc	BEM	Crime	1974
Griffiths, Willis	Pc	GM	Rescue	1941
Grigg, David L	Ps	GM	Rescue	1941
Grose, Reginald G	Pc	GM	Rescue	1941
Ground, Frederick W	Pc	KPM	Crime	1939
Grove, Brian E	Pc	QGM	Crime	1979
Grove, Frederick A	Pc	QC	Crime	1957
Gulliver, John A	Pc	BEM	Crime	1954
Gunn, Richard	Pc	GM	Rescue	1940
Gurney, Peter E S	Expo	BEM	Defusing bomb IRA	1973
Gurney, Peter E S	Expo	GM	Defusing bomb IRA	1983
Hack, Albert E	Ps	GM	Rescue	1944
Hack, William G	Pc	GM	Rescue	1940
Hadaway, David	Ps	QGM	Crime	1991
Haggerty	Wpc	RHS	Rescue	1983
Hainsby, George	Pc	KPM	Rescue	1928
Hales, Charles A	Ps	GM	Rescue	1941
Hall, Charles	Pc	KPM	Crime	1921
Hall, Harry	Pc	KPM	Crime	1930
Hall, Leonard D	Pc	GM	Rescue	1941
Hall, David	Pc	QC		1997
Hall	Pc	RHS	Rescue	1958
Hamblin, William	Pc	KC	Crime	1945
Hammerton, Richard D	Wrpc	KC	Civil defence	1940
Hammond, Derrick O	Pc	QC	Crime	1974
Hamovitch, Joseph	Wrpc	C	Rescue	1941
Hancock, Frederick	Pc	RHS	Rescue	1916
Harding, Robert	Pc	KPM	Runaway horse	1925
Hardy, Alfred	Wrpc	KC	Civil defence	1941
Hardy, James	Pc	KPM	Crime	1918
Harfield, James E	Pc	QC	Crime	1973

Harlow, Paul	Pc	QC	Crime	1993
Harness, John	Pc	QC	Crime	1969
Harper	Ps	C	Rescue	1919
Harris, Arthur W	Pc	C	Rescue	1924
Harris, John R	Pc	BEM	Crime	1957
Harrison, Norman	Pc	GM	Craig and Bentley	1953
Harrison		QC		1975
Harrison, Tordiff	Ds	QC	Crime	1969
Hatch, Anthony M	Pc	QC	Crime	1979
Hawkes, Frederick E	Pc	KPM	Crime	1934
Hawkins, Richard V	Capt	BEM	Defusing bomb IRA	1973
Haxell, Geoffrey A	Ps	QC	Crime	1976
Hayes, Harry	Pc	KPM	Rescue	1921
Hayes, Harry	Pc	C	Rescue	1921
Hayes, John	Pc	KPM	Crime	1923
Haynes, Thomas J	Pc	KPM	Runaway horses	1934
Haynes, Thomas J	Pc	C	Runaway horse	1932
Haytread, George	Pc	KPM	Crime	1911
Haywerd, Andrew	Pc	RHS	Rescue	1999
Hayward, Ernest V	Pc	KPM	Defused a bomb	1940
Haywood-Trimming, Colin	Supt	QC	Protection duty	1996
Healey, John A	Pc	QGM	Crime	1991
Healing, Terence E	Pc	QC	Crime	1971
Hearn, John	Pc	KPM	Rescue	1938 MM
Hearn, Walter	Pc	KPM	Runaway horses	1920
Heaton, Derek	Pc	BEM	Crime	1966
Hedges, James	Ps	KPM	Crime	1926
Heggie, James	Pc	QC		1995
Hemley, George E	Ps	KPM	Crime	1939
Henderson, Donald V	Major	GM	Defusing bomb IRA	1976
Henderson, John M	Pc	QC	Crime	1987
Henley, Malcolm J	Pc	QGM	Crime	1983
Herrington, Jeffrey	Pc	QC	Crime	1965
Heyes, Gordon	Pc	QGM	Crime	1979
Hibbitt, Charles E	Wrpc	KC	Civil defence	1941
Hickman	Pc	RHS	Rescue	1924
Hickson	Pc	QC		1971
Hide, Robert H	Pc	KPM	Crime	1949
Hierons, John	Pc	RHS	Rescue	1902
Highgate, Albert	Pc	KPM	Rescue	1930
Hill, Charles G	Insp	KC	Civil defence	1945
Hill	Pc	C	Rescue	1919
Hill, Basil E	Pc	BEM	Rescue	1941
Hill-Cottingham Leslie G	Ps	KC	Civil defence	1945
Hills, Michael J	Pc	GM	Kidnap attempt	1974
Hine	Pc	QC		1983
Hilton, William M	Pc	QC	Crime	1996
Hitchings, Julie	Wps	QC	Crime	1995
Hite, Vernon T	Spc	GM	Rescue	1941
Hobbs, Roy A	Pc	BEM	Crime	1964

Hobbs, Walter	Ds	KPM	Crime	1924
Hobday, Peter John	Pc	QC	Crime	1972
Hodgson, William B	Pc	KPM	Fire at munitions factory	1918
Hogarth, Thomas	Ps	KC	Civil defence	1940
Hoggard, Philip	Pc	QC	Fire	1958
Holleyman, Charles F	Pc	QC	Crime	1973
Holloway, William J	Insp	BEM	Rescue	1944
Holyhead, Rodney V	Wrpc	BEM	Rescue	1944
Honey, Richard	Pc	BEM	Rescue	1969
Honour, William A	Supt	BEM	Rescue	1941
Hood, Joseph, H	Pc	KPM	Runaway police vehicle	1937
Hood, Joseph, H	Pc	C	Runaway vehicle	1936
Hooper, Derek	Pc	QC		1997
Hopkins, William	Pc	KPM	Runaway horse	1926
Horswood, Stephen D	Pc	QC	Crime	1986
Howells, Martin	Pc	QGM	Broadwater Farm Riot	1988
Howorth, Kenneth R	Expo	GM	Defusing bomb IRA	1983 P
Hughes, Albert	Pc	KPM	Runaway horses	1916
Hughes, Albert	pc	C	Runaway horses	1915
Hughes, Leslie F	Pc	GM	Rescue	1941
Hughes, Paul D	Dc	QC	Crime	1994
Hughes, Robert	Pc	QC	Rescue	1980
Humm, Frank H	Pc	QGM	Crime	1974
Humphries, Robin	Pc	QC	Crime	1980
Hunter, Norman R C	Ps	QC	Crime	1976
Hunter, Randolph S	Pc	QC	Crime	1976
Huntley, Robert	DI	BEM	Crime	1963
Hurley, Dermot E	Pc	QC	Rescue	1968
Huse, Henry J	Ps	QC	Crime	1969
Hutchings, Harry	Pc	KPM	Runaway horse	1923
Hutchings, Harry	Pc	C	Runaway horse	1922
Hutchins, Frederick G	Ps	QPM	Crime	1961 P
Hyde, David	Insp	QC	Crime	1987
Irvine, Alexander M	Pc	KPM	Crime	1931
Iusignea, Herbert C	Insp	BEM	Operations during air raids	1940
Jackson, Alfred W	Insp	BEM	Rescue	1941
Jackson, Edward W T	Pc	GM	Rescue	1940
Jackson, Ernest P	Pc	QC	Crime	1973
Jackson, William F	Pc	QC	Crime	1969
Jacobi, Ernest	Pc	KPM	Rescue	1931
Jacobi, Ernest	Pc	C	Rescue	1930
Jacobs, Peter D	Pc	QC	Crime	1968
Jaffray, Alexander	Pc	KPM	Crime	1921
Jaggs, Robert J W	Pc	BEM	Craig and Bentley	1953
James, Alfred C	Pc	KPM	Crime	1931
James, Evan J	Ps	GM	Rescue	1941
James, John P	Pc	GM	Rescue	1941
Jameson, George	Pc	KPM	Crime	1914
Jardin, Alan	Pc	QC	Crime	1976
Jarvis, Malcolm	Ps	RHS	Rescue	1993

Jenkins, Anthony E	Pc	QC	Crime	1976
Jenkins, John	Pc	Stanhope Medal		1882
Jenkins, Reginald A	Dc	BEM	Crime	1969
Jenkins	Insp	KPM		1945
Jenkinson, John	Pc	QC	Crime	1995
Jessiman, William	Pc	KPM	Runaway horse	1911
Jewell, Martin C	Pc	QC	Crime	1973
Johnson, Paul	Pc	RHS	Rescue	2002
Johnson, Stanley W	Pc	GM	Rescue	1941
Jones, Christopher	Pc	KPM	Runaway horse	1927
Jones, Edward	Pc	RHS	Rescue	1894
Jones, Julie	Wpc	QC	Crime	1995
Jones, Noah	Pc	KPM	Rescue	1914
Jones, Peter R	Pc	QC	Crime	1983
Jones, Reginald G	Dc	KPM	Crime	1930 MM
Jones, Ronald D	Pc	QC	Crime	1976
Jones, Russell	Pc	BEM	Rescue	1970
Jones, Stephen R	Pc	QC	Crime	1986
Jones, Stuart	Pc	BEM	Crime	1966
Jordan, Albert C G	Pc	QC	Crime	1967
Jordan	Pc	QC		1971
Joslin, Joseph	Pc	KPM	Rescue	1911
Juniper, Arthur L	Pc	C	Rescue	1931
Juniper, Arthur L	Pc	RHS	Rescue	1931
Kane, John	Sps	KPM	Crime	1942
Karn, George W	Pc	GM	Crime	1958
Kay, John	Pc	BEM	Crime	1957
Kay, Harry P	Pc	KPM	Crime	1948
Kearns, Janet M	Wpc	QC	Crime	1982
Keenan, Stephen M	Pc	QC	Crime	1984
Keery, William J	Pc	GM	Rescue	1941
Kellett, Robert	Pc	QC	Crime	1969
Kelly, Brian C	Pc	KC	Civil defence	1940
Kelly, David J	Ps	QC	Crime	1984
Kemp, Charles	Pc	KPM	Rescue	1916
Kemp, Charles	Pc	C	Rescue	1915
Kemp, Edward	Pc	QGM	Crime	1995
Kemp, Harold G	Pc	BEM	Rescue	1944
Kenwood, Thomas J	Pc	KPM	Rescue	1931
Kerr, David M	Pc	QC	Crime	1974
Kerrison, Edward P	Pc	GM	Rescue	1940
Keylock, Frank V	Dc	BEM	Rescue	1963
Keyte, Andrew	Pc	QC		1996
Kidd, Charles	Pc	KPM	Rescue	1919
Kidd, Charles	Pc	C	Rescue	1918
Kielty, Patrick	Pc	QGM	Crime	1995
Kielty, Patrick	Ps	QGM	Crime	1997
Kiff, Raymond P	Pc	GM	Crime	1977
Killick, Harry	Pc	RHS	Rescue	1906
King, Alan D	Ps	QC	Crime	1995 P

King, Ivan S	Pc	GM	Crime	1951
King, William F	Pc	KPM	Rescue	1934
Kingdom, Zara J	Wpc	QC	Crime	1994
Kinniburgh, William	Pc	QGM	Crime	1977
Kirby, Colin E	Pc	QC	Crime	1974
Kirkup, George R	Pc	KC	Runaway horse	1945
Knapp, Alan J	Ds	QC	Crime	1992
Knapp, Alan J	Ds	GM	Crime	1992
Knight, Malcolm J	Pc	BEM	Crime	1971
Knight, Stephen P	Pc	QGM	Balcombe Street siege	1977
Lamb, Mark S P	Pc	QC	Crime	1982
Lambert, Frederick W	Pc	C	Runaway horse	1919 P
Lambert, William	Pc	KPM	Rescue	1910
Lambert, William	Pc	RHS	Rescue	1909
Lambert	Pc	RHS	Rescue	1974
Landy, Matthew	Dc	KPM	Rescue	1918
Landy, Matthew	Pc	C	Rescue	1917
Lane, John K	Ps	BEM	Crime	1965
Laurence, John M	Spc	BEM	Rescue	1963
Law, Alberta M			See entry for Watts	
Lawson, Jennifer J	Wpc	QC	Crime	1994
Lawson, Peter L	Ps	BEM	Crime	1969
Lee, Charles G	Ps	KC	Civil defence	1941
Lee, Charles H	Spc	BEM	Rescue	1941
Lee, Frederick W	Pc	KPM	Crime	1942
Leeder, Paul	Pc	QC	Crime	1969
Lees, Bernard	Pc	GM	Rescue	1940
Lemmon, James	Pc	KPM	Runaway horse	1934
Lennox, William B	Pc	BEM	Rescue	1969
Leslie, James W C	Pc	GM	Rescue	1941
Levy, Isaac	Wrpc	KC	Civil defence	1941
Lewin, Robert F W	Pc	KC	Civil defence	1940
Lewis, Jack	Pc	KPM	Crime	1921
Lewis, John A	Pc	BEM	Crime	1956
Lewis, Nigel J	Pc	QC	Crime	1970
Lewis	Wrpc	C	Rescue	1942
Lindsell, Charles	Pc	KPM	Crime	1943
Little, Thomas	Pc	KPM	Rescue	1913
Lock, Trevor J	Pc	GM	Iranian Embassy siege	1981
Lock, Victor J	Dc	BEM	Crime	1967
Lockwood, William	Pc	KPM	Runaway horse	1914
Long, Timothy J	Pc	QC	Rescue	1988
Longhead, Thomas A J	Pc	QC	Crime	1971
Longhurst, William	Pc	KPM	Rescue	1917
Lovegrove, Harry	Pc	KPM	Runaway horse	1924
Lovejoy, Ronald K	Dc	KPM	Rescue	1930
Lowe, Bernard J	Ps	QC	Crime	1969
Lowery, Bernard	Pc	KC	Civil defence	1940
Lowes, Alfred T	Ps	KC	Civil defence	1940
Lowndes, Anthony	Ps	BEM	Crime	1952

Loxley, Norman G	Ps	GM	Rescue	1956
Ludford, John	Pc	RHS	Rescue	1902
Lyddon, Leslie	Pc	KPM	Rescue	1927
Lyddon, Leslie G	Pc	C	Rescue	1927
Mabbott, Adrian	Pc	QC		1997
Macaskill, John	Pc	QC	Crime	1996
Mace, Benjamin	Pc	C	Runaway horse	1921
Mackaness, Paul A J	Pc	QC	Crime	1974
Mackey, Leslie J	Sps	BEM	Rescue	1963
Mackin, Peter H	Pc	QC	Rescue	1972
MacLeod, Alasdair C F	Pc	GM	Crime	1966
MacRae, Kenneth A	Pc	QC	Crime	1971
Mahir, Thomas E	Insp	GM	Rescue	1941
Maloney, Denis M	Pc	QC	Crime	1977
Manley, Donald	Pc	QC	Rescue	1966
Mann, Charles G T	Pc	GM	Rescue	1941
Mann, Graham F	Pc	QC	Crime	1975
Manns, Leslie V	Pc	BEM	Crime	1967
Mansfield, William	Ps	QGM	Balcombe Street siege	1977
March, Walter	Pc	KPM	Crime	1923
Marlow, Frederick C	Pc	QC	Crime	1967
Marr	Pc	RHS	Rescue	1963
Marsh, Peter	Insp	BEM	Crime	1971
Marshall, James W	DI	BEM	Crime	1969
Marshall, William	Pc	KPM	Rescue	1928
Marshall, William	Pc	C	Rescue	1926
Martin, Albert V	Ps	GM	Rescue	1941
Martin, Charles	Dc	KPM	Crime	1923
Martin, David B	Insp	QGM	Crime	1979
Martin, Jasper	Ps	GM	Rescue	1941
Martin, Stephen	Pc	QGM	Broadwater Farm Riot	1988
Martin	SOCO	B	Crime	1987
Matthews, R G	Pc	BEM		1976
Marvin, Drummond G	Insp	QC	Crime	1979
Mawer, Stuart	Pc	KC	Civil defence	1940
May, Percival T F	Pc	KC	Civil defence	1941
Mayger, Herbert G	Ps	KPM	Crime	1945
McCallum, John K	Pc	GM	Crime	1951
McDonald, James C	Pc	GM	Craig & Bentley	1953
McDonald, John D	Pc	QC	Crime	1976
McDonald, William A	Insp	KC	Civil defence	1944
McDonough, Clarence L	Insp	GM	Rescue	1953
McDoull, Percy	Dc	KPM	Crime	1923
McDowell, Gordon G	Insp	BEM	Crime	1967
McFall, Terrence F	Pc	GM	Crime	1967
McFarlane, Neil R	Ps	GM	Rescue	1941
McGlinchey, Kevin W D	Pc	QC	Crime	1998
McKay, Albert	Pc	QC	Rescue	1972
McKechnie, Albert	Sps	KC	Civil defence	1940
McKenning, John E	Pc	GM	Rescue	1941

McKenzie, James A	Pc	GM	Crime	1952
McKitterick, Arthur J	Pc	KPM	Rescue	1939
McKitterick, Arthur J	Pc	C	Rescue	1937
McLaren, Laurie A	Pc	KPM	Rescue	1934
McVeigh, Murtach P	Ps	GM	Balcombe Street siege	1977
McVernon, John	Dc	KPM	Crime	1942
Mead, John W T	Pc	GM	Rescue	1941
Mead, Thomas	Pc	KPM	Runaway horse	1926
Meager, William J	Ps	BEM	Rescue	1944
Meldrum, Alan	Pc	QC	Crime	1983
Melton, Robert M	Pc	KPM	Rescue	1918
Mewton, William	Pc	KPM	Fire on train with explosives	1920
Miles, Sidney G	Pc	KPM	Craig and Bentley	1953 P
Miller, John	Pc	BEM	Crime	1970
Millett, Kenneth J	Pc	QC	Crime	1972
Mills, C	Pc	RHS	Rescue	1902
Mills, Guy S	Ps	QC	Crime	1974
Milne, Kenneth	Pc	QGM	Broadwater Farm Riot	1988
Milne, Stewart	Pc	RHS	Rescue	1901
Minnis, Robert H	Pc	KPM	Rescue	1931
Minnis, Robert H	Pc	C	Rescue	1930
Mitchell, Ian D T	Pc	QC	Rescue	1968
Mockeridge, Donald	Pc	C	Runaway horse	1950
Moffatt, D'Arcy B	Pc	KPM	Fire at munitions factory	1918
Mogford, John	Pc	BEM	Crime	1971
Monnery, William	Pc	KPM	Fire on train with explosives	1920
Monteith, William	Dc	KPM	Crime	1942
Monti, Frank R	Pc	QC	Crime	1974
Moody, William A	Insp	KPM	Crime	1949
Moore, Francis	Pc	KPM	Crime	1920
Moore, Lesley Allison	Wpc	Stanhope Medal		1991
Morcock, Leonard C	Pc	QC	Crime	1957
Morgan, Wyndham D	Pc	BEM	Crime	1956
Morgan,	Ps	RHS	Rescue	1968
Morgan	Pc	RHS	Rescue	1933
Morley, William J	Pc	RHS	Rescue	1902
Morris, Edward	Pc	KPM	Runaway horses	1936
Morris, Edward	Pc	C	Runaway horse	1934
Morris, Stanley	Pc	QC	Crime	1970
Morris, Walter	Pc	KPM	Rescue	1935
Morrison, Gordon D	Pc	KPM	Crime	1940
Morrison, James	Dc	QGM	Kenneth Noye incident	1994 P
Morrison, Thomas A	Wrpc	GM	Rescue	1941
Morse, Dennis C	Pc	QC	Crime	1969
Moseley, Henry	Ps	BEM	Rescue	1945
Mounce, Reginald E R	Pc	KPM RHS C	Rescue	1937
Mountney, Harry J	Pc	C	Runaway horse	1923
Muggeridge, Frederick	Ps	KPM	Crime	1931
Muggleton, Alan C	Pc	QC	Crime	1976
Muliken, Robert E	Pc	KC	Civil defence	1940

Mulvaney, Thomas F	Pc	KC	Civil defence	1941
Munroe, Brian R	Pc	QC	Crime	1970
Murphy, Dennis H	Pc	KPM	Rescue	1931
Murphy, Dennis	Pc	C	Rescue	1930
Murphy, Donal J F	Wrpc	KC	Civil defence	1941
Murphy, Joseph A	Ps	KC	Civil defence	1940
Murray, Charles E	Ps	KC	Civil defence	1941 P
Murray, Philip	Pc	RHS	Rescue	1997
Murrock, Stanley A	Pc	QC	Crime	1973
Myers, George T	Pc	KPM	Runaway horse	1941
Myring, Paul T	Expo	QC	Crime	1995
Naish, Philip H	Pc	QC	Rescue	1965
Newing, Cecil	Pc	KPM	Rescue	1929
Newman, Charles J	Pc	C	Tottenham Anarchist Outrage	1910
Newsham, Richard	Pc	KPM	Fire at munitions factory	1918
Nicholls, Cyril C	Ds	BEM	Crime	1954
Nicholls, David	Pc	QC	Crime	1994
Nicholson, Charles	Pc	GM	Rescue	1940
Nicod, William H	Pc	C	Tottenham Anarchist Outrage	1910
Nield, William A	Pc	BEM	Crime	1967
Nightingale, Gordon E	Pc	QC	Rescue	1976
Nightingale, John C	S/Insp	BEM	Rescue	1941
Noble, Ronald	Insp	GM	Rescue	1941
Norman, James W	Pc	QC	Crime	1957
Norman, Percival	Pc	KPM	Runaway horse	1925
Oakes, George A	Pc	KPM	Fire at munitions factory	1918
Oakes, Reginald I	Pc	GM	Rescue	1941
O'Brien, Mark J	Pc	QGM	Crime	1996
O'Brien, Patrick L	Ds	BEM	Crime	1969
O'Calligham, Denis	Pc	QC	Crime	1964
O'Driscoll, Walter	Pc	QC	Crime	1974
O'Rourke, Brian A M	Pc	QC	Crime	1974
O'Rourke, Stephen J	Pc	QC	Crime	1986
O'Neill, Francis J	Pc	QGM	Crime	1983 P
Ockey, Edward M	DI	KPM	Crime	1930
Offord, Harold D	Pc	QC	Rescue	1972
Oldroyd-Jones, Barry	Pc	QC	Crime	1996
Olds, David	Pc	QC	Crime	1983
Olds, Phillip M	Pc	QGM	Crime	1982
Oliver, Christopher	Pc	RHS	Rescue	1999
Oliver, Roger K	Dc	BEM	Crime	1966
Oliver, Thomas	Pc	GM	Rescue	1956
Oliver, William	Ps	KPM	Crime	1942
Orr, Charles R	Insp	BEM	Rescue	1941
Osborne, Alexander D	Ps	KC	Civil defence	1940
Ost, Frederick	Pc	KPM	Crime	1920
Outram, Herbert	Pc	RHS	Rescue	1898
Packman, Ernest A	Dc	BEM	Crime	1966
Page, Terrence J	Ps	BEM	Crime	1968
Page, Tom A	Wrpc	KPM	Crime	1944

Painter, Francis L	StnPs	BEM	Rescue	1945
Pandya, Ricky	Pc	QGM	Broadwater Farm Riot	1988
Parker	Ps	RHS	Rescue	1975
Parker, Hugh H	Pc	QC	Crime	1970
Parker, William J	Pc	KC	Civil defence	1941
Parrott, Kathleen F	Wpc	GM	Acted as decoy	1955
Parsons, Albert G	Wrpc	GM	Rescue	1940
Parsons, Brian	Ps	BEM	Crime	1972
Pateman, Alfred J	Pc	KPM	Crime	1941
Pateman	Insp	KPM		1944
Pattenden, Sidney	Pc	KPM	Crime	1933
Pawley, Bernard E W	Pc	GM	Crime	1979
Pawsey, Phillip	Insp	QPM	Crime	1961 P
Paxton, William D	Pc	KPM	Rescue	1939
Payne, Gerald F	Insp	BEM	Rescue	1941
Peacock	Pc	BEM		1971
Peacock,	Pc	QC		1972
Pearce, Michael J	Pc	QC	Crime	1965
Pearce, Peter E	Pc	QC	Crime	1973
Peckover, Harold	Pc	KPM	Runaway horses	1925
Pedrick, Brinley T	Wrpc	GM	Rescue	1941
Peffer, Michael T	Ps	QGM	Crime	1975
Pegler, Henry	Pc	KPM	Crime	1928
Pengelly, David H	Ps	GM	Broadwater Farm Riot	1988
Penn, Charles	Pc	KPM	Runaway horses	1918
Penrose, Peter J H	Pc	KC	Runaway horse	1952
Perigo, Lawrence A	Pc	KPM C	Runaway horse	1937
Perkins, John J	Pc	QC	Crime	1958
Perry, Howard J	Pc	KPM	Rescue	1938
Perry, Roger C	Pc	QC	Crime	1969
Phelan, Patrick R	Dc	QC	Crime	1992
Phillips	Pc	QC		1971
Phillips, John A	Wrpc	KC	Civil defence	1941
Phillips, Rodney	Pc	BEM	Crime	1971
Phipps, Richard	Pc	QC		1995
Pickford, Derek C	Expo	QGM	Bomb, Rubens Hotel	1989
Pillar, Elliott	Pc	KPM	Crime	1939
Piper, Jeffrey A	Pc	QC	Crime	1972
Pitcher, John	Pc	QC	Crime	1964
Plackett J	Pc	RHS	Rescue	1902
Pointer, Alan K	Pc	QGM	Crime	1974
Pope, Edwin J	Pc	GM	Rescue	1941
Porter, Arthur W	Ps	BEM	Crime	1966
Porter, David W	Dc	QC	Crime	1994
Porter, George	Pc	KPM	Rescue	1914
Porter, Lambert E	Wrpc	GM	Rescue	1941
Potter, William	Ps	KPM	Crime	1942
Powell, Bernard J	Pc	QC	Crime	1964
Powell, Harry	Pc	KPM	Rescue	1921
Price, David H	Pc	QC	Crime	1970

Price, James	Insp	KPM	Crime	1944
Price, John D	Pc	BEM	Crime	1971
Price, Michael W	Pc	QC	Crime	1979
Price, Royston N	Pc	QC	Crime	1968
Priddle, Michael	Insp	QC	Crime	1986
Pritlove, Thomas J	Pc	KPM	Crime	1941
Proctor, Martin S	Pc	QGM	Rescue	1988
Prout	Pc	RHS	Rescue	1932
Pulham, John C	Insp	GM	Rescue	1941
Pulley, Frank	Pc	BEM	Crime	1968
Purfett, Alfred	Pc	KPM	Rescue	1911
Purnell, John F	Insp	GM	Balcombe Street siege	1977
Quincey, John J	Sub Div Insp	KC	Civil defence	1941
Quinnell, Leonard H	Pc	QC	Crime	1977
Rackham, Cecil	Ps	KPM	Crime	1939
Rainsford, Philip	Pc	QGM	Crime	1991
Ralph, Augustus	Pc	KPM	Rescue	1918
Ralph, Augustus	Ps	C	Rescue	1917
Ravening, Thomas	Pc	KPM	Runaway horse	1913
Raymond, Walter E	Pc	KPM	Rescue	1931
Redford, Peter	Dc	QC	Crime	1996
Redpath, David	Pc	QC	Crime	1969
Redwood, Henry C	Pc	Reward		1830
Rees, Hubert M	DCI	BEM	Crime	1962
Reeve, George	Pc	Reward	Crime	1859
Reynolds, Anthony	Pc	BEM	Crime	1971
Richardson, George	Pc	KPM	Crime	1920
Rich, Anthony Paul	Pc	BEM	Crime	1968
Riches, Frederick	Pc	KPM	Crime	1920
Riddle, Matthew	Pc	GM	Rescue	1941
Riley, Brian D	Insp	QC	Crime	1974
Ritchie, Carl	Pc	QC	Crime	1996
Roach, Lawrence T	Insp	QC	Crime	1973
Robb, John A	Pc	BEM	Rescue	1968
Roberts, George	Pc	KPM	Runaway horses	1915
Roberts, George	Pc	C	Runaway horse	1913
Roberts, James D	Pc	QC	Crime	1956
Roberts, Percival	Pc	KPM	Crime	1928
Roberts, Maxwell	Pc	QGM	Broadwater Farm Riot	1988
Robertson, Derek J	Ps	QGM	Crime	1996 P
Robertson	CI	RHS	Rescue	1980
Robertson,	Pc	KC		1945
Robertson, J	Ps	RHS	Rescue	1905
Robins, William A	Pc	KPM	Crime	1934
Robinson, Charles F	Pc	KPM	Rescue	1936
Robinson, George	Pc	RHS	Rescue	1906
Robinson, James	Pc	KC	Civil defence	1941
Robson, A	Ds	BEM	Crime	1966
Robson, James A	Ps	GM	Rescue	1944
Robson, James A	Ps	RHS	Rescue	1950 GM

Rook, James R	Pc	QC	Crime	1995
Root, Joseph	Pc	KPM	Rescue	1913
Root, Joseph	Pc	RHS	Rescue	1911
Rose, Michael J	Ps	GM	Crime	1966
Rose, Thomas	Wrpc	KC	Civil defence	1944
Rose, Sexton	Pc	GM	Rescue	1940
Rosie, George M	Ps	GM	Rescue	1941
Ross, John D	Pc	BEM	Crime	1968
Ross, Michael B	Pc	QC	Crime	1972
Rowe, James	Insp	RHS	Rescue	1895
Rowell, Charles E	Pc	QC	Crime	1979
Rowland, Alexander	Pc	RHS	Rescue	1892
Rowswell, Bertie	Pc	KPM	Crime	1947
Ruddock, Bertram W	Pc	KPM	Runaway horse	1935
Rumble, David R	Pc	BEM	Crime	1973
Russell, Arthur G	Pc	KPM	Rescue	1935
Russell, G E	Pc	RHS	Rescue	1903
Russell, John G	Pc	BEM	Crime	1963
Rutherford, John	Dc	KPM	Crime	1924
Ryall, Sidney	Pc	KPM	Crime	1912
Ryland, Leonard J	Ds	BEM	Crime	1969
Sadgrove, Charles	Pc	KPM	Rescue	1924
Saint, Alfred G	Pc	RHS	Rescue	1909
Saley, Richard	Sps	KC	Civil defence	1945
Sallabank, Lawrence P	Dc	QC	Crime	1969
Salmon, Alfred C	Pc	KPM	Crime	1944
Salmon, John C	Pc	KPM	Rescue	1944
Salter, Percy H	Pc	KPM	Crime	1943
Sample, George R	Pc	KC	Civil defence	1941
Sargent, Edwin R	Pc	QC	Crime	1964
Saunders, Graham	Pc	QC	Crime	1987
Sayer, Cecil	Dc	KPM	Crime	1923
Sayers	Pc	QC		1952
Scheide, Alfred	Pc	KPM	Rescue	1933
Schermuly, William J C	Pc	GM	Rescue	1941
Scott, Conrad	Pc	RHS	Rescue	1907
Scott, Eric B	Pc	QC	Crime	1979
Scott, Laurence	Pc	GM	Crime	1967
Searle, George C	Wrpc	KPM	Crime	1949
Seeds, Angela	Wpc	QC	Crime	1983
Setter, James H	Pc	RHS	Rescue	1907
Seprini, Anthony J	Pc	QC	Crime	1971
Sexton, Archibald E	Wrpc	GM	Rescue	1944
Sexton-Munns, Alan	Pc	QC	Crime	1984
Shacklock, Ronald	Pc	BEM	Crime	1970
Shadrack, Michael J	Insp	QC	Crime	1974
Shelah, Edward E O	Ps	KPM	Runaway horse	1935
Shepherd, Derek H	Pc	QC	Crime	1998
Shepherd, Michael	Pc	QGM	Broadwater Farm Riot	1988
Shepherd, Ralph D	Ps	KPM	Crime	1948

Shepherd, Thomas C	Pc	KPM	Crime	1940
Sherlaw, James A	Ps	GM	Rescue	1041
Shillingford, Stanley J	Spc	KC	Civil defence	1941
Shipton, Alfred L	Insp	KC	Civil defence	1940
Shipton, Alfred L	Insp	GM	Crime	1952
Siddall, Harold	Pc	RHS	Rescue	1916
Silver, William	Pc	KPM	Crime	1913
Simister, Richard M	Pc	QC	Crime	1983
Simmons, Fred	Pc	RHS	Rescue	1895
Simpson, Neil	Pc	QGM	Crime	1993
Sinclair, George A	Pc	GM	Crime	1954
Slessor	Pc	RHS	Rescue	1973
Slimon, Peter	Pc	GM	Crime	1973
Slipper, Thomas	Pc	KPM	Runaway horses	1917
Sloan, Daniel D	Pc	KPM	Fire at munitions factory	1918
Sloan, William	Insp	BEM	Rescue	1941
Sloman, David G	Ps	QC	Crime	1984
Slowley, Roy V E	Pc	GM	Rescue	1941
Skinner	Pc	RHS	Rescue	1968
Skinner, John	Pc	QC	Crime	1987
Smith	Supt	KPM		1945
Smith, Albert	Pc	RHS	Rescue	1901
Smith, Alfred	Pc	C	Rescue	1917 P
Smith, Claude D	Insp	KPM	Crime	1935
Smith, Clive	Pc	C	Runaway horse	1911
Smith, Frank	Pc	QC	Crime	1974
Smith, George	Pc	KPM	Rescue	1921
Smith, George	Pc	C	Rescue	1921
Smith, Harry	Pc	C	Rescue	1932
Smith, James	Dc	BEM	Crime	1974
Smith, Leslie A	Pc	GM	Crime	1951
Smith, Malcolm McL	Wrpc	KC	Civil defence	1941
Smith, Robert	Pc	RHS	Rescue	1893
Smith, Stephen	Pc	KC	Civil defence	1940
Smith, Thomas	CI	QC	Crime	1976
Smithers, Cecil	Ps	KPM	Rescue	1916
Smithers, Cecil	Ps	C	Rescue	1915
Sneddon, Alexander	Ps	BEM	Rescue	1941
Snelling, Cecil	Pc	KPM	Crime	1947
Snitch, Edward N	Pc	GM	Crime	1953
Snooks, Frederick A	Pc	QC	Crime	1972
Sowden, Anthony	Dc	QC	Crime	1986
Sparkes, Henry G	Pc	KPM	Runaway horse	1929
Spencer, Bertie	Pc	KPM	Runaway horse	1913
Springett, George	Pc	KPM	Rescue	1912
Spinks, John F	Ps	QC	Crime	1977
Spooner	Pc	KC	Civil defence	1944
Squibb, Jason P	Dc	QC	Crime	1994
Staines,	Pc	C	Rescue	1919
Stamper, Roy	Pc	BEM	Crime	1964

Starkey, Robert M	Pc	KPM	Rescue	1938
Steele, Henry M	Pc	QC	Crime	1969
Steele, Kenneth W L	Pc	KPM	Rescue	1936
Stephens, F	Ps CID	RHS	Rescue	1902
Stephenson, Peter W	Pc	QC	Crime	1976
Stevens, Henry W	Pc	GC	Crime	1958
Stevens, Maurice A	Pc	KC	Civil defence	1940
Stevens	Pc	QC	Crime	1964
Stiff, Arthur	Aps	KPM	Runaway Horse	1914
Stone, Frederick M	Pc	KPM	Rescue	1928
Stone, Frederick M	Pc	C	Rescue	1927
Stone, Frederick M	Pc	GM	Crime	1952
Stone, Leon	Pc	GM	Rescue	1941
Strange, Norman	Pc	KPM	Crime	1947
Street, Robert R	Ps	QC	Crime	1974
Strood, Peter E	Ps	QC	Crime	1960
Stubbs, Francis	Pc	KPM	Crime	1919
Stubbs, Michael	Ds	QC	Crime	1996
Stiff, Arthur	A/Ps	KPM	Runaway horse	1914
Stratford, Ernest A	Pc	C	Rescue	1945
Sulaiman, John	Ps	QC	Rescue	1989
Sullivan, Maurice	Pc	KPM	Crime	1920
Summerfield, David V	Pc	QC	Rescue	1972
Swan, Robert	Pc	KPM	Crime	1933
Swayne, Ernest W	Pc	KPM	Crime	1938
Sweet, Ernest A	Pc	C	Runaway horse	1930
Sweet, Percy	Pc	KPM	Crime	1921
Swinfield, John	Ds	QC	Crime	1996
Tanner, Thomas	Wrpc	GM	Rescue	1941
Tappy, Alan	Pc	QGM	Broadwater Farm Riot	1988
Tarbit, Osmond E A	Insp	BEM	Rescue	1941
Tarling, Michael R	Pc	QC	Crime	1970
Tarry, William	Pc	KPM	Crime	1940
Taylor, Ernest	Pc	RHS	Rescue	1899
Taylor, Joseph	Pc	C	Rescue	1912
Taylor, Joseph G	Pc	KPM	Rescue	1910
Taylor, Joseph G	Pc	RHS	Rescue	1909
Taylor, Samuel	Pc	KPM	Rescue	1921
Taylor, Thomas	Pc	KC	Rescue	1950
Taylor, Walter G	Pc	GM	Rescue	1941
Telfer, Robert	Pc	KC	Civil defence	1941
Terry, Leslie H	S Insp	KPM	Crime	1944
Thomas, David C	Pc	KC	Crime	1948
Thomas, Ian W	Ps	QGM	Crime	1989
Thomas, John	Ps	KPM	Rescue	1921
Thomas, Richard W	Pc	BEM	Rescue	1963
Thomas, Stephen A	Ds	GM	Crime	1992
Thompson, James E	Pc	KC	Civil defence	1940
Thompson, James W	Pc	KPM	Rescue	1936 P
Thompson, Thomas C	Pc	BEM	Crime	1957

Thorne, Leonard W	Pc	GM	Rescue	1941
Tibble, Stephen A	Pc	QPM	Crime	1976 P
Tierney, Michael R	Pc	QC	Crime	1979
Till, John W	Pc	QC	Rescue	1989
Tilly, Percy E H B	Pc	KC	Civil defence	1944
Timmins, Harry	Pc	KPM	Rescue	1935
Todd, Lindsay C	Ps	QC	Crime	1975
Todd, Walter H	Pc	KPM	Crime	1934
Tomlin, Geoffrey C	Pc	QC	Crime	1971
Tomlinson, David A	Pc	QC	Crime	1955
Tribe, William	Pc	C	Runaway horse	1922
Tribe, William J	Insp	BEM	Rescue	1944
Tricker, Ernest J	Pc	GM	Rescue	1941
Trim, Harry R W	Pc	KC	Civil defence	1940
Trollope, Arthur	Pc	KC	Civil defence	1945
Tucker, Derek	Pc	QC	Crime	1970
Tucker, Charles	City Police	KPM	Sidney Street	1911
Tucker	Pc	KC	Civil defence	1945
Turnbull, Ronald	Pc	BEM	Crime	1971
Turnell, Harry J	Pc	KPM	Rescue	1938
Turner, G T	Pc	RHS	Rescue	1900
Turner, Michael	Pc	QC	Crime	1977
Turner, William B C	Pc	QC	Rescue	1973
Turpin, Albert	Pc	KPM	Rescue	1928
Turpin, Albert	Pc	C	Rescue	1927
Tween, William	Pc	KC	Crime	1948
Tyson, Albert W	Pc	C	Runaway horse	1930
Tyson, Richard E	Pc	QC	Accident	1981
Usher, Gordon	Pc	QGM	Crime	1974
Utley, David B	Pc	QC	Accident	1956
Vibart, Jasper P	Ps	QC	Crime	1958
Vincent, Harold	Pc	KPM	Crime	1925
Voizey, George A J	Wrpc	GM	Rescue	1941
Von, Charles B	Dc	BEM	Crime	1967
Waddell, Douglas R	Pc	QC	Crime	1971
Waldron, Percy	Fireman			1936
Walker, John	Pc	KPM	Crime	1915
Wall, Anthony G	Pc	BEM	Crime	1956
Wallen, Robert	Ps	KPM	Rescue	1933
Walsh, Christopher P	Pc	QC	Crime	1994
Walter	Spc	KC	Civil defence	1945
Walton, Frederick C	Pc	KPM	Runaway Horse	1940
Wannell, Clifford A	Pc	QC	Crime	1983
Ward, Albert	DI	KPM	Crime	1926
Ward, Robert	Pc	QC	Crime	1974
Warren, Edward F	Pc	KC	Runaway horse	1945 MM
Warren, Edward F	Pc	C	Runaway horse	1944
Warrilow, Eva	Wpc	QC	Crime	1976
Waterhouse, Timothy P	Insp	QC		1990
Waters, Edmund	Ps	KPM	Rescue	1913

Watkins, Wyndham V	Pc	BEM	Rescue	1941
Watt, Joseph	Pc	C	Runaway horse	1913
Watt, Thomas F	Pc	BEM	Crime	1962
Watts, Alberta M	Wps	KPM	Acting as a decoy	1947
Wearing, William A	Pc	KPM	Fire at munitions factory	1918
Webb, Ronald P N	Pc	QC	Crime	1973
Webber, Albert	Pc	KPM	Rescue	1920
Webster, Bruce I	Pc	QC	Rescue	1965
Weeks	Pc	RHS	Rescue	1955
Wells, Albert F	Ds	BEM	Crime	1952
Wells, James R	Insp	QC	Balcombe Street Siege	1977
West, Frederick	Pc	KPM	Rescue	1915
West, Henry J	Pc	RHS	Rescue	1898
Wetherell, John M	Pc	QC	Crime	1966
Wharton, Arthur J	Pc	QC	Crime	1962
Wharton, John S N	Pc	GM	Crime	1969
Wheal, David	Pc	QC	Crime	1977
Wheeler, Brian E	Pc	BEM	Crime	1967
Wheeler, Dennis E	Pc	KPM	Crime	1949
Wheeler, Edmund J S	Pc	BEM	Rescue	1951
Wheelhouse, Michael J	Pc	GM	Crime	1966
Whife, James S	Wrpc	BEM	Rescue	1945
White, Raymond J	Pc	C	Rescue	1976
Whiteford, Angus C	Pc	QC	Crime	1966
Whitehead, John P	Pc	BEM	Rescue	1971
Whitham, Douglas	Pc	GM	Crime	1966
Whitmore George	Pc	GM	Rescue	1941
Whiting, Michael A	Pc	QPM	Crime	1974 P
Whyte, William	Pc	QC	Runaway horse	1965
Wiles, Peter M	Pc	QC	Crime	1973
Wilkinson, Anthony	Pc	Reward		1829
Wilkinson, Victor L H	C Supt	QC	Crime	1973
Will, Stuart	Ps	C	Rescue	1973 P
Williams, David J	Insp	QC	Rescue	1976
Williams, Harold	Pc	KC	Crime	1952
Williams, Harry	Pc	KPM	Crime	1920
Williams, Phillip J D	Pc	GM	Crime	1969
Williams, Tom	Pc	QC	Runaway horse	1953
Williams, Wesley	Pc	BEM	Crime	1971
Williams, William	Pc	KPM	Crime	1920
Willmott, Barry J	Pc	QC	Crime	1972
Wilson, Peter J	Pc	QC	Balcombe Street siege	1977
Wilson, Robert G	Pc	KPM	Runaway horses after air raid	1918
Wilson, Robert M	Pc	QC	Crime	1980
Wilson, T	Ps	RHS	Rescue	1898
Wiltshire, Peter J	Ps	QGM	Crime	1994
Winter, Stewart J	Pc	BEM	Crime	1958
Winton, Albert	Pc	KPM	Rescue	1913
Wolfenden, David A	Pc	BEM	Rescue	1974
Wood, David A	Pc	QC	Crime	1977

Wood, David E	Pc	GM	Crime	1956
Wood, Michael V	Pc	QC	Crime	1971
Wood, Wallace	Pc	KPM	Rescue	1927
Woodhams, Ernest C	City Police	KPM	Sidney Street	1911
Woodhams,	Pc	RHS	Rescue	1974
Woodhouse, Nicholas	Pc	QC	Crime	2004
Woodmore, Peter A	Ds	GM	Crime	1966
Woodroffe, Evelyn	Pc	RHS	Rescue	1997
Woodrow, Robert A	Pc	QC	Crime	1962
Wordsworth, Alan	Ps	QGM	Crime	1974
Worthy	Pc	Reward		1858
Wright, Alan T	Pc	QC	Crime	1974
Wright, Charley H	Ps	GM	Rescue	1944
Wright, Deborah	Wpc	QC		1996
Wright, Frederick	Insp	AM	Rescue	1918
Wright, Frederick	Pc	KPM	Crime	1920
Wright, Jonathan L	Pc	QC	Crime	1998
Wright, Maurice H	Pc	KPM	Crime	1940
Wright, Norman A R	Pc	QGM	Crime	1977
Wright, Thomas	Pc	KPM	Crime	1915
Wright	Pc	KC	Civil defence	1944
Young	Insp	RHS	Rescue	1982
Young, Alfred	Pc	KPM	Crime	1910
Young, Harold I W	Sps	GM	Rescue	1940
Young, James F	Pc	KC	Rescue	1947
Young, John R	Pc	QGM	Crime	1974
Young, Reginald J	Pc	QC	Crime	1968
Young, Robert J	Pc	QC	Rescue	1957
Young, Thomas	Pc	BEM	Crime	1960
Young, William H	Wrpc	GM	Rescue	1941
Ziething, Alexander	Pc	C	Tottenham Anarchist Outrage	1910

Appendix 5

Index of Roll of Honour

Abrahams, Israel	Pc	see entry for Jack Morgan	1939
Acerman, Desmond M	Pc	Road traffic accident	1967
Addison, Ronald A	Pc	Heart attack	1960
Adams, Royston E	Pc	Accident	1958
Aldridge, William	Pc	Assaulted	1839
Allaway, Joseph A	Pc	Road traffic accident	1936
Allen, Edgar G	Pc	Road traffic accident	1958
Allen, George W	Pc	Road traffic accident	1931
Arbuthnot, Jane	Wpc	Harrods Bomb	1983
Atkins, Frederick	Pc	Shot	1881
Avery, Jack W	Pc	Stabbed	1940
Bacon, William	Ps	Drowned	1881
Baker, Thomas L	Pc	Assaulted	1866
Baldwin, James	Pc	Stabbed	1898
Barrett, David	Pc	Road traffic accident	1954
Basseby	Pc	Road traffic accident	1922
Batley	Ps	Flying accident on Special Protection duties	1945
Baxter, Alan M	Pc	Road traffic accident	1977
Beazer, Robert	Pc	Road traffic accident	1971
Beckerson, Douglas F	Pc	Fell through glass roof	1971
Bell, Martin B	Pc	Road traffic accident	1986
Bell, Samuel	Pc	Accident	1875
Bellenie, Frank	Pc		1983
Bennett, Alfred	Pc	Assaulted	1873
Benton, William G	Pc	Road traffic accident	1929
Berry, Herbert	Pc	Assaulted	1918
Birkmyre, John	Pc	Fire	1844
Blake	Wrpc	WW2 bomb	1941
Blakelock, Keith	Pc	Broadwater Farm Riot	1985 QGM
Bottomley, Derek J	Pc	Road traffic accident	1977
Bowler, James	Pc	Drowned	1872
Bradstock, Daniel	Insp	Stabbed	1868
Breen, Paul M	Pc	Road traffic accident - during ambulance dispute	1989
Bridgewood, Peter G	Dc	Road traffic accident	1961
Brooks, Henry T	Pc	Accidentally shot by police revolver	1940
Brown, George	Pc	Accident	1860
Brown, Laurance P	Pc	Shot	1990
Brownhill	Pc	Long range rocket explosion	1945
Bruce, Alexander	Wrpc		1940
Bryant, Frank	Pc	During rescue	1919 KPM
Campbell, William	Pc	Crushed on crowd duty	1903

Carroll, James	Pc	Assaulted with own truncheon	1841
Carson, Cornelius	Supt	Rescue - overcome by fumes	1957
Carter, James R	Pc	Road traffic accident	1934
Carter, Leonard	Ps	Fell into uncovered pit	1927
Cautherlay, Harry	Pc	Road traffic accident	1931
Chaplin, Henry James	Pc	Assaulted by mob	1851
Cherry, Paul R	Pc	Road traffic accident	1967
Choules, Alan	Tdc	Drowned	1971
Clark, George	Pc	Stabbed	1846
Clarke, Daniel	Pc	Road traffic accident	1981
Clarke, Dennis P	Pc	Assaulted	1867
Clarke, John A	Pc	Road traffic accident	1977
Claxton, Percy J	Pc	Gas explosion	1954
Cockbury, Thomas O B	Wrpc		1940
Cole, George	Pc	Shot	1882
Cole, George	Pc	Hit by runaway horse	1891
Collins, Henry	Ps	Thrown from police horse	1866
Collis, James	Pc	Runover by train	1879
Cook, Percy E	Pc	Overcome by sewer fumes	1927
Cook, Richard	Pc	Fell from police horse	1878
Cooper, George R	Pc	Road traffic accident	1950
Cordwell, Albert E	Pc	Pensioned - died of injuries	1922
Cornish, Gordon	Pc	Road traffic accident	1983
Cowell, Dennis E	Pc	Drowned	1965
Cox, Charles	Pc	Drowned	1870
Coyne, Roger E	Ps	Road traffic accident	1979
Crawley, Steven F	Pc	Road traffic accident	2001
Croake, Patrick A	Pc	Road traffic accident	1978
Croft, William	Pc	Fell into pit while chasing burglars	1905
Culley, Robert	Pc	Stabbed	1833
Dale, George A	Pc	Road traffic accident	1968
Daly, Timothy	Pc	Shot	1842
Daniels, Joseph	Pc	Choked on his teeth after an arrest	1892
Davies, Melvyn	Pc	Road traffic accident	1959
Davies, Michael John	Pc	Stabbed	1969
Davey, William John	Pc	Shot	1863
Day, Ashley	Pc	Road traffic accident	1990
Dean, Thomas	Pc	Drowned	1888
Deeks, Alfred	Insp	Collapsed	1912
Demmon, Leonard	Ps	Terrorist incident Cyprus	1956 QPM
Dench, David E	Dc	Road traffic accident	1972
Dennis	Spc	Bomb explosion	1944
Diboll, George A	Pc	Collapsed and died	1935
Dixon, George	Insp	Drowned	1893
Dodd, Stephen	Insp	Harrods bomb explosion	1983
Donovan, Michael	Pc		1917
Dorney, Edward R	Pc	Dog handler struck by a train	1960
Dunne, Patrick	Pc	Shot	1993
Eden, Maurice	Ps	Terrorist incident Cyprus	1956 GM
Edgar, Nathaniel	Pc	Shot	1948

Edmonds	Pc	Long range rocket explosion	1945
Eite, Joseph	Pc	Assaulted	1868
Ellis, Alfred	Pc	Drowned	1888
Ellis, William A	Spc	Drowned	1916
Ezobi, Tokunbo	Pc	Road traffic accident	2003
Fitnum, Henry	Pc	Drowned	1882
Fitzgerald, Patrick G	Pc	Road traffic accident	1948
Fitzgerald, William	Pc	Assaulted	1866
Fletcher, Yvonne	Wpc	Shot	1984
Ford, David	Pc	Fell through roof	1929
Fordham, John W	Dc	Stabbed	1985
Fox, Geoffrey	Pc	Shot - crew of Foxtrot one one	1966
Free, Frederick W	Pc		1911
Frick, Noel C	Pc	Road traffic accident	1993
Fulker, James	Pc	Found dead on his beat	1842
Fuller, William	Pc	Thrown from police horse	1859
Funnell, George S	Pc	Fire	1900
Furnell, Terrence D	Pc	Road traffic accident	1960
Free, Frederick W	Pc	Drowned	1911
Garner, David	Ps	Heart attack	1892
Gisbourne, David G	Insp	Collapsed 2 days after public disorder	1974
Gladwell, Robert C	Pc	Assaulted	1991
Glasby, Harold	Pc	Drowned	1934
Goad, Roger	Expo	Defusing a bomb	1975 GC BEM
Goddard, William	Pc	Drowned	1882
Goggins, George	Ps	Road traffic accident	1956
Goulder, William	Pc	Drowned	1900
Graham, Henry	Pc	Accident	1892
Grantham, Joseph	Pc	Assaulted	1830
Green, Thomas	Sps	Epsom Police Station Siege	1919
Greenoff, Edward G B	Pc	Explosion	1917 KPM
Groombridge, David	Ps	Assaulted	1887
Groomes, Thomas	Pc	Drowned	1877
Grout, William	Sps	Road traffic accident	1942
Groves, Henry A	Pc	Thrown from police horse	1935
Guest, Arthur C	Spc	Shot during firearms training	1941
Haines, Anthony I	Pc	Road traffic accident	2001
Hall, George	Pc	Fell from police horse	1846
Hallett, William G	Pc	Road traffic accident	1921
Hamilton, Richard K	Pc	Road traffic accident	1977
Hammond, George P	Pc	Died of injuries received in 1985	1995 QPM
Hard, William	Insp		1862
Harding, Harry	Pc	Road traffic accident	1949
Hardy, James	Pc	Road traffic accident	1918 KPM
Hart, Thomas	Pc	Drowned	1829
Hastie, James	Pc	Assaulted	1846
Hawkins, Albert V	Pc	Road traffic accident	1949
Head, Christopher T	Ds	Shot - crew of Foxtrot one one	1966
Healey, Arthur	Pc	Fell through glass roof	1902
Heath, Walter J	Ps	Shot while unloading revolver	1912

Herbert, Ian	Dc	Road traffic accident	1998
Higgs, George W	Pc	Road traffic accident	1972
Hird, Royston W	Pc	Road traffic accident	1958
Holdaway, Arthur	Pc	Road traffic accident	1924
Holden, Brian B J	Pc	Road traffic accident	1963
Howell, Henry C E	Pc	Road traffic accident	1944
Howell	Wrpc	Long range rocket explosion	1945
Howorth, Kenneth	Expo	Defusing a bomb	1981 GM
Hubbard, Daniel	Insp	Road traffic accident	1916
Hughes, Joseph	Insp	Thrown from police horse	1882
Hutchins, Frederick G	Ps	Shot	1961 QPM
Ince, Michael E D	Pc	Road traffic accident	1971
Ives	Ps	WW2 bomb explosion	1941
Jackson, Thomas	Ps	Assaulted	1864
Jamieson, Alan D	Insp	Road traffic accident	2001
Janeway, Page M	Pc	Injuries received from Epsom Police Siege	1920
Johnson, George	Pc	Assaulted	1914
Jones, David A	Pc	Road traffic accident	1964
Jones, Stephen	Pc	Road traffic accident	1984
Joyce, Joseph	Ds	Shot	1892
Judge, George H R	Pc	Road traffic accident - failed to stop	1918
Keller	Wrpc	Bomb explosion	1944
Kelliher, Kevin	Pc	Road traffic accident	1979
Kelly, James	Pc	Shot	1920
Kemp, William J	Dc	Assaulted	1897
Kidd, Frederick	Pc	Drowned	1900
King, Alan D	Ps	Stabbed	1991
Lambert, Frederick W	Pc	Hit by runaway horse	1919
Lane, Noel	Ps	Harrods bomb explosion	1983
Langford, Daniel	Pc	Assaulted	1864
Lawes, Arthur	Pc	Road traffic accident	1930
Leeuw, Ronald I	Pc	Heart attack after violent prisoner arrested	1984
Lewis, Michael	Pc	Ruptured Heart	1888
Lillicrap, Richard	Pc		1862
Lloyd, John	Pc	Of injuries received	1925
Lock, Edward	Pc	Road traffic accident	1924
Lock, Samuel	Pc	Shot while cleaning pistol	1950
London, John	Pc	Road traffic accident	1966
Long, John	Pc	Stabbed	1830
Lord	Pc	Enemy air raid	1944
Luke, David	Pc	Collapsed while swimming at Hendon	1981
MacDougall, Neil	Ps	Shot during police revolver practice	1901
Macey, James	Pc	Collapsed after arrest	1904
Mackay, Nina	Wpc	Stabbed	1997
Madigan, Michael	Pc	Drowned	1852
Marnie, Alexander A	Spc	Fractured skull after fall	1915
Martin, Robert G	Pc	Road traffic accident	1950
Maughan, John B	Dc	Road traffic accident	1964
May, Arthur	Pc	Injuries received after a fall	1892
May, James B	Pc	Road traffic accident	1967

McCarthy, Charles	Pc	Knocked down by a horse	1846
McCloskey, Ronal K A	Pc	Road traffic accident	1987
McFadzean, Thomas A	Ps	Fall	1950
McGaw, Robert	Pc	Kicked by police horse	1887
McKinnon, Alexander	Pc		1940
McLaughlan, Eric	Pc	Road traffic accident	1965
Meehan, Leslie V	Pc	Thrown from suspects motor vehicle	1960
Mercer, Robert	Pc	Road traffic accident	1982
Miles, Sidney G	Pc	Shot (Craig & Bentley)	1952 KPFSM
Mitchell, Raymond	Pc	Road traffic accident	1928
Moir	Pc	Bomb explosion	1944
Monk, Daniel Harker	Pc	Assaulted with his own truncheon	1848
Morgan, Henry	Pc	Assaulted	1848
Morgan, Jack	Wrpc	Road traffic accident	1939
Morrison, James	Dc	Stabbed	1991 QGM
Moulton, Thomas E	Pc	Injured on duty	1927
Munroe, Roderick M	Pc	Road traffic accident	1962
Nazer, William S	Pc	Drowned	1879
Need, Thomas	Dc	Road traffic accident	1993
Newbold, James	Pc	Drowned	1901
Nice, James	Pc	Assaulted	1869
Nicholls, Charles	Pc	Dropped dead	1842
O'Neill, Francis J	Pc	Stabbed	1980 QGM
Packer, Albert E	Pc		1933
Parncutt, Frederick	Spc		1937
Parrott, Moses	Pc	Dropped dead	1872
Parsonson, Matthew J	Pc	Road traffic accident	1994
Pasker, William	Pc	Drowned	1890
Patrick, Frederick W	Pc	Drowned	1863
Pawsey, Phillip	Insp	Shot	1961 QPM
Pearce, Charles	Pc	Drowned	1864
Pecker, Albert E	Pc	Died on injuries	1933
Peers, Mark	Pc	Drowned - underwater search team	1989
Pell, Ronald R	Pc	Road traffic accident	1969
Percy, Frederick	Pc	Road traffic accident	1933
Perkins, Gilbert E	Pc	Road traffic accident	1947
Perry, Michael	Pc	Road traffic accident	1993
Perry, Thomas W	Pc	Collapsed after an arrest	1905
Pickett, Harry	Pc	Road traffic accident	1943
Pike	Pc	Assaulted	1922
Pinder, David J	Pc		1969
Pinder, Stuart A	Ds	Road traffic accident	1978
Pirnie, Gail D	Wpc	Collapsed at Hendon during training	1994
Popps, James J C	Spc	Collapsed	1914
Price, Douglas J	Pc	Road traffic accident	1972
Prior, David J	Pc	Road traffic accident	1969
Purdy, Raymond W	Ds	Stabbed	1959
Queenie	Police Dog	Harrods bomb explosion	1983
Quemby, Arthur E	Pc	Road traffic accident	1948
Quibell, Lawrence	Pc	During fire engine practice	1917

Quinnell, John	Spc	Drowned	1914
Randall, Thomas	Pc	Fighting with another police constable	1859
Randall, William	Pc	Road traffic accident	1972
Reynolds, Charles	Pc	Drowned	1842
Richardson, Harold	Pc	Drowned	1886
Ricketts, Frank	Pc	Drowned	1916
Rivett, Frederick J	CI	Fell from a police horse	1919
Robertson, Derek J	Ps	Stabbed	1994 QGM
Robins, George	Ps	Kicked by a horse	1870
Robson, William	Insp	Drowned	1884
Rolfe, Francis H	CI	Fell dead from blood poisoning	1914
Ross-Myring, Herbert G	Spc	Road traffic accident	1940
Rowland, Thomas E B	Pc	Fractured skull	1919
Russell, Leonard	Pc	Collapsed after an arrest	1904
S'dhu Kulwant S	Pc	Fell through a roof while chasing suspect	1999
Saunders, George E	Ps	Drowned	1864
Saunders, Raymond V	Pc	Road traffic accident	1952
Sawyer, Henry W	A/Ps	Assaulted	1918
Scandrett, Jeremy	Pc	Road traffic accident	2001
Scott, Alexander	Pc	Assaulted	1850
Seager, Sidney	Pc	Road traffic accident	1966
Self, John	Pc	Assaulted	1929
Shannon, Malachi	Pc	Thrown from police horse	1856
Sharp,	Pc	Long range rocket explosion	1945
Shepherd, George	Pc	Thrown from a moving vehicle	1938
Sibley, William	Pc	Collapsed and died	1849
Silvey, William	Pc	Fell from a wagon	1883
Simpkins, Mark	Pc	Road traffic accident	1983
Smith, Alan E	Pc	Road traffic accident	1980
Smith, Alfred	Pc	Assaulted	1914
Smith	Ps	Bomb explosion	1944
Snowdon, James R B	Pc	Road traffic accident	1980
Southworth, George R	Pc	Fell	1939
Spooner, George E	Ps	Drowned	1913
Spooner, Wayne D	Pc	Road traffic accident	1986
Stoker, Francis	Pc	Rescue attempt	1855
Stone, Edwin	Pc	Heart attack	1896
Sullivan, Anthony	S/Ps	Accidental injuries	1927
Summers, Raymond H	Pc	Stabbed	1958
Sunnucks, Grant C	Pc	Road traffic accident	1984
Sutch, William	Spc	Road traffic accident	1941
Swan, Edward W	Pc	Assaulted	1918
Taylor, Albert	Pc		1937
Taylor, Ernest	Wrpc	Fell from a wall	1940
Thompson, Albert	Pc	Hit by horse and cart	1885
Thompson, Ernest	Pc	Stabbed	1900
Thompson, James W	Pc		1935 KPM
Thompson, Leslie E	Pc	Road traffic accident	1947
Thompson, Oscar	Sdi	Road traffic accident	1947
Tibble, Stephen A	Pc	Shot by the IRA	1975 QPM

Tipple, Reginald	Ps	Shot	1956
Towers, Edwin	Pc	Road traffic accident	1942
Tralau, Walter	Pc	Accident	1944
Tring, Michael	Pc	Road traffic accident	1994
Tullett, Arthur V	Insp	Road traffic accident	1929
Tutt, Bernard	Pc	Road traffic accident - crushed saving children	1937
Twinn, William	Pc	Hit by runaway horse	1879
Tyler, Alfred J	Pc	Road traffic accident	1920
Tyler, William	Pc		1909 KPM
Vincent, Leslie	Pc	Road traffic accident	1960
Walker, Stephen	Pc	Road traffic accident	1983
Walters, Phillip	Pc	Shot	1995
Ware, William G	Pc	Drowned	1931
Waring, George F	Pc	Assaulted	1870
Weatherstone, Vernon R	Tdc	Road traffic accident	1974
Welch, John	Pc	Suffocated in sewer	1849
Westney, David E	Ps	Road traffic accident	1967
Whatley, Harold J	Ds	Road traffic accident	1953
Wheeler, William J	Spc		1917
White, George E	Pc	Road traffic accident	1964
White	Wrpc	WW2 bomb explosion	1941
Whiting, Michael A	Pc		1973 QPM
Whitney, Tom L	Ps	Died on injuries received on duty	1926
Wiley, J A	Spc	Collapsed	1915
Wilkinson, Kenneth C	Pc	Road traffic accident	1966
Will, Stuart	Ps	Drowned	1973
Williams, Stephen R	Pc	Road traffic accident	1996
Williamson, Joseph	Pc	Assaulted	1908
Williamson, William	Pc	Accident	1915
Wilson, Victor J	Pc	Died of injuries received on duty	1926
Wombwell, Stanley B	Dc	Shot - crew of Foxtrot one one	1966
Wright, Charles	Pc	Accident	1895
Wright, John	Pc	Fire	1844
Wright, Robert	Pc	Fire	1893
Wroth, David	Pc	Died of injuries received on duty	1921
Young, Alfred	Pc	Shot	1915 KPM